Dedicated to Carol "my song"
and to our children:
Jeanne, Patricia, Deborah, David and Jonathan

Also, a special thanks to Dave
for his help in editing **Strange Work**.

Strange Work

A COMMENTARY ON THE BOOK OF REVELATION

BY

Rev. Herbert Melville Munson, Jr.

*For the Lord shall rise up as in Mount Perazim,
He shall be wroth as in the Valley of Gibeon,
that He may do His work, His*
strange work,
and bring to pass His act.

Isaiah 28:21(KJV)

Copyright 2010 Rev Herbert Melville Munson, Jr.

ISBN 978-0-557-31890-2

Revised and edited March 24, 2013

TABLE OF CONTENTS

PROLOGUE: ABOUT THE AUTHOR — ix
INTRODUCTION — xi

REVELATION 1: THE GLORIFIED CHRIST — 1

REVELATION 2 – 3: CHRIST MIDST HIS CHURCHES — 29

    Ephesus — 31
    Smyrna — 37
    Pergamos — 41
    Thyatira — 49
    Sardis — 59
    Philadelphia — 66
    Laodicea — 77

REVELATION 4 – 5: GOD'S THRONE IN HEAVEN — 86

    The Throne Sitter — 88
    The Scroll and the Lamb — 101

REVELATION 6: THE SEAL JUDGMENTS BEGIN — 111

    The First Seal: The White Horse Rider — 112
    The Second Seal: The Red Horse Rider — 115
    The Third Seal: The Black Horse Rider — 116
    The Fourth Seal: The Pale Horse Rider — 117
    The Fifth Seal: The Souls under the Altar — 119
    The Sixth Seal: The Great Tribulation Begins — 121

REVELATION 7: THE 144,000 AND
    THE GREAT MULTITUDE — 129

The 144,000	129
The Innumerable Multitude	136

REVELATION 8 – 9: THE TRUMPET JUDGMENTS BEGIN — 141

The First Trumpet: Hail Mingled with Fire	146
The Second Trumpet: The Fiery Mountain Cast into the Sea	149
The Third Trumpet: Wormwood	150
The Fourth Trumpet: Darkness for 1/3rd of the Day and Night	151
The Angel with the Three Woes	153
The Fifth Trumpet and First Woe: The Bottomless Pit Opened	154
The Sixth Trumpet and Second Woe: Four Demons Loosed	161

REVELATION 10 – 11:14: THE INTERLUDE BETWEEN THE SIXTH AND SEVENTH TRUMPETS — 169

The Mighty Angel	169
The Mystery of God	174
The Little Book	175
The Temple	180
The Two Witnesses	182

REVELATION 11:15 – 19: THE SEVENTH TRUMPET SIGNALS THE BEGINNING OF THE END — 191

REVELATON 12: THE WOMAN AND THE DRAGON — 199

The Woman, Israel	200
The Dragon, Satan	201
The Man Child, Christ	205
The Flight of Israel	206
The War in Heaven	208

REVELATION 13: ANTICHRIST AND THE FALSE PROPHET — 217

- The Beast from the Sea — 217
- The Beast from the Earth — 227

REVELATION 14: HEAVEN'S MOUNT ZION AND THE CYCLE JUDGMENTS — 235

- The 144,000 — 235
- The Preaching Angel with the Gospel — 240
- The Proclaiming Angel about Babylon — 241
- The Warning Angel concerning the Mark of the Beast — 242
- The Reaping of the Vine by Christ — 246
- The Gathering of the Vine by the Angels — 250

REVELATION 15 – 16: THE POURING OUT OF THE BOWL JUDGMENTS — 255

- The Choir in Heaven — 255
- The First Bowl: Sores — 259
- The Second Bowl: The Sea Turned to Blood — 260
- The Third Bowl: All Fresh Water Turned to Blood — 260
- The Fourth Bowl: The Sun's Heat Intensified — 263
- The Fifth Bowl: Absolute Darkness — 263
- The Sixth Bowl: The Call to Armageddon — 264
- The Seventh Bowl: Hail and the Universal Earthquake — 269

REVELATION 17: THE GREAT WHORE ON THE SCARLET BEAST — 273

- The Harlot Dressed in Purple and Scarlet — 274
- The Scarlet Beast — 278
- The Ten Kings — 282

REVELATION 18: THE REMAINS OF
              FALLEN BABYLON   289

REVELATION 19: THE SECOND RETURN
              OF THE LORD JESUS CHRIST   299

    The Marriage Supper of the Lamb   301
    The Return of the King of Kings
            and Lord of Lords   306
    The Battle of Armageddon   315
    The Demise of Antichrist and
            the False Prophet   316

REVELATION 20: THE THOUSAND YEAR REIGN
              OF CHRIST   319

    The Chaining of Satan   321
    The Millennial Reign of Christ   329
    The Loosing of Satan   332
    The Battle of Gog and Magog   334
    The Great White Throne Judgment   337

REVELATION 21:1 – 22:5: THE ETERNAL HOME
              OF THE SAINTS   345

    The New Heavens and the New Earth   345
    The New Jerusalem   353

REVELATION 22:6 – 21: THE EPILOGUE   369

APPENDIX A: A TIME LINE CHART OF
              THE TRIBULATION   381

APPENDIX B: A DISCUSSION OF THE
          SEVEN YEAR TRIBULATION PERIOD   383

SCRIPTURE VERSES QUOTED IN STRANGE WORK   389

PROLOGUE

ABOUT THE AUTHOR

Who am I? Well, I'm a husband, a dad, a grandpa, a guy who loves God's Word, but most of all I am a believer in the Lord Jesus Christ. I have been a pastor of four churches and led numerous bible studies over the years. I have two degrees, a BS in Biblical Literature from Multnomah University (at the time known as Multnomah School of the Bible) in Portland, Oregon, and a BA in English Literature from New Mexico State University in Las Cruces, New Mexico.

    I have also been a truck driver, a courier for a hospital, a manager of two real estate offices, a mortgage broker and a medical office manager. Right now, I am semi-retired and live in San Antonio, Texas, where I work with my son, Dave, in his Saddleback Leather Company … an Internet business Dave set up to support missions. He and his wife, Suzette, manufacture and sell the world's coolest handmade leather products including luggage, briefcases, duffle bags, travel cases, backpacks, satchels, iPad sleeves, gadget pouches, wallets, desk pads and so on. You can check them out at: http://www.saddlebackleather.com. Oh yeah, and don't miss Dave's tribute to his black lab, Blue, there. He was Dave's constant companion during his single years and the founding of Saddleback.

Carol and I have five children: Jeanne, Patricia, Deborah, David and Jonathan. We also have fourteen grandchildren and two great grandchildren. Our oldest daughter, Jeanne, and her husband, Tim, live in Keller, Texas, near Fort Worth. They adopted a little girl from Russia, named Maria, bringing their family to five. Patricia has four children and also lives in Keller. She and her husband, Dennis, own Chamberlain Shipping, LLC, a fulfillment shipping company that handles all of Saddleback Leather Company's quality control and shipping. Debbie has three children and lives in San Antonio. Jonathan, our youngest, served in the Marine Corps as a Marine Security Guard at the American Embassies in London and also in Tunis, Tunisia, graduated from Wheaton, and currently works with

Chamberlain Leather Milk (**http://www.leather-milk.com/**) in development and marketing.

Our first great-grandchild, Avalyn Kay Franklin, came along to our grandson, Aiden and his wife, Cinnamon, and our second, Wyatt Clanton, to our grandson, Jacob and his wife Renee. Truly, our cup *runneth over*!

Finally, one of my life goals is to write commentaries on four books of the Bible (Genesis, Daniel, Matthew and Revelation), and make them available in a set. These four books are uniquely linked together in presenting the whole picture of end time prophecy in the Bible. The Genesis commentary I call *First Work*. Daniel is *Kingdom Work*. Matthew is *King's Work*. Revelation is *Strange Work*.

INTRODUCTION

Nearly three millennia ago, the prophet Isaiah predicted that **the Lord God of hosts** would **rise up** one day and do a **strange work** on the Earth. Furthermore, he prophesied that when it came it would come as **a destruction upon the whole earth** (Isaiah 28:21-22). The last thing that mankind expects today is that the true and living God will actually rise up and initiate such an intervention. Yet, with one voice, the prophets of the Bible predict that is exactly what He will do. The book of Revelation is the most detailed of the Bible's prophecies concerning that fast approaching supernatural intervention. The lion's share of the book of Revelation (chapters 6 through 18) give us in-depth details about the events, personalities and sequences of that inevitable future day of reckoning in our world's history.

Someone has dubbed the book of Revelation, *The prophetic Grand Central Station of the Bible*. That is a good way to describe it because all of the great eschatological themes of the Bible run to the book of Revelation like train-tracks to a central hub. Therefore, as far as prophecy is concerned, the book of Revelation is the most important and relevant book of the Bible ... and especially so for us twenty-first century believers who are living way down here in these last days of world history.

On September 24, 2007, Mahmoud Ahmadinejad, current President of Iran (speaking in Arabic at Columbia University), began his remarks with this prayer:

In the name of God, the compassionate, the merciful ... Oh, God, hasten the arrival of **Imam al-Mahdi** *and grant him good health and* **victory** *and make us his followers and* **those** *to attest to his rightfulness.*

His prayer was a call for the Shia Islamic Messiah, **Imam al-Mahdi**, (the *Twelfth Imam*) to appear and conquer the world (**victory**) ... and for Ahmadinejad's audience at Columbia (**those**) to one day bow their knees (**attest to his rightfulness**) to this long anticipated, Islamic world dictator. Disturbingly, Amadinejad has said that he would like to hasten the Twelfth Imam's appearing by personally starting the last great World War that Shia Moslems believe will usher in their Islamic Messiah. Moslems of Ahmadinejad's sect believe they can hasten the coming of the Twelfth Imam by starting a war of genocide to defeat the *Little Satan* (Israel) and its ally, *The Great Satan* (U.S.A.). As recent as March of 2011, Ahmadinejad's regime published a video for distribution to the Islamic world called *The Coming Is Near*. In it, the case is made that all the unrest in the Middle East is a sign of the Mahdi's soon coming.

Meanwhile, across the Middle East, North Africa and Asia, fanatic Islamic *Holy Warriors* continue to carry out their centuries old agenda of converting infidels with the sword as they await their Imam Al-Mahdi to come and fulfill the dream of their religion being the only religion on planet Earth. Over the centuries, thousands upon thousands of people have lost their lives to these fanatics. Their single purpose and unchanging ultimatum is that every *infidel* (non-Moslem) must convert to Islam or be exterminated. It is simple as that. Disturbingly, on a world-wide scale, their cause appears to be on the increase.

Here, in the United States, we too have felt the sword of Islam. Nearly three thousand innocent lives were lost on 9/11 alone at the bombing of our World Trade Centers and that tragedy was not the first time we had experienced it. Consider all of the American lives lost by the bombing of the Marine barracks in Lebanon, the past attacks on various U.S. Embassies, the bombing of the Cole, the earlier bombing of the World Trade Center and last, but not least, the thousands of American lives that have since been lost on the battle fields of Iraq and Afghanistan. Truly, as the Bible predicts:

...in the last days, perilous times will come… Second Timothy 3:1b

Standing at the heart of Islam's hatred, and in the way of its goals however, is the little nation of Israel. For decades, the eyes of the world have been drawn to this tiny country and its capital at Jerusalem. When Israel was established by the United Nations in 1948, for the first time in nearly two millennia large numbers of Jews began returning to their ancient homeland. Immediately, war erupted as surrounding Islamic states attempted to eradicate the fledgling new nation. They were not successful, however. But, war after war has continued to erupt over that tiny land. Arabic nations, the Palestinians, and a host of Islamic fundamentalist terrorist organizations have done their best to destroy Israel but, somehow, she has managed to survive. Today, her existence is threatened more than ever. As we speak, skirmish after skirmish is being fought from Gaza between Hamas (backed by Iran) and Israel which has resulted in hundreds of lives being lost. On every side, the red hatred of the enemies of the Jews continues to seethe and build while Mahmoud Ahmadinejad and other Islamic fascists continue to avow to *push Israel into the sea*. Iran's current crash program to develop nuclear weapons and ballistic missiles is predicated on this all-consuming goal ... and the launching of their first satellite into orbit (2/8/2009) was a huge step in Iran's ability to launch its nuclear weapons when they are completed.

The Bible predicts that in the last days the ancient nation of Babylon is going to rise again. According to Scripture, **Babylon** will be Antichrist's world capital and the name of his worldwide empire (Rev. 17:18). Geographically, ancient Babylon was located at the head of the Persian Gulf where Iran, Iraq and Kuwait are situated today. It was at ancient Babylon, under King Nebuchadnezzar, that man-worship first raised its ugly head (Daniel 3) when Nebuchadnezzar made a statue of himself and commanded that everyone in his empire must fall down and worship it. However, three young Hebrews ... Shadrach, Meshach and Abednego ... refused to do so. So, Nebuchadnezzar had them thrown alive into a super-heated fiery furnace. However, the one true and living God intervened and miraculously rescued them and, when the three young Hebrews walked out of Nebuchadnezzar's furnace, not a single hair on their bodies had been singed! Nor, was there even the smell of smoke on them! If you would like to read about it further, go to my commentary on Daniel at: **biblebookofdaniel.com/chapter3.htm**.

Now, coming back to the subject of Iran, fast-forward with me to our present day. Iran has long desired to conquer its neighbors. The last war that Iran initiated against Iraq cost over a million lives. And, had it not been for the assistance of the United States, Iran would have prevailed. If Iran could succeed in conquering Iraq, much of the territory of the ancient Babylonian Empire would be reconstituted.

Let me set forth a possible scenario. If the Rapture of the Church were to occur today, the United States of America (presently the most powerful country on Earth) would be devastated. Millions of Christians, who presently occupy key and strategic positions throughout our nation would suddenly and instantly vanish from off the earth. The result would be utter chaos throughout every area of American infrastructure and society. Communications ... transportation ... utilities ... government ... and, most importantly, the United States military would be severely disrupted and crippled in the blink of an eye. In an atom of time, our nation would be thrown into paralysis and chaos. Not so, however, in the Muslim world. Those nations would lose almost no one. Then, with the Christian nations of the world disabled and in utter chaos, the Islamic world would be free to quickly unite and make its long desired move for world domination ... and ancient Babylon could quickly rise again. Under those circumstances, *The Man of Sin* (Antichrist) could step forth upon the world scene, declaring that he is the *Twelfth Imam*, and billions of fanatic Muslim adorers would instantly be available to march beside him to conquer the world. Three and a half years later, he would invade Israel breaking his treaty with them and seize the temple at Jerusalem and make his claim to be God. Then, once again, in the mold of Nebuchadnezzar of old, man-worship would be imposed upon the world (Rev. 13) and that worst of all manifestations of idolatry would have come full circle. Man-worship, having begun in Babylon, would once again be centered at Babylon ... in one last great Gentile, blasphemous, world dominating theocracy.

In Daniel 11:37-38 (a passage that refers to the coming Antichrist), we read:

__Neither shall he regard the God of his fathers__, nor the desire of women, nor regard any god: for he shall magnify himself above all. But in his estate shall he honor __the God of forces__ and a god whom his fathers knew not shall he honour with gold, and silver, and with precious stones, and pleasant things. (KJV)

Many believers have puzzled over that passage and sought to interpret it. If Antichrist were to be a Moslem, however, the phrase **the God of his fathers** (from whom he will turn away), would be referring to Allah ... and **the God of forces** (to whom he will turn), would refer to Satan. According to the Bible, this switch of allegiance will occur when Antichrist seizes the Jew's temple at Jerusalem (midway through the Tribulation). Then, he will declare himself to be God and demand to be worshipped there by all (Daniel 11:36; Matthew 24:15; 2 Thessalonians 2:3-4). We will discuss this in greater depth when we come to Revelation 13.

As for the nation of Israel, she too would be little affected by the Rapture of the Church. Very few of her people would go missing as well. At this time, Israel is the sole, though undeclared, nuclear armed Middle Eastern power. Therefore, she too would emerge from the Rapture as a power to be reckoned with. Perhaps this will be the key reason that Antichrist will enter into a treaty with her before he sets forth to conquer the rest of the world (Daniel 9:27). That prophetic treaty will insure the peaceful existence of the Jews in their homeland during the first three and a half years of the Tribulation and give them the authority and time to rebuild their temple.

This is one possible scenario of what could happen in the aftermath of Christ's removal of his believers from planet Earth (the Rapture of the Church).

Believers everywhere are asking, *Are the world events I am witnessing today the fulfillment of Biblical prophecy?* Not too long ago, on cable television, I heard two well known Bible expositors state that the Bible's prophetic battles of **Armageddon** and **Gog and Magog** were virtually upon us. In their opinion, this was evidenced by what we are witnessing on the chaotic world scene today. The book of Revelation, however, clearly states that is not the case. It places the battle of **Armageddon** at the end of the Great Tribulation (Rev. 16), and the battle of **Gog and Magog** at the end of the Millennium ... over a thousand years later (Rev. 20). Neither **Armageddon** nor **Gog and Magog** are upon us at all. However, another great world war that the Bible predicts **is** most certainly gathering on our horizon today. In my opinion, what we are witnessing is the beginning stirrings of that war's inexorable approach. It is **the great world war that will bring Antichrist to power**. Immediately after the Rapture, the Bible predicts that Antichrist will quickly arise and seize the whole world by military force (Rev. 6:2). The history of Earth is fast approaching this great prophetic event. When it actually begins to occur in time, like passengers on a runaway train, the peoples of the world will be thrust into the amazing and perilous days of the Tribulation that Daniel and Jesus foretold and that are so precisely described in Christ's book of Revelation.

Now, let me say a few words about this commentary...

First, *Strange Work* is unique among commentaries on Revelation because it takes the position that the visions of the book are in the exact **chronological order** of their future fulfillments. I am not aware of any other commentary that recognizes that fact. Although this may seem unimportant, this unique insight adds a wealth of new and fresh information to many things that heretofore have seemed very mysterious and difficult to interpret. Four examples come to mind:

a. In *Strange Work* you will find a unique interpretation of the judgment of the **sixth seal** as to its timing, centrality, literal character and future significance (Rev. 6:12-17).

b. In *Strange Work* you will find a fresh and well supported interpretation of the judgment of the two **sickles** in Revelation 14:14-20, that clearly demonstrates that this is the judgment of wicked Israel (resurrected Jews from all time combined with all the wicked Jews who are still alive during the closing days of the Great Tribulation).

c. In *Strange Work* you will find a probable identification of the **seven kings** of Revelation 17, who were ancient Caesars of the Roman Empire and are types of the coming Antichrist.

d. In *Strange Work* you will find a possible key to understanding the mysterious number of the **beast** ... ***666*** ... (Revelation 13:17-18), when applied to binary code as it is used to transmit data over the Internet.

Second, *Strange Work* holds strictly to **sound principles of biblical exegesis**. Only when one follows a literal, grammatical, historical method of interpretation the Bible does it consistently yield its truths to its readers (Second Timothy 2:15b).

Third, I have made every attempt to ground *Strange Work* on **sound principles of hermeneutics**. Hermeneutics is the science of interpretation. This is a big word that simply means that when you are interpreting the Bible (or any other writing for that matter) you must always follow common sense rules of interpretation in order to correctly understand what the author is saying. For example, one of the rules of hermeneutics is the *rule of context*. Only by consistently studying and acknowledging what was said before and after the point where one is reading can we correctly understand the meaning of the thought of the writer. Violations of sound hermeneutical principles never yield correct interpretations of the Word of God or any other writing for that matter. They invariably lead one away from the meaning that an author intended rather than **to** the meaning of what was written.

Fourth, throughout *Strange Work* the biblical text, along with the majority of the scriptures that are cited, are printed out for you so that everything is at the reader's finger tips. You will not need to look up anything or necessarily even have a Bible on hand to study Revelation.

For the most part, I have used the New King James Version of the Bible in *Strange Work* and have taken the liberty to underline and bold print it for added emphasis. For what it is worth, I also consulted the NIV but, it being an *equivalent translation* rather than a *literal* one, I concluded that the NKJV was the better text to use for our study. When interpreting prophecy, each and every word can be of vital importance, you see. One seeks to know exactly what God has said ... not roughly what he said ... when studying prophecy and a literal translation is far more helpful in that regard than an *equivalent* version.

Fifth, throughout *Strange Work,* where the latest Greek scholarship throws new light on the text, the reader will find the designation *NU* inserted and the scripture updated at that point. This abbreviation refers to two classic works on the original languages and manuscripts of the New Testament. The *N* stands for the twenty-sixth edition of the *Nestle-Aland Greek New Testament* and the *U* stands for the third edition of the United Bible Societies' Greek New Testament, *The New Testament Text.* So, as you read along, you will be able to see where the latest Greek scholarship has clarified or improved on the translation of the New King James Version. This is in accordance with another sound principle of hermeneutics, by the way. It is called the rule of *the priority of the original languages.* This rule states that, when one is handling a translation from one language to another and a question arises, the only reliable way to discover the answer is to consult the original language. In the Bible, that would be Greek in the New Testament and Hebrew and a smattering of Aramaic in the Old. *NU* helps us a great deal in that regard.

Sixth, I have written **Strange Work** with three groups of people in mind. First, it is written to edify (build up) the Church of Jesus Christ. So, primarily, it is written for believers today. Second, it is my prayer that it will be used of the Lord to speak to lost men and women as well ... so that they might be saved. Third, it is written for the Tribulation Saints who are going to come to Christ during the dark days of the coming Tribulation (Revelation 7:9-17). Nothing would thrill me more than if any of those saints in that future day were to find access to this commentary and discover God's plan and will, comfort and help, during the dark days of Earth's two thousand five hundred and twenty day trial.

Finally, I have written *Strange Work* in the style of how I speak ... as if the reader and I were just chatting together ... seated in front of a cheery fireplace in a cozy room. Therefore, if you find the grammar and punctuation not exactly according to rule ... it is on purpose ... for easy reading and my own way of communicating.

I realize that the book of Revelation can be a bit intimidating at times. But, I would strongly encourage each reader to stick with it. The blessings and rewards for doing so are beyond measure. There are very few unsolved mysteries in the book of Revelation. After all, it **is *the Revelation of Jesus Christ***. It is not a book that is hard to interpret. The difficulty is in simply believing what it so plainly says.

Now, let me acknowledge some of those who have helped me along in my understanding of the Bible and in my study of Revelation. I absolve them of any responsibility, however, for any interpretations in *Strange Work* with which they might not agree or deem inaccurate. I gratefully thank and acknowledge the following men of God who have helped me in my understanding as well as helped me with my own walk with the Lord by sharing with me their love for the Savior and His Word ... either by their writings or in person.

A Study in the Revelation ... E. F. Webber, D.D., F.R.G.S. Dr. Webber's book was the first on Revelation that I read as a teenager. My saintly grandmother, Mrs. H.C. Hudson, who often listened to Dr. Webber's radio broadcasts, sent it to me.

A Revelation of Jesus Christ ... J. B. Smith

The Apocalypse ... J. A. Seiss

Things to Come ... J. Dwight Pentecost

The Revelation of Jesus Christ ... John F. Walvoord

The Rapture Question ... John F. Walvoord

Thru the Bible with J. Vernon McGee ... J. Vernon McGee

Dr. Stanley A. Ellison ... Western Seminary, Portland, Oregon

Dr. Earl D. Radmacher ... Western Seminary, Portland, Oregon

Dr. John G. Mitchell ... Multnomah School of the Bible (Now: Multnomah University and Biblical Seminary), Portland, Oregon

Dr. Roger D. Congdon ... Multnomah School of the Bible, Portland, Oregon

Before we begin, here is an outline of the book of Revelation that I have found helpful. It would be a good one to memorize. The lion's share of it came from Dr. Stanley Ellison:

I. The vision of Jesus Christ in Glory (Chapter 1)
II. The vision of Jesus Christ midst his Churches (Chapters 2-3)
III. The vision of Jesus Christ in Coronation (Chapters 4-5)
IV. The vision of Jesus Christ in Judgment (Chapters 6-18)
V. The vision of Jesus Christ in Return (Chapters 19-20)
VI. The vision of Jesus Christ in Eternity (Chapters 21-22)

Are you ready to begin? Well then, fasten your spiritual seat belt because we are about to experience the most spectacular, eye-popping, into the future, ride of our spiritual lives!

Scripture taken from the New King James Version. Copyright © 1982 by Thomas Nelson, Inc. Used by permission. All rights reserved.

REVELATION 1

THE GLORIFIED CHRIST

Rev. 1:1-3

The **Revelation** *of Jesus Christ, which God* **gave** *him* **to show his servants***; things which must shortly take place. And he sent and signified it by his angel to his servant John, who bore witness to the* **word of God***, and to the* **testimony of Jesus Christ***, to all things that he saw. Blessed is he who reads and those who hear the words of this prophecy, and keep those things which are written in it; for the time is near.*

1:1

First and foremost, **Revelation** is from **Jesus Christ** himself. The Greek word translated **Revelation** here is Αποκαλυψις (*apocalupses*). It means *unveiling* or *uncovering*. It is the same word that is used in Second Thessalonians 1:7b-8:

... *rest with us when the Lord Jesus is* **revealed** *from heaven with his mighty angels, in flaming fire taking vengeance on those who do not know God, and on those who do not obey the gospel of our Lord Jesus Christ.*

So, the first two words of the book tell us what it is about. It is an unveiling ... or pulling back of the curtain from things that were previously hidden and unknown. Many new things will be given to us from our Lord here, including a far greater understanding of His person and future work. Up to this point in the Bible, Christ Jesus has been set forth as the **Lamb of God** ... appointed for sacrifice ... the meek and lowly one who quietly went to his cross like a sheep to the slaughter. But, what a contrast we will find in him here in the Revelation. In these pages, he steps forth as the **Lion of the tribe of Judah** (Revelation 5:5) who roars over the Earth and shakes it to its foundations. Revelation reveals Jesus as he now is ... and evermore shall be ... the Son of God glorified ... **King of Kings and Lord of Lords** ... **Lion of the Tribe of Judah**. When he walked among us on Earth, two thousand years ago, his glory was veiled and hidden. He steps forth on these pages in all the blinding glory of *the sun shining in his strength*.

Second, this book is the ***Revelation** ... **which God gave him**.* When Jesus was on Earth, he told his disciples there were things locked away in the heart of his Father that even he did not know. For example, concerning the timing of his Second Coming he said,

*But of that day and hour knoweth no one, not even the angels of heaven, **neither the Son**, but the Father **only**. Matthew 24:36*

These words indicate that the things we are about to read are things that were previously unknown even to Christ Jesus himself. Notice the sequence of how they have come down to us. Verse one says they came from the Father to the Son ... then from the Son to his angel ... then from his angel to John. John, in turn, has passed them down to you and me, Christ's *servants*, via this book of Revelation. How it must have thrilled Jesus' heart when he received these things from his Father to pass on to us. It also reveals that the Father's heart is identical to that of his Son when it comes to you and me ... Christ's blood bought children. So, these words are the Father's gift to the Son for you and me, the Son's *servants*. Keep in mind that this function is not something new to the Son of God. Jesus has always been passing on the Father's words. He is the revealer of all that God is and has said (John 1:18; Hebrews 1:13). As he put it in *John 17:6-8,*

*I have **manifested your name** to the men whom you have given me out of the world. They were yours, you gave them to me, and they have kept your word. Now they have known that all things, which you have given me, are from you. **For I have given to them the words which you have given me;** and they have received them, and have known surely that I came forth from you; and they have believed that you sent me.*

Third, this book is a ***Revelation*** of things which ***must shortly come to pass.*** The word ***shortly*** may seem a bit puzzling at first. After all, it has been over nineteen hundred years since these prophecies were first penned ... and they have yet to come to pass. How is it then that our Lord could say they ***must shortly come to pass***? I believe the answer lies in the fact that the Spirit is speaking to us here from God's perspective rather than from our human perspective. From God's point of view, everything is just down the block, so to speak. As Peter so aptly put it,

But, beloved, do not forget this one thing, that **with the Lord one day is as a thousand years**, *and a thousand years as one day. Second Peter 3:8*

In this respect, someone has said *The whole era of human experience to God is like a momentary flash of a meteor across the skies of eternity.* Nevertheless, with every tick of the clock ... for the past two thousand years our world has drawn closer and closer to the fulfillment of the things which we are about to read.

May we step aside for a moment? I find it very intriguing that from Adam to Abraham was a period of approximately two thousand years and from Abraham to Christ was approximately two thousand years and from Christ to where you and I are sitting today has been approximately two thousand years. So, according to the Bible, approximately six thousand years of human history has expired since the Creation. If Christ were to return during our generation and begin his thousand year reign on Earth (Revelation 20:4), Earth's full history, before it passes away, will have been an even seven thousand years. A nice round number, wouldn't you say? Going back to Peter's statement that **with the Lord one day is as a thousand years**, and considering that God's dealings have often been in cycles of seven (the seven day creation; the institution of a seven day work week; the coming seven year Tribulation period, etc.), it seems to me to be more than probable that you and I are living on the very brink of the end of this present age and on the edge of the Millennial reign of Christ. This is not a prophecy ... it is just something that, in my opinion, has a very high and biblically based probability. Whether or not this is correct, however, the things of which we are about to read will indeed ***shortly come to pass*** as far as the Lord is concerned.

Last, verse one says that this book of Revelation was ***sent and signified ... by his*** [Christ's] ***angel to his servant John.*** John was the human agent at the end of the chain whom Christ chose to give us these words. There has always been a man involved in the transmission of the Word of God, by the way. Peter says,

*...for prophecy never came by the will of man, but **holy men of God spoke** as they were moved by the Holy Spirit. Second Peter 1:21*

Now, the question arises, "Which **John** are we talking about here?" It was generally held by the early church fathers that the man referred to here is John, the Apostle. This is also supported by a good deal of internal evidence in the book of Revelation. The Apostle John wrote the gospel of John, First, Second, and Third John, and the book of Revelation.

1:2

In verse two, John adds his own solemn witness to the authenticity of this book. Here, unequivocally states that the things we are about to read are **the word of God** and the **testimony of Jesus Christ** ... things that he *saw* with his own eyes. The book of Revelation is a firsthand, eyewitness account.

1:3

In verse three, a blessing is pronounced upon all who ***read**, **hear*** and cherish the things written in this book. No other book of the Bible pronounces such a blessing upon its readers and hearers. Are you ready to be ***blessed***, dear reader? You surely will be if you read or just hear ... and tuck away in your heart ... the wonderful and amazing things that are in this book. You and I have God's word on it.

Rev. 1:4-6

*John, **to the seven churches** which are in Asia: Grace to you and peace **from him who is and who was and who is to come**, and from the **seven spirits** who are before his throne, and from Jesus Christ, the faithful witness, the firstborn from the dead, and the ruler over the kings of the earth. To him who* [**NU changes "*loved us and washed*" to "*loves us and freed*"**] *us from our sins in his own blood, and has made us* [**NU changes "*kings*" to "*a kingdom of priests*"**] *to his God and Father, to him be glory and dominion forever and ever. Amen.*

1:4

Although Revelation is written to all of Christ's servants of all ages, the first ones to receive it were located at seven local churches that existed in John's day. They were located in the country we know today as Turkey. They are named individually in verse eleven and each church has a personal letter from the glorified Jesus Christ recorded in chapters two and three.

Picking up with verses four through six, we have the greeting or salutation of the book. It begins with the words, **Grace to you and Peace.** Isn't that a wonderful greeting? You have to be a child of God to be able to grasp the full impact of these two words. That's because we children of the living God experience these two things on a daily basis. So, with these two warm and meaningful words, three separate entities step forward on the page here to greet us.

The first to greet us with *grace and peace* is He *who is and who was and who is to come.* This is one of the complex names of God the Father. Let's break it down. He is:

...the one who is. This emphasizes the **present tense** reality of God. Do you remember the name that God gave to Moses at the burning bush in Exodus 3? When Moses asked, *Who are you?* God replied, *I Am that I Am.* The one who greets us here is that very one. He is the One who simply is ... the self-existent, God the Father ... the great *I Am that I Am* ... the One who, at any given point in time ... simply **is**.

...who was. The second part of the name turns our thinking backward in time to God's **past tense**. As the God who *was*, he is the One who has always been ... the One who inhabits eternity. As far back in time as you might wish to go, you will find the One *who was* is there. As you have it in *Psalm 90:2,*

*Before the mountains were brought forth, or ever you had formed the earth and the world, even **from everlasting to everlasting**, you are God.*

...who is to come. The third part of his name directs our thinking forward in time out into the future. He is the God of the **future tense** ... the One who will always be. As far as you might want to go out into the future, you will find the one *who is to come* there. As you have it in *Isaiah 57:15,*

*For thus says the High and Lofty One **who inhabits eternity**, whose name is Holy: 'I dwell in the high and holy place, with him who has a contrite and humble spirit, to revive the spirit of the humble, and to revive the heart of the contrite ones.'*

So, the first greeter who welcomes us with the words ***grace and peace*** is none other than the ever present ... from eternity past to eternity future ... God the Father. Awesome! Aye?

The second to greet us here with ***grace and peace*** is actually the combined voices of a group. We read, ***and from the seven spirits which are before his throne.*** Now, who do you suppose they might be? That is a good question and it brings to mind an important principle of Biblical interpretation. When we don't immediately understand something we read in God's Word, the best thing to do is to wait until our Bible sheds more light on the subject. This very important principle, simply stated, is: *Always be ready to reserve judgment*. Good Bible interpreters reserve judgment until they have the whole picture before they come to a conclusion about something in the Word of God. We don't have enough information yet to form an opinion as to just who these ***seven spirits*** are who are greeting us here. All we have at this point is a very warm ***grace and peace*** from the ***seven spirits which are before his throne***. If we are patient, we will learn, later in Revelation, a great deal more about who they are. We will encounter them more than once in the pages to follow and will learn why they play such a prominent role in the future events that Revelation will unfold to us.

1:5

The third and final greeter to welcome us with ***grace and peace*** is the Lord Jesus Christ himself. John will expound a good bit more on this greeter than he does the other two. I believe that is because the Father has decreed that in this present age in which you and I live, the Son of God is to have the preeminence. He is to occupy center stage in all things. As you have it in *Colossians 1:18*,

And he is the head of the body, the church, who is the beginning, the firstborn from the dead, ***that in all things he may have the preeminence****.*

In keeping with this, the Holy Spirit, through John, will give us a very moving description of the Preeminent One who is greeting us here. He says he is:

...*the faithful witness.* The Lord Jesus never spoke a word that the Father didn't give him to speak, nor did he ever do a single thing that the Father didn't direct him to do. Truly, Jesus is ***the faithful witness***. He was and is, at all times, in perfect sync with his Father. As he himself put it in *John 7:16-18,*

***My doctrine is not mine, but his who sent me**. If anyone wants to do his will, he shall know concerning the doctrine, whether it is from God or whether I speak on my own authority. He who speaks from himself seeks his own glory; but **he who seeks the glory of the One who sent him is true**, and no unrighteousness is in him.*

...*the firstborn from the dead*. Now, there were several people who were raised from the dead before Christ. Three that come to mind are: Lazarus (John 11:43-44), Jairus' daughter (Mark 5:35-43), and the widow's son (Luke 7:11-15). There were also some in the Old Testament times. How then can it be said that Jesus is the ***firstborn from the dead***? Let's answer that by asking a question. What happened to the people who were raised from the dead before Christ? They died again. They were put back into a grave. And, where are their bodies right now? They are still in their graves ... but, not Jesus. He was the first to be permanently resurrected from the dead and now has an eternal resurrection body. At this very moment, as you are reading this, there is a Man with an eternal, resurrected body seated at the right hand of the Majesty on High ... the ***firstborn from the dead***! This word ***firstborn***, by the way, speaks of the fact that there are more to follow. That's music to my ears, how about your's? All of Christ Jesus' saints who have died are going to follow him in like resurrection to his own one day. As you have it in *Romans 8:11,*

*But if the Spirit of him who raised Jesus from the dead dwells in you, he who raised Christ from the dead **will also give life to your mortal bodies** through his Spirit who dwells in you.*

And again, in *First Corinthians 15:20,*

*But now Christ is risen from the dead, and has become the **firstfruits** of those who have fallen asleep.*

When Christ died for you and me, his blood purchased us lock, stock and barrel ... body, soul and spirit. Our bodies belong to Christ. They were purchased with his own blood. That's why he's going to return for them one day. God's people will not truly be complete until that day arrives. As you have it in *Philippians 3:20-21*,

For our citizenship is in heaven, from which we also eagerly wait for the Savior, the Lord Jesus Christ, who will **transform our lowly body** *that it may be conformed to his glorious body, according to the working by which he is able even to subdue all things to himself.*

Great news, aye?

...the prince of the kings of the earth. Jesus is the Supreme Potentate of all authorities that have ever ruled or ever will rule on planet Earth. His Father has exalted him far above any and all of this world's rulers and authorities. As you have it in *Philippians 2:9-10*,

Therefore God also has highly exalted him and given him the name which is above every name, that **at the name of Jesus every knee should bow**, *of those in heaven, and of those on earth, and of those under the earth...*

Now, notice here that at the end of verse five, we come to an unexpected break in John's description of Christ. Apparently, as John was writing down these stirring descriptions of our Lord and Savior, he just couldn't help but burst out in praise! Listen closely to the penned praises of our brother as he worships his Lord here. He exclaims:

...*Unto him that loves us.* The Greek word *loves* here is αγαπωντι (*agapontai)*. It comes from the root word for God's love, αγαπη (*agape*). It is in the present tense which means that Jesus' love for you and me began at a point in time in the past and continues on and on to this very moment. The thought is something like this, "unto him who loved us in eternity past, was loving us when he died for us on the cross (Romans 5:8), and is loving us right now at this very moment." All of that is inherent in this one sublime Greek word. Isn't that a wonderful truth? Does it stir your heart like it stirred John's? To God be the glory for Jesus' deep and abiding love for you and me, brother and sister. His love is unchanging, unceasing and unquenchable. As you have it in *Romans 8:38-39*,

*For I am persuaded that neither death nor life, nor angels nor principalities nor powers, nor things present nor things to come, nor height nor depth, nor any other created thing, shall **be able to separate us from the love of God which is in Christ Jesus our Lord**.*

John's praise continues:

...and freed us from our sins in his own blood. Now there's a subject for ceaseless praise, is it not? As the song says, *There is a fountain filled with blood drawn from Emanuel's veins! And sinners plunged beneath that flood lose all there guilty stains*! All praise and all glory to our wonderful Lamb who so freely and lovingly poured out his blood for you and me. It has freed us from our sins, both from their penalty (Romans 6:23), and from their bondage (Romans 6:14), and it will one day free us even from their very presence. As you have it in *Hebrews 9:12,*

Neither by the blood of goats and calves, but by his own blood, he entered in once into the holy place, have obtained eternal redemption for us. (KJV)

1:6

...and has made us a kingdom of priests. Here is another great cause for praise to the people of God. How wonderfully Christ has elevated us. Think of it. *First Peter 2:9,* says,

*But you are a chosen generation, **a royal priesthood**, a holy nation, his own **special people**, that you may proclaim the praises of him who called you out of darkness into his marvelous light...*

Jesus has made us his ***kingdom of priests***. As such, we have the great and unsurpassed honor of representing him to the world around us. John concludes:

...to him be glory and dominion forever and ever. Amen. Amen, indeed!

Rev. 1:7-8

*Behold, he is **coming with clouds**, and **every eye will see him**, even they who pierced him. And all the tribes of the earth will mourn because of him. Even so, Amen. '**I am the Alpha and the Omega**',*

[**NU omits**: *"the Beginning and the End"*] *says the Lord God, 'who is and who was and who is to come, the Almighty.'*

1:7

Verse seven is a prophetic statement prompted from the previous words ... **to him be glory and dominion forever and ever**. The Father himself, **the Alpha and the Omega**, is the one who speaks up here with these words. In response to John's praises of the Savior, the Father boomed out this statement. It is a promise from the lips of the Father concerning his Son. It is a thumbnail description of the main event toward which all of human history and all the things found in the book of Revelation are headed. Namely, the sure triumph over all peoples, principalities and spirits by his conquering Son, the Lord Jesus Christ, at his Second Coming.

Let's step aside for a moment and do a bit of defining of terms here. The Bible teaches there are two comings of the Lord Jesus Christ yet to occur. The first will be when he appears in the sky and removes his Church from the Earth ... taking his people back with him to His Father's house in Heaven. Theologians call this *the Rapture of the Church*. It is an event that is entirely different from the **Second Coming**. They are two separate events altogether. The Rapture could occur at any moment. When it does, Christ will suddenly appear in the skies of Earth and call his Church out of this world. At that time, believers (whether living or dead), will be caught up together into the clouds to meet their Lord and Savior *in the air*. As you have it in *First Thessalonians 4:16-17*,

For the Lord himself shall descend from heaven with a shout, with the voice of the archangel, with the trump of God: **and the dead in Christ shall rise first: then we which are alive and remain shall be caught up together with them in the clouds, to meet the Lord in the air***: and so shall we ever be with the Lord.* (KJV)

So the Rapture of the Church is not to be confused with the Second Coming that the Father is talking about here in verse seven. The Second Coming will occur **after** the Rapture at the end of the Tribulation. At that time, Christ will literally return to the earth to rule and reign here for a thousand years ... his feet literally touching down on the earth. Zechariah prophesied this very specifically saying,

*And in that day **his feet will stand on the Mount of Olives**, which faces Jerusalem on the east. And the Mount of Olives shall be split in two, from east to west, making a very large valley; half of the mountain shall move toward the north and half of it toward the south. Zechariah 14:4*

You will remember that it was from the Mount of Olives that Jesus left the Earth and ascended back into Heaven (Acts 1:11-12). It will also be to the Mount of Olives that he will return one day. What happens in between these two events is … this present Church age in which you and I live … plus the vast majority of what is about to be described to us here in the book of Revelation. All of chapters four through eighteen take up the subject of that latter time period. Here is a simple presentation of Christ's past and yet future appearances that might prove helpful in putting things into perspective.

Christ's First Coming and life on Earth

(4 or 5 BC to AD 29)

[born in Bethlehem; died on a cross at Jerusalem; rose from the dead; ascended back to Heaven from the Mount of Olives]

Christ's Next Appearance in the skies to Rapture out his Church

(AD 2013+)

Christ's Second Coming to Earth to rule and reign after of the seven year Tribulation

(AD 2020+)

Christ's Thousand Year Reign on Earth

(AD 2020+ to 3020+)

Verse seven then, is one of many prophecies in Scripture that predict Christ's Second Coming. Let's take a closer look at its details. The Father says,

*…**he is coming with clouds***. We need to go back to the prophet Daniel for this ***cloud*** aspect of the Lord Jesus Christ's Second Coming.

I was watching in the night visions, and **behold, One like the Son of Man, coming with the clouds of heaven**! *He came to the Ancient of Days, and they brought him near before him. Then to him was given dominion and glory and a* **kingdom** *that* **all peoples, nations, and languages should serve him**. *His dominion is an everlasting dominion, which shall not pass away, and his kingdom the one which shall not be destroyed. Daniel 7:13-14*

Keep in mind that the event Daniel saw in the scripture above was not the Second Coming. Rather, it was the future day when Christ will come to his Father's throne to formally receive his kingdom after the Rapture. We will see that day greatly magnified for us in Revelation four and five. Daniel's prophecy does, however, give us the **clouds of heaven** aspect of the movements of the Son of God in his glorified state. You might say Christ is Heaven's **Cloud Rider**. When he is on the move, the Shekinah glory clouds of Heaven accompany him. Both at the Rapture of the Church and at Christ's Second Coming, the Bible says Jesus will be accompanied by clouds. As you have it in *First Thessalonians 4:17a,*

Then we who are alive and remain shall be caught up together with them **in the clouds** *to meet the Lord in the air.*

These glory clouds were observed several times in Old Testament as well. Ezekiel saw and described them as follows:

And I looked, and, behold, a whirlwind came out of the north, **a great cloud, and a fire infolding itself, and a brightness was about it, and out of the midst thereof as the colour of amber, out of the midst of the fire**... *Ezekiel 1:4* (KJV)

What a sight they must be! Doubtless, this is what Jesus had in mind when he prayed,

Father, I will that they also, whom thou hast given me, be with me where I am; that they may **behold my glory**... *John 17:24a*

...every eye will see him, even they that pierced him. And all the tribes of the earth will mourn because of him. At Jesus' Second Coming, every living person on Earth will see him coming, as well as **they also that pierced him**. The Father's words here, **they also which pierced him**, sets before us two possibilities. He might simply be speaking about Jews in a general sense or he could be referring specifically to the actual Jews who were involved in the crucifixion. I take it to be the latter. At Jesus' trial, the Lord told Caiaphas that he personally would one day see him *coming in the clouds*. Let's look at that passage for a moment. Caiaphas said,

*'I put you under oath by the living God: tell us if you are the Christ, the Son of God!' Jesus said to him, 'It is as you said. Nevertheless, I say to you, hereafter **you** will **see** the Son of Man **sitting at the right hand of the Power**, and **coming on the clouds of heaven**.' Matthew 26:63b-64*

I suspect that the first part of the Lord's words to Caiaphas, were fulfilled when Caiaphas died. At that time, when Caiaphas' spirit returned to God, he probably witnessed Jesus **sitting at the right hand of the Power**. But, what about the second part of Jesus' statement that Caiaphas would also see him *coming on the clouds of heaven*? Since that clearly refers to Christ's Second Coming, it follows that Caiaphas himself will be present at that time to see it. Zechariah, speaking many years before Christ's birth, also prophesied that the Jews who crucified Christ would be present at his Second Coming.

And I will pour on the house of David and on the inhabitants of Jerusalem the Spirit of grace and supplication; ***then they will look on me whom they pierced****. Yes, they will **mourn** for him as one mourns for his only son, and grieve for him as one grieves for a firstborn. And one will say to him, 'What are these wounds between your arms?' Then he will answer, 'Those with which I was wounded in the house of my friends.' Zechariah 12:10; 13:6*

These and other scriptures indicate that the resurrection of Israel will take place just prior to Christ's Second Coming. At that time, all Jews from all time, including Caiaphas and those who were involved in Jesus' crucifixion, will find themselves beholding him as he is about to descend to Earth in the glory clouds of heaven. Then, suddenly, all wicked Jews will be removed from Earth by Christ's angels. This will be developed further when we get to Revelation 14.

...all the kindreds of the earth shall wail because of him. The wailing aspect of Christ's Second Coming is also prophesied in Zechariah 12, above. And, the Jews will not be the only ones to mourn at his coming. That future day will cause everyone around the globe to wail and mourn as well. Jesus spoke of this in *Matthew 24:29-30,*

Immediately **after the tribulation of those days** *the sun will be darkened, and the moon will not give its light; the stars will fall from heaven, and the powers of the heavens will be shaken. Then the sign of the Son of Man will appear in heaven, and then* **all the tribes of the earth will mourn***, and* **they will see the Son of Man coming on the clouds of heaven** *with power and great glory.*

Notice, in the above scripture, that Jesus places his Second Coming *after the tribulation of those days*. We need to tuck that important detail away in our memory banks. The Father's prophecy of the Second Coming here ends with John's prayerful exclamation (and, I trust, yours and mine as well) ... **Even so, Amen.**

1:8

Immediately after John's **Amen**, the Father's voice was once again heard. He exclaimed **I am Alpha and the Omega.** Alpha and Omega are the first and last letters of the Greek alphabet. This is like saying *I am the A and the Z.* With these words, he is declaring that he is everything, the beginning and the end, and everything in-between. May I say to you, very sincerely, that anyone who does not come to know the true and living God through faith in his Son, Jesus Christ, has missed out on absolutely everything. The chief end of man is to know God and to enjoy and glorify him forever. He is the **Alpha and the Omega**, you see.

He continued ... **who is, who was, and who is to come, the Almighty**. This confirms to us that the One speaking here is the same one who greeted us back in verse four, namely, God the eternal and everlasting Father.

Rev. 1:9-11

I, John, **[NU omits "both"]** *your brother and companion in the tribulation and kingdom and patience of Jesus Christ, was on the island that is called* **Patmos** *for the* **word of God** *and for the* **testimony of Jesus Christ***. I was* **in the Spirit on the Lord's Day***, and I heard behind me a loud voice, as of a* **trumpet***, saying,* **[NU omits "'I am the Alpha and the Omega, the First and the Last,' and,"]** *'What you see,*

***write** in a book and **send it to the seven churches** [**NU omits, "which are in Asia:"**] to Ephesus, to Smyrna, to Pergamos, to Thyatira, to Sardis, to Philadelphia, and to Laodicea.'*

1:9

At the time that John wrote these words, the Romans had put him in exile out on the little island of Patmos. It is a small rocky island off the coast of Turkey out in the Aegean Sea. John had been the Pastor of the church at Ephesus ... just across the water from Patmos which was now his island prison. He tells us here that he had been imprisoned out there for two reasons:

...for the word of God. Apparently, John had been exiled for his writings of the Word of God. He had written four books of the Bible and it seems they had gotten him into hot water with the Romans. Domitian, the Roman Caesar at that time, was a notorious persecutor of believers in Christ.

...for the testimony of Jesus Christ. John was also exiled for his mouth. He was a bold and unashamed witness for the Lord Jesus Christ. Both his writings and his preaching had landed this great Apostle in the clink. Someone has asked ... *If it were illegal to be a Christian would there be enough evidence to convict you?* There was plenty of evidence to convict John. What he wrote and what he said made it abundantly clear that Christ was his life and the Romans put him away for it ... way out there on Patmos.

1:10

He continues:

...I was in the spirit. The most natural and consistent interpretation of this statement is that John is referring to the fact that he had a unique, Spirit initiated, experience. I take this to be a reference to the Holy Spirit. In chapter four, verse two, he uses this same phrase, ***in the spirit***, to describe how he was caught up into Heaven. The Apostle Paul recounted a similar experience when he also was taken up to Heaven (2 Corinthians 12:2). In that passage he says that he couldn't tell if he was in his body or out of it. Now, mystics have often claimed such experiences as well, but they are deceived. A drug related or transcendental experience is not the same as the Spirit controlled experiences that John and Paul had. Their experiences were *the real McCoy.*

...on the Lord's day. This is an idiomatic phrase which was coined by the first century Church. It was the name the first century believers used to describe their day of worship. Today, most people just call it *Sunday*. They called it *the Lord's day*. They called it that because it was the day their Lord and ours arose from the dead. It was observed on Sunday, the first day of the week, as opposed to the Sabbath, which fell on Saturday. It also was chosen to emphasize that the Church was no longer obligated to keep the Law with its Sabbath day requirements but was now under grace.

Let's use our imagination here for a moment. Picture, John. He's lean, having had to endure the hard life of a Roman exile. Picture him sitting ... all alone ... on the stony seashore of his island prison. He's been staring out across the sea toward Ephesus. He's thinking and praying over his little flock over there across the water. Suddenly, he finds himself *in the spirit* and behind him a great voice like *a trumpet* spoke. It is the same voice, by the way, that you and I will hear one day, dear saint. This *trumpet* voiced One will cause us to forget all our troubles, aye!? His words rang in John's ears:

1:11

...what you see, write in a book and send it to the seven churches.

Rev. 1:12-16

*Then I turned to see the voice that spoke with me. And having turned I saw **seven golden lampstands**, and in the midst of the seven lampstands **One like the Son of Man**, **clothed with a garment** down to the feet and girded about the chest with a **golden band**. His head and hair were **white like wool**, as white as snow, and his **eyes like a flame of fire**; his feet were like **fine brass**, as if refined in a furnace, and his **voice as the sound of many waters;** he had in his right hand **seven stars**, out of his mouth went a sharp **two-edged sword,** and his countenance was **like the sun** shining in its strength.*

1:12

No doubt, John abruptly turned to see who had spoken with such power and authority and, when he turned, he found himself gazing upon a scene and a Person extraordinaire. He saw **seven golden lampstands**. The Koine Greek word here for **lampstands** is λυχνιας (**luxnias**). It is a word that means **pedestals**. These were stands that people sat their oil lamps on so they would yield maximum light in a room. Doubtless, each one had a lamp burning atop of it. One translation renders this word *torches*. After seeing the lamp-stands, John's eyes moved to the amazing person who was standing in their midst.

1:13

He says he saw:

...One like the Son of Man. This is one of the major prophetic titles of Messiah in the Old Testament. It comes from *Daniel 7:13*,

I was watching in the night visions, and behold, **One like the Son of Man***, coming with the clouds of heaven! He came to the Ancient of Days, and they brought him near before him.*

This Messianic title emphasizes Christ's humanity as well as his future reign. It is a well-recognized Jewish designation for their future King and Messiah. When the Son of Man came into our world and lived among us, he took upon himself human flesh. He became one of us. As you have it in *Hebrews 2:14* and *16-17*,

Inasmuch then as the children have partaken of flesh and blood, he himself likewise shared in the same, that through death he might destroy him who had the power of death, that is, the devil...

For indeed he does not give aid to angels, but he does give aid to the seed of Abraham. Therefore, **in all things he had to be made like his brethren***, that he might be a merciful and faithful High Priest in things pertaining to God, to make propitiation for the sins of the people.*

Luke's gospel also emphasizes this aspect of the person of Jesus Christ. There, Jesus repeatedly refers to himself as **the Son of Man**. As you have it in *Luke 19:10*,

... for the **Son of Man** *has come to seek and to save that which was lost.*

At this very moment, there is a *Man* seated at the right hand of the Majesty on High. He is one of us. He has been here, done that. He knows all about us. He knows our trials, our temptations, our weaknesses, our fears, our frailties and our troubles. He knows what it is to be human. As you have it in *Hebrews 4:14-16,*

*Seeing then that we have a great high priest, that is passed into the heavens, Jesus the Son of God, let us hold fast our profession. For **we have not an high priest which cannot be touched with the feeling of our infirmities**; but was in all points tempted like as we are, yet without sin. Let us therefore come boldly unto the throne of grace, that we may obtain mercy, and find grace to help in time of need.* (KJV)

*...**clothed with a garment down to the feet.*** He was wearing the long, flowing robe of a priest. As you have it in *Hebrews 5:6,*

*You are a **priest** forever according to the order of Melchizedek.*

And again in *Hebrews 4:14,*

*Seeing then that **we have a great High Priest** who has passed through the heavens, Jesus the Son of God, let us hold fast our confession.*

You may wish to read Hebrews 5, just to refresh your thinking concerning Jesus, our great High Priest, who God has appointed a Priest forever after the order of Melchizedek (Psalm 110:4). Melchizedek was the king/priest to whom Abraham paid tithes in Genesis 14. We learn from Hebrews that his priesthood is separate from ... and far superior to ... the Aaronic priesthood of the Law. Jesus couldn't have been an Aaronic priest because he was not from the tribe of Levi. He was from the tribe of Judah. Therefore, God appointed him a priest forever after the order of Melchizedek. And guess what, child of God ... since Christ has made you and me *a kingdom of priests* (Rev.1:6; 1 Peter 2:9), by virtue of the fact that we are in Christ, we also have been placed into the priesthood of the order of Melchizedek of whom our Savior is High Priest. Our priesthood predates and is far superior to the Aaronic priesthood of the Law of Moses. So, if anyone ever asks what kind of priest you are ... just tell them you are of the order of Melchizedek.

*...**girded about the chest with a golden band***. The One who stood before John wore a *golden band* around his waist. I believe

this speaks of the fact that John was standing in the presence of a *king*. Few people wore such a unique and expensive thing as this unless they were a king. To be specific, the One standing before John was *the King of the Jews*. At his crucifixion, in mockery and jest they nailed a sign to Jesus' cross that said in Greek, Latin, and Hebrew,

*This is **the King of the Jews** Luke 23:38b*

Standing before John was that very King. And, although I believe this was the primary emphasis, he certainly was far more than that. He was also the King of kings of *Daniel 7:14*,

Then to him was given dominion and glory and a kingdom, that all peoples, nations, and languages should serve him. His dominion is an everlasting dominion, which shall not pass away, and his kingdom the one which shall not be destroyed.

1:14

*...**His head and hair were white like wool, as white as snow**.* This speaks of the fact that the One standing before John was the Eternal One as well ... the very incarnation of the Ancient of Days ... the everlasting God. The prophet Micah, prophesying about Jesus' birth, said,

*But you, Bethlehem Ephrathah, though you are little among the thousands of Judah, yet out of you shall come forth to me the one to be Ruler in Israel, **whose goings forth are from of old, from everlasting**. Micah 5:2*

His white ***head and hair*** also emphasized this was the One who is Wisdom itself. First Corinthians 1:31, says that Jesus is the ***wisdom of God***. That being the case, it is Jesus himself who spoke through Solomon's pen in Proverbs 8. There, Wisdom personified says,

*I, **wisdom**, dwell with prudence, and find out knowledge and discretion.' 'I love those who love me, and those who seek me diligently will find me. Proverbs 8:12, 17*

Ruth Paxton, one of God's great saints and writers about the Holy Spirit, is said to have received Christ as her Savior when she realized that the Wisdom who was speaking in Proverbs 8, was none other than the Lord Jesus Christ himself. What an amazing Person stood before

John that day. There was standing none other than the white-haired, eternal Ancient of Days ... Wisdom himself!

...his eyes were like a flame of fire. When John's eyes met the eyes of the one standing before him ... how unsettling it must have been. His eyes penetrated John like a laser causing John to immediately look away. They were the eyes of the One who possessed both absolute knowledge and absolute holiness. They were the eyes of the Omniscient Holy One. As you have it in *Jeremiah 23:24a*,

*Can anyone hide himself in secret places, so I shall not **see** him? says the* LORD.

And again, as you have it in *Hebrews 4:13*,

And there is no creature hidden from his sight, but all things are naked and open to the eyes of him to whom we must give account.

In Psalm 139, we read of the extent to which he is intimately acquainted with each one of us. Nothing about us escapes him. It says there that he sees our retiring at night and our getting up in the morning and that he reads all of our thoughts from afar.

1:15

It was no accident that John's eyes fell swiftly away to the ground from the fiery-eyed One who stood before him. I believe your eyes and mine will fall away from them as well, one day. With bowed, John now found himself staring at the feet of the Son of Man. Then, he says:

...His feet were like fine brass, as if refined in a furnace. The brassy feet that stood before John spoke of **judgment**. They were the **hardened** feet of the One who will one day tramp out the **winepress of the fierceness and wrath of Almighty God** (Rev.19:15b). In short, it was the **Judge of the whole Earth** who was standing before John. As you have it in *John 5:22-23*,

For the Father judges no one, but has committed all judgment to the Son, that all should honor the Son just as they honor the Father. He who does not honor the Son does not honor the Father who sent him.

...his voice as the sound of many waters. My, what a voice. John describes it as having the same awesome quality as cataracts of thundering waters. Doubtless, it causes a physical sensation of raw power when heard. This is the One who speaks the Word of God ...

the Omnipotent One himself. There is a whole Psalm written about this voice, by the way. It is Psalm 29. There, we read in verses three and four,

*The **voice** of the* LORD *is over the waters; the God of glory **thunders**; the* LORD *is over many **waters**. The voice of the* LORD *is powerful; the voice of the* LORD *is **full of majesty**.*

1:16

...He had in his right hand seven stars. This is the second symbol that we have encountered so far in Revelation. The first were the lampstands. Before we go on, let me say a word about interpreting symbols. The general rule is, when a symbol is *obscure*, the Bible will explain it to us (with the exception of certain things that are not for us to know but are written for our brothers and sisters in a yet future day). On the other hand, if a symbol is *obvious*, and clearly refers to a known thing in the Scripture, the text will not explain it. We are expected to understand those symbols from our knowledge of the Word of God. These two symbols, the **lampstands** and the **seven stars**, are *obscure* symbols. We are not expected to know the meaning of them. Therefore, they will be explained to us later in the chapter.

...out of his mouth went a sharp two-edged sword. This is the third symbol in this opening chapter. However, it is an *obvious* one and does not need to be explained. Can you decipher it? As a student of the Word of God, we are expected to recognize this symbol. This **sword** represents the Word of God. In several places in the Bible, a sword is used as a metaphor for the Word of God. For example, as you have it in *Hebrews 4:12*,

*For the **word of God** is living and powerful, and sharper than any **two-edged sword**, piercing even to the division of soul and spirit, and of joints and marrow, and is a discerner of the thoughts and intents of the heart.*

And again, in *Ephesians 6:17*, we read,

*And take the helmet of salvation, and **the sword of the Spirit, which is the word of God**...*

Standing before John was the One who speaks the sharp sword of the Word of God. How amazing and powerful his words are ... how irresistible, eternal, and unstoppable! By the words from those lips the universe was spoken into existence and, I might add, is presently being held together. *Hebrews 11:3,* says,

*By faith we understand that the worlds were framed by the **word of God**, so that the things which are seen were not made of things which are visible.*

And again, in *Colossians 1:16* (speaking of Christ), we read,

***For by him were all things created**, that are in heaven, and that are in earth, visible and invisible, whether they be thrones, or dominions, or principalities, or powers: all things were created by him, and for him and he is before all things and **by him all things consist**.* (KJV)

And again, in *Hebrews 1:3,*

*Who being the brightness of his glory, and the express image of his person, and **upholding all things by the word of his power**, when he had by himself purged our sins, sat down on the right hand of the Majesty on high...*(KJV)

Oh, the raw power of the Word of God!

...His countenance was like the sun shining in its strength. In blinding glory, the One who possesses all glory stood before John on that day. John had seen a fleeting glimpse of his glory on the Mount of Transfiguration (Matthew17; Mark 9), but what a difference it was on this day. Jesus' prayer in John 17, had been answered, you see.

*And now, O Father, **glorify me** together with yourself, with the **glory** which I had with you before the world was. John 17:5*

The Christ who stood before John that day was standing in all the fullness of the glory of God. John saw him as he is right now and as you and I will see him one day ... the utterly resplendent One. Struggling to describe him, John can only say he was *like the sun shining in its strength*. In *First Timothy 6:15-16* we read,

*He will **manifest** in his own time, he who is the blessed and only Potentate, the King of kings and Lord of lords, who alone has immortality, **dwelling in unapproachable light**, whom no man has seen or can see, to whom be honor and everlasting power. Amen.*

So, there we have it. In Revelation 1, we are given a description of the glorified Christ as seen nowhere else in the Bible. He steps forth here, in awesome and resplendent majesty. An unveiling indeed, wouldn't you say?

Rev. 1:17-20

*And when I saw him, I fell at his feet as dead. But he laid his right hand on me, saying to me, 'Do not be afraid; I am the **First and the Last**. I am he who lives, and was dead, and behold, I am alive forevermore.' Amen. 'And I have the keys of Hades and of Death.* **[NU adds "*Therefore*"]** *write the things which you have seen, and the things which are, and the things which will take place after this. The mystery of the seven stars which you saw in my right hand, and the seven golden lampstands: The seven stars are the **angels** of the seven churches, and the seven **lampstands** **[NU omits "which you saw"]** are the seven churches.'*

1:17

When Christ was on earth, John had often reclined affectionately against him at meal times. We read in John 13, that he did so at the Last Supper. Now, however, he fell before his Lord like a sack of potatoes. Compassionately, Jesus reached down and touched his old friend and disciple and said, **Do not be afraid.** Immediately, John was strengthened. Jesus then continued:

...I am the First and the Last. With these seven words, Jesus took to himself the unmistakable title of deity from *Isaiah 44:6,*

Thus says the LORD, the King of Israel, **and** *his Redeemer***, the LORD of hosts***: 'I am* **the First** *and I am* **the Last***; besides me there is no* **God***.'*

Notice how this scripture says that **both** the *Lord*, who is the **King of Israel**, **and** his **Redeemer**, **the LORD of hosts** ... share the same name ... **the First** and **the Last** ... and that, together, they are the one and only true **God**. There are several names of the Deity that are used interchangeably between the Father and the Son, by the way. In this way they declare their equality in the godhead and their oneness of essence. In *Isaiah 9:6,* for example, the prophet speaks specifically of Jesus Christ saying,

For unto us a child is born, unto us a son is given; and the government will be upon his shoulder. And his name will be called **Wonderful***,* **Counselor***,* **Mighty God***,* **Everlasting Father***,* **Prince of Peace***.*

1:18

...I am he who lives, and was dead, and behold, I am alive forevermore. Amen. And I have the keys of Hades and of Death. The NIV more correctly translates this, *I am the Living One; I was dead.* If we didn't know who this was by now, these words make his identity crystal clear. He identifies himself as the One who *was dead* but *behold, I am alive forevermore*. The Greek literally says *I am alive to the ages of the ages!* This is the risen Christ. I'm so glad that you and I serve a living Savior, aren't you? All the founders of man's bogus religions are dead as a door-nail. They are all lying in their graves at this very moment. But our Savior, Christ Jesus, is *alive*. He is the Living One, you see. He alone can say, *I have the* **keys** *of Hades and of Death* because he has conquered them both. As he put it in *John 5:26-29*,

*For as the Father has life in himself, so he has granted the Son to have life in himself, and has given him authority to execute judgment also, because he is the Son of Man. Do not marvel at this; for **the hour is coming in which all who are in the graves will hear his voice and come forth**; those who have done good, to the resurrection of life, and those who have done evil, to the resurrection of condemnation.*

The Apostle Paul writes in *First Corinthians 15:55-57,*

*O Death, where is your sting? O Hades, where is your victory? The sting of death is sin, and the strength of sin is the law. But **thanks be to God, who gives us the victory through our Lord Jesus Christ**.*

Matters of life and death and the grave (*Hades*) are held exclusively in the hands of Christ Jesus our Lord. He owns them. He has the *keys*.

1:19

In verse nineteen, the Lord once again commissioned John to be his designated writer of the book of Revelation. He tells him to *write the things which you have seen, and the things which are, and the things which will take place after this.* These words form Christ's own outline of the book of Revelation. It is as follows:

1.	***The things which you have seen***	Chapter 1 (Past things, which John had just seen)
2.	***the things which are***	Chapters 2-3 (Present things, that John will shortly hear about concerning the seven churches.)
3.	***the things which will take place after this***	Chapters 4-22 (Future things, things to come.)

1:20

Last, here in verse twenty we come to the Lord's explanation of the two obscure symbols ... the ***seven stars in His right hand*** ... and the ***seven golden lampstands*** in the midst of which Christ was standing. Let's consider them separately.

He says ... ***The seven stars are the angels of the seven churches.*** The word ***angel***, in the Greek here, is αγγελοι (***angeloi***). Each one of the letters to the seven churches in chapters 2 and 3 begin with the words ... ***unto the angel of the church at*** (such and such) ***write***. This Greek word is usually translated ***angel*** in the Bible. Its basic meaning, however, is *messenger* and is sometimes translated that way as well. It is a word that is used for men (who are sent out as messengers) as well as for God's angels. I do not believe that our Lord is speaking here of angels. So, the translation, ***angels***, in the KJ and NKJ is inaccurate. Nowhere in Scripture are angels said to be assigned to or have any special function in regard to a local church. Rather, an angel's function is to minister to individual believers (Hebrews 1:11). So, it doesn't make sense for Christ to address his letters in chapters 2 and 3 to angels. On the contrary, it is far more reasonable that Christ is addressing his letters to specific men who would actually receive them and read them to their congregations. The better translation then, is ***unto the messengers of the seven churches, write*** ... and ... ***To the messenger of the church at __ write.*** And so it is correctly translated in several other translations of the Bible.

Having said that, who are these ***messengers*** then that, symbolically, our Lord is holding in his hand? Well, they probably represent the chief elders or pastor-teachers of the seven churches. Logically, such men would receive and read to their congregation any communication that was received. Also, they were, in a very Biblical sense, Christ's ***messengers*** to his churches because they were men who Christ himself had sent to them. As you have it in *Ephesians 4:11*,

*And he himself **gave** some to be apostles, some prophets, some evangelists, and some **pastors and teachers**...*

One of the tragic things about the church culture of our day is that many do not see their pastor-teacher for what he is … gifts and messengers to them from the Lord Jesus Christ himself. Take it for what it is worth, I believe this is the best translation of ***angeloi*** here. It refers to the local elder, pastor-teacher at each of the seven churches that existed in John's day and to which Christ is about to address in specific letters.

Now, concerning the symbol of the ***lampstands***, in the midst of which our Lord was standing, Christ says they represent ***the seven churches*** themselves. What a wonderful and appropriate symbol he chose for his churches. In Jesus' eyes, each one of these churches were pedestals upon which a light was to be placed in order to dispel the darkness around them. As you have it in *Matthew 5:15-16*,

*Neither do men light a candle, and put it under a bushel, **but on a candlestick**; and it giveth light unto all that are in the house. Let your light so shine before men, that they may see your good works, and glorify your Father which is in heaven.* (KJV)

Philippians 2:15-16a, says,

*… that you may become blameless and harmless, children of God without fault in the midst of a crooked and perverse generation, among whom **you shine as lights in the world, holding fast the word of life**…*

Jesus is the Light of the World. Right now, however, he is seated at the right hand of the Majesty on High and shines forth in this present dark world through his churches. Every true church is a lampstand for Christ.

In conclusion, you will remember that when John first turned to see the Trumpet-Voiced One, he saw the Lord standing ***in the midst*** of the ***lampstands***. This too is quite significant. It was the job of the High

Priest in the Old Testament to tend the lamp-stands in the Holy Place. It was his responsibility to trim their wicks, replenish their oil and keep them burning brightly. Christ Jesus, standing *in the midst of the seven lampstands*, was a beautiful picture of the relationship between himself, as High Priest, and the churches, his lamp-stands. As our *great high priest*, he is always in the midst of his churches tending to each one so that its light might shine to its maximum potential.

REVELATION 2 - 3

CHRIST IN THE MIDST OF HIS CHURCHES

We come now to the second division of the book of Revelation, THE VISION OF JESUS CHRIST MIDST HIS CHURCHES. Following Jesus outline back in 1:19, John will now write down *the things which are*. This section contains seven letters from Christ to seven of his local churches that existed in John's day. This section will not be just dry history, however. We will discover that the things Christ said to these churches are as relevant to us 21st century Christians as today's newspaper. Doubtless, it is Christ's intention that each one of these letters should apply to all of his believers throughout history. He makes that abundantly clear when at the end of each letter he exhorts the reader, *he that has an ear, let him hear what the Spirit says to the churches.*

In *Matthew 13:16*, Jesus said to his disciples,

*But blessed are your eyes, for they see: **and your ears**, **for they hear**.*

He was speaking about his disciples' ability to perceive and receive spiritual truth ... in contrast to the majority of other Israelites at that time who had no such ability. When he spoke those words, he had just finished quoting *Isaiah 6:9-10*, which says,

By hearing ye shall hear, and shall not understand; and seeing ye shall see, and shall not perceive: for this people's heart is waxed gross, and their ears are dull of hearing, and their eyes they have closed; lest at any time they should see with their eyes, and hear with their ears, and should understand with their heart, and should be converted, and I would heal them.

Spiritual truth can only be received and understood by spiritual people. This is what our Lord is referring to when, at the end of each of these letters, he says, *he that has an ear, let him hear what the Spirit says to the churches*. Cleary our Lord had many more readers of these letters in mind than merely their original recipients. They are meant for all of his believers of all time ... folks like you and me ... those who have **ears to hear**.

Also, I am convinced that these letters are not placed here at the beginning of the book of Revelation by accident. Jesus, the Head of the Church, put them here for a purpose. His purpose is so that those who continue on to read the deep, complex, amazing and eye opening prophecies of this book would be spiritually prepared to receive them. This is very important. The letters to the seven churches are placed here by design ... so that we readers of the Revelation have the opportunity for a spiritual tune-up, so to speak, before we proceed on with the book. The Apostle Paul, speaking to the Corinthian church, said,

*And I, brethren, could not speak unto you as unto **spiritual**, but as unto **carnal**, even as unto **babes** in Christ. I have fed you with **milk**, and not with **meat**: for hitherto you were not able to bear it, neither yet are you able. First Corinthians 3:1-2* (KJV)

Carnal believers and **babes** have little appetite for ... and little ability to ... receive and understand the Word of God. Those abilities are tied to the condition of one's heart. When a believer's heart is right toward God, the Word of God becomes his or her delight and their necessary food for daily living. Here in chapters 2 and 3, we readers of the Revelation are going to receive a great blessing. As we read Christ's letters to the churches, we will be given the opportunity to receive a renewing of our hearts. Jesus, our loving and all-knowing Great Physician, will give each of us a spiritual examination. He will take our spiritual temperature. There will be no holding back. Then, when he is finished, he will simply tell us his findings and prescribe the precise cure that we may need. By the end of chapter 3, if we will comply with his words we will be spiritually running on all eight cylinders and completely ready to receive all the wonderful revelations that our loving Lord and his Father so eagerly want to convey to us. Are you up for this? Ready or not, here we go. It would serve us well to enter these next two very special chapters with the prayer of David on our lips,

Search me, O God, and know my heart: try me, and know my thoughts: and see if there be any wicked way in me, and lead me in the way everlasting. Psalm 139:23-24 (KJV)

One more thing before we begin ... let me quickly point out that there are other views as to how these letters were intended. Probably the most common is that each letter is simply a snapshot of a particular **period** in Church history. Personally, I find no indication of that, either in the text or in church history. The danger in that view, in my opinion, is that it diverts the reader's attention away from what the Lord is actually trying to say to us here and, instead, sidetracks the reader's attention away to the academic exercise of sorting through the often dry leaves of church history ... trying to find a fit for each letter.

EPHESUS

THE COLD CHURCH

Rev. 2:1-17

To the angel of the church of Ephesus write, 'These things says he who holds the **seven stars** *in his right hand, who* **walks in the midst of the seven golden lampstands***: I know your works, your labor, your patience, and that you cannot bear those who are evil. And you have tested those who say they are apostles and are not, and have found them liars; and you have persevered and have patience, and have labored for my name's sake and have not become weary. Nevertheless, I have this against you, that you have* **left your first love***. Remember therefore from where you have fallen;* **repent** *and do the first works, or else I will come to you quickly and remove your lampstand from its place; unless you repent. But this you have, that you hate the deeds of the* **Nicolaitans***, which I also hate. He who has an ear, let him hear what the Spirit says to the churches. To him who overcomes I will give to eat from the tree of life, which is in the midst of the Paradise of God.'*

Ephesus was a beautiful and wealthy cultural center in its day. It used white marble extensively in its buildings. It had a theater that held twenty thousand and an amphitheater with a capacity of an hundred thousand. Historians tell us that, on occasion, one to two million people were inside the city. I suspect that the Ephesian church was a wealthy church.

2:1

THE SALUTATION

First, notice that Christ opens each one of his seven letters with one or more key descriptions of himself. These descriptions are designed to be powerful reminders to the readers of just who the letter is from. In most of the letters, the description that Christ uses to identify himself comes directly out of chapter one. In addition, each unique salutation is tailored specifically for the situation of the particular church that he is addressing.

The Lord addresses the Ephesian church as **he who holds the seven stars in his right hand, who walks in the midst of the seven golden lampstands.** This description emphasizes that Christ is the **head of the Church**. The Ephesians had heard that before. In Paul's letter to them, he said that Christ is **head over all things to the church** (Ephesians 1:22b). Apparently, they needed to hear that truth again.

Now, you will remember that Jesus explained these symbols back in chapter one. There, Christ said that the **stars** represented the **messengers** of the churches. Using that symbol again here, Jesus is emphasizing again that he is the one who gave this church their pastor (he came **from** his hand) and also that he was guiding him as well (he is **in** his hand). Is that the way you view your pastor? That's the way Christ sees him.

Then, he says that he **walks in the midst of the golden lampstands**. Back in chapter one, you will remember that the **lampstands** were symbols of the seven churches themselves. By bringing up this second symbol to the Ephesians, Christ is emphasizing his absolute headship over the Church and is reminding them of how intimately he is involved in its day to day life. Christ walks in the midst of his churches ... controlling, inspecting, advising, encouraging, sanctifying, interceding, nurturing, chastening, coaching and judging each and every one. Sometimes, a pastor or some church member or board member might begin to think of themselves as the head of their particular church. When that occurs, it is tragic. Invariably, it leads to bad consequences. Jesus alone is the head of the Church. In real life, when properly applied, the truths portrayed by these two symbols balance themselves in the life of a healthy church.

2:2-3

THE COMPLIMENT

I know your works, your labor, your patience, and that you cannot bear those who are evil. And you have tested those who say they are apostles and are not, and have found them liars; and you have persevered and have patience, and have labored for my name's sake and have not become weary.

Jesus is very positive about his church at Ephesus. Let's look at his commendations here for a moment. He says:

...I know your works, your labor. They were a **working** church ... busy for their God ... fulfilling the admonition of *First Corinthians 15:58,*

Therefore, my beloved brethren, be steadfast, immovable, always **abounding in the work of the Lord***, knowing that your* **labor** *is not in vain in the Lord.*

...you cannot bear those who are evil. They were a **separated** church. They didn't run with the wrong crowd and found those who practiced evil to be unbearable and totally unsuitable to fellowship with.

...you have tested those who say they are apostles and are not, and have found them liars. They were a **theologically sound** church. They knew their Bibles and weren't easily taken in by the *wolves in sheep's clothing* who came bearing lies and false doctrines. Our Lord is pleased with his serving, separated and doctrinally sound churches.

2:4-5

THE PROBLEM

...Nevertheless I have this against you, that you have left your first love. How hard it must have been for the Ephesians to hear these words. He who reads the heart and mind can surely put his finger on a problem, can he not? This sounds serious ... and it is. What do you think this *first love* is, that our Lord is so concerned about? No doubt, the Ephesians asked themselves that same question. Well, isn't it first love that most marriages begin with? When a marriage falls by the

wayside, it is certain that the two partners have left their first love. As with a marriage, the *first love* of any believer is his or her first love for the Savior. Jesus is every believer's first love. Somehow, at Ephesus, the entire church had let that fact slip. Amazing. These folks, who crossed all their doctrinal "ts" just right ... and who were separated from the world and busy as bees in the work of the Lord were living out their Christian lives with a fatal flaw. Their hearts had grown cold toward the Savior that had bought them and called them into fellowship with himself! Before we jump on them too hard, however, let me say that this is one of the easiest things in the world to happen to a believer. Our relationship with Christ can become cool and stale so very quickly. Have you not found it to be so? It is a very subtle thing. Frankly, if you and I are not in love with Jesus Christ, everything else we do is simply emptiness and vanity. A heart grown cold toward Christ ... is a heart in serious trouble.

THE REMEDY

...*Remember therefore from where you have fallen; repent and do the first works*. Our Lord is very practical here. He points the way back for these Ephesian believers from their "spiritual Siberia" in no uncertain terms. For the heart that has grown cold toward him, the Great Physician offers a three step cure.

First, he says to **Remember.** Can you remember when you first fell in love with the Savior? Think back for a moment. Remember how excited you were about him? Jesus says this is step one ... **Remember.**

Second, he says, **repent.** Coldness toward Christ is a sin that must be confessed and forsaken (First John.1:9). If your relationship with Christ has grown old and cold, the way back is to call a spade a spade and **repent**, dear child of God. It is our own fault if we have allowed our relationship with Christ to deteriorate into spiritual frostbite. However, although our love for Christ may have waned, his love for us has not changed at all. As we learned back in chapter one, he is loving us at this very moment ... even with these words.

Third, the Lord says, **do the first works**. The Ephesians were doing many good works, but they weren't doing the most important ones. They weren't doing the *first works*. He is speaking here about the kind of things they did when they first fell in love with him. Do you remember your first works? Think for a minute about someone that has recently come to Christ and is all aglow with the fire of his or her newfound relationship with him. What kind of things do they do? A few years ago, there was a fellow I worked with who came to Christ. His fervency and absolute love for the Savior was almost embarrassing. He talked to Jesus constantly ... and read his Bible ... my goodness ... sometimes all night long! Also, he talked incessantly about Jesus to anyone and everyone who would listen. A year and a half later, (6/2003), he was still calling me up all excited about the things he had found in the Bible and just wanting to share them with me. New love just can't keep its mouth shut, can it? How natural it is to tell people when we've found that special someone that we've fallen in love with. How's your relationship with the Savior? Have you been sitting at his feet by reading his Word? Have you been talking to him a lot in prayer? Have you been telling others about him? Those are *first works*, beloved.

May we pause here for a moment? Would you be willing to take a bit of a spiritual inventory along with me? When was the last time you or I told Jesus that we loved him? Has it been a while? My, we believers are so easily infected with the *spiritual cold virus*. And, when we get that way, it affects everything we say and do, as well as everyone else around us. When our love for Christ turns cold, we become like a window in the Church left open in winter. We tend to freeze everyone else who is in the room! Don't be a window letting in the cold, be a heater that keeps your home and church warm for Christ. Above all else, we must keep our *first love* burning as warmly as the first day we came to know Jesus. This is primary in the Christian life. If the Spirit is speaking to you about this, would you like to take a moment and repent and just throw your arms around his neck, as it were, and tell him that you are sorry and that you love him? Good. Now, we can get back to doing the *first works*, aye!?

THE WARNING

How important is this? If their first love is not restored, Jesus says, *I will come to you quickly and remove your lampstand from its place*. When coldness toward Christ is a church-wide problem, it is a disaster. The Head of the Church is threatening here to shut this church down if their first love is not restored. I believe entire denominations are being shut down by the Head of the Church today because they have left their first love. Where once mighty congregations thrived on the Word of God and prayed and evangelized, there is little left but empty pews. God forbid that it should happen to your church or mine.

2:6

After this painful but profitable expose', the Lord returns now to the things that please him at Ephesus. He begins by commending them for hating **the deeds of the Nicolaitans**, which he says, **I also hate**. I know of no solid historical information about this sect. Exactly what the Nicolaitans practiced or believed, we do not know. Suffice it to say that Jesus is pleased with any church that stands firmly against groups, clubs, sects and cults who hold bold heresies or practice immorality and wickedness. It's a good thing to hate what Jesus hates.

2:7

THE ADMONITION AND THE PROMISE

Our Lord's closing words to the church at Ephesus instructs all those who read this **to hear what the Spirit says to the churches**. Then, he closes with the promise saying, **To him that overcomes I will give to eat from the tree of life which is in the midst of the Paradise of God**. An *overcomer*, by the way, is anyone who is a true believer in the Lord Jesus Christ. As you have it in *First John 5:5*,

*Who is he who **overcomes** the world, but he who believes that Jesus is the Son of God?*

Christ promises all his **overcomers** here that one day they will eat from **the tree of life** in the midst of God's green Heaven. I'm up for that. How about you? We'll take a closer look at this tree when we come to chapter 22.

SMYRNA

THE SUFFERING CHURCH

Rev. 2:8-11

*And to the angel of the church in Smyrna write, 'These things says the **First and the Last, who was dead, and came to life**: I know your works, tribulation, and poverty (but you are rich); and I know the blasphemy of those who say they are Jews and are not, but are a synagogue of Satan. Do not fear any of those things which you are about to suffer. Indeed, the devil is about to throw some of you into prison, that you may be **tested**, and you will have tribulation ten days. **Be faithful until death**, and I will give you the crown of life. He who has an ear, let him hear what the Spirit says to the churches. He who overcomes shall not be hurt by the second death.'*

2:8

THE SALUTATION

Christ addresses the Smyrna church as ***the First and the Last, who was dead, and came to life***. So, he greets them not only as God of very God, but also as the one who, himself, has suffered and died but came back to life. It is good for suffering believers to be reminded that they are following in the footsteps of their God and suffering Savior, Jesus Christ. And, like Christ himself, though they might even be killed for their faith, their future is truly bright and secure. These truths can be of great comfort to those saints who are enduring fiery trials for his name's sake. *Philippians 1:29* says,

*For to you it has been granted on behalf of Christ, not only to believe in him, but also to **suffer** for his sake...*

2:9

THE COMPLIMENT

Christ tells them, ***I know your works, tribulation and poverty***. It is comforting to know that our Lord sees and cares about every situation and trouble of his children. The **works** of the saints at Smyrna did not lack the solid foundation of love for the Savior that was the case at Ephesus. These Smyrnites were a bunch of on-fire believers for Christ. But, in their day to day lives, this had brought about great difficulty. Persecution was the order of their day and it had complicated their lives with economic loss and destitution. Christ tells them that he is aware of their **poverty**. Jesus knows all about poverty, by the way. Once, he told a scribe who was thinking of following him,

*The foxes have holes, and the birds of the air have nests; but **the Son of man hath not where to lay his head**. Matthew 8:20*

Our Lord's words to his believers at Smyrna indicate they had lost material possessions for his name's sake, possibly even their homes and livelihoods. If they were alive today, some misguided soul might say to them *It is because you aren't tithing*! (Sic). What a crock those misguided purveyors of the Law and the Prosperity Doctrine are promoting. It is common for God's people to suffer poverty for his name's sake, brother. But, Christ assures them they **are rich**. Once, I had the privilege of visiting a little Mexican village named La Cuba. It was a tiny little place set down in a valley and built along a small stream. It is located about seven hours south of Juarez. How poor the Lord's saints were who lived there. But, how proud they were of their little dirt floored church where their livestock took shelter at night! But, oh my, how rich they were in the Lord. The only true wealth we believers possess is Christ, beloved. Amen? *Proverbs 13:7* says,

*There is one who makes himself rich, yet has nothing; and one who makes himself poor, yet has **great riches**.*

The church at Smyrna was of the latter.

Jesus continues, ***I know the blasphemy of those who say that they are Jews and are not, but are a synagogue of Satan***. Satan is always the instigator of the persecution of the saints. When Jesus was on earth, he said to a group of Pharisees who were persecuting him,

Why do you not understand my speech? Because you are not able to listen to my word. ***You are of your father the devil***, *and the desires of your father you want to do. He was a murderer from the beginning, and does not stand in the truth, because there is no truth in him. When he speaks a lie, he speaks from his own resources, for he is a liar and the father of it. John 8:43-44a*

2:10

THE INSTRUCTION

The Lord counsels his impoverished flock at Smyrna, *do not fear any of these things which you are about to suffer. Indeed, the devil is about to throw some of you into prison, that you may be tested, and you will have tribulation ten days*. Jesus knows all about persecution and the people Satan uses to bring it. We American believers know little of such things. However, more and more, we surely will if our society continues its current downward spiral into paganism. Jesus tells these believers not to fear their persecutors. He assures them their trial will only last *ten days*. I believe that Christ meant this as a figure of speech meaning, in the mind of God, a very brief period of time. Suffering and persecution may seem to last forever to a believer when it is occurring down here on earth but, in reality, it is very very brief. In light of eternity and the rewards it will bring to those who suffer persecution ... the time is both short and priceless. Are you suffering for Christ's sake, dear saint? Then, you are greatly blessed! It is a huge honor and an unspeakable privilege to suffer for his name's sake. *First Peter 4:12-13* says,

*Beloved, do not think it strange concerning the **fiery trial** which is to try you, as though some strange thing happened to you; but **rejoice to the extent that you partake of Christ's sufferings**, that when his glory is revealed, you may also be glad with **exceeding joy**.*

The Apostle Paul says in *Romans 8:18*,

*For I consider that the **sufferings** of this present time are **not worthy to be compared** with the **glory** which shall be revealed in us.*

Jesus said in *Matthew 5:11-12*,

***Blessed** are you when they revile and persecute you, and say all kinds of evil against you falsely for my sake. **Rejoice and be exceedingly glad**, for **great is your reward in heaven**, for so they persecuted the prophets who were before you.*

2:11

THE PROMISE

Christ continues ... *be faithful until death, and I will give you the crown of life*. He is not talking about salvation here. He is promising that one day he will bestow kingly rewards on all of his suffering saints (Second Corinthians 5:10). The suffering saints at Smyrna are scheduled for *crowns*! In the New Testament, crowns always refer to rewards. Let me take a moment and list them for you. There is the:

Crown of life ... This crown is found here in the letter to Smyrna and in James 1:12. It awaits those who suffer and endure temptation, persecution and trials.

Incorruptible Crown ... This crown is found in First Corinthians 9:25. It awaits those who have run their race well in living for Christ.

Crown of Rejoicing ... This crown is found in First Thessalonians 2:19. It has been called *the soul winner's crown*. It awaits those who have faithfully worked to get the Word of God out and have been instrumental in helping precious souls to come to Christ.

Crown of Righteousness ... This crown is found in Second Timothy 4:8. It will be given to those who *love his appearing* ... who are eagerly watching and waiting for Christ to come.

Crown of glory ... This crown is found in First Peter 5:4. It is the teacher and/or pastor's crown. It will be awarded to those faithful saints who have diligently fed God's people with the Word of God.

Jesus had nothing negative to say to his church at Smyrna. She was his suffering church. People and churches who are suffering for Christ and his gospel, almost without exception are spiritually right where they are supposed to be. He promises them a crown.

The Lord concludes, *He who overcomes will not be hurt by the second death*. Hebrews 9:27 says,

*...it is appointed for men to **die** once, but after this the judgment...*

That scripture is speaking about the physical death that all mankind experiences. The *second death*, however, is defined for us in *Revelation 20:14*,

Then Death and Hades were cast into the lake of fire. This is the **second death**.

The ***second death*** is an eternal and irreversible state. It will be the place and circumstance of all the wicked of all time who end up in the Lake of Fire. There, they will find themselves eternally separated from God. That is real death, brother. For multitudes of people, the ***second death*** begins for them at the point of their physical death. It is the state that awaits all who are not ***overcomers*** by faith in the Son of God. Its final manifestation will come after the Great White Throne judgment (Revelation 20). At that time, all who are not found written in the ***Lamb's Book of Life*** will be cast into the Lake of Fire. It was the avoidance of the ***second death*** that Jesus was referring to when he said to Martha,

*I am the resurrection and the life. He who believes in me, though he may die, he shall live. And whoever lives and believes in me shall **never die*** [experience the ***second death***]. *Do you believe this? John 11:25-26*

Dr. D. L. Moody, speaking of the necessity of being born again through faith in Jesus Christ said, *He who is born once will die twice, but he who is born twice will die once.* Christ assures his suffering believers at Smyrna that, as ***overcomers***, they will never be hurt by the ***second death*** ... the only real and permanent loss anyone has to fear.

PERGAMOS

THE HERETIC INFESTED CHURCH

Rev. 2:12-17

*And to the angel of the church in Pergamos write, 'These things says he who has the sharp two-edged sword: I know your works, and where you dwell, where Satan's throne is. And you hold fast to my name, and did not deny my faith even in the days in which **Antipas was my faithful martyr**, who was killed among you, **where Satan dwells**. But I have a few things against you, because you have there those who hold the **doctrine of Balaam**, who taught Balak to put a stumbling block before the children of Israel, to eat things sacrificed to idols, and to commit sexual immorality. Thus you also have those who hold the **doctrine of the Nicolaitans**, which thing I hate. **Repent**, or else I will come to you quickly and will fight against them with the sword of my* mouth. *He who has an ear, let him hear what the Spirit says to the churches. To him who overcomes I will give some of the hidden manna to eat. And I will give him **a white stone**, and on the stone a new name written which no one knows except him who receives it.'*

Pergamos was located about fifty-five miles (89 km) northwest of Smyrna and fifteen miles (24 km) inland from the sea. It was a Roman city that sat on a mountainside. It got its name from the paper (*pergamena*) that was made there. It is said that Caesar Augustus loved to come to this mountain retreat to dry out. It had a 20,000 volume library which Mark Anthony later gave to Cleopatra which, in turn, became the foundation of the great library at Alexandria. There was also a medical school at Pergamos. For nearly seven hundred years, people traveled there to its hospital for treatments. In addition, it was a city filled with idol temples. Aklepios, the god of healing, had a temple there. Zeus, Athena and Dyonesis had their temples there. It also was a center of emperor worship, sporting a temple dedicated to the worship of Octavius Caesar.

2:12

THE SALUTATION

Jesus addresses this church as *he who has the sharp two-edged sword*. This is an obvious symbol for the Word of God. The church at Pergamos had a habit of tolerating heretics and their false teachings. Heretics are best scattered by the *sharp two-edged sword* of the Word of God.

2:13

THE COMPLIMENT

Like the churches at Ephesus and Smyrna, Christ begins by noting that the church at Pergamos was busy for him. We should never underplay the importance of good works. Those who are busy doing good works are glorifying their Father who, himself, is constantly doing good things (James 1:17). *Titus 2:13-14,* speaks to this saying,

*...looking for the blessed hope and glorious appearing of our great God and Savior Jesus Christ, who gave himself for us, that he might redeem us from every lawless deed and **purify for himself his own special people, zealous for good works**.*

And also, as you have it in *Titus 3:8, 14*,

*This is a faithful saying, and these things I want you to affirm constantly, that those who have believed in God should be **careful to maintain good works**. These things are good and profitable to men.*

And let our people also learn to maintain good works, to meet urgent needs, that they may not be unfruitful.

Jesus said,

*By this my Father is glorified, that you bear **much fruit**; so you will be my disciples. John 15:8*

Our Lord desires for his people to be engaged in good works. He compliments the saints at Pergamos for theirs.

He continues ... **and did not deny my faith even in the days in which Antipas was my faithful martyr, who was killed among you**. Christ further commends these brothers and sisters for their courage and perseverance. He knew how difficult it was for them to live for him in Pergamos where they faced an incredibly hostile environment that had resulted in the violent death of Antipas, one of their brothers in Christ. All we know about this man, Antipas, is what is written here. Jesus calls him **my faithful martyr**. That is enough, is it not? The Greek word used here for **martyr** is μάρτυς *(martus)*. It has been transliterated into our like sounding word, martyr. The root meaning of this word is **witness**. Antipas was a good witness for the Lord Jesus Christ. That was probably why he was killed. It pleased the Lord that the church at Pergamos continued to stand firm even though one of their own was murdered for his witness in their midst. These words of Christ indicate that the enemies of Christ had come right into a church meeting and cut Antipas down. Remember that name ... **Antipas**. He is a member of a very elite group in the Church of Jesus Christ. You will want to get acquainted with him one day. He is one of Christ's *faithful* martyrs.

I take this phrase, **where Satan's seat is**, to be literal. The word translated **seat** here is the Greek word for **throne**. I believe that Pergamos was actually Satan's headquarters on Earth at the time of the writing of the book of Revelation. The prolific idol and man-worship that took place at Pergamos speaks loud and clear of Satan's dominion there. Talk about a tough environment for believers! The Bible teaches that Satan is the god of this world. He rules over all the nations in his dark kingdom and manipulates all their lost populations as he sees fit (Matthew 4:8-9; Luke 8:12; 1 Peter 5:8-9; Ephesians 2:2). Satan is not in Hell as popular secular opinion often thinks. He is loose in Heaven as well as on the earth and he has hoards of demons at his beck and call. This statement that Satan's throne was at Pergamos is one of a number of indications in Scripture that Satan's dominion on Earth is organized into specific geographic territories. You might recall that the demons which Jesus cast out of the man of Gadara, in Mark 5, begged him not to **send them away out of the country**. Why did they request that, do you think? The only reason I can think of is because they had been assigned there and would get into hot water if they left and went anywhere else.

In the book of Daniel, we read that an angel (probably Gabriel) was hindered from coming to Daniel by a demonic being called the **Prince of Persia** (Dan.10:13). Clearly, there was an evil demonic principality over the nation of Persia in Daniel's day just as, I might add, there still is today. This may well explain why American is having such a go of it with the nations of Iran, Iraq, Afghanistan and Pakistan. The greatest thing at stake in those dark countries, by the way, is not *the war on terror* but, as a result of that conflict, whether or not those nations will open up so that the gospel can be preached there. Satan and his demons would not be happy about that and they have surely pulled out all stops against it. *Ephesians 6:12* says,

For we wrestle not against flesh and blood, but against principalities, against powers, against the rulers of the darkness of this world, against spiritual wickedness in high places. (KJV)

Our Lord continues his compliment of the believers at Pergamos by noting that they were **holding fast to my name**. That is, they were holding firm to the truth of who Jesus Christ truly is. They tenaciously held to both the humanity and to the deity of the Lord Jesus Christ. *First Timothy 2:5* and *3:16,* could have been inscribed on the wall of their church,

...For there is one God, and one mediator between God and men, the **man Christ Jesus**... *(KJV)*

And without controversy great is the mystery of godliness: **God was manifested in the flesh**, *justified in the Spirit, seen by angels, preached among the Gentiles, believed on in the world, received up in glory.*

I am often amazed at how many Christians are fuzzy about the person of the Lord Jesus Christ. He is the God-Man. He is both the Son of God and the Son of Man. This church had those truths down pat. They were holding fast to his **name**.

2:14-15

THE PROBLEM

...But I have a few things against you, because you have those who hold the doctrine of Baalam and those who hold the doctrine of the Nicolaitans, which thing I hate. In spite of the many good things at Pergamos, the Lord points out that there were some serious cancers there that needed to be dealt with. The church was tolerating heretics in their midst. How subtle Satan is. What he couldn't accomplish from outside through persecution and intimidation, he was accomplishing from inside by planting his heretics in the church. There is a good deal of this going on in the Church today. Heretics are people who teach lies and half-truths to God's people. The Lord insists that such people need to be confronted and, if they won't repent, they should be expelled. As you have it in *Titus 3:10-11*,

A man that is an **heretic**, [αἱρετικὸν **(heretikon)**], *after the first and second admonition* **reject**; *knowing that he is subverted, and sinneth, being condemned of himself.* (KJV)

There were people in the church at Pergamos who held serious deviations from the moral and/or central doctrines of the Word of God. The church should have dealt with them but it hadn't. The Lord put his finger on those troublemakers. He names them. They were the Baalamites and the Nicolaitans. Doubtless, the believers at Pergamos knew exactly who Jesus was referring to. It's a bit tougher for us. Let's take a moment and take a closer look at these two groups.

Balaam

In Numbers 22-25 and 31 we read about a prophet named Balaam who advised the king of Moab as to how to destroy the Israelites. He did it for money. His counsel was that the king of Moab should promote intermarriage with the Israelites. Intermarriage with the heathen was strictly forbidden in God's Law. Balaam knew the heathen Moabite women would then lead Israel off into idolatry. Then, Balaam reasoned, God would judge his people for this and they could all be destroyed.

Apparently, there was a group of people at Pergamos who were propagating the same error that Balaam advised by encouraging intermarriage between believers and heathen idol worshipers. There are a lot of such Baalamites in the Church today. They lead people away from the Lord by promoting and condoning unholy marriages. Watch out for this all too popular position. God's Word says,

***Do not be unequally yoked together with unbelievers**. For what fellowship has righteousness with lawlessness? And what communion has light with darkness? And what accord has Christ with Belial? Or what part has a believer with an unbeliever? Second Corinthians 6:14-15*

Nicolaitans

This is the same sect that was mentioned in the letter to the Ephesians (2:6). Again, we do not know what their doctrine entailed. Perhaps it was something similar to the doctrine of the Masons that is so invasive in many congregations today. Many church members are joined to the Masons and there is a great deal of praise for their good works. However, the core **doctrine** of this organization is an abomination and if it is being openly propagated in a church, must be dealt with. Masonic doctrine teaches that there is a brotherhood of all religions because, they say, all religions have come from one pure but previously lost, original source. Hence, it is irrelevant in their view whether the Bible or a Koran is on a Masonic altar. Deeply committed Masons believe they have rediscovered man's original religion whose god they call *the great Architect* in lower levels of Masonry. Those higher up, claim they hold the original and one true religion of man in its pure form (as opposed to the entire rest of the world's watered down and contaminated versions, including Christianity). They teach that

God's secret and original name was *Jebulon*, a composite name made up of the Jehovah of the Hebrews, Baal of the Canaanites and Osiris of the ancient Egyptians. It is said that some Masons in the higher levels of Masonry worship *Jebulon* around their altar.

If we could ask our Lord how he feels about his pure covenant name, **Jehovah**, being lumped together with the utterly pagan idols of Baal and Osiris and their abominable child sacrifices and historic immorality, he would unquestionably say that it is a doctrine **which thing I hate**. Make no mistake about it, Masonic doctrine is heresy and it is false. And, as with all of man's false doctrines and religions, it negates and obscures the truth of the gospel of the Lord Jesus Christ. Jesus is the only way to God (John 14:6) and his Church alone holds the pure and only true religion in the world today. For further information on the modern day heresies of the Masons, most Christian bookstores offer books for the buying. *The Secret Teachings of the Masonic Lodge* by John Ankerberg and John Weldon, Moody Press, is one that comes to mind. We 21st Century churches need to be very careful that we too are not tolerating those who teach and promote things that our Lord hates. Peter says,

But there were also false prophets among the people, even as ***there will be false teachers among you****, who will secretly bring in* ***destructive heresies****, even denying the Lord who bought them, and bring on themselves swift destruction. And* ***many will follow their destructive ways****, because of whom* ***the way of truth will be blasphemed****. Second Peter 2:1-2*

Someone has said, *The Church in America today is overrun with heresy and heretics*. How true. We believers must stand upon the fundamental truths of the Word of God when confronting them (Jude 3-4), and not allow their teachings to go unchallenged when they infiltrate the Church.

2:16

THE INSTRUCTION AND THE WARNING

Jesus' remedy for these believers who have been tolerating heretics in their midst is the same as his remedy prescribed to the Ephesian church. He tells them ... ***repent***. Repentance means to have a change of mind and direction ... to do a *one-eighty*. The Pergamos believers needed to tell the Lord, *We were wrong for tolerating heresies and for not dealing with the people who were teaching them to us. We humbly ask you Lord ... for forgiveness.*

Jesus says if they will not hear him on this ... **I will come to you quickly and *fight against them with the sword of my mouth*.** The Lord himself will take measures against a church's heretics if it will not act. What measures might he take? He says he will simply use his sword against them. The one who speaks the Word of God can easily deal with a church's heretics. He is a jealous God (Exodus 34:14). He will act. He is jealous of the truth and jealous of his blood bought people. Well ... should a church *just let Jesus take care of it* then? No ... by no means. By the time Jesus must take care of it, countless lives may have been permanently damaged. The church should repent and take care of it long before the Lord is forced to do so. It's a matter of urgent necessity before precious blood-bought believers have been damaged.

2:17

THE PROMISES

Finally, he says, **he who has an ear let him hear what the Spirit says to the churches.** This is followed by two more wonderful promises to his overcomers.

First, he promises them **hidden manna.** I believe this is best understood in the light of John 6:48-58, where Jesus said, **I am the living bread which came down from heaven: if any man eat of this bread, he shall live forever**. Jesus is God's **hidden manna**. Blessed indeed, are all who continuously partake of him. They will live forever in a continuous spiritual feast on Christ.

Second, he promises his overcomers the gift of **a white stone**. On it, he says, a **new name which no man knows but him who receives it** will be written. I believe this stone will be a literal one. In Asia, at the time that John was writing this book, it was a custom to give an intimate friend a **tessara** which was a small smoothed stone or piece of ivory with writing on it. It became the secret private possession for the one who received it from the one who gave it. In like manner, I believe Jesus is speaking here of a heavenly *tessara* that will be inscribed with a secret and private **new name** that each child of God will be given from his hand one day. These individualized stones will ever remind us of the intimate and utterly unique ... one on one ... relationship that we have with our Lord Jesus Christ. It's my opinion that these special names will not be for everyday use in Heaven ... but only on those occasions when we are enjoying one on one fellowship with our Lord himself. The great old hymn is right on which says, *There's a new name written down in glory and its mine! Oh yes, its mine!*

THYATIRA

THE IMMORAL CHURCH

Rev. 2:18-29

*And to the angel of the church in Thyatira write, 'These things says the Son of God, who has **eyes like a flame of fire**, and his **feet like fine brass**: I know your works, love, **service**, faith, and your patience; and as for your works, the last are more than the first. Nevertheless I have* **[NU omits "*a few things*"]** *against you,* **[NU omits "*because you allow*"]** *that you tolerate that woman Jezebel, who calls herself a prophetess,* **to teach** *and seduce my servants* **to commit sexual immorality** *and eat things sacrificed to idols. And I gave her time to repent of her sexual immorality, and she did not repent. Indeed I will cast her into a sickbed, and those who commit adultery with her into* **great tribulation**, *unless they repent of their deeds. I will kill her children with death, and all the churches shall know that I am he who searches the minds and hearts. And I will give to each one of you according to your works. Now to you I say,* **[NU omits "*and*"]** *to the rest in Thyatira, as many as do not have this doctrine, who have not known the depths of Satan, as they say, I* **[NU omits "*will*"]** *put on you no other burden. But hold fast what you have till I come. And* **he who overcomes**, *and keeps my works until the end, to him* **I will give power over the nations**; *he shall rule them with a rod of iron; they shall be dashed to pieces like the potter's vessels'; as I also have received from my Father;* **and I will** *give him the morning star. He who has an ear, let him hear what the Spirit says to the churches.'*

Thyatira sat at a crossroads between two valleys. It was a military and commercial center. Its coins depicted a warrior on a charger armed with a battle-axe. Its main claim to fame was its commercial guilds (unions), which are mentioned in the inscriptions found there. Lydia, the merchant lady who Paul won to the Lord at Phillipi, was from Thyatira. She was selling turkey-red dye when Paul first met her (Acts 16:14).

2:19

THE SALUTATION

The Lord addresses this church as, **the Son of God** whose eyes are like a ***flame of fire*** and whose feet are like ***fine brass***. This is another conclusive proof that the one John saw back in chapter one was, indeed, the Lord Jesus Christ. He specifically calls himself here **the Son of God**. His reference to his *eyes* and his *feet* both speak of judgment. He alone is the Judge of both believers and non-believers. The Bible says that God has committed all judgment into the hands of the Son (John 5:22). Concerning us believers, *Second Corinthians 5:10* says,

*For we must **all appear** before the **judgment seat of Christ**, that each one may receive the things done in the body, according to what he has done, whether good or bad.*

This is further emphasized in *First Corinthians 3:11-15*,

*For no other foundation can anyone lay than that which is laid, which is Jesus Christ. Now if anyone builds on this foundation with gold, silver, precious stones, wood, hay, straw, each one's work will become clear; for the day will declare it, because it will be revealed by **fire**; and the fire will **test each one's work**, of what sort it is. If anyone's work which he has built on it endures, he will receive a **reward**. If anyone's work is burned, he will **suffer loss**; but he himself will be saved, yet so as through fire.*

Dr. McGee, commenting on this Corinthian 3 passage, says, *Some Christians leaving the judgment seat of Christ will smell like they were bought at a fire sale!* Many of the Thyatiran believers were fleshly. They were a carnal people who spent their lives stacking *wood, hay and straw* on the foundation of Christ. Sadly, many in the Church today follow in their footsteps.

THE COMPLIMENTS

Amazingly, the Lord lists six virtues of this church. He commends them for:

...their **works**. These are the credentials of all true believers, by the way (James 2:17-18).

...their **love**. This is another wonderful characteristic of real believers. It is a fruit of the Spirit.

...their **service**. The Greek word here is διακονίαν (*diakonian*), the word from which we get our word *deacon* which speaks of ministry. It literally means *one who makes a dust by hastening.* They were a ministering church (James 1:27).

...their *faith*. They were a believing church, trusting completely in the Lord Jesus Christ.

...their **patience**. Patience only comes as the result of having walked through fiery trials in life (Romans 5:3). The Thyatiran believers had been *over the mountain,* as Louis L'Amour would say.

...their **works**. Their works were increasing ... **the last are more than the first**. It is a very healthy sign when a local church's good works are continually increasing. Wow! I wouldn't mind belonging to a church like this, would you?

2:20-21

THE PROBLEM

Nevertheless, he says, ***I have a few things against you, because you allow that woman Jezebel, who calls herself a prophetess, to teach and seduce my servants to commit sexual immorality and eat things sacrificed to idols***. The Lord goes right to the source of the problem at Thyatira. The church was allowing a woman named Jezebel to teach them to commit sexual immorality.

By the way, isn't it amazing how often a church refuses to discipline its people? The Corinthian church looked the other way while one of its members openly practiced incest in their midst (1 Corinthians 5:1). Likewise, the church at Thyatira was looking the other way while Jezebel was actually teaching the saints there to engage in sexual immorality! Now, it is my opinion that our Lord is taking exception to the fact that Jezebel was **teaching** in the church at all ... as well to **what** she was teaching. This would be in line with those passages in the Word that prohibits women to *teach or to usurp authority over the man* (I Timothy 2:11-14). Again, as you have it in *First Corinthians 13:34-35,*

Let women keep silence in the churches: for it is not permitted unto them to speak; but to be under obedience, as also says the Law. And if they will learn anything, let them ask their husbands at home: for it is a shame for women to speak in the church. (KJV)

Let me clarify this. I believe our Lord's objection to Jezebel's teaching in the first place is an indicator that she was a **married woman** which would have placed her under the above referenced rules for married women in the Church. I know this is certainly not, "PC" today. However, it is my understanding that the biblical role of married women in the Church is to be in submission to their husbands at all times. This is especially important in the setting of a church meeting. Whenever a married woman **takes it upon herself** to dominate a meeting of the saints with instruction or statements and questions apart from any consideration of the Scripture or her husband ... she is out of bounds and brings shame on herself and the husband to whom she is supposed to be in subjection.

These rules do not apply to single women and widows, however. Their status as single women allows them the freedom to freely speak out in the Church and, in the beginning of the Church, they sometimes even held the role of prophetesses (see I Corinthians 11:5; Luke 2:36 and Acts 21:8-9). When they married, however, they lost that freedom and ministry, having assumed a new role as wife, with all of the new obligations and blessings that entailed. Are there exceptions to these rules? Yes. If a married woman is asked by the elders and has the approval of her husband ... she certainly can speak and teach the saints. Also, Scripture reveals that married women can and should, in fact, teach other women and children in the Church (Titus 2:3-4). Some may disagree with what I have said here. It is more of a knotty issue in some circles than others. Bottom line though ... Jezebel had clearly taken the bit in her teeth and was teaching whenever and whatever she pleased to the church at Thyatira.

Continuing on with our text, some say that Jezebel was not this woman's actual name but I take it that it was. The famous Jezebel of the Old Testament was the wicked wife of King Ahab found in First Kings 16. She introduced idol worship and its accompanying sexual immorality to Israel. These two biblical Jezebels were two peas in a pod. The words here, **and eat things sacrificed to idols**, suggest that Jezebel was luring the saints to the local idol temples to consummate her false teachings by participating in the feasting and drinking there followed by unbridled sexual immorality.

Jezebel had a logical justification for this practice and promoted herself as a ***prophetess***. There are only two other mentions of this word ***prophetess***, by the way, in the New Testament. One is where it is used of Anna, a godly widow who was present at the dedication of the baby, Jesus (Luke 2:36). The other is where it is used in the plural, referring to Phillip's four virgin daughters in Acts 21:9. Jezebel's character was certainly the opposite of those five dear saints. She was of the false prophet school that Peter so explicitly warns about in *Second Peter 2:1, 14, 18-19...*

But there were also false prophets among the people, **even as there will be false teachers among you***...*

...having eyes full of **adultery** *and that cannot cease from sin,* **enticing** *unstable souls. They have a heart trained in covetous practices, and are accursed children.*

For when they speak great swelling words of emptiness, **they allure through the lusts of the flesh, through lewdness**, *the ones who have actually escaped from those who live in error. While they promise them liberty, they themselves are* **slaves of corruption**; *for by whom a person is overcome, by him also he is brought into bondage.*

The Lord says that he gave Jezebel **time to repent of her sexual immorality**, but she refused to respond. This is amazing, is it not?

Jesus is gracious and longsuffering even toward the Jezebels who are polluting his Church!

2:22-23

THE WARNING

In verses 22 and 23, the Lord confronts Jezebel and her associates.

First, he warns he will *cast* her into *a bed of sickness*. This is in contrast to Jezebel's warm sensuous beds of adultery and fornication. The Lord tells Jezebel he is about to discipline her with sickness. I take it ... because of the nature of Christ's warning here ... that Jezebel was a Christian. I assume that because:

a. He gave her time to *repent*. Repentance is a very Christian thing and is a common remedy offered to believers by Christ in order for them to set things straight and restore their fellowship with him (I John 1:9-10).

b. He threatens her with *illness*. This too, is a common thing that the Lord uses to chasten stubborn and rebellious believers. As you have it in *First Corinthians 11:30-32,*

*That is why many among you are weak and **sick**, and a number of you have fallen asleep* [died]. *But if we judged ourselves, we would not come under judgment.* ***When we are judged by the Lord, we are being disciplined*** *so that we will not be condemned with the world.* (NIV)

Second, he says that he will **cast ... those who commit adultery with her into great tribulation, unless they repent of their deeds**. I take this second part of Christ's warning to refer to the **unbelievers** up at the temple that Jezebel and her disciples had been practicing sexual immorality with. Unquestionably, we have the first mention of the Great Tribulation here in the book of Revelation (referring to the second half of the seven year Tribulation period). The Greek words are θλῖψιν μεγάλην *(thelipsin megalain)*. Jesus is using these words in their technical theological sense, just as he used them in Matthew 24:21, where he was defining that future time of trouble that will come upon the earth after the Rapture of the Church. This warning would also apply to any phony believers at the church at Thyatira, by the way. Such people would find themselves left behind if the Rapture occurred. Therefore, Christ's words would apply to all unbelievers (outside or inside the church at Thyatira) who were indulging in Jezebel's orgies. Christ emphatically warns these unsaved people that he will **cast** them **into great tribulation** if they do not repent of their wicked ways.

As for the phony believer element that existed in the Thyatiran church (professors ... but not possessors ... of real faith in the Lord Jesus Christ). They, along with all the other non-Christian participants in Jezebel's practices, could expect nothing less than to find themselves on a fast track to the ***great tribulation*** in the event of the Rapture of the Church. Such hypocrites have always been present in the Church to plague it. Blatant and habitual immorality is one of the signatures of false brethren, by the way. As you have it in *First John 3:7-8*,

Little children, let no one deceive you. He who ***practices righteousness*** *is righteous, just as he is righteous.* ***He who sins*** [habitually] ***is of the devil****, for the devil has sinned from the beginning. For this purpose the Son of God was manifested, that he might destroy the works of the devil.*

By way of application to the Church today, let me just say that, after the Rapture occurs, the unsaved Jezebel element will find itself left behind and on a fast track to the Great Tribulation right along with all their non-Christian chums. If the Rapture were to occur today, phony Christians who play church but practice immorality would be doomed to enter the Tribulation which will rapidly worsen into the Great Tribulation. I believe that to be the thought here. Although this second part of Christ's warning was aimed primarily at the unsaved crowd up at the temple, it also included any unsaved Jezebel elements that existed inside the church at Thyatira as well. This reminds us of the parable of the ***wheat*** and the ***tares*** in Matthew 13, does it not?

Third, Christ says he will ***kill*** Jezebel's ***children with death***. I take this to refer to the Christian followers of Jezebel's doctrine who had adopted her teachings and were propagating it on to others. In that sense, they would truly be ***Jezebel's children***. This is a stern warning indeed. One of our Lord's options, in chastening believers who go too far into sin, is the option of instituting their physical death. The passage above from First Corinthians 11, demonstrates this truth. Some at Corinth had died as a discipline and a grace from the Lord. James speaks to this issue also in *James 5:19-20*,

*Brethern, if any of you do err from the truth, and one convert him [turns him back]; let him know, that he which converteth the sinner from the error of his way, shall save a soul from **death**, and shall hide a multitude of sins.* (KJV)

The Lord adds **and all of the churches shall know that I am he who searches the minds and hearts. And I will give to each one of you according to your works**. These words strengthen my contention that Jezebel and many of her followers were believers. Christ is clearly referring to them here in context of being members of his Church. His discipline of them would not go unnoticed by all of the other churches, just as the death of Ananias and Sapphira made quite an impact on the Church in Acts 5. Make no mistake about it, if the Lord carried through and judged Jezebel and her followers, all the other churches heard about it ... especially since they had all been given a heads up when this book of Revelation was sent out to them. God is a holy and just God and a loving disciplinarian. He will not hesitate to discipline those he loves and, if necessary, take them home rather than allow them to continue to destroy themselves and others. As you have it in *Hebrews 12:5-6*,

*And you have forgotten the exhortation which speaks to you as to son 'My son, do not despise the chastening of the Lord, nor be discouraged when you are rebuked by Him; for **whom the Lord loves He chastens, and scourges every son whom He receives**.'*

2:24-25

COMFORT

Jesus continues ... ***Now unto you I say, and to the rest in Thyatira, as many as do not have this doctrine, who have not known the depths of Satan, as they say***. Now, keep in mind here that these letters were addressed to individual pastors of the churches. So, when Christ says ... ***Now unto you***, he is speaking to the pastor at Thyatira. Also, standing with him, were ***the rest*** of the saints who were not participating in Jezebel's immorality. This phrase ... **who have not known the depths of Satan, as they say** ... tells us something of Jezebel's teaching and her justification for it. Have you ever run across someone who said, Y*ou really need to experience evil to truly know and understand it!*? That was Jezebel's line. She taught that everyone needed to taste **the depths of Satan** so that they could fully know and appreciate Good from Evil. Watch out, beloved. That is an old lie from the pit. Satan used it on Eve in the Garden of Eden. He is still using it today.

*Then the serpent said to the woman, 'You will not surely die. For God knows that in the day you eat of it your eyes will be opened, and you will be like God, **knowing good and evil.**' Genesis 3:4-5*

Eve didn't end up knowing good and evil like God knows it. No, she ended up knowing evil in an experiential way with all its black trappings. It cost Eve both her spiritual and her physical life. We don't need to experience evil to know it, nor for us to know what is truly good. Our sinless Lord never experienced sin in order to know it nor to know what was good. God's Word was sufficient for him to know good and evil and it is sufficient for you and me as well.

One more thought before we move on here. Heretics love to boast about their perceived superior spirituality. Jezebel went around pronouncing that she was a ***prophetess***. With this boast, she gathered a following. Watch out for people who want you to enter into their little, exclusive, super-spiritual club. Usually, those groups are a one-way street to Jezebel City. The Church of Jesus Christ is the exact opposite of this. It is a completely open ... all-inclusive ... everyone growing and knowing ... together ... unified ... body of believers. Secret societies, sectarianism, prejudice, spiritual pride and exclusiveness have no place in the lives of God's people. STAY AWAY FROM THEM. Those who promote these little clubs are carnal, fleshly and they are hazardous to one's spiritual health.

Finally here, Christ says, **Hold fast what you have till I come**. Dear believer, if you are in the midst of a mess like the one that was being played out at Thyatira, this word is for you. **Hold fast** until he comes. Keep looking up. Your redemption draws nigh. As you have it in *James 5:7,*

*Therefore be patient, brethren, **until the coming of the Lord**. See how the farmer waits for the precious fruit of the earth, waiting patiently for it until it receives the early and latter rain.*

2:26-29

THE PROMISE

Christ leaves two more wonderful promises here for his **overcomers** who **keep my works until the end**. Christ's **works** are always in stark contrast to the things that the Jezebel element likes to promote.

First, he promises they will have **power over the nations** and **shall rule them with a rod of iron**. This is not the only place our Lord has promised this to his people, by the way. *Second Timothy 2:12a*, says,

*If we endure, we shall also **reign with him**.*

And again, in *First Corinthians 6:2*, we read,

*Do you not know that the saints will **judge the world**? And if the world will be judged by you, are you unworthy to judge the smallest matters?*

What an exciting and exalted future awaits the Lord's overcomers. They will be given **power over the nations** to rule them with a **rod of iron**. He is speaking of his Millennial reign and the strict exercise of his laws at that time against those who pursue lawlessness, disobedience and harm toward others.

The second thing our Lord promises his overcomers is the **Morning Star**. This name refers to Christ himself. It is rooted in an Old Testament prophecy found in *Numbers 24:17a*,

*I see him, but not now; I behold him, but not near; a **Star** shall come out of Jacob; a Scepter shall rise out of Israel...*

In that prophecy, Moses foresaw the arrival of Christ to rule and reign on Earth one day. Here, Jesus adds the word ***Morning*** to it, which he also does in *Revelation 22:16*,

*I, Jesus, have sent my angel to testify to you these things in the churches. **I am** the Root and the Offspring of David, the Bright and **Morning Star**.*

Christ's reference to himself as the **Morning Star** magnifies the certainty of his future visible presence on Earth as well as in eternity. Have you ever wondered what that day will be like ... that glorious day when we will physically see Jesus and regularly and walk with him by sight? If you have ever gone out very early in the morning and seen the last and brightest star ... still shining, it will be something like that. Throughout his Millennial reign and throughout all of eternity, our Lord will always be right there, always visible ... always beautiful ... always shining in his unquenchable and matchless glory. This is the unspeakable treasure that awaits his overcomers. As he put it to Abraham in *Genesis 15:1b*,

Do not be afraid, Abram. ***I*** *am your shield,* ***your exceedingly great reward****.*

SARDIS

THE DEAD CHURCH

Rev. 3:1-6

And to the angel of the church in Sardis write, These things says he who has the seven Spirits of God and the seven stars: 'I know your works, that you have a name that you are alive, but ***you are dead****. Be watchful, and* ***strengthen the things which remain, that are ready to die****, for I have not found your works perfect before my God.* ***Remember*** *therefore how you have received and heard; hold fast and repent. Therefore if you will not watch, I will come upon you as a thief, and you will not know what hour I will come upon you. Nevertheless, you have a few names* **[NU omits "even"]** *in Sardis who have not defiled their garments; and they shall walk with me in white, for they are worthy. He who overcomes shall be clothed in white garments, and I will not blot out his name from the* ***Book of Life****; but I will confess his name before my Father and before his angels.' He who has an ear, let him hear what the Spirit says to the churches.*

Sardis was the capital of the province of Lydia and the first city to mint gold and silver coins. It was also known for its arts and crafts. The Lydian kings were so rich that they were legendary. An earthquake leveled

Sardis in AD 17, and it never fully recovered after that, even though the Romans gave it ten million sesterces (1/4 of a denarius each) in relief.

3:1

THE SALUTATION

Christ addresses the church at Sardis as the one who *has the seven spirits of God* and *holds the seven stars*. This is a reference to the same *seven spirits of God* that greeted us back in chapter one. Later in the book, we will learn that they are the angels of the Trumpet Judgments who will carry out the Lord's final judgments of the Great Tribulation and beyond. When they have finished blowing their trumpets, everything will have been wrapped up. Our Lord refers to them here because they speak of his approaching judgments. As the one who controls (*holds*) these seven spirits, Christ is emphasizing that he is the one who is about to intervene on the earth and set things straight.

As for the *seven stars*, you will remember that they are symbols of the messenger/pastors of the seven churches. Since Christ holds the pastors of the churches in his hand, it follows that he holds his churches accountable for their teaching and example. These twin concepts ... judgment and accountability ... are themes that are often found in the New Testament. For example, Christ judged a number of folks at Corinth because of their casual and blasphemous attitude toward the Lord's Table. Concerning this matter of Jesus judging his churches, we looked at that in our analysis of the church at Thiatira.

Now, as for a church's accountability for the leadership that Christ sends to it, *Hebrews 13:17,* commands,

***Obey** those who rule over you, and be submissive, for they watch out for your souls, as those who must give account. Let them do so with joy and not with grief, for that would be **unprofitable** for you.*

At the Judgment Seat of Christ, I would not want to be the pastor who will have to give an account for the sorry condition of the church at Sardis. Nor, would I want to be a member of that church, or any other church, who deliberately chose not to heed their godly pastor's teaching and leadership.

THE PROBLEM

Sadly, there is no compliment here for the dead church at Sardis. There was nothing to compliment. So, Christ simply goes directly to their problem.

He says ... *I know your works, that you have a name that you are alive, but you are dead*. What a rebuke. This church was a shell, a phony. I once lived in a little eastern Oregon town near the Eagle Cap wilderness where the movie *Paint Your Wagon* was made. After the filming was over, the producer invited the public to come up and tear down the sets and haul away whatever materials they wanted ... free of charge. So, a fellow pastor and I got a big truck and went up to the site to glean materials for our church camp. After the long drive on a mountainous dirt road, we finally arrived in a beautiful high mountain valley. The first thing that met our eyes was a magnificent water wheel turning slowly in the stream below us. Then, all around in the little valley was what looked to be a mining town right out of the Old West. My friend, Fred, and I drove down its main street and parked in front of a building that read, *General Store*. Then, we got out, opened the front door and stepped inside. Immediately, we began to laugh. Once inside, we found that we had stepping right back into the forest on the other side! The structure was just a front. It was not a building at all. The water wheel had the same problem. It turned and turned, but it wasn't actually doing anything!

The church at Sardis was like that mockup town. It had a name that it was a living, breathing church but, in reality, it was just a sham. I fear there are far too many churches like that today.

May we step aside again for a moment? A church building, by its very presence in a community, says something to all who see it. By its very presence it declares, *This is a place where God is known, loved and served*. But, unfortunately that is not always the case. Our righteous Lord will judge such churches for their hypocrisy. Dead churches do a great deal of damage to the cause of Christ. They seek to fool their community and sometimes even manage to fool themselves but they can't fool their Lord. The church at Sardis probably said, *The Bible is the Word of God* but, they didn't read it, love it, study it, meditate on it, obey it or experience its life-changing, sanctifying power. They may have had a plaque on the wall that said, *Prayer changes things*, but they never met for prayer. They probably said, *Jesus save*s ... but they never got around to speaking of him to the poor lost folks they encountered. They probably said they loved one another but were notorious for fighting over ... just about everything. The great identifying mark of a dead church is its hypocrisy. Jesus said to his church at Sardis, **you have a name that you are alive, but you are dead**.

3:2-3

THE INSTRUCTION

What an optimist our wonderful Savior is. Even his dead churches, he never views as hopeless! There is no such thing as a hopeless church, as far as Jesus is concerned ... if it is willing to listen to him and obey his instructions. Christ's words to the dead church at Sardis are fourfold.

First, he says, **be watchful**. The first thing a dead church needs to do is to open its eyes, wake up, and honestly evaluate itself. If it is willing to do that, it will discover some unpleasant things but they will be very good for it. For example, it will discover that it hasn't really been seeing anything, hearing anything or doing anything that matters. It hasn't even recognized that it was dead. The first step back for a dead church is to **be watchful**. Wake up! *Ephesians 5:13-16,* says,

But all things that are ***exposed*** *are made manifest by the* ***light****, for whatever makes manifest is light. Therefore he says: 'Awake, you who sleep, arise from the **dead**, and Christ will give you **light**.' See then that you walk circumspectly, not as **fools** but as wise, redeeming the time, because the days are evil.*

Second, he says, **strengthen the things which remain, that are ready to die**. After waking up, a dead church needs to ask itself, *Exactly what do we have left that hasn't gone down the drain? Do we still believe in justification by faith, the authority of the Word of God and our obligation to the Great Commission? What's left*? Jesus instructs this church to look at what they still possess that is authentic Christianity and then strengthen and build on those things **which remain**.

Third, he says, ***remember therefore how you have received and heard***. Another very essential step for a dead church is to remember ***how*** they heard and got saved in the first place. Peter says,

*...having been **born again**, not of corruptible seed but incorruptible, through the **word of God** which lives and abides forever. First Peter 1:23*

Have you forgotten how you received Christ and heard about him? It was through the communication of the Word of God, was it not? The Sardis church was not reaching others with the Word of God like they themselves had been reached with it. Somewhere along the line, they abandoned that priority. When a church stops preaching and evangelizing with the Word of God, it has become a dead church. Any church that continues to be obedient in getting the Word of God to lost humanity around them will never come to the sorry state of deadness that the church at Sardis was in. No one will ever hear the Lord say, *Well, where you went wrong was ... you spent too much time, energy and resources getting the Word of God out to poor lost sinners so that they could get saved!*

Finally, Christ says, **hold fast and repent**. There is no healing for a patient until he or she agrees with the diagnosis of their physician and submits to the remedy the doctor prescribes. Christ's prescription for the church at Sardis was **repentance**. Any dead church that is willing to take that medicine has taken a giant step on the path to a glorious comeback.

THE WARNING

He says, ***Therefore if you will not watch, I will come upon you as a thief***. When a dead church persists in its hypocrisy and refuses to wake up, it opens itself up to the Lord's judgment. He told his church at Sardis that he will come upon them like ***a thief in the night***. This certainly will be true for many people at the Rapture. Someone has said, *The Rapture will not be rapturous for the disobedient and slothful*. Although it will be a day of rejoicing and reward for many, it doubtless will be a bitter day for others. *First John 3:18-19,* says,

*My little children, let us not love in word or in tongue, but in deed and in truth. And by this we know that we are of the truth, **and shall assure our hearts** before him.*

Real, authentic Christianity brings assurance to the hearts of believers toward their Lord, both in the here and now as well as when they will stand in his presence one day.

3:4

THE COMPLIMENT

He says, **You have a few names, even in Sardis who have not defiled their garments**. Normally, not everyone in a dead church is **dead**. Even in the deadest churches, a few good people can usually be found who are obedient and have a real vibrant and obedient love toward the Savior. Such was the case at Sardis. **A few**, he says, **have not defiled their garments**. A few were living clean and separated lives for Christ. They were separate from the world and from the spiritual deadness of their church. Now, it's an axiomatic truth that deliberate disobedience to the revealed will of God leads to impurity of life. These two things go together like bread and butter. When people are not obeying the Word of God and abiding in Christ, there is only one other alternative ... they become caught up in carnality and sin. A victorious Christian life is a Christ centered, Word centered, Spirit filled and empowered **way of life**. Where this is not taking place, flesh and sin always take over. We read in *Galatians 5:16*,

I say then: **walk in the Spirit***, and you shall* **not** *fulfill the lust of the flesh.*

Let's step aside here for a moment. The Bible says there are **three different lifestyles** that are in the world today. First Corinthians 2:14-3:3, gives them to us.

First, there is the *natural man*. This is the unsaved man. He does not and cannot receive the things of God because they are *foolishness to him*.

Then, there is the *spiritual* man. He is the saved man who consistently has, and is enjoying, a real walk with Christ. He sees clearly and is able to discern all things.

Finally, there is the *carnal* man. He also is a saved man ... but he has built his life apart from walking with Christ. Therefore, he continues to act like the same old natural man that he was before he got saved.

It is very important to understand that all three of these are **chosen** life styles. Every believer chooses to be either a spiritual man or a carnal man. The *spiritual man* is the one Jesus is addressing here at Sardis in verse four. He was in the vast minority, as he is in many churches today. He was living a life of purity and the Lord speaks here in glowing terms of the future of such people. He says, *They shall walk with me in white, for they are worthy*. I believe that he is speaking about a position of future privilege in Heaven where spiritual saints will enjoy a deeper and more intimate walk with Christ. Apparently, not everyone will know such a high level of relationship. The child of God who has walked with Christ down here, will one day enjoy a level of fellowship and service with their Savior above that many disobedient and carnal believers may never know. This is the heart of our Lord's promise and comfort here to his handful of spiritual saints at Sardis who had not *soiled their garments*.

3:5-6

THE PROMISE

Finally, our Lord sets forth three more wonderful promises here to his **overcomers**.

First, he says, they will be *clothed in white*. Although all of Christ's saints will one day be clothed in white (Romans 4:22-25), the white garments spoken of here will be quite different. We will discuss these garments further when we get to the Marriage Supper of the Lamb in chapter 20.

Second, he promises, *I will not blot his name from the Book of Life.* Some have been quick to jump on this statement, thinking they can prove that Christians can lose their salvation. In reality, however, it is teaching the exact opposite. This is a wonderful verse on assurance. In the Greek here, Jesus uses a **double negative**. It is very significant. To fully appreciate its meaning it would have to be translated like this: *I will **never** ever, surely not **ever**, **never**, never, never, never, never, never, never* (ad infinitum) *blot out **any** overcomer's name from the Book of Life!* So, this verse is another great anchor for eternal security. It teaches that a believer's position in Christ is permanent, irrevocable and eternally secure. Once your name is in this book, brother, the Lord assures you it will never **ever** be blotted out. We have the Word of God on it.

Third, he promises, *I will confess his name before my Father and before his angels*. Jesus also spoke of this to his disciples.

*Therefore **whoever confesses me before men**, him **I will also confess** before my Father who is in heaven. But whoever denies me before men, him I will also deny before my Father who is in heaven. Matthew 10:32-33*

Isn't that a wonderful promise? Can you picture it? One day, the Lord Jesus himself ... standing before the awesome presence of his Holy Father and all of his mighty angels ... will confess each and every one of his saints individually by name (Luke 12:8-9). That will certainly be a red-banner day in the life of each of us believers, will it not? What a moment that will be in your history and mine. ***He who has an ear, let him hear what the Spirit says to the churches***.

PHILADELPHIA

THE BIBLE CHURCH

Rev. 3:7-13

*And to the angel of the church in **Philadelphia** write, 'These things says he who is holy, he who is true, he who has the key of David, he who opens and no one shuts, and shuts and no one opens: I know your works. See, I have set before you an open door,* **[NU omits "and"]** *which no one can shut* **[NU omits "it"]**; *for you have a little strength,* **have kept my word** *and have not denied my name. Indeed I will make those of the synagogue of Satan, who say they are Jews and are not, but lie; indeed I will make them come and worship before your feet, and to know that I have loved you. Because you* **have kept my command** *to persevere, I also will keep you **from** the hour of trial which shall come upon the whole world, to test those who dwell on the earth.* **[NU omits "Behold"]** *I am coming quickly! Hold fast what you have, that no one may take your crown. He who overcomes, I will make him a pillar in the* **temple** *of my God, and he shall go out no* *more. And I will write on him the name of my God and the name of the city of my God, the New Jerusalem, which comes down out of heaven from my God. And I will write on him my new name. He who has an ear, let him hear what the Spirit says to the churches.'*

The Greek word for Philadelphia is **Φιλαδελφεία** (*filadelfia*). It means **brotherly love**. Philadelphia was a Lydian city founded by King Attalus II, which he named Philadelphus because of his devotion to his brother. It was located at the foot of Mount Tmolus but, unknown to King Attalus, it was situated on a major fault that caused it to be prone to earthquakes. The great earthquake of AD 17, completely devastated the city. Afterwards, it was re-named, Neocaesarea. Philadelphia was situated in a great vine growing area. Down through the centuries, the Christian witness remained strong at Philadelphia. No doubt, that is because it was so well grounded in the Word of God. The church remained there throughout medieval times and, in spite of the Moslem invasion and takeover of the area, Christians were still found there into modern times.

3:7

THE SALUTATION

We come here to a marked change in salutations of Christ to his churches. This is the first church that Christ doesn't use a description of himself from chapter one. I believe that is because of the very special relationship the Lord enjoyed with these Philadelphian believers. Let's look at it.

First he says, **These things says he who is holy**. When the angel announced Jesus' birth to the virgen Mary, he said,

...the Holy Spirit will come upon you, and the power of the Highest will overshadow you; therefore, also, that **Holy One who is to be born** *will be called the Son of God. Luke 1:35b*

Those who know a deep personal relationship with the Lord Jesus Christ are acutely aware that he is the **holy one of God** (Mark 1:24). Christ once challenged the Pharisees saying, **which one of you convinceth** [can convict] **me of sin?** His question was met by stony silence. No one could think of anything. The Psalmist, prophesying about Jesus' death and resurrection, said,

For you will not leave my soul in Sheol, nor will you allow your **Holy One** *to see corruption. Psalm 16:10*

The Apostle Paul says of Christ,

For he made him **who knew no sin** *to be sin for us, that we might become the righteousness of God in him. Second Corinthians 5:21*

The writer to the Hebrews proclaims,

Therefore he is also able to save to the uttermost those who come to God through him, since he always lives to make intercession for them. For such a High Priest was fitting for us, **who is holy**, *harmless,* **undefiled, separate from sinners**, *and has become higher than the heavens... Hebrews 7:25-26*

People who do not walk with Christ do not know much about the holiness of their Lord. In fact, they know very little about his true nature and little of what the Word of God says about him. It's not too uncommon to even run across believers who think that Jesus may have sinned a little! That's abysmal ignorance, brother and sister. The Philadelphian believers were not of that group. So, when he addressed them as the **Holy One** ... they knew exactly who was talking to them.

Second, the Lord addresses them as, **He who is true**. Jesus said in *John 14:6,*

I am the way, the **truth**, *and the life. No one comes to the Father except through me.*

The Apostle John says,

And the Word became flesh and dwelt among us, and we beheld his glory, the glory as of the only begotten of the Father, full of grace and **truth**. *John 1:14*

The believers at Philadelphia knew the One who is Truth incarnate. That fact escapes carnal believers.

Lastly, he addresses the Philadelphians as, **He who has the key of David, he who opens and no one shuts, and shuts and no one opens**. As soon as their Pastor read that, I can picture someone in the congregation calling out, *That's Isaiah 22:22. It's from our Lord, alright!* In Isaiah 22, God says of his Son,

The **key of the house of David** *I will lay on his shoulder; so he shall* **open**, *and no one shall shut; and he shall* **shut**, *and no one shall open. I will fasten him as a peg in a secure place, and he will become a glorious* **throne** *to his* **father's** *house. Isaiah 22:22-23*

Holy ... true ... heir to the throne of *David* ... the one *who opens and no one shuts, and shuts and no one opens* ... these are the words of the warm and special greeting Jesus used to greet his church at Philadelphia.

3:7-8

THE COMPLIMENTS

Christ begins ... *I have set before you an open door*. This statement, in itself, is a great compliment. Someone has said, *Prayer moves the hand of God.* The fact that Jesus had opened a door for the Philadelphians is moot testimony to the prayer life of this church. Being a people of the Book, they had come to know the Lord's will and were able to pray accordingly. That, in turn, caused the Lord to gladly open a door on their behalf. The Apostle Paul requested, in *Colossians 4:3*,

*...meanwhile **praying** also for us, that God would open to us a **door** for the Word, to speak the mystery of Christ, for which I am also in chains...*

Notice, the great Apostle Paul himself requested that the Colossians pray to the Lord that he would provide a door of opportunity for him *to speak the mystery of Christ.* Frankly, only a spiritual person or church would even think to ask for such a thing. That's praying according to the will of God, brother. A Bible church is a praying church. Having come to know God's will in his Word, it petitions the Throne accordingly. The Lord set an open door before the Philadelphian believers because they had asked according to the will of God. Do you ask God to open doors for you and your church to share the mystery of Christ? *First John 5:14-15,* says,

*Now this is the confidence that we have in him, that if we **ask** anything according to his **will**, he hears us. And if we know that he hears us, whatever we ask, we know that we **have** the petitions that we have asked of him.*

Christ continues ... *you have a little strength*. This is another great compliment. The Philadelphian believers would be the first to tell you that they were weak and that all their strength came from the Lord. People of the Book learn quickly that they are weak but, he is strong. And, they learn to depend totally upon the strength of their Omnipotent Lord. Paul says,

*But God has chosen the **foolish things** of the world to put to shame the wise, and God has chosen the **weak** things of the world to put to shame the things which are mighty; and the **base things** of the world and the **things which are despised** God has chosen, and the **things which are not**, to bring to nothing the things that are, that no flesh should glory in his presence. First Corinthians 1:27-29*

Again, in *Second Corinthians 12:9-10*, we read,

*And he said to me, 'My grace is sufficient for you, for **my strength is made perfect in weakness.'** Therefore most gladly **I will rather boast in my infirmities, that the power of Christ may rest upon me**. Therefore I take pleasure in infirmities, in reproaches, in needs, in persecutions, in distresses, for Christ's sake. For when I am **weak**, then I am **strong**.*

When Jesus noted that these Philadelphian believers had *a little strength*, it was a great compliment and an encouragement. In relation to the Omnipotent One, **they had a little strength** and, brother, that is **a whole lot of strength**! In relation to him *who holds all things together by the word of his power* (Hebrews 1:3) it was little ... but the Omnipotent One knows strength when he sees it and they had it ... from him. They were experiencing being **strengthened with all might according to his glorious power** (Colossians 1:11)!

Then, he says, *you ... have kept my word.* What a wonderful compliment that is. Twice here, the Lord says they have *kept* his Word (v. 8 and v. 10). This shows the Philadelphia church to be the most spiritual of the seven churches, in my opinion. They had to have been a biblically literate church to know the Word of God and keep it. And, oh, the raw power of the Word of God in the life of a believer and church. It cannot be overestimated. It is the Word of God that produces spiritual people and spiritual churches. It is the key to the new birth, Christian maturity, wisdom, knowledge, understanding, freedom, the filling of the Holy Spirit, spiritual growth, sanctification (purity), and a fruitful walk with Christ. Let's look at a few scriptures that speak to these truths.

...having been born again, not of corruptible seed but incorruptible, **through the word of God** *which lives and abides forever... First Peter 1:23*

You are already clean because of the **word** *which I have spoken to you. John 15:3*

As newborn babes, desire the pure milk of the **word**, *that you may* **grow** *thereby... First Peter 2:2*

Blessed is the man who walks not in the counsel of the ungodly, nor stands in the path of sinners, nor sits in the seat of the scornful; **but his delight is in the law of the LORD, and in His law he meditates day and night**. *He shall be like a tree planted by the rivers of water, that brings forth its fruit in its season, whose leaf also shall not wither; and whatever he does shall prosper. Psalm 1:1-3*

The proverbs of Solomon the son of David, king of Israel: To know **wisdom** *and instruction, To perceive the* **words** *of* **understanding**... *Proverbs 1:1-2*

Then Jesus said to those Jews who believed him, 'If you abide in my **word**, *you are my disciples indeed. And you shall know the truth, and the truth shall make you* **free**.*' John 8:31-32*

If you abide in me, and my **words** *abide in you, you will ask what you desire, and it shall be done for you. By this my Father is glorified, that you bear much* **fruit**; *so you will be my disciples. John 15:7-8*

Now, let's compare two verses and note the relationship between the intake of the Word of God in the life of a believer and the filling of the Holy Spirit.

Let the **word** *of Christ dwell in you richly in all wisdom, teaching and admonishing one another* **in psalms and hymns and spiritual songs, singing with grace in your hearts to the Lord**. *Colossians 3:16*

And do not be drunk with wine, in which is dissipation; but be **filled with the Spirit**, *speaking to one another in psalms and hymns and spiritual songs, singing and making melody in your heart to the Lord... Ephesians 5:18-19*

Did you notice that the results of **letting the Word of God dwell in one's life richly and being filled with the Spirit are identical**? That's because they are two sides of the same coin. The filling of the Holy Spirit and the intake of the Word of God cannot be separated.

You cannot have the one without the other. How can someone be filled with the Holy Spirit and not be filled with his Word? How can someone be filled with his Word and not be filled with his Holy Spirit? There is no substitute in the life of a believer for the Word of God. No experience can duplicate its multifaceted and indispensable work. Have you been reading your Bible? It's the sanctifying life-changing Word of God you know. It can and will change your life when you take it in, cherish it in your heart and let it take deep root ... way down in your soul. Jesus, in his prayer for us in *John 17:17*, prayed to his Father,

Sanctify *them by your truth. Your* **word** *is truth.*

There is no road to spirituality and maturity outside of the Word of God ... no road at all.

3:9-10

THE PROMISES

The Lord promises two things to the Philadelphians. First, that he will vindicate them in the presence of their enemies. Like the church at Smyrna, these believers had been suffering at the hands of ungodly Jews in their city. The Lord aims a thunderbolt at their enemies here, calling them **the synagogue of Satan**, just as he spoke of the unrighteous Jews at Smyrna back in 2:9. He says, **they say are Jews and are not, but lie**. This parallels the thought in *Romans 2:28-29*,

For **he is not a Jew** *who is one outwardly, nor is circumcision that which is outward in the flesh; but he is a Jew who is one inwardly; and circumcision is that of the heart, in the Spirit, not in the letter; whose praise is not from men but from God.*

A true Jew, by God's definition, is a spiritual person, a person who is truly godly. The Jews who were persecuting the believers at Philadelphia were just outward Jews and not God's people at all or they would have acted like God's people. The Lord's promise to the Philadelphians is that he would one day compel those phonies to fall at their **feet** and **worship** and **know that I have loved you**. What an occasion that will be. When Jesus vindicates his suffering saints, it will certainly be in no uncertain terms.

Second, Christ promises, *I also will keep you from* **the hour of trial which shall come upon the whole world, to test those who** *dwell on the earth*. Eschatologically speaking (doctrine of end things), these words are very important. The Greek word translated *from* here is the word ἐκ (*ek*), which means *out of*. The import of this little two letter word is great. Christ is promising to keep these Philadelphian believers **out of the time period itself**. He will accomplish that by removing his saints from the earth before the day of God's wrath begins. I take this term, *the hour of trial*, to refer to the entire seven year Tribulation that will commence after the Rapture of the Church. This is further proof that the Church will not be on Earth when God's day of wrath comes.

Now, the church at Philadelphia has long vanished from the scene, yet the coming *hour of trial* has yet to arrive. One might ask then, *How could this have been relevant to them*? The answer lies in the fact that the return of Jesus Christ for his Church has always been an eminent one. He could have come for the Philadelphian believers at any time but, in retrospect, he didn't. Therefore, this statement has now come to apply to Christ's Universal Church of all ages as evidenced by his words, *he that has an ear let him hear what the Spirit says to the churches*. These words are strong proof for the pre-tribulation Rapture of the Church. In essence, they teach us that **no church** will enter into that time period. This is in line with the whole of scripture on this subject as well. For example, as you have it in *First Thessalonians 1:10*,

*...And to wait for his Son from heaven, whom he raised from the dead, even Jesus who **delivers us from the wrath to come***.

It is the legitimate and biblical expectation for every church, of every age, that they will not go through the coming day of God's wrath, the Tribulation. They will all go out ahead of it.

The Lord further clarifies what he means by the ***hour of trial*** by saying it will be sent *to test those who dwell on the earth*. The coming Tribulation will test mankind under the severest conditions imaginable. It will be designed to see which way men will turn under extreme conditions. It will be a time of refining for Jews and Gentiles alike. Out of those days, God will call out the last of his people for his name's sake. Every possible man, woman and child who will turn to the Savior and be saved will come to him during those dark days. Millions will respond during God's great day of testing. It will bring about the greatest revival the world has ever seen. In chapter 7, we will be introduced to the believers who will come out of the Great Tribulation. A passage from Isaiah's prophecy, at this point, is helpful in defining what our Lord means by *testing*. Because of its importance, here is *Isaiah 24,* in its entirety.

Behold, the LORD makes the earth empty and makes it waste, *distorts its surface and scatters abroad its inhabitants. And it shall be: as with the people, so with the priest; as with the servant, so with his master; as with the maid, so with her mistress; as with the buyer, so with the seller; as with the lender, so with the borrower; as with the creditor, so with the debtor.* **The land shall be entirely emptied and utterly plundered, for the LORD has spoken this word**. *The earth mourns and fades away, the world languishes and fades away; the haughty people of the earth languish. The earth is also defiled under its inhabitants, because they have transgressed the laws, changed the ordinance, broken the everlasting covenant. Therefore the curse has devoured the earth, and those who dwell in it are desolate. Therefore* **the inhabitants of the earth are burned, and few men are left**. *The new wine fails, the vine languishes, all the merry-hearted sigh. The mirth of the tambourine ceases, the noise of the jubilant ends, the joy of the harp ceases. "They shall not drink wine with a song; strong drink is bitter to those who drink it. The city of confusion is broken down;* **every house is shut up**, *so that none may go in. There is a cry for wine in the streets,* **all joy is darkened**, *the mirth of the land is gone. In the city desolation is left, and the gate is stricken with destruction. When it shall be thus in the midst of the land among the people,* **it shall be like the shaking of an olive tree, like the gleaning of grapes when the vintage is done**. *They shall lift up their voice, they shall sing; for the majesty of the LORD they shall cry aloud from the sea. Therefore glorify the LORD in the dawning light, the name of the LORD God of Israel in the coastlands of the sea. From the ends of the earth we have heard songs: "Glory to the righteous!" But I said, "I am ruined, ruined! Woe to me! The treacherous dealers have dealt treacherously, indeed, the treacherous dealers have dealt very treacherously.* **Fear and the pit and the snare are upon you, O inhabitant of the earth**. *And it shall be that he who flees from the noise of the fear shall fall into the pit, and he who comes up from the midst of the pit shall be caught in the snare; for the windows from on high are open, and the foundations of the earth are shaken. The earth is violently broken, the earth is split open,* **the earth is shaken exceedingly. The earth shall reel to and fro like a drunkard**, *and shall totter like a hut; its transgression shall* *be heavy upon it, and it will fall, and not rise again. It shall come to pass in that day that the LORD will punish on high the host of exalted ones, and on the earth the kings of the earth. They will be gathered together, as prisoners are gathered in the pit, and will be shut up in the prison; after many days they will be punished. Then the moon will be disgraced and the sun ashamed; for the LORD of hosts will reign On Mount Zion and in Jerusalem and before his elders, gloriously.*

Truly, mankind is scheduled for an *hour of trial* indeed.

3:11

THE WARNING

The Lord concludes with a three-part warning to the church at Philadelphia.

First, he says, **behold, I am coming quickly**. The Rapture of the Church will be an instantaneous event. There will be no time to get ready. As you have it in *First Corinthians 15:51-52,*

Behold, I tell you a mystery: we shall not all sleep, but we shall all be changed; ***in a moment, in the twinkling of an eye****, at the last trumpet. For the trumpet will sound, and the dead will be raised incorruptible, and we shall be changed.*

Second, he says, **hold fast what you have**. The Philadelphians were a spiritual and fruitful people. The greatest danger to a Bible reading and practicing church is that it can become a non-Bible reading, unspiritual and fruitless church by simple neglect. **Hold fast to what you have** is very good advice indeed, both for them and for you and me as well.

Third, he says, **that no one take your crown**. As I have mentioned before, crowns are rewards. The Philadelphians were to be careful not to let anyone influence them to let the Word of God slip. This could result in tragic loss of reward for them. Paul likewise warns in *Colossians 2:8,*

Beware lest ***anyone cheat you*** *through philosophy and empty deceit, according to the tradition of men, according to the basic principles of the world, and not according to Christ.*

Employment, money, family, friends, professors and teachers and a host of other things can sidetrack believers from what is really important in life. Don't allow it to happen to you, dear saint. Hold fast to the Word of God until he comes.

3:12

THE PROMISES

Christ closes his letter with two more promises to his overcomers.

First, he says, *I will make him a pillar in the temple of my God, and he shall go out no more*. Pillars are the very visible, ornate and central structures in great buildings and palaces. So it will be with the child of God in his Father's house. The Greek word for *temple* here is ναῷ (*naoh* from *naos*). It is the word for the inner Holy of Holies in the temple of God. It was in the *naos* that the Ark of the Covenant stood and where God dwelt between the golden cherubim of its lid, the Mercy Seat. One day, you and I will regularly walk in a city that, chapters 21 and 22 tell us, will be the **naos** of God ... side to side ... and top to bottom ... a Holy of Holies ... in the very visible presence of God. We will be pillars there, *fixtures*, if you please, in that holy and awesome city. Peter, using a similar analogy, says of us believers in Christ,

Coming to him as to a living stone, rejected indeed by men, but chosen by God and precious, you also, **as living stones**, **are being built up a spiritual house**, *a holy priesthood, to offer up spiritual sacrifices acceptable to God through Jesus Christ. First Peter 2:4-5*

Second, he says, *I will write on him the name of my God, and the name of the city of my God ... and I will write on him my new name.* This is precious. I don't know about the visibility or location of these identifying marks on the child of God, but we learn here that they will be written on every child of God with the finger of Christ himself. The implication is that they will be visible forever for all to see. They will display our identity and declare our legitimacy in Heaven. God's name, Heaven's name, and Christ's new name ... all three will be written on God's children. What an honor it will be to bear them. Do you know Christ's new name, by the way? No? Neither do I, but we will, one day. It will be written upon us. As Christ's overcomers, we shall uniquely display them before all created beings throughout eternity, showing that we are Christ's and he is ours.

One more thought before we leave the church at Philadelphia. Let's you and I resolve to be a Word centered people, O.K.? Let's get to know our Bibles. Let's be a people of the Book. Have you read your Bible today? Out of it stems all that God has for us. You and I will one day spend eternity with the Living Word of God who spoke each and every word of it. Treasure it, study it, memorize it, cherish it and do not let it slip.

LAODICEA

THE WISHY WASHY CHURCH

Rev. 3:14-22

And to the angel of the church **[NU omits *"of the Laodiceans"*]** *in Laodicea write, 'These things says the Amen, the Faithful and True Witness, the **Beginning** of the creation of God: I know your works, that **you are neither cold nor hot**. I could wish you were cold or hot. So then, because you are lukewarm, and neither cold nor hot, **I will vomit you out of my mouth**. Because you say, 'I am rich, have become wealthy, and have need of nothing'; and do not know that you are wretched, miserable, poor, blind and naked; I counsel you to buy from me gold refined in the fire, that you may be rich; and white garments, that you may be clothed, that the shame of your nakedness may not be revealed; and anoint your eyes with eye salve, that you may see. **As many as I love, I rebuke** and chasten. Therefore be zealous and repent. **Behold, I stand at the door and knock**. If anyone hears my voice and opens the door, I will come in to him and dine with him, and he with me. To him who overcomes I will grant to sit with me on my throne, as I also overcame and sat down with my Father on his throne. He who has an ear, let him hear what the Spirit says to the churches.'*

Laodicea was probably the wealthiest of the seven churches. It was situated on a major trade route and was a commercial banking center. It had so much money that after the great earthquake of AD 17, it refused aid from the Roman Senate. Like the Laodicean church, the city itself seemed to *have need of nothing*. It also had a medical school that produced and marketed a famous eye salve. Jesus will allude to that salve in his comments to this church.

3:14

SALUTATION

Christ addresses this church as the, **Amen**. This is the only place in the Bible where this name of Christ is found. *Amen* means, *so be it,* or *it is true.* In effect, Jesus is saying, *The one writing to you is the one who has the last and true word on all thing,* the One who will have the final word ... like a period at the end of a sentence. Now, complacent people, as well as complacent churches, are usually arrogant in their coldness, apostasy and compromising life styles. They live as if they have no accountability at all. So, the ***Amen*** addresses them here in no uncertain terms. They would do well to listen. He is the One who will have the last word on every life and church throughout all time. All will give account to him. Jesus is the ***Amen*** of God.

Also, He addresses them as **the Faithful and True Witness**. Jesus never pulled a punch on anyone. He always told it like it was. He is God's **Faithful and True Witness**. When he was on earth, Jesus said,

*...When you have lifted up the Son of man, then shall ye know that I am he, and that **I do nothing of myself**; but as my Father hath taught me, I speak these things. And he that sent me is with me: the Father hath not left me alone; **for I do always those things that please him**. Jn. 8:28-29*

*..the words that I speak unto you **I speak not of myself: but the Father that dwelleth in me**, he doeth the works. Jn. 14:10b*

Jesus never deviated from faithfully expressing and doing the will of his Father. He was always faithful. The Laodicean church was far from that and his opening words here were designed to bring these folks up short. In response, they should have asked themselves, *Are we faithful and true witnesses?* In *John 20:21b,* Jesus said,

Peace to you! As the Father has sent me, ***I also send you****.*

And, in *Acts 1:8*, we read,

*But you shall receive power when the Holy Spirit has come upon you; and you shall be **witnesses** to me in Jerusalem, and in all Judea and Samaria, and to the ends of the earth.*

Last, he addresses them as **The Beginning of the creation of God**. The Greek word here for **beginning** is ἀρχή (*arke*). It means origin or the original cause of something. Contrary to the beliefs of the Mormons and Jehovah Witnesses who teach this verse says that Jesus was a created being, Jesus is actually saying that he is the Creator himself. The scriptures also clearly testify to this fact. Here are a few of them.

Speaking of Jesus, *Colossians 1:15-16*, says,

*He is the image of the invisible God, the firstborn over all creation. For **by him all things were created** that are in heaven and that are on earth, visible and invisible, whether thrones or dominions or principalities or powers. **All things were created through him and for him**.*

Hebrews 1:2-3 says God,

*...has in these last days spoken to us by his Son, whom he has appointed heir of all things, **through whom also he made the worlds**; who being the brightness of his glory and the express image of his person, and **upholding all things by the word of his power**, when he had by himself purged our sins, sat down at the right hand of the Majesty on high...*

Christ Jesus is the Creator and the originator of all things. Yet we live in a day when secular society (and often ho-hum Christianity) has chosen to adopt the theory of Evolution and the eternality of matter as their preferred hypothesis of origins. The Word of God disagrees. As you have it in *Exodus 20:11*,

*For in **six days** the LORD made the heavens and the earth, the sea, and all that are in them, and rested the seventh day. Therefore the LORD blessed the Sabbath day and hallowed it.*

And again, in *Hebrews 11:3*,

*By faith we understand that **the worlds were framed by the word of God**, so that the things which are **seen were not made of things which are visible**.*

I do not know what theory of creation the Laodicean church may have held. It wouldn't surprise me though if some of them held the popular Greek myth of their day which said that the earth was hatched by a giant chicken! Jesus points out to this lukewarm church that **he** is their Creator ... with all that that implies.

3:15-16

THE PROBLEM

Our Lord begins by saying ... *I know your works, that you are neither cold nor hot. Because you are lukewarm, and neither cold nor hot, I will vomit you out of my mouth*. Well, that's right to the point, isn't it? Jesus didn't mince words. The word picture he used is a vivid one. It is a picture of someone who assumes they are taking a cool drink of water but they discover that it is like warm saliva and immediately spews it out of their mouth. A lukewarm church is a sickening thing to the Head of the Church. Let's look a bit more closely at his words.

What is *hot*? I would define a *hot* church as one that is fervent in prayer, witnessing, good works, love for one another, Bible study and, most of all, love for the Savior.

What is *cold*? A *cold* church is one that possesses little or none of the above.

What is *lukewarm*? A *lukewarm* church is a group of saints that agree with the things of a hot church. Yet, they are so complacent and indifferent to them that they seldom give them a second thought. So, a lukewarm church is a church that performs *Churchianity* as opposed to living Christianity on a daily basis. Jesus says of such a church, *You make me sick!* He literally says to them, *I will vomit you out of my mouth*. I take this to mean that Christ is threatening to suddenly dissolve their church like an involuntarily physical reaction on his part. This is not just a threat to remove them like he threatened to do to the Ephesian church. He is saying, *Frankly, I don't know how much longer I can stomach you*.

3:17

THE WARNING

He continues ... *Because you say I am rich, and increased with goods, and have need of nothing*...

The source of the problem at Laodicea appears to be materialism. Materialism, in the life of a church or individual Christian, is a devastating thing. It has a way of creeping up on people. It brings a false sense of security and an independence from God that totally distracts from living and walking with the Savior. Consider these scriptures.

No one can serve two masters; for either he will hate the one and love the other, or else he will be loyal to the one and despise the other. **You cannot serve God and mammon** [money]. *Matthew 6:24*

And having food and clothing, with these we shall be content. But those who desire to be rich fall into temptation and a snare, *and into many foolish and harmful lusts which drown men in destruction and perdition.* **For the love of money is a root of all kinds of evil**, *for which some have* **strayed from the faith** *in their greediness, and pierced themselves through with many sorrows. First Timothy 6:8-10*

As dedicated materialists, the Laodiceans thought they had it made, but the Lord says they are **wretched, miserable, poor, blind and naked**. What an indictment. Many have likened this church to the Church in America because of her materialism.

May I step aside here for a moment? One must never assume that material prosperity is synonymous with spiritual success. This is one of the great errors taught in our day, as it was in Jesus' day. Prosperity doctrine preachers are constantly pounding the drum on this. They are up to their ears in the error of the Laodiceans. Riches are never a sign of either spirituality or spiritual success. Solomon said,

Remove falsehood and lies far from me; **Give me neither poverty nor riches**; *Feed me with the food allotted to me; Lest I be full and deny you, and say, 'Who is the LORD?' Or lest I be poor and steal, and profane the name of my God. Proverbs 30:8-9*

That is very good advice. The writer to the Hebrews also speaks pointedly to this issue.

Still others had trial of mockings and scourgings, yes, and of chains and imprisonment. They were stoned, they were sawn in two, were tempted, were slain with the sword. They **wandered about in sheepskins and goatskins, being destitute**, *afflicted, tormented; of whom the world was not worthy. They wandered in deserts and mountains, in dens and caves of the earth. And all these, having* *obtained a good testimony through faith, did not receive the promise... Hebrews 11:36-39*

The lives of the majority of God's greatest saints have not been marked by health and wealth, brother. They have been marked by faith and sacrifice, poverty and suffering, and yes ... even sickness. The Laodiceans confused riches and prosperity with God's blessing ... an error the Pharisees held and so did Job's misguided friends.

3:18

THE INSTRUCTION

Since the Laodiceans were of the *shop until you drop* crowd, Jesus tells them they should pick up a couple of things while they are out and about doing their shopping. He counsels, **buy from me gold refined in the fire, that you may be rich**. He is saying, *Come to me if you want true riches, I have them and I'll show you how to get them.* Faith, the fruit of the Spirit, laboring under duress, suffering in the fires of persecution, serving under thankless conditions and sacrificing along with Christ is where real riches lie, beloved. Those are things that will remain. They are **gold tried in the fire**.

Next, he counsels them to acquire **white garments** from him so that **the shame of your nakedness may not be revealed**. Saints who are long on materialism and short on righteousness will find themselves very much underdressed in Heaven one day and it will very much be to their shame. Christ is referring here to the time, after the reward seat of Christ, when the literal clothing of the saints will reflect the things they accomplished for and with him when they were alive on Earth. If there was precious little kingdom living down here, there will not be a whole lot to wear up there. *Revelation 19:7-8,* says,

Let us be glad and rejoice and give him glory, for the marriage of the Lamb has come, and his wife has made herself ready. And to her it was granted to be arrayed in fine linen, clean and bright, **for the fine linen is the righteous acts of the saints**.

Last, the Lord counsels them to drop by his pharmacy and get some eye medicine. He says **anoint your eyes with eye-salve that you might be able to see**. This should have really struck home with the Laodiceans because there was a famous eye-salve factory there. What's he getting at? Well, I hate to keep pounding the drum of the importance of the Word of God, but it's the only eye-salve that I know of. Meditate on these verses and see if it isn't so.

*Your **word** is a lamp to my feet and a light to my path. Psalm 119:105*

*The entrance of your **words** gives light; it gives understanding to the simple. Psalm 119:130*

*So now, brethren, I commend you to God and to the **word** of his grace,* **which is able to build you up and give you an inheritance among all those who are sanctified**. *Acts 20:32*

The cure for poor, blind, lukewarm believers is liberal applications of the *eye-salve* of the Word of God. This was Jesus' formula for a turnaround for the Laodiceans.

3:19-20

The final words of Christ to his **lukewarm** church at Laodicia are surprising, touching and deeply moving. He says, **As many as I love, I rebuke and chasten: therefore be zealous and repent**. These are loving and marvelously gracious words, are they not? Up to this point, if I were a part of the Laodicean church, I might have been just about ready to throw in the towel. But listen, in spite of the sorry condition this church was in, the Head of the Church does not hesitate to declare his love for them. Amazing. As you have it in *Hebrews 12:6-9,*

*For whom the LORD **loves** he chastens, and scourges every son whom he receives. If you endure chastening, God deals with you as with sons; for what son is there whom a father does not chasten? But if you are without chastening, of which all have become partakers, then you are illegitimate and not sons. Furthermore, we have had human fathers who corrected us, and we paid them respect. Shall we not much more readily be in subjection to the Father of spirits and **live**?*

And, not only does he declare his love for them but he also **offers them his fellowship**. He declares, **Behold, I stand at the door and knock**. This is a wonderful word picture. It is a verse that is often quoted to persuade non-Christians to come to Christ but it was actually spoken to believers. Jesus tells the Laodiceans that he is knocking on their door and He deeply desires entrance to fellowship with them.

This is a wonderful thing about Jesus. He desires our fellowship ... even when we don't desire his. The English artist, Holman Hunt, painted a famous picture based on this verse that pictures Christ knocking upon a door. It is said, when he first displayed it, a woman remarked that he had forgotten to put a handle on the door. He replied, *This door is a picture of the human heart. The handle is on the inside.* This is true of every believer. No matter how badly we foul up, Christ still desires our fellowship. But, it is entirely up to us. Jesus is either inside fellowshipping with us or he's outside, knocking on our door.

To sum up, the Lord's cure here for ho-hum Christianity is threefold ... **repentance** ... followed by a liberal applications of the **Word of God** ... followed by genuine **fellowship with Christ**. All who take him up on this remedy will surely bless the day they did. They will be transformed from lukewarm to warm to hot for God and the things of God.

3:21-22

THE PROMISE

Now, we come to Christ's final promise to his overcomers in these wonderful letters. He says that he will grant his overcomers *to sit with me on my throne*. Say what!? Can you believe this? What an honor. No one knows yet the full import of this promise but, at a minimum, it speaks of reigning with Christ in his glorious Kingdom on earth one day. What an amazing offer to such a poor excuse for a church, aye? That's grace, brother. We saw this same promise back in *Revelation 2:26-27*,

And he who overcomes, and keeps my works until the end, to him ***I will give power over the nations; he shall rule them*** *with a rod of iron; they shall be dashed to pieces like the potter's vessels; as I also have received from my Father...*

This brings us to the end of this section, THE VISION OF JESUS CHRIST MIDST HIS CHURCHES. Christ is in the midst of your church and mine. All that he has said here in chapters 2 and 3 is directed to each one of us and to our churches for our spiritual profit and edification. I believe that he put these chapters here so that we might truly be 100 percent in fellowship with him when we move on to the unfolding mysteries that he is about to impart to us in the pages that follow. There certainly is much to think and pray about here. Perhaps the most important thing was his words to the Ephesian church, though ... since he put them first in the order of churches. ***He who has an ear, let him hear what the Spirit says to the churches.***

REVELATION 4 - 5

GOD'S THRONE IN HEAVEN

Rev. 4:15

*After these things I looked, and behold, a **door** standing open in heaven. And the first voice which I heard was like a trumpet speaking with me, saying, '**Come up here**, and I will show you things which must take place **after this**.' Immediately I was in the Spirit; and behold, a **throne** set in heaven, and **One sat on the throne**. And He who sat there was like a jasper and a sardius stone in appearance; and there was a rainbow around the throne, in appearance like an emerald. **Around the throne were twenty-four thrones**, and on the thrones I saw twenty-four **elders** sitting, clothed in white robes;* [NU omits "and they had"] *with crowns of gold on their heads. And from the throne proceeded lightnings, thunderings, and voices. **Seven lamps of fire were burning before the throne, which are the seven Spirits of God**.*

We have now arrived at the largest section of Revelation, THE VISION OF JESUS CHRIST IN JUDGMENT. It takes up all of chapters 4 through 18, and is the meat and lion's share of the book.

4:1

Suddenly, John saw *a door standing open in Heaven* and the trumpet voiced One said, *Come up here, and I will show you things which must take place after this*. The Greek words, *after this*, are μετὰ ταῦτα *(meta touta)*. These are the same words that Jesus used back in 1:19, when he told John what he could expect to be writing down. These words tip us off that, from this point on, Christ will be revealing future things to us.

Immediately, John was transported through a door in Heaven by means of the powerful voice that came from above. This reminds me of the Rapture of the Church, does it you? One day, all of us believers will hear this same trumpet-like voice that John heard and we too will be *immediately* transported up and out of this world. As you have it in *First Thessalonians 4:16-17,*

*For the Lord himself shall descend from heaven with a shout, with the voice of the archangel, and with the trump of God: and the dead in Christ shall rise first: then we which remain **shall be caught up** together with them in the clouds, to meet the Lord in the air: and so shall we ever be with the Lord.*

4:2-3

Upon arrival above, John's senses were flooded with stimuli. Heaven is a real place, even more real than where you and I are right now. There, John was confronted with amazing realities ... realities of substance, color, noises, voices, angels, people and thrones. Quickly, his eyes were drawn to a great central *throne* upon which sat an awesome Throne Sitter. He exclaimed, **behold, a throne set in heaven, and One sat on the throne**. The Throne Sitter was a visible manifestation of the Father, by the way. We know this to be the case because Jesus will approach him in chapter 5. John says that the Throne Sitter's appearance was like the sparkling luminescence of a *jasper stone*, combined with the blood red of a *sardius stone* (named after Sardis, the area around which it is found).

There is a wonderful significance to the colors of these two stones that were emanating from the Father's person upon his throne. In Old Testament times, twelve stones were sewn on the High Priest's vest ... one for each of the twelve tribes of Israel. The *jasper* and *sardius* stones were the first and last stones on the vest. The jasper stone stood for the tribe of Reuben. Ruben's name meant, *behold a son*. The sardius stone stood for the tribe of Benjamin. His name meant, *son of my right hand*. The fact that the Father was emanating the colors of these two stones is significant. Both the Father and the Son reflect one another, you see. That's because, in essence, they are truly one. The Lord Jesus perfectly reflected his Father when he was on Earth. As you have it in *Hebrews 1:3a,*

*Who being the brightness of his glory, and **the express image of his person**, and upholding all things by the word of his power, when* *he had by himself purged our sins, sat down on the right hand of the Majesty on high...* (KJV)

And again in *John 1:18*, we read,

No one has seen God at any time. The only begotten Son, who is in the bosom of the Father, **he has declared him**.

In *John 14:9*, when Philip asked to see the Father, Jesus replied,

Have I been with you so long, and yet you have not known me, Philip? **He who has seen me has seen the Father**; *so how can you say, 'Show us the Father'?*

Here, in the heavenly scene that met John's eye, we find that the reverse is also true. He that has seen the Father, has also seen the Son. Doubtless, this is why the Father is reflecting the colors that are associated with his Son whose throne this is as well.

Next, John's eyes lifted upward to behold a magnificent emerald **rainbow** that encompassed the Father's throne. You will recall that God designated the rainbow to be the sign of his Noahic Covenant, within he promised never again to destroy the Earth by water (Genesis 9:8-13). Every rainbow that has appeared, from that day to this, has a reminder of that covenant. This particular rainbow, that surrounds God's throne in Heaven, is there as a permanent reminder that the one true and living God, who occupies this throne, is a covenant and promise keeping God.

Now, I have a question about this scene. Where is Jesus? Shouldn't he be seated at the right hand of this Majesty on high? But he isn't, is he? Where do you think he is, then? To answer the question, let's begin by asking ourselves ... *Where is Jesus right now, at this very minute*? Why, he is seated on this very throne, is he not? As you have it in *Hebrews 1:3*,

...who being the brightness of his glory and the express image of his person, and upholding all things by the word of his power, when he had by himself purged our sins, **sat down at the right hand of the Majesty on high**...

And again, as we had it back in *3:21*,

To him who overcomes **I will grant to sit with me on my throne**, *as I also overcame and* **sat down with my Father on his throne**.

The fact that Christ is not present on this throne suggests that there is something uniquely unusual about this scene indeed. May I say to you that Christ was not present at the point in time when John arrived ... because he had left his Father's throne? In the immediate future, Jesus will only leave his Father's throne for one of two reasons. First, he will temporarily leave it to go and personally fetch his Church from off the earth and bring it back to Heaven (First Thessalonians 4:16). Or, second, he will leave his Father's throne to return to Earth to rule and reign here for a thousand years (Zechariah 14:34; Rev. 20:4). It will become apparent, as we gather more information about this scene, that Jesus is not seated with the Father because of the Rapture of the Church. Time-wise, John had arrived in Heaven just **after** the Rapture ... and just **before** Christ had returned to the throne.

4:4

Next, John says, *Around the throne were twenty-four thrones, and on the thrones were twenty-four elders sitting*. Can you identify these men? Let's see if we can do so by taking a closer look at them.

First, they are called *elders*. The Greek word used here for *elders* is the word πρεσβυτέρους *(presbuteros)*. In the New Testament, this term is one that is used for the spiritual leaders of the Church. It describes their office. The other Greek word, used for Church leaders, is ἐπίσκοποσ *(episkopos)*, translated *bishop* or *overseer*. This word describes the function of the office.

Second, there were *twenty four* of them. What might be the significance of this particular number? Well, the old Aaronic priesthood was divided into twenty-four divisions (I Chronicles 24:1-19). They forfeited their priesthood, however, when they rejected their Messiah and his work for them on the cross and were subsequently *cut off* (Romans 11:17-22). The Lord then turned to the Gentiles and they, along with a small remnant of Messianic Jews, took the place of the former Aaronic priesthood. You will remember back in 1:6, believers are called a *kingdom of priests*. I believe these *twenty-four elders* who were sitting around God's throne here are representatives of a transferred right of priesthood. They are probably individual heads of a twenty-four division, Melchizedecan, priesthood in Heaven (Hebrews 7:16-17). If that is the case, then their individual divisions could well be assigned specific times and tasks of service, as were their ancient Aaronic counterparts on Earth. In any case, everything about them speaks of the fact that they are representatives of the Church. This is further confirmed in 5:9, where John hears them singing to the Lamb ... ***You ... have redeemed us to God by your blood.***

Third, they themselves were seated upon ***thrones***. Only the Church is promised ***thrones*** in Scripture. Jesus promised them to his disciples in *Matthew 19:28,*

*Assuredly I say to you, that in the regeneration, when the Son of Man sits on the throne of his glory, you who have followed me **will also sit on twelve thrones, judging the twelve tribes of Israel**.*

The above scripture may help us to speculate as to who some of these twenty-four elders might be. I don't think we would be far from wrong if we said that twelve of them are the Lord's Apostles, fulfilling Matthew19:28, above. They would, then, be representing the Jewish side of the Church. Then, it would make sense that the other twelve are ***elders*** who represent the Gentile side of the Church. If that is the case, we should find the major founders and nurturers of the Gentile Church seated there as well ... such men as Paul, Barnabas, Timothy, Silas, Luke, Mark, Titus, Aquila, Gaius, Aristarchus, Epaphroditus and Sopater.

Fourth, they were ***clothed in white robes***. Back in 3:5, Jesus said, ***He who overcomes shall be clothed in white garments***. Only Church saints are promised white clothing in the Bible. Both of these words, ***garments*** and ***robes***, are translations of the same Greek word, by the way.

Last, they were each wearing ***crowns of gold***. Only the Church is promised ***crowns*** in the Bible. They will be given as rewards. The fact that these elders are seen as already **crowned** is very important. It tells us that the Judgment Seat of Christ (II Corinthians 5:10), has already taken place and its rewards given out.

So, there is more than ample evidence here that these men who are seated upon thrones round about the throne of God are representatives of Christ's Church. Not only had John been caught up into Heaven ... but he had been caught up to a future time and event that he was needed to witness ... a time and an event where the Church was all present and accounted for. This is in agreement with the words of the One who called John up there in the first place saying, ***Come up here, and I will show you things which must take place after this***.

4:5

Having observed the elders and their thrones, next John's senses were confronted by sudden and ominous sounds coming from the throne. Like a summer storm, unexpectedly bearing down on a countryside, God's throne rumbled to life with **lightnings**, **thunderings** and **voices**. John's eyes, having been riveted back to the throne by these awesome sounds and flashes, saw that there were now, **Seven lamps of fire ... burning before the throne, which are the Seven spirits of God**. This reminds me of that verse over in *Hebrews 1:7*, which says,

*And of the angels he saith, who maketh his **angels spirits, and his ministers a flame of fire**.* (KJV)

These are the same *spirits* that greeted us back in chapter one. Now, however, John sees them *burning* before the throne of God. What a sight! It is becoming apparent from these descriptions that this is a throne preparing for judgment. At long last, the one who sits upon this throne is about to intervene upon the earth. He is about to step in and do something about evil and wickedness and unbelief. These ominous rumblings and flashes of lightening, coming out from the Father's throne, speak of the fact that God, at this point in time, is coming to the end of His patience and long-suffering. Like a nuclear reactor approaching critical mass, this throne was becoming unstable. The balance between longsuffering and justice was tilting toward an overriding demand for justice. That being the case ... and I believe that it is ... the *voices* John heard emanating from the throne were probably the stored up cries of countless thousands of God's saints who, down through the ages, cried out to God as they were being beaten, robbed, raped, tortured and murdered and finally cast off like so much garbage. We can rest assured that God has not forgotten a single such cry. *Proverbs 15:3,* says,

The eyes of the LORD are in every place, keeping watch on the evil and the good.

And, again in Deut. 32:25,

Vengeance is Mine, and recompense;
Their foot shall slip in due time;
For the day of their calamity is at hand,
And the things to come hasten upon them.'

At long last, the God of the whole earth was about to rise up and take action ... and his seven avenging angels were ablaze before his throne, standing ready to carry out their God's bidding. The point in time that John had arrived in Heaven was on the very brink of the fulfillment of the words of *Romans 12:19b*,
   *...it is written, **'Vengeance is mine**, **I will repay**,' says the Lord.*

Rev. 4:6-8

Before the throne there was **[NU adds "*something like*"]** *a sea of glass, like crystal. And in the midst of the throne, and around the throne, were four **living creatures** full of eyes in front and in back. The first living creature was like a **lion**, the second living creature like a **calf**, the third living creature had a face like a **man**, and the fourth living creature was like a flying **eagle**. The four living creatures, each having six wings, were full of eyes around and within. And they do not rest day or night, saying: '**Holy, holy, holy, Lord God Almighty**, Who was and is and is to come!'*

4:6-7

As John's attention continued to be riveted upon the throne, he observed that four **living creatures**, ζῶα *(zoa)*, were present there as well. In Scripture, these awesome beings are almost exclusively found in association with the throne of God. The only exception was when one of them was placed at the entrance of the Garden of Eden to guard the way to the Tree of Life (Genesis 3:24). Ezekiel 1 and 10 are key chapters to study for a more detailed description of these magnificent beings and their throne related functions. The first time Ezekiel saw them, they were coming out of the wilderness carrying this same throne of God Almighty. We learn from that account, that they not only bear God's throne but they are also its protectors ... flashing around about it like lightning and with wings that thunder with deafening noise (Ezek.1:14, 24). It would be time well spent to read those chapters to get the complete picture of the Lord's mighty and awesome Zoa.

Now, John saw the ***living creatures*** as one-dimensional because he only observed them from one angle. Therefore, to him, each one seemed to have a different face. Ezekiel, however, tells us that each one of the *zoe* are four sided beings and each have all four faces. Standing together, apparently they are always so situated that anyone who approaches the throne of God will see all four faces and makes them appear to be looking in all directions at all times. Furthermore, just as the colors from the Father represent the Son, so also the specific aspects of the ***living creatures*** reflect the Son as well. For example, each of the four **faces** of the Zoa, speak of a specific **function** of the person and work of the Lord Jesus Christ. Let's look at them and see if it is not so.

THE LION FACE

The *lion* faces of the living creatures emphasize that the one whose throne they bear, protect and surround, is the King of Israel ... ***The Lion of the Tribe of Judah***. This, by the way, is the theme of book of Matthew. Matthew's argument is that Jesus is the King of the Jews. Matthew's genealogy traces Christ's lineage back to King David, establishing Jesus' legal right to the throne of Israel.

THE CALF FACE

The *calf* faces of the ***living creatures*** emphasize the fact that the Lord, whose throne they surround, is God's prophesied and beloved **Servant**. A calf or ox is a serving beast. In Isaiah, God said of his Son,

Behold! my Servant *whom I uphold, my Elect One in whom my soul delights! I have put my Spirit upon him; he will bring forth justice to the Gentiles. Isaiah 42:1*

The argument of the book of Mark is that Jesus is God's **Servant**. As Jesus himself, put it in *Mark 10:45,*

...For even the Son of Man did not come to be served, but to **serve***, and to give his life a ransom for many.*

Consistent with Mark's theme, there is no genealogy of Christ found in Mark ... for who would care about the lineage of a servant?

THE MAN FACE

The *man* faces of the *living creatures* emphasize the fact that the Lord, who's throne this is, is a human ... the one who *became flesh and dwelt among us* (John 1:14). He was and is *the man, Christ Jesus* (First Timothy 2:5). Ever since our Lord's return to Heaven, a man has been seated at the right hand of the majesty on high! This is the theme of Luke's gospel. That's why Luke gives us such a detailed account of the birth of Jesus and traces his lineage all the way back to Adam. Over and over again in Luke, Jesus refers to himself as *the son of Man*.

THE EAGLE FACE

The *eagle* faces of the *living creatures* emphasizes the fact that the Lord, whose throne they bear is God of very God. Make no mistake about it, Jesus Christ is deity. In the Old Testament, Jehovah God is often likened unto an *eagle*. Boaz used this metaphor when he said to Ruth,

*The LORD repay your work, and a full reward be given you by the LORD God of Israel, under whose **wings** you have come for refuge. Ruth 2:12*

Psalm 91:4, says,

He shall cover thee with his feathers, and under his wings shalt thou trust... (KJV)

The theme of John's gospel is the straight up proposition ... *Jesus is God*. He takes it up with the very first verse,

*In the beginning was the Word, and the Word was with God, and **the Word was God**.* (KJV)

And, in verse fourteen, he says,

*...and the **Word became flesh** and dwelt among us.*

4:8

Also, each of the living creatures had *six wings*. In Ezekiel's account, he said the creatures flashed from place to place like *lightening* (Ezekiel 1:14). This speaks of the fact that the one whose throne they bear and protect is the Omnipresent One. The One who is anywhere and everywhere, all at the same time.

Next, John says that each of the living creatures were *full of eyes in front and in back*. The Zoa's myriad of eyes speak of the fact that the Lord on this throne is the Omniscient One. Jesus is all-knowing and all-seeing. As you have it in *Luke 6:8a,*

But he knew their thoughts… (KJV)

Last, John says that the living creatures never ceased, night and day, to proclaim, **Holy, Holy, Holy, Lord God Almighty, which was and is and is to come**. At the point in time where John arrived, the **living creatures** will be continuously, spontaneously and loudly proclaiming God's holiness … around the clock. That is because the judgments that Christ will shortly unleash upon the earth are rooted in his holy nature. Jesus is *the Holy One of God*.

To sum up, what John saw was a throne set for judgment. It was rumbling like a volcano … emitting flashes of lightening … as four living creatures that surrounded it ceaselessly thundered, **Holy, Holy, Holy** … and seven angels were burning like fire before it. What a sight, aye? And, what a day it will be when you and I see this exact event for ourselves, when the long delayed justice and retribution of God is about to be unleashed upon the earth!

Let's step aside here for a moment. Jesus came into our world to save poor lost sinners from the wrath of God that is to come (First Thessalonians 1:10). For that reason, he shed his precious blood on the cross in order to reconcile estranged and sinful men and women to Holy God. Because the holiness of God demands that sin be punished, Christ's death was absolutely necessary. As we have it in *Romans 3:25-26,* (speaking of Jesus),

*…whom God set forth as a **propitiation** by his blood, through faith, to demonstrate his **righteousness**, because in his forbearance God had passed over the sins that were previously committed, to demonstrate at the present time his righteousness, **that he might be just and the justifier of the one who has faith in Jesus**.*

Make no mistake about it, it was the holiness of God that sent Jesus to the cross and it was at the cross where God's just demands against sin were satisfied and met. Jesus paid it all. He experienced and absorbed God's wrath against sin … for us all … and then, and only then, was Holy God propitiated (satisfied) and able to throw open the door for man to come to him. Propitiation is a good Bible word that is not often used in our modern vocabulary. It simply means that when God's wrath against sin fell on his Son at the cross, God felt and became satisfied. Christ Jesus alone had the infinite capacity to absorb his Father's wrath against sin on our behalf. It should have been poured out on us. We were the offenders, but it was poured out on God's Lamb instead. Christ bled and died in our place. He paid the penalty of death for each and every one of your sins and mine. It was a penalty that Holy God demanded. As you have it in *Romans 6:23a*,

For the wages of sin is death...

Only after that sacrifice, could God freely justify and forgive sinners their debt. Only **after** the cross, could God remain holy and just in pardoning and receiving sinful men and women to himself (Romans 3:25-26). Amazing plan, amazing grace! Also, we need to keep in mind that it will be the justice of God that will be the eternal undoing of all those who turn away in unbelief from this great gift of forgiveness and salvation God has so freely and graciously provided through his Son. The awful consequences of spurning Christ will be set before us in the pages to follow.

Rev. 4:9-11

*Whenever the **living creatures** give glory and honor and thanks to him who sits on the throne, who lives forever and ever, the twenty-four elders fall down before him who sits on the throne and worship him who lives forever and ever, and **cast their crowns** before the throne, saying: **You are worthy**, [**NU omits "O" and adds "our" Lord "and God"**], to receive glory and honor and power; For you created all things, and by your will they existed and were created.*

4:9-11

After observing God's throne set for judgment, all of Heaven was suddenly caught up in a great outpouring of worship. Beginning as the four *living creatures* were crying, **Holy, Holy, Holy** ... suddenly the twenty-four elders left their thrones and fell down before the Throne Sitter ... and began casting their crowns at his feet. The NIV says that they **lay their crowns before the throne** but, Dr. Zodhiates says the

Greek verb *cast*, βαλοῦσιν (*balousin*), used here ... *in all its applications retains the idea of <u>impulse</u>*. What uninhibited worship takes place in Heaven! Aye? What a contrast it must be to so much that purports to be worship down here. Real uninhibited and spontaneous worship is a rare and precious thing here but, praise God, it is the norm up there. I'm looking forward to that, aren't you?

Again, keep in mind that this event that John is telling us about was a real one that is yet to take place in the future ... and you and I are actually going to be there when it occurs in history. On that day, we will be participants in this very worship that John saw and that we are reading about here. Doubtless, it will be worship so complete and so sublime that it is presently almost beyond our comprehension. You and I will really worship on that day. We will speak to our dear Lord with utter abandon and adoration with all our hearts confess what he means to us and what he has done for us. He loved us, he saved us and he kept us. It was his plan, his grace, his mercy, his Son, his Spirit and his Word by which he rescued us to himself. Then, on that day, we will spontaneously *cast* our crowns at his feet with utter and glorious delight.

John heard the elders cry out, **You are worthy O Lord to receive glory and honor and power for you created all things**. Our great God and Father is worthy of worship simply because he is our Creator as well. It is fundamental to a creature to praise its Creator. May I ask you a question? Are you glad that God created you? Are you thankful to him for your existence? Isn't it wonderful that he called you and me into being? Life ... the gift of existence ... is a priceless treasure, brother and sister. Thank you, Jesus. My, how we will worship our wonderful Creator on that day!

In conclusion, let me suggest that a helpful way to remember the content of a chapter in the Bible is to simply assign a key word to it. Here, in chapter 4, a good key word would be *Holy*. This is the central theme of the chapter. God's holiness is at the core of his nature and will be fundamental to the judgments of the Tribulation that are about to be unfolded before us.

Rev. 5:1-4

*And I saw in the right hand of him who sat on the throne **a scroll written** inside and on the back, sealed with seven seals. Then I saw a strong angel proclaiming with a loud voice, **'Who is worthy to open the scroll** and to loose its seals?' And **no one in heaven or on the earth or under the earth was able to open the scroll, or to look at it**. So I wept much, because no one was found worthy to open* **[NU omits "and read"]** *the scroll, or to look at it.*

5:1

Although this is a new chapter, the words *And I saw* tells us that we are still at the same scene which began back in 4:1. John is continuing his record of this yet future and incredible day at which he stood. In fact, here in chapter 5, we will discover the key to the entire event.

John's attention is now drawn to a mysterious *scroll* in the Throne Sitter's right hand. As he looked more closely, he saw that it was full of writing on its front and on its back. There was no room left anywhere upon it for more to be written. In this regard, it was exactly like the book in *Ezekiel 2:9-10*,

*Now when I looked, there was a hand stretched out to me; and behold, a scroll of a book was in it. Then he spread it before me; and **there was writing on the inside and on the outside**, and written on it were lamentations and mourning and woe.*

However, these are two different scrolls (books) altogether. Ezekiel's scroll contained a prophecy of impending judgments on Israel. This one, we will learn, contains the prophecy of impending judgments on the whole world. Ezekiel was instructed to preach the contents of his scroll to Israel to warn them that, if they did not repent, judgment would come. The Throne Sitter's scroll also contains warnings of judgment to come but this time they will be upon the whole earth. These judgments will unfold before us as the scroll's seals are broken off by Christ in chapter 6.

5:2-4

Now, there was something very unusual about the scroll in the Throne Sitter's hand. John heard a ***strong angel*** with a ***loud voice*** cry out ... ***Who is worthy to open the scroll and to loose its seals?*** But ... ***no one was found worthy to open the scroll, or to look at it***. This was a unique book indeed. It was for *one's eyes only ... and his hands alone*. If he could be found, he could open it and the program it contained could be initiated to bring about the defeat of all of God's enemies and usher in God's long awaited kingdom and everlasting dominion on Earth. This book belonged to one alone ... the worthy One. It was his title deed, as it were, to the earth and all of its inhabitants.

But, the strong angel's cry was met with silence. No one came forth. This was precisely as it was supposed to be, by the way. The reason for the delay was to point out that there was absolutely no **other** man nor angel who was qualified to take this book ... no one at all. John was devastated. If no one came forth to take the scroll, evil would continue on and on. The world would go on and on in endless cycles of sin, violence, chaos, war, pain, bitterness, injustice, sickness and death! John began to weep ***much***. His deeply emotional response is evidence that he recognized the nature of the scroll in the Throne Sitter's hand and its unsurpassed importance to the event at which he stood. Doubtless, the Holy Spirit had revealed it to him. The light may have come on when he first saw the book in the Throne Sitter's hand.

No doubt, the angel's call for one worthy to receive it, echoed throughout every nook and cranny of the universe ... emphasizing that, among men, there is no one else to whom this scroll belongs. There is only One who is worthy and qualified to receive it and to carry out all that is written within it. One solitary man possesses the moral quality and precise credentials to open and carry out the judgments and program that are contained in this document. He is a perfect and righteous Man, for he who enforces holiness must himself be Holy. He, who judges sinners, must himself be without sin. In John 8, when a woman was caught in the act of adultery and dragged before Jesus by the Pharisees, he told them, ***He that is without sin let him cast the first stone***. Do you remember what happened next? All her accusers slunk away, did they not? No one could judge her because no one was any better than she was. The Scripture says, **all have sinned and come short of the glory of God** (Romans 3:23). All but One, that is ... the One who will do the stone casting one day ... for, in that he is sinless, righteous and just, he is **worthy** to do so. The one who opens this scroll will unleash the judgments of God upon the earth and the only one worthy to do that is the Lord Jesus Christ, who died for the sins of the world and has, for centuries, offered himself to mankind as the way out through his blood!

*And he is the propitiation for our sins: and not for ours only, but also for the **sins of the whole world**. First John 2:2*

This whole scene was the exact same one that Daniel saw concerning that future and momentous day when the Son of Man would receive his kingdom and authority and dominion from the hand of the *Ancient of Days*, you see. As you have it in *Daniel 7:13-14*,

*I was watching in the night visions, and behold, **One like the Son of Man, coming with the clouds of heaven! He came to the Ancient of Days**, and they brought him near before him. Then **to him was given dominion and glory and a kingdom, that all peoples, nations, and languages should serve him**. His dominion is an everlasting dominion, which shall not pass away, and his kingdom the one which shall not be destroyed.*

Revelation 4 and 5 are no more, nor less, than the expanded account of that future day of Christ's coronation and commissioning ... the expanded version of the thumbnail sketch of it that Daniel saw. John was standing in the middle of it and he knew it! The scroll in the Throne Sitter's hand contained Christ's authority, title and right to dominion over all the earth. It was his legal and authoritative edict from the *Ancient of Days* to take rule and reign over all peoples and nations. It contained the detailed agenda, judgments, personages and events that would put all of Christ's enemies under his feet. It is the most significant and crucial document of all time.

Rev. 5:5-7

*But one of the elders said to me, 'Do not weep. **Behold, the Lion of the tribe of Judah, the Root of David**, has prevailed to open the* *scroll and* **[NU omits *"to loose"*]** *its seven seals.' And I looked, and behold, in the midst of the throne and of the four living creatures, and in the midst of the elders,* **stood a Lamb** *as though it had been slain, having seven horns and seven eyes, which are the seven Spirits of God sent out into all the earth. Then* **he came and took the scroll out of the right hand of him who sat on the throne**.

5:5

Someone approached the weeping John and told him to dry his tears because, indeed, One had been found who was worthy and qualified to take and to open the scroll. Then, as John was drying his eyes, suddenly ... there He was. A **Lamb** appeared in the midst of the Throne. This was his rightful place, by the way. An elder cried out, **Behold, the Lion of the Tribe of Judah, the Root of David has prevailed to open the scroll and to loose its seven seals**. Won't that be something, when we hear these very words for ourselves one day?

Those two Old Testament titles for Messiah speak of the fact that the kingdom that Jesus will establish on Earth will be a Jewish kingdom, presided over by the King of Israel. Let's look at them.

First, the Lamb is called, **the Lion of the Tribe of Judah.** You will remember that when Jacob was blessing his sons and came to Judah, he prophesied that a king would come from Judah's line who would be called **Shiloh**. He said,

Judah is a lion's whelp; from the prey, my son, you have gone up. He bows down, he lies down as a lion; and as a lion, who shall rouse him? **The scepter shall not depart from Judah**, *nor a lawgiver from between his feet,* until **Shiloh** *comes; and* to **him** *shall be the obedience of the people. Genesis 49:9-10*

Because of Jacob's prophesy, a **Lion** became the symbol of the tribe of Judah. Jesus was born of that tribe and **Shiloh** is one of his names. It means *rest*. One of the great blessings of Christ's Millennial reign on Earth will be that he will provide rest to the earth and to his people. There is a great need for that today, is there not? Our world is in such endless turmoil. It will not experience rest, however, until **Shiloh** comes. Peter, preaching to the Jews in *Acts 3:19-21*, said,

Repent therefore and be converted, that your sins may be blotted out, so that **times of refreshing** *may come from the presence of the*

Lord, and that he may send Jesus Christ, who was preached to you before, **whom heaven must receive until the times of restoration of all things**, which God has spoken by the mouth of all his holy prophets since the world began.

Second, the Lamb is called, **the Root of David**. This further identifies the one who John saw appear on the throne that day and take the scroll from the Throne Sitter's hand. This Messianic title emphasizes that Jesus is from the royal line of David. He is the descendent of David's father, **Jesse**. And, as such, the Bible says he will one day come to rule the world in righteousness. Let's look at another wonderful prophecy concerning this coming Davidic King. It is found in *Isaiah 11:1-10*,

*There shall come forth a **Rod from the stem of Jesse**, and a **Branch** shall grow out of his **roots**. The Spirit of the LORD shall rest upon him, The Spirit of wisdom and understanding, the Spirit of counsel and might, the Spirit of knowledge and of the fear of the LORD. His delight is in the fear of the LORD, and he shall not judge by the sight of his eyes, nor decide by the hearing of his ears; but with **righteousness** he shall judge the poor, and decide with equity for the meek of the earth; **he shall strike the earth with the rod of his mouth**, and **with the breath of his lips he shall slay the wicked**. **Righteousness shall be the belt of his loins**, and faithfulness the belt of his waist. The wolf also shall dwell with the lamb, The leopard shall lie down with the young goat, the calf and the young lion and the fatling together; and a little child shall lead them. The cow and the bear shall graze; their young ones shall lie down together; and the lion shall eat straw like the ox. The nursing child shall play by the cobra's hole, and the weaned child shall put his hand in the viper's den. They shall not hurt nor destroy in all my holy mountain, for **the earth shall be full of the knowledge of the LORD as the waters cover the sea**. And in that day there shall be a **Root of Jesse**, who shall stand as a **banner** to the people; for **the Gentiles shall seek him**, and **his resting place shall be glorious**.*

When the angel Gabriel announced Jesus' birth to the virgin, Mary, he said,

*He will be great, and will be called the Son of the Highest; and **the Lord God will give him the throne of his father David**. And he*

will reign over the house of Jacob forever, and of his kingdom there will be no end. Luke 1:32-33

5:6-7

John testifies, **in the midst of the throne ... stood a Lamb as it had been slain.** What a paradox, the great conquering King of kings appears in Heaven before his Church as a Lamb ... **slain**. To them, he is God's **Lamb**, first and foremost, you see. Later, he will reign as King. So, there standing on the throne in full view of his entire Church, his saints, and all of God's holy angels, stood Christ, the Lamb of God. What a moment that will be when it actually occurs, aye? To us believers, by the way, he will ever be our dear, precious, sacrificed Lamb. I believe that he will forever bear the marks of his sacrificial death before us and we will forever be reminded by them of what he did for us and how much he loved us. Let's take a moment here to look at a few scriptures that speak it.

The next day John saw Jesus coming toward him, and said, 'Behold! ***The Lamb of God*** *who takes away the sin of the world!' John 1:29*

...knowing that you were not redeemed with corruptible things, like silver or gold, from your aimless conduct received by tradition from your fathers, but with the precious blood of Christ, as of a ***lamb*** *without blemish and without spot. First Peter 1:18-19*

He was oppressed and he was afflicted, yet he opened not his mouth; he was led as a ***lamb*** *to the slaughter, and as a sheep before its shearers is silent, so he opened not his mouth. Isaiah 53:7*

The Lamb had now returned to his Throne. Let's look closer at John's description of him.

First, he says he had **seven horns**. In the Bible, horns are often used as symbols for power. The idea is that the strength of a horned creatures reside in their horns. This Lamb, by having seven horns, is symbolically declaring that he possesses all power. Make no mistake about it, the Lamb of God possesses all power. By the raw power of his Word alone ... the entire universe is presently being held together. As you have it in *Hebrews 1:3,*

...who being the brightness of his glory and the express image of his person, ***and upholding all things by the word of his power,*** *when*

he had by himself purged our sins, sat down at the right hand of the Majesty on high...

Now that's POWER, brother. This Lamb is the Omnipotent One himself!

Second, the Lamb had *seven eyes*. Here, the symbolism is explained to us. John says his *eyes* are the *seven spirits of God sent out into all the earth*. Again, this is referring to the same *seven spirits* that greeted us in chapter one and who were, at that moment, burning before the Throne (4:5). The Lamb's eyes are symbols of these *spirits* because they are the ones who will, as extensions of Christ, carry out his judgments on the earth when they blow their *seven trumpets* (8:6).

Then, the great moment came. The Lamb took the *scroll* from the Throne-Sitter's hand. I can almost hear the low gasps and exclamations of all those who witnessed it that day, can't you? Words fail to describe the profound significance that this moment will one day bring in Heaven. We'll just have to see it for ourselves. Oh yeah ... and we will!

Rev. 5:8-14

Now when he had taken the scroll**, the four living creatures and the **twenty-four elders** fell down before the Lamb, each having a harp, and golden bowls full of incense, which are the prayers of the saints. And they sang a new song, saying: "You are worthy to take the scroll, and to open its seals; for you were slain, and have redeemed us to God by your blood out of every tribe and tongue and people and nation, and have made **[NU changes "us kings"] them a kingdom** and priests to our God; and **[NU omits "we"] they** shall reign on the earth. Then I looked, and I heard the voice of **many angels** around the throne, **the living creatures**, and the **elders**; and the number of them was ten thousand times ten thousand, and thousands of thousands, **saying** with a loud voice: "Worthy is the Lamb who was slain to receive power and riches and wisdom, and strength and honor and glory and blessing! And **every creature which is in heaven and on the earth and under the earth and such

as are in the sea, and all that are in them, *I heard saying: "Blessing and honor and glory and power be to him who sits on the throne, and to the Lamb, forever and ever! Then the four living creatures said, "Amen!" And the* [**NU omits** *"twenty-four"*] *elders fell down and worshipped* [**NU omits** *"him who lives forever and ever"*].

5:8

When Jesus receives his commission to judge the earth and establish his eternal kingdom here, it will be the greatest turning point in all of human history. It can't happen too soon, Amen? So, when he took the book from his Father's hand, the greatest praise and worship session Heaven will likely ever see broke out. First, the Church, represented by the twenty four elders, fell down before the Lamb and began to sing to him. Then, the living creatures accompanied by a myriad of angels exuberantly began to speak forth their praises. Then, all of God's created creatures joined in the mounting thunder of praise. This was topped off by the biggest and loudest **Amen** ever uttered from the combined voices of the four living creatures. Handel's *Hallelujah Chorus* will not be able to hold a candle to the crescendo of praise and song that will break forth in Heaven the day the Lamb takes his scroll from his Father's hand! Because this event is so important, it is worth our while to examine it even more closely.

First, the elders ***fell down before the Lamb.*** They had fallen before the Throne Sitter in chapter 4, but now they fall before the Lamb. As they are falling, they are seen to be holding two things. John says they had:

...***Harps***. Since these elder are representatives of the Church, I believe this implies that all of us believers will be given one of these instruments one day. Now, I'm a guitar player of sorts. My two boys can out-play me now, but I have used my guitar to facilitate my own praises as well as those of others many times. Nevertheless, I can't wait to get my hands on one of these ***harps*** in heaven. I believe they are specifically designed by God to be facilitators of the praises of his people. Don't worry about being able to play it though ... you'll do just fine.

...***golden bowls full of incense***. They had golden bowls of incense. The symbolism of the incense is explained here. John says that the golden bowls of incense were the ***prayers*** of the saints. Soon, that of which we are only reading about here will actually come to pass in history and will issue in Christ's long awaited reign on Earth. This has been the dream, yes, the prayer of God's people, both Jews and Gentiles, from ancient times. God has not lost one of those prayers. And, at this exact point in time they will be poured out afresh before his throne by the elders of the Church. What an event. The time will have come to answer them, you see. I am sure that many of your prayers are in those bowls. Have you ever prayed, *thy kingdom come, thy will be done on earth as it is in Heaven?* Those prayers of yours will surely be mingled in with all the others in those golden bowls which will be poured out afresh before God on that momentous day.

5:9

Second, the Church began to sing to their Lamb. These verses continue to nail down the Lamb's identity beyond question. The song that the elders sang was about the redemption that their precious Lamb had provided for them. They sang, ***you were slain and have redeemed us to God by your blood out of every tribe and tongue and people and nation***. I can't wait to put that to melody, along with the rest of the saints, can you? This word, ***redeemed***, means to be purchased *out of the slave market of sin in order to be set free*. As you have it in *Titus 2:13-14,*

...looking for the blessed hope and glorious appearing of our great God and Savior Jesus Christ, who gave himself for us, that he might ***redeem*** *us from every lawless deed and purify for himself his own special people, zealous for good works.*

By the blood of Christ, you and I were redeemed out of the slave market of sin and set free! Glory to God!

Third, innumerable ***angels*** joined in ... speaking their praises to the Lamb. The NIV says the angels ***sang***. But, they didn't. The Greek word here should be properly translated ***saying***. It is λέγοντες **(*legontes*)**. Old traditions are hard to break, I guess. Angels are never found singing in Scripture. *Not even when the Shepherds heard them that night in Bethlehem?* you ask. I'm afraid so. Apparently, of all of God's created beings, only you and I have the capability to sing to God.

Let's step aside here for a moment. Music is an amazing and wonderful thing. I love all kinds of music from classical to jazz, from country to gospel, from rock to blues. I like it all. But I love instrumentals the best. Maybe that is because when man puts words to a melody or rhythm his words all too often just foul it up! Where do you think music came from in the first place? What was its origin? The obvious answer is that it came from the Creator, the source of all things ... our Lord Jesus Christ. Music finds its origin and nature in God himself. Did you know the Scripture says that God himself will sing to his people one day? We find it in *Zephaniah 3:17*,

The Lord thy God in the midst of thee is mighty; he will save, he will rejoice over thee with joy; he will rest in his love, **he will joy over thee with singing**.

God himself is musical. Man, having been made in the **image** of God, is musical as well. Problem is, fallen man's music is all too often centered solely upon himself, and as such, is often perverted and foul. Nevertheless, even man's worst music has elements of the image of God in it. I wish the Church would utilize a broader spectrum of music in its worship and praise, by the way. A good Bluegrass instrumental, for example, with its guitars, banjos and mandolins, can really make one's heart sing! Take it for what it's worth ... all music has a divine element to it.

Now, I believe that this is why you never find angels singing in the Bible. They can't. They were not made in the image of God, you see. So, it says here that the angels joined in, **saying with a loud voice ... Worthy is the Lamb who was slain to receive power and riches and wisdom and strength and honor and glory and blessing**. Notice also, that they do not speak about redemption. That is because they have not and cannot experience it. Christ Jesus did not die for the angels. But, they do know **worthy** when they see it. So they speak loud and clear to their great Sovereign Lord of his worthiness.

Then, all living creatures chimed in. *Do you think that every creature will actually speak praises to the Lamb on that day?* you may ask. Yes, I believe they will. At his triumphal entry, didn't Jesus say that if his disciples stopped praising him (as the Pharisees demanded) that **these very stones would cry out** (Luke 19:40)? John heard all the creatures saying, **Blessing and honor and glory and power be to him**

that sits on the Throne and to the Lamb forever and ever. The animal kingdom will play a significant role in our Lord's future kingdom, by the way. They are mentioned in many Old Testament prophesies. *Romans 8:19-22,* speaks of this as well.

For the earnest expectation of the **creation** *eagerly waits for the revealing of the sons of God. For the creation was subjected to futility, not willingly, but because of him who subjected it in hope; because the creation itself also will be delivered from the bondage of corruption into the glorious liberty of the children of God. For we know that the whole creation groans and labors with birth pangs together until now.*

Last, the four living creatures capped it all off with a thundering ***Amen!!!*** The scene closes with the Church still worshipping. At long last, their precious ***Lamb*** was about to rise up and reign.

A good key word to help remember the content of this chapter 5 would be the word, *"**Worthy**"*. Jesus is the only man worthy to take the scroll and to open its seals. Sinners who choose to reject him and his great salvation must one day face him as their Judge. He died for them and has done everything possible to save them. Therefore, he is worthy to judge them. The ***Lion***, not the ***Lamb***, is the one who those who persist in unbelief will have to face one day. Furthermore, it is to this ***Lion*** who entire new generations of sinners will have to answer and obey during his one thousand year reign on Earth.

REVELATION 6

THE SEAL JUDGMENTS BEGIN

In chapters 4 and 5, when John was caught up into Heaven, he was transported forward in time to that future momentous day when Christ will receive the authority and program for his kingdom from the hand of his Father. Finding himself standing at that unparalleled event, John saw Christ take a scroll from his Father's hand. Here, in chapter 6, the Lamb begins to open that scroll by breaking off each of its seven seals ... one by one. As each is broken away, the amazing drama of its unique, future, preordained event or events will unfold before us. Before we begin this chapter, let's take a moment and talk a bit about the concept of the coming Tribulation it will describe.

Time-wise, the Bible prophesies that the Tribulation will last for seven years. It is divided into two halves, each consisting of three and a half years. The last three and a half year segment is called the *Great Tribulation*. The scriptural basis for these time periods is discussed in Appendix B. During the seven year Tribulation, three great series of judgments will come upon the Earth, initiated by the Lamb's breaking off of the seals from his scroll. They are the *Seal*, the *Trumpet* and the *Bowl Judgments*. Each series consist of seven judgments. Also, the last judgment of the first two series introduces the first judgment in the next series. So, the breaking of the seventh Seal introduces the first Trumpet judgment and the blowing of the seventh Trumpet introduces the first Bowl judgment. After the pouring out of the seventh Bowl judgment, Christ will immediately return to Earth with great power and glory and rule and reign here for a thousand years.

When Christ breaks the first seal off his scroll, the seven year Tribulation period will commence down on Earth. The breaking of the first five Seals will each result in five *indirect* judgments on Earth. When these judgments come, the world may not realize that they are of supernatural origin or from Christ. People may just assume that the terrible things they are experiencing are merely due to fate or circumstance. The sixth Seal, however, will be the eye-opener. It will be the first of God's *direct* interventions on the earth. During the spectacular judgment of the sixth Seal, the world will arrive at the beginning of the second half of the Tribulation ... the *Great Tribulation*. The first six Seals cover the first half of the Tribulation and they are all found here in Revelation 6.

The gospel accounts that contain Jesus' words about the coming Tribulation are found in Matthew 24 and 25, Mark 13, and Luke 17 and 21. The material we find in those scriptures exactly parallels the much expanded view that we find in Revelation 6 through 19. The coming Tribulation is referred to by:

Daniel, as **the 70th week** (Daniel 9:26)

Jeremiah, as **the time of Jacob's trouble** (Jeremiah 30:7)

Joel, as **the great and terrible day of the Lord** (Joel 2:31)

Jesus, as **great tribulation** (Matthew 24:21)

Paul, as **the day of wrath and revelation of the righteous judgment of God** (Romans 2:5)

THE FIRST SEAL BROKEN ...
THE WHITE HORSE RIDER

Rev. 6:1-2

*Now **I saw when the Lamb opened one of the** [NU adds "seven seals"]; and I heard one of the four living creatures saying with a voice like thunder, 'Come and see.' And I looked, and **behold, a white horse. He who sat on it had a bow**; and a **crown** was given to him, and he went out conquering and to conquer.*

6:1-2

When the Lamb broke the first seal off his scroll, John saw the first of the famous *Four Horsemen of the Apocalypse* ride forth down upon the earth. The scene has shifted here from Heaven down to the earth but the event itself was triggered from above. The first Seal judgment from the Lamb came forth in the form of a man. In symbol, John saw him ride forth on a *white horse* carrying a *bow* (as in bow and arrow) and he was given a *crown*, after which, he immediately went out *conquering and to conquer*. Notice that we are not given any explanation as to this man's identity. That is because the reader is expected to understand his symbol based on his or her previous knowledge and study of the Scriptures. Who is he? He is the symbol of a future person (and events related to him) that is predicted in the Bible in several places. The symbol itself is an oriental one, depicting a military conqueror. In chapter 19, we will see Christ himself riding a white horse, but that is the only similarity between these two. This rider is not Christ for the following reasons:

1. It is Christ who sends this rider forth.
2. This rider appears at the *beginning* of the Tribulation; Christ will appear at its *end*.
3. This rider uses conventional weapons, *a bow;* Christ will fight with *the sword of His mouth* (19:15).
4. This rider wears a *victor's crown,* στέφανος *(stephanos)*; when Christ appears, he will be wearing *many diadems,* διαδήματα *(diademata)* (19:12).
5. This man *initiates* wars; Christ will *end* them.
6. This man goes forth *unnamed*; but, when Christ appears, *he will be wearing his name* for all to see...**King of Kings and Lord of Lords** (19:16).

Who then is this white horse rider? The one who best fits the description, as well as the placing here in the book of Revelation, is called, among other names in the Bible, Antichrist. Very early in the Tribulation, at the breaking of the first seal, Antichrist will begin his rise to power by means of military might and will ultimately *conquer* the world ... becoming its undisputed ruler and dictator. Here are some scriptures that foretell the coming of this powerful, future world ruler:

And in the latter time of their kingdom, when the transgressors have reached their fullness, **a king shall arise**, *having fierce features, who understands sinister schemes.* **his power shall be mighty**, *but not by his own power;* **he shall destroy fearfully**, *and shall prosper and thrive; he shall destroy the mighty, and also the holy people. Through his cunning he shall cause deceit to prosper under his* **rule**; *and he shall exalt himself in his heart. He shall destroy many in their prosperity. He shall even rise against the Prince of princes; but he shall be broken without human means. And the vision of the evenings and mornings which was told is true; therefore seal up the vision, for* **it refers to many days in the future**. *And I, Daniel, fainted and was sick for days; afterward I arose and went about the king's business. I was astonished by the vision, but no one understood it. Daniel 8:23-27*

Then the **king** *shall do according to his own will: he shall exalt and magnify himself above every god, shall speak blasphemies against the God of gods, and* **shall prosper till the wrath has been accomplished**; *for what has been determined shall be done. He shall regard neither the God of his fathers nor* **the desire of women**, *nor regard any god; for he shall exalt himself above them all. But in their place* **he shall honor a god of fortresses**; *and a god which his fathers did not know he shall honor with gold and silver, with precious stones and pleasant things.* **Thus he shall act against the strongest fortresses** *with a foreign god, which he shall acknowledge, and advance its glory; and he shall cause them to rule over many, and divide the land for gain. Daniel 11:36-39*

And then **the lawless one will be revealed**, *whom the Lord will consume with the breath of his mouth and destroy with the brightness of his coming. Second Thessalonians 2:8*

Little children, it is the last hour; and as you have heard that the **Antichrist is coming**, *even now many antichrists have come, by which we know that it is the last hour. First John 2:18*

So they worshipped the dragon who gave authority to the beast; and they worshipped the beast, saying, 'Who is like the beast? **Who is able to make war with him?'** *Revelation 13:4*

These scriptures prophesy the coming of Satan's man, Antichrist. They predict he will be a warrior who will conquer the world and become its undisputed dictator. His rise to power will be the first terrible indirect judgment of the Lamb on an unbelieving world who has consistently and stubbornly rejected Christ's lordship over them.

Before we move on, I would like to add a comment about the Daniel prophecy just quoted in regards to the phrase **He shall regard neither the God of his fathers nor the desire of women**. I believe that this **desire of women**, spoken of here, refers to the desire that women, in general, have for a husband. In my opinion, this may well indicate that Antichrist will be a homosexual. His dual rejection of **the God of his fathers** and **the desire of women** follows the same pattern that is found in Romans 1:21, 24-27. There we read, **when they knew God, they glorified him not as God.** Then, we read the following results... **God gave them up to uncleanness through the lusts of their own hearts ... the men leaving the natural use of the woman, burned in their lust one toward another; men with men working that which is unseemly.** (KJV). The tremendous explosion of homosexuality in our world today and the ongoing and unprecedented push to legitimatize it in every realm of society may well be laying the foundation for the future acceptance and, indeed, adoration of Antichrist. In a very short period of time, homosexuality has become an accepted lifestyle and is now aggressively being endorsed on a world-wide scale. This may well be in preparation for the arrival of Antichrist.

THE SECOND SEAL BROKEN ... THE RED HORSE RIDER

Rev. 6:3-4

*When he opened the **second seal**, I heard the second living creature saying, 'Come.'* **[NU omits *"and see"*]** *Another horse, fiery red, went out. And it was granted to the one who sat on it to take peace from the earth, and that people should kill one another; and there was given to him a great sword.*

When the Lamb broke the second Seal from his scroll, another indirect judgment began to unfold down on Earth. John saw a rider come forth who was mounted on a fiery **red horse** who would **take peace from the earth**. This symbol is pretty straightforward. It is a symbol for war. Upon the rise of Antichrist, every nation on Earth will quickly become embroiled in red war. This is the logical and sure result of the rise of the warrior, Antichrist, who was loosed by the first Seal. Jesus, commenting on this judgment in *Matthew 24:6-7*, said,

*And **you will hear of wars and rumors of wars**. See that you are not troubled; for all these things must come to pass, but the end is not yet. For **nation will rise against nation, and kingdom against kingdom**. And there will be famines, pestilences, and earthquakes in various places.*

Early in the Tribulation, multiple and devastating wars will break out on the Earth as a result from the Lamb's breaking of the second Seal. Is this World War III? Yes, if you wish to call it so. Whatever its actual number will be, however, when the Lamb breaks the second seal from his scroll the whole world will become embroiled in war and, ultimately, even our beloved and powerful United States military will fall to Antichrist! I will comment a bit more on that when we get to Revelation 13.

THE THIRD SEAL BROKEN ... THE BLACK HORSE RIDER

Rev. 6:5-6

*When he opened **the third seal**, I heard the third living creature say, 'Come and see.' So I looked, and **behold, a black horse**, and he who sat on it had a pair of scales in his hand. And I heard a voice in the midst of the four living creatures saying, 'A quart of wheat for a denarius, and three quarts of barley for a denarius; and do not harm the oil and the wine.'*

Again, the symbol is a straightforward one. Famine will spread across the earth after Christ breaks off the third Seal. In Matthew 24:6, just quoted as it relates to the second seal, you will notice that Jesus also said that famines would follow the ***wars and rumors of wars***. Famine is typically the result of war. We see its ugly head all across the world today where wars are raging. Take Darfur, for example.

Wherever men are engaged in fighting, there is no time for planting and harvesting.

This specter of the black horse rider is a graphic one. He rides forth clutching a set of food scales and, as he rides, the Father speaks from the midst of the four living creatures setting the exact conditions of this worldwide famine by saying, *A quart of wheat for a denarius, and three quarts of barley for a denarius; and do not harm the oil and the wine*. With these words, the Lord insures a great scarcity of food on Earth during those days. And, may I say to you, what the Father decrees in heaven is always a done deal. A **denarius** was a whole day's wage in Jesus' day. During the days of the black horse rider, a whole day's wages will only buy enough food for one person. Further, the Father commands no one **harm the oil and the wine**. These words accentuate the thought that these usually abundant items will become so rare and precious that special care will have to be taken to handle them.

THE FOURTH SEAL BROKEN ... THE PALE HORSE RIDER

Rev. 6:7-8

*When he opened the fourth seal, I heard the voice of the fourth living creature saying, 'Come and see.' So I looked, and **behold, a pale horse. And the name of him who sat on it was Death, and Hades followed with him. And power was given to them over a fourth of the earth, to kill with sword, with hunger, with death, and by the beasts of the earth**.*

6:7-8

When the Lamb broke the fourth Seal from his scroll, John saw the personification of Death itself ride forth. It was seen riding a sickly yellowish green horse. The Greek word here translated *pale* is χλωρός (*cloros*). We get our word *chlorine*, a pale greenish chemical, from this Greek word. Notice that Death was closely followed by **Hades**, the Greek word that designates the holding place of all the wicked dead. Someone has said *Death never travels alone. Heaven or hell is always on its heels.* This was a terrifying apparition indeed. Can you picture it? Hell, loping along behind Death, eagerly gobbling up all those who Death was destroying! This is a reminder that, as spiritual beings made in the image of God, all humans will live somewhere ... for all eternity. The only question that remains is, *Where*? You definitely will not want it to be Hades. Our text says, **And power was given to them over a fourth of the earth, to kill...** One quarter of Earth's population will perish following the Lamb breaking of the forth Seal. We are told here that death will come from one of four quarters: **the sword** (war); **hunger** (famine); **death** (includes all other sources ... sickness, heart attacks, old age, accidents, etc.); and **wild beasts**. Wild beasts are notorious for becoming ferocious when they have fed on human flesh. Man-eating tigers in Asia have well demonstrated that fact. Ezekiel also spoke of four elements of judgment that came upon wicked Israel in his day.

*For thus says the Lord GOD: 'How much more it shall be when I send my **four severe judgments on Jerusalem**; the **sword** and **famine** and **wild beasts** and **pestilence**; to cut off man and beast from it?' Ezekiel 14:21*

In summary, after the Lamb has broken the first four Seals off his scroll, the results will be the worst decimation by war and its by-products the world has ever seen. If it were to take place today, over a billion and a quarter people would lose their lives. Hopefully, these judgments will have a sobering and eye-opening effect on many people in that day. These judgments are not merely designed to carry out the vengeance of God on a wicked and unbelieving humanity. They will also be sent to awaken the consciences of sinners. Disasters can be powerful wake-up calls from God.

May we step aside here for a moment? One of the terrible things about this age of grace in which you and I are presently living is the fact that multitudes of people slip away each day into a Christless eternity. They live out their lives blithely unaware and uncaring of the eternal doom that awaits them just around the corner. This alone is more than ample reason to be against the push for euthanasia in our day. People without Christ who are assisted in taking their own lives think they are being delivered from their pain and suffering. Nothing could be further from the truth. They merely awake on the other side to discover that their real pain and suffering has just begun. How tragic! The Bible says,

...For to him that is joined to all the living there is hope: for a living dog is better than a dead lion. Ecclesiastes 9:4

Christ is really going to turn up the heat on mankind with his four Seal judgments during the opening days of the Tribulation. And, I believe they will drive many sinners to reconsider and turn to Christ. Jude 23, speaks of this method of reaching people.

*...but others save with **fear**, pulling them out of the fire, hating even the garment defiled by the flesh.*

THE FIFTH SEAL BROKEN ... TRIBULATION MARTYRS ARE REVEALED

Rev. 6:9-11

*When he opened the **fifth seal**, I saw under the altar the souls of those who had been **slain for the Word of God and for the testimony which they held**. And they cried with a loud voice, saying, 'How long, O Lord, holy and true, until you judge and avenge our blood on those who dwell on the earth?' Then a white robe was given to each of them; and it was said to them that they should rest a little while longer, until both the number of their fellow servants and their brethren, who would be killed as they were, was completed.*

6:9-11

At the breaking of the fifth Seal, the scene shifts back from Earth to Heaven. Up there, throughout the first three and a half years of the rise of Antichrist, murdered saints have been continuously arriving from down below. The Greek word used here, translated ***slain***, is εσφαγμενων **(*esthagmenown*)**. This word speaks of a death by violence. The tense of this Greek participle is perfect passive meaning, *having been slain*. It alludes to the fact that these saints were murdered because they were considered a nuisance. But, up in Heaven, John sees them ***under the altar***, which speaks of the fact that God views them as sacrifices.

This is our first encounter in Revelation with Tribulation saints. It will be costly to believe in Christ during the rise of, and under the reign of, Antichrist. Those days will really separate the men from the boys. Many are Christians today because it costs them nothing. In that day it will cost people everything. Second Thessalonians 2:6-7, tells us that in that day the restraints on sinful man will be lifted. That being the case, men will more cruel and pitiless than ever ... as cruel as their depraved natures dictate. It will be Satan, and his Antichrist's, day. Both Daniel and Jesus prophesied that the saints would be given into Antichrist's hand in that day.

*I was watching; and the same horn was **making war against the saints, and prevailing against them**... Daniel 7:21*

*He shall speak pompous words against the Most High, **shall persecute the saints** of the Most High, and shall intend to change times and law. **Then the saints shall be given into his hand** for a time and times and half a time. Daniel 7:25*

***Then they will deliver you up to tribulation and kill you**, and you will be hated by all nations for my name's sake. Matthew 24:9*

The question arises, *In what sense is the fifth Seal a judgment of the Lamb then, since it is his own saints who are being killed*? I believe the answer lies within the fact that those who are doing the murdering of God's people are **storing up for themselves vengeance against the day of vengeance** (Romans 2:5). As Christ's murdered Saints continue to swell in number in Heaven, the wrath of God will be continuing to swell up above as well. *Psalm 9:12,* says,

*When he avenges blood, **he remembers them; he does not forget** the cry of the humble.*

Having suffered the horrors of execution by Antichrist, John heard the Tribulation martyr's cry out to their Lord for vengeance. This resulted in the handing out of **white robes** to each one, followed by the Lord's words to them **that they should rest a little while longer, until both the number of their fellow servants and their brethren, who would be killed as they were, was completed**. What a longsuffering God our Lord is! Even in that awful day when his own beloved people are being slaughtered by the score ... he will continue to delay his wrath for his great mercy's sake.

THE SIXTH SEAL BROKEN ... HEAVEN IS OPENED

Rev. 6:12-17

*I looked when he opened the **sixth seal**, and* [**NU omits** *"behold"*] *there was a great **earthquake**; and the sun became black as sackcloth of hair, and the* [**NU adds** *"whole"*] *moon became like blood. And the **stars of heaven fell to the earth**, as a fig tree drops its late figs when it is shaken by a mighty wind. Then **the sky receded as a scroll** when it is rolled up, and **every mountain and island was moved** out of its place. And **the kings of the earth, the great men, the rich men, the commanders, the mighty men**, every slave and every free man, **hid themselves** in the caves and in the rocks of the mountains, and **said to the mountains and rocks, 'Fall on us and hide us from the face of him who sits on the throne and from the wrath of the Lamb!'** For the great day of his wrath has come, and who is able to stand?*

6:12-14

We come now to a spectacular and very significant future turning point in history. It is during the events of the sixth Seal that the Great Tribulation (the second half of the Tribulation) will begin. The judgments of the sixth Seal are the first direct judgments we have encountered in the book of Revelation and their nature fits like a glove with all the other judgments that are prophesied to occur during the Great Tribulation (the last three and a half years of the Tribulation). Today, you and I are living in the Age of Grace. It began at the cross, closing the Old Testament dispensation of the Law, and continues on to this very hour. During this Age of Grace, direct supernatural judgments from God have virtually been unheard of. It has been well over two millennia since mankind has witnessed any direct supernatural judgments from God on Earth. Today, the only sin God is holding mankind accountable for is unbelief. As you have it in *Second Corinthians 5:19,*

To wit, that God was in Christ, reconciling the world unto himself, **not imputing their trespasses unto them**; *and has committed unto us the ministry of reconciliation.*

I repeat. The only sin that God is holding men and women accountable for today is the sin of **unbelief** in his Son ... a horrendous sin that has not yet brought direct judgment on mankind ... but one day will. At the end of the Age of Grace, it will come. As you have it in *Second Thessalonians 1:7-9,*

And to you who are troubled rest with us, when the Lord Jesus shall be revealed from heaven with his mighty angels, **in flaming fire taking vengeance on them that know not God, and that obey not the gospel of our Lord Jesus Christ**: *who shall be punished with everlasting destruction from the presence of the Lord, and from the glory of his power...*

And again, in *John 3:36,*

He that believeth on the Son has everlasting life: and he that believeth not the Son shall not see life; but **the wrath of God abideth on him**.

God has directly intervened in judgment on the earth in ages past. Before the Law was given, he judged mankind in Noah's day leaving only nine people alive on the earth. During the age of the Law, God intervened many times in judgment during Moses and Joshua's day and during the days of the prophets. However, from those times up to today, his judgments have been muted. That will dramatically change when Christ breaks away the sixth Seal from his scroll. At that time, the world will experience the first direct intervention by God in judgment that has taken place here on the Earth in nearly three thousand years. If you accept the supernatural, you will have little trouble with the description of his judgments from this point on in the book of Revelation. If not, you will have a good deal of difficulty with what the book of Revelation predicts is coming to planet Earth. Let's look at this one. Jesus was also speaking of the judgment of the sixth Seal when he said in *Luke 21:11,*

And there will be great earthquakes in various places, and famines and pestilences; **and there will be fearful sights and great signs from heaven**.

The judgments of the sixth Seal will fulfill Jesus' prediction of *fearful sights and great signs in heaven*. When Christ breaks the sixth Seal off his scroll in Heaven, things will occur around the globe like nothing ever before recorded in human history. Our text says it will come as follows:

1. ...a world-wide *earthquake*
2. ...a total blackout of the *sun*
3. ...a change in the nature of the *moon* that will cause it to become a light source, glowing with the hue of red *blood*
4. ...a change in the nature of the universe that will result in actual *stars* falling to the Earth like overripe *figs*
5. ...the displacement of *every mountain and island* on earth from their present geographic locations
6. ...and (the finale) ... the rolling back of the *sky* above, revealing God Almighty and His Lamb seated upon their throne for all to see. Needless to say, these events will be undeniably supernatural by the earth-dwellers of that day. Let's look a bit closer at these prophesied events.

Now, a worldwide *earthquake* is scientifically impossible. Earthquakes are caused by the shifting of the tectonic plates in the Earth and thus only occur in specific and very limited locations. A worldwide earthquake cannot occur apart from the supernatural. Also, a temporary and total darkening of the *sun* is scientifically impossible. It just couldn't occur apart from the supernatural. The reversal of Earth's primary light source from the sun to the *moon* is scientifically impossible. One can only imagine the effect on the scientific community when, for a period of time, the moon will be earth's only source of light! *Stars* falling to the earth is scientifically impossible. Many would say that the very fact that such a thing is stated in the Bible is proof that it is a scientifically inaccurate book. They would strenuously object, saying, *Real stars falling to the Earth? Do you realize the nature and size of a star? You Christians are so ignorant and so unscientific! Why, if this **literally** were to occur, the stars wouldn't **fall to the earth** ... the earth would be sucked into the first star that even got close and then burn up like a moth in a flame!*

The shifting and relocation of every *mountain* and **every island** is scientifically impossible. How could that be? Yet, it shall. Finally, the rolling back of the heavens like *a scroll* is scientifically impossible. But that too will occur.

Puny ... oh so scientific man ... politically correct man ... sophisticated, modern, civilized man ... is scheduled for a rude awakening when Christ breaks the sixth Seal from off his scroll. God exists, you see, and man has been living in God's supernatural universe for millennia ... but he has stubbornly refused to acknowledge its true nature. How great and powerful our God is! He is the Omnipotent One. As Gabriel, the archangel, once said to a young girl who had been told she was scheduled to have a baby apart from the normal impregnation by a man ... **with God nothing shall be impossible** (Luke 1:37). Do you really think that he who holds the whole universe together *by the Word of His power* (Hebrews 1:3) could not do the things that are so clearly described here in the sixth Seal judgment? *Jeremiah 32:7,* says,

Behold, I am the LORD, the God of all flesh. Is there **anything too hard** *for me?*

If God so desired, with a mere thought he could cause every star in the universe to fall to Earth and bounce along the ground like so many fiery marbles ... just as, it appears, many actually will at the breaking of the sixth Seal. At that time, God will arise and bear his right arm, you see, and the supernatural will become a matter of undeniable fact. Can you picture what effect these things will have on unregenerate men and women when they see such contradictions of their so-called *laws of nature*!?

We Christians do not need to scientifically prove that stars can fall to the earth, by the way. Nor, do we need to scientifically prove how the heavens could roll back like a scroll. We just need to believe the Word of God, dear saint ... whether it makes sense to us or not. The burden of proof is on the skeptics. They must prove that these things will **not** occur as prophesied here in the Word of God. By the way, it doesn't say that all the stars fell to the earth although, under the omnipotent hand of Almighty God, they certainly could. Later in the book, and subsequent to this event, we will still find stars shining in the heavens. But, it's my opinion that a large number of them will be conspicuously absent from their places in Earth's skies above. After the Lamb sets in motion the amazing events of the breaking of the sixth Seal, mankind will have a very difficult time indeed denying the supernatural. These events will be powerful blows to proud, haughty, scientific man and none too soon in my opinion. At the breaking of the sixth Seal, men who have obstinately viewed the universe from the vantage point of uniformitarian, naturalistic, humanistic, evolutionary ideology ... will be proven the fools they are.

6:15-17

Now let's look at the profound results that these events will have on earth-dwellers in that day. John says, **And the kings of the earth, the great men, the rich men, the commanders, the mighty men, every slave and every free man, hid themselves in the caves**. What abject panic and utter bedlam this judgment will cause. The sixth Seal will truly shut men's mouths. They will only have one thing to say on that day ... and it will be said to the mountains and the rocks around them ... **Fall on us and hide us from the face of him who sets on the throne and from the wrath of the Lamb**. Isaiah also prophesied of the chaos that the sixth Seal will bring saying,

Enter into the rock, and hide in the dust, from the terror of the LORD and the glory of his majesty. **The lofty looks of man shall be humbled, the haughtiness of men shall be bowed down**, and the LORD alone shall be exalted in that day. For the day of the LORD of hosts shall come upon everything proud and lofty, upon everything lifted up; and it shall be brought low; upon all the cedars of Lebanon that are high and lifted up, and upon all the oaks of Bashan; upon all the **high mountains**, and upon all the hills that are lifted up; upon every high tower, and upon every fortified wall; upon all the ships of Tarshish, and upon all the beautiful sloops. **The loftiness of man shall be bowed down**, and the haughtiness of men shall be brought low; the LORD alone will be exalted in that day, but the idols he shall utterly abolish. **They shall go into the holes of the rocks, and into the caves of the earth, from the terror of the LORD and the glory of his majesty, when he arises to shake the earth mightily.** In that day a man will cast away his idols of silver and his idols of gold, which they made, each for himself to worship, to the moles and bats, **to go into** *the clefts of the rocks, and into the crags of the rugged rocks, from the terror of the LORD and the glory of his majesty, when he arises to shake the earth mightily.* Isaiah 2:10-21

May we step aside here for a moment? Did you notice that when this actually occurs, men will not simply stare curiously up at God Almighty and the Lamb above them. No. What will they do? They will attempt to do everything in their power to **get away and hide** themselves from the presence of God and his Lamb. Anyone who thinks that they can look upon Holy God and his Lamb **apart from the spiritual protection which the imputed righteousness of Christ provides** (1 Corinthians 5:21) is very sadly mistaken. Notice that when men look upon the Holy Ones above in that day, their only motivation will be to flee away from their presence. Sinners cannot stand in the presence of Holy God and his Righteous Lamb unless they have been specifically and supernaturally prepared for it by being ***born again*** (John 3:3). We sinners must be re-made into a new creature, having our sins washed away by faith in Christ and having received the very righteousness of Christ himself by imputation (Romans 4:20-24). This alone prepares a man or woman to be able to stand unharmed and unafraid before Holy God. Any other scenario or scheme of man to prepare to meet his Maker will inevitably result in abject panic and ultimate destruction. Are you prepared to stand in the presence of Holy God and his Holy Lamb? Jesus can make you ready.

Now, the question arises, *How long will the judgment of the sixth Seal last*? It doesn't say here. But I expect its events will be comparatively brief in duration, especially when the heavens are rolled back for unregenerate men to see God and his Lamb above. In conclusion, let me say that the events of the sixth Seal are critical to the understanding of the rest of the book of Revelation. At the end of the sixth Seal judgment, when the heavens are rolled back like a great scroll, mankind will have historically arrived at the halfway point of the Tribulation (three and a half years in) and the Great Tribulation will have begun. There is an important verse in Joel that applies here. *Joel 2:30-31,* quotes God as saying,

And I will show wonders in the heavens and in the earth, blood, and fire, and pillars of smoke. The sun shall be turned into darkness, and the moon into blood **before** *the great and the terrible* **day of the Lord** *come.*

At the beginning of the sixth Seal judgment, Joel's prophetic words, ***The sun shall be turned into darkness*** and ***the moon into blood***, will be fulfilled. Note that he says that these things will take place ***before*** the ***great and the terrible day of the Lord come***. The ***great and the terrible day of the Lord*** refer to the Great Tribulation (the second half of the Tribulation). When we read that the sun was darkened and the moon turned to blood in verse thirteen, we are still in the first half of the Tribulation. But, when the *sky* is rolled back like a scroll, in verse fourteen, we have entered into the second half of the Tribulation, the *Great Tribulation* ... Joel's ***great and terrible day of the Lord***. So, the words men cried out at the sight of God's throne and the Lamb ... are eschatologically (doctrine of end time things) correct and "right on". They cried ... ***For the great day of his wrath is come; and who shall be able to stand?*** Although they will not be thinking of the timing of these end-time events when they say this, they will have hit the nail on the head ... for ***the great day of his wrath*** will have ***come*** indeed. And, although they will assume that they themselves are *toast*, it will not yet be the case. For just as suddenly as it all began, it will also come to an end and they will crawl out from their holes and hiding places to find that things are relatively back to normal ... except for the aftermath of these terrible judgments including a good number missing stars from the heavens above.

Now, let's think for a moment about the effect that these things will have on God's chosen people, the Jews, who will be living at that time. I believe that the supernatural events of the breaking of the sixth Seal will result in the conversion of thousands of Jews in that day. Along with the rest of mankind, they too will climb out from their holes having visibly seen their God and his Christ seated on their throne in Heaven. It will be very difficult, after that point in time, for a Jew to deny Christ is his Messiah and the King of Israel. The breaking of the sixth Seal will be the turning point, in my opinion, for many Jews ... and a certain 144,000 in particular ... who we will shortly meet just a few verses from now.

In closing, let me say again that you and I currently live in a very stable and relatively predictable world today. God's natural laws have been unchanging and consistent for a very long time. So much so, that men have almost universally adopted a uniformitarian secular mindset and have taken it upon themselves to deny altogether the supernatural nature of the universe and world in which we live ... and, often, even the existence of God himself. They proudly declare that all things consist and merely function by predictable laws of nature apart from God whatsoever. At the breaking of the sixth Seal, our Lord will dramatically confront them with the error of their thinking.

REVELATION 7

THE 144,000 AND THE INNUMERABLE MULTITUDE

Rev. 7:1-8

After these things I saw four angels standing at the four corners of the earth, **holding** *the four winds of the earth,* **that the wind should not blow** *on the earth, on the sea, or on any tree. Then I saw another angel ascending from the east, having the seal of the living God. And he cried with a loud voice to the four angels to whom it was granted to harm the earth and the sea, saying, 'Do not harm the earth, the sea, or the trees* **till we have sealed the servants of our God** *on their foreheads.' And I heard the number of those who were sealed.* **One hundred and forty-four thousand of all the tribes of the children of Israel** *were sealed: of the tribe of* **Judah** *twelve thousand were sealed; of the tribe of* **Reuben** *twelve thousand* **[beginning with "Reuben," NU omits 10 of the** *"were sealed"* **words of reference]***; of the tribe of* **Gad** *twelve thousand; of the tribe of* **Asher** *twelve thousand; of the tribe of* **Naphtali** *twelve thousand; of the tribe of* **Manasseh** *twelve thousand; of the tribe of* **Simeon** *twelve thousand; of the tribe of* **Levi** *twelve thousand; of the tribe of* **Issachar** *twelve thousand; of the tribe of* **Zebulun** *twelve thousand; of the tribe of* **Joseph** *twelve thousand; of the tribe of* **Benjamin** *twelve thousand were sealed.*

Here, in chapter seven, we come to a pause in the action before the events of the Great Tribulation continue to be revealed to us. Specifically, this is the first of four **interludes** in the book of Revelation ... the **interlude between the sixth and seventh Seals**. In this chapter, we will be given vital and important information about two groups of people who will live during the dark days of the Great Tribulation. We will also read about the sealing of one of these groups before God allows any further judgments to proceed on the Earth. The people that are to be sealed are Jews. This is our first encounter with

Israelites in the book of Revelation. Truly, God is not through with his people, the Jews, yet. No, not by a long shot, as we see here and as the Apostle Paul so clearly teaches in Romans 9-11. During the Great Tribulation, God will once again be working with and through his chosen covenant people of old. A careful study of the scriptures regarding the Jewish people reveals that the primary purpose of the Tribulation is the re-commissioning, refining, restoration and vindicating of the Jews. Here are a few scriptures that prophesy to that effect.

*For thus says the LORD: 'We have heard a voice of trembling, of fear, and not of peace. Ask now, and see, whether a man is ever in labor with child? So **why do I see every man with his hands on his loins like a woman in labor**, and all faces turned pale? Alas! For that **day** is great, so that **none is like it**; and **it is the time of Jacob's trouble**, **but he shall be saved out of it**. For it shall come to pass in that day,' says the LORD of hosts, 'That I will break his yoke from your neck, and will burst your bonds; foreigners shall no more enslave them. But they shall **serve** the LORD their God, and David their king, whom I will raise up for them. Therefore **do not fear, O my servant Jacob**,' says the LORD, **'Nor be dismayed, O Israel**; for behold, I will save you from afar, and your seed from the land of their captivity. Jacob shall return, have rest and be quiet, and no one shall make him afraid. For **I am with you,' says the LORD, 'to save you; though I make a full end of all nations where I have scattered you**, yet I will not make a complete end of you. But I will **correct you** in justice, and will not let you go altogether unpunished'. Jeremiah 30:5-11*

***I will bring the one-third through the fire**, will **refine** them as silver is refined, and **test** them as gold is tested. They will **call** on my name, and **I will answer** them. I will say, 'This is My people'; and each one will say, 'The LORD is my God.' Zechariah 13:9*

*For I do not desire, brethren, that you should be ignorant of this mystery, lest you should be wise in your own opinion, that blindness in part has happened to Israel **until the fullness of the Gentiles has come in**. And so all **Israel will be saved**, as it is written: 'The Deliverer will come out of Zion, And He will turn away ungodliness from Jacob; for this is My **covenant** with them, when I take away their* sins.' Concerning the gospel they are enemies for your sake, but concerning the election they are beloved for the sake of the fathers. For **the gifts and the calling of God are irrevocable**. Romans 11:25-29

But Zion said, 'The LORD has forsaken me, and **my Lord has forgotten me.**' Can a woman **forget** her nursing child, and not have compassion on the son of her womb? Surely **they may forget, yet I will not forget you**. See, **I have inscribed you on the palms of my hands**; your walls are continually before me. Isaiah 49:14-16

The Tribulation will initiate a whole new ball game for God's people, Israel. It will commence a whole new age and program for them. The Church will be gone from the earth and the Church Age will be over and past. It is very significant that the word *church* is not found one time from Revelation 4 through 21. That is because, during those days, it will not exist on Earth. The Church will have been removed and God will once again be working with his ancient covenant people, the Jews. At that time, according to Zechariah 13:9 just quoted, God will bring one-third of his people, the Jews, through the fire to **refine** them. As Jeremiah put it, **it is the time of Jacob's trouble, but he shall be saved out of it.** During those days, the Jews will once again begin to call on the **name** of their God (Christ, the Jehovah of the Old Testament) and he will answer them. These are amazing prophecies and they will be literally fulfilled during the dark days of the Great Tribulation.

Now, I believe the Jews that we see here in Revelation 7, were saved by direct confrontation. That was the manner in which the Apostle Paul was converted. The confrontation that turned these 144,000 Jews occurred during the sixth Seal judgment. Were those traumatic events effective? Well ... here they are ... just a few sentences away from seeing their Messiah with their own eyes ... seated at the right hand of the majesty on high! Everyone on earth were crying to the rocks and mountains, **Fall on us and hide us from the face of him who sits on the throne and from the wrath of the Lamb**. Those cries have barely died down when we come here to the startling revelation that **144,000 Jews are now standing ready to serve the Lord Jesus Christ**! In verse four, we read ... **And I heard the number** *of those who were sealed. One hundred and forty-four thousand of all the tribes of the children of Israel were sealed.*

Let's step aside for a moment. The Apostle Paul is the only man in history who was ever saved by a direct confrontation. His story is found in Acts 9. There, on the road to Damascus, as he was traveling to Damascus to arrest and persecute believers in Christ, this zealous Pharisee and Christian hater was literally struck to the ground and spoken directly to by the risen Christ. Jesus said to him, **Saul, Saul, why are you persecuting me?** (Acts 9:4) Paul answered, **Who are you, Lord?** Jesus said, **I am Jesus whom you are persecuting.** Direct confrontation was what it took to turn Saul of Tarsus to the true and living God. Later, he spoke about it this way,

Then last of all he [Christ] *was seen by me also, as by one **born out of due time**. First Corinthians 15:8*

What did Paul mean by, **as by one born out of due time**? He was saying that his conversion experience was an anomaly. It was out of place in regards to the age in which he lived. It was out of sequence in the pages of the history of God's dealings with men. Paul knew that his conversion experience was like a man who had been born in the wrong time period. He understood that the method of direct confrontation that Christ had used to save him was a method that belonged to a different age than the Church Age. It belonged in the yet future age of the Great Tribulation. It belonged to the time of the aftermath of the sixth Seal … as evidenced by all these Jews we are looking at here in chapter 7.

Someone may ask, *Will all the Jews in that day turn to the Lord because of the confrontation of the sixth Seal*? The answer, of course, is, *No*. Even direct intervention and confrontation by God will not be sufficient to change the minds of two thirds of the Jews who will be living on Earth at the middle of the Tribulation. However, many will respond in faith, as the Apostle Paul did. Zechariah prophesied that a third would be brought through the Tribulation and be refined. Doubtless, that will be millions of Jews. Here in chapter 7, we encounter an elite 144,000 of them. The Green Berets, so to speak, of the Jews in that day. Immediately after the sixth Seal, we find them standing here, absolutely committed to Christ. The flabbergasted Paul, while still with his face in the dirt on the road to Damascus, responded, **Lord what would you have me to do?** (Acts 9:6) No doubt, these Jews have asked their Lord the same question and they are now standing ready to be sent out in Christ's name into the perilous days of the Great Tribulation. Doubtless, as with the Apostle Paul before them, they will be a zealous lot, whole-heartedly carrying out their work for their Messiah in the spirit Paul demonstrated in *Philippians 1:20-21*,

*...according to my earnest expectation and hope that in nothing I shall be ashamed, but with all **boldness**, as always, so now also **Christ will be magnified** in my body, whether by life or by death. **For to me, to live is Christ, and to die is gain**.*

Armed with that same zeal and commitment, the 144,000 witnesses will surely turn their world upside down during the days of their ministry. Let me share one more thought as to the timing of this great, future conversion of so many Jews. *Romans 11:25*, says,

*...blindness in part has happened to Israel **until the fullness of the Gentiles** has come in.*

This term, *the fullness of the Gentiles*, refers to the time of the Great Tribulation. It is talking about the **time period** of the last three and a half years of the Tribulation. It will be the time of Antichrist's reign. It is called *the fullness of the Gentiles* because it will be the pinnacle of Gentile reign on the earth. When that reign begins, as clearly stated in Romans 11:25, and as clearly demonstrated here in Revelation 7, the supernatural *blindness* of *Israel* ... which exists today and was instituted when the Jews rejected their Messiah ... **will be lifted**. *The fullness of the Gentiles* is the final phase of what Jesus referred to as *the times of the Gentiles* in Luke 21:24. The *times of the Gentiles* began when God's Theocracy on Earth was terminated and the Glory of the Lord departed back to Heaven from Jerusalem, as recorded in Ezekiel 8-11:3. At that time, Nebuchadnezzar and his Babylon took over dominion of the earth, being the first of a procession of Gentile kingdoms that have continued down through history to our day. For a more detailed discussion of this subject, see my commentary on Daniel at: **http://www.biblebookofdaniel.com/chapter1_2.htm**.

7:1-3

Returning to our text, notice that this is a new vision. First, John saw four angels holding back the four winds of heaven. As he continued to watch, another angel appeared out of the east and shouted to the original four, **Do not harm the earth, the sea, or the trees till we have sealed the servants of our God on their foreheads**. The word translated **harm** here, makes it clear that the **winds** are intended to be symbolic. These **winds** are speaking of God's judgments that will shortly come upon the earth. Wind is a very appropriate symbol in this regard. In excess, wind is irresistible, unpredictable and devastating. Often, tornadoes sweep across the plains and southern states of our nation that have winds in excess of two hundred miles per hour. Needless to say, little is left after they have passed by. Here, the symbolic **winds** of God's judgments are put temporarily on hold until the **angel ... from the east** seals God's servants. This seal will protect them from the judgments God is about to send upon the Earth. When they come, they will not affect these 144,000 chosen and sealed servants of Christ. This whole scene is reminiscent of the night when Israel was delivered from Egypt, is it not? You will remember that God commanded his people to mark their door-posts with lamb's blood so that the approaching death angel would not harm them (Exodus 12:23). We read in *Exodus 12:13,*

*Now the blood shall be a **sign** for you on the houses where you are. And **when I see the blood, I will pass over you**; and the plague shall not be on you to destroy you when I strike the land of Egypt.*

The future sealing of God's Jewish servants will function in the same manner as the blood did on Israel's door-posts of old. In 9:4, we will read of its effectiveness. There, demon locusts are instructed to hurt **only those men who do not have the seal of God on their foreheads**. God's judgments on the wicked are never designed to be inflicted upon his own people. *Revelation 14:1,* tells us what this seal is.

*Then I looked, and behold, a Lamb standing on Mount Zion, and with him one hundred and forty-four thousand, **having his Father's name written on their foreheads**.*

7:4-8

Now, let's take one more look at the identity of these 144,000 servants of God. The Jehovah's Witnesses claim this scripture is talking about some of them, but obviously these are not Jehovah's Witnesses. Our text specifically says that they are **the children of Israel**. You can't make the Bible mean just anything you want it to mean. It says what it means and it means what it says. Furthermore, lest there be any misunderstanding as to who these people are, we are told that they are individuals from twelve specific tribes of Israel and each tribe is listed for us. Twelve thousand are sealed from each tribe. By the way, there are no *lost tribes of Israel*. Our omniscient God knows exactly where all of his people are and to which tribe each one belongs. When the sealing of the 144,000 takes place, an Old Testament prayer will have been answered.

O LORD, why have you made us stray from your ways, and hardened our heart from your fear? **Return** *for your servants' sake, the tribes of your inheritance. Isaiah 63:17*

Notice that the angel *from the east* calls these Jews, **the servants of our God**. All through the dark days of the Tribulation, they will be serving him. Doing what? No doubt, they will be busy getting the Word of God out ... the message of the gospel of Jesus Christ. This is what God intended for them to do from the day he originally chose them to be his people. That's why, in Matthew 5:13-14, Jesus called them **the salt of the earth** and the **light of the world**! This has always been God's plan for the Jews ... that they would be spokespersons for him. At the middle of the Tribulation, his purpose for his people will finally begin to come to fruition when the 144,000 commit their lives and fortunes to the Savior. These fellows are going to be amazing. Like 144,000 Apostle Pauls, they will spread out over the earth with the message of Christ. In the second half of this chapter, we find an innumerable multitude of Gentiles who have come out of the Great Tribulation having **washed their robes and made them white in the blood of the Lamb.** They are not positioned there by accident. Where did they hear about **the blood of the Lamb**, do you suppose? Well, from the 144.000 for one. This great multitude of believers is found in the second half of this chapter as evidence, in my opinion, of the effectiveness of the future ministry of Christ's 144,000.

Strange Work

Before we move on, please notice that one tribe of Israel is conspicuously missing from the list of the 144,000. It is the tribe of Dan. That tribe has been replaced or substituted by the half tribe of **Manasseh**. You will find the original list of the twelve tribes of Israel in Genesis 49. There, the scripture specifically says, **these are the tribes of Israel** (Genesis 49:28). What is the explanation for the omission of Dan and the substitution of the half tribe of Manasseh? I believe it is this. I believe that the tribal privilege of Dan to serve Christ in that future day has been revoked due to their past history of unfaithfulness to their God. The other half tribe, Ephraim, and the tribe of Dan were both responsible for having originally introducing idolatry to Israel. They set up golden calves in Dan and Bethel which eventually lead the entire nation away from God and into judgment (Judges 18:30; Hosea 4:17; 1 Kings 12:28). This may well be why they will not be allowed to serve during the Great Tribulation. Service is a privilege that is all too often taken for granted by God's people, is it not? Willful rebellion and failure to follow Christ may well risk disqualification from serving him at some future date and time. I believe that is the case here.

Rev. 7:9-17

After these things I looked, and behold, **a great multitude which no one could number, of all nations, tribes, peoples, and tongues, standing before the throne and before the Lamb**, *clothed with white robes, with palm branches in their hands, and crying out with a loud voice, saying, 'Salvation belongs to our God who sits on the throne, and to the Lamb!' All the angels stood around the throne and the elders and the four living creatures, and fell on their faces before the throne and worshipped God, saying: 'Amen! Blessing and glory and wisdom, thanksgiving and honor and power and might, be to our God forever and ever. Amen.' Then one of the* **elders** *answered, saying to me,* **'Who are these arrayed in white robes**, *and* **where did they come from?'** *And I said to him,* **[NU changes "Sir" to "My Lord"]**, *you know.' So he said to me,* **'These are the ones who come out of the great tribulation, and washed their robes and made them white in the** *blood of the Lamb. Therefore they are before the throne of God, and serve him day and night in his temple. And he who sits on the throne will dwell among them. They shall neither hunger anymore nor thirst anymore; the sun shall not strike them, nor any heat; for the Lamb who is in the midst of the throne will shepherd them and lead them to* [**NU** changes *"living fountains of waters"* to *"fountains of the waters of life."*] *And God will wipe away every tear from their eyes.'*

7:9-10

Now, John's attention shifts from Earth's scene and the sealing of the 144,000, back up to Heaven. Up there, he finds an innumerable multitude standing before God's throne. They are from every ethnic group on Earth. They were wearing **white robes**. You will remember that the martyrs of the fifth Seal were given **white robes** and told to wait for the arrival of the rest of their brethren that would be killed. The fact that these people are in Heaven, dressed in **white robes**, indicates that they are those very **brethren** spoken of back there in 6:11. Again, let me emphasize it will be very difficult to be a Christian during the Great Tribulation. It will literally cost people their lives to follow Christ in that day. John heard the multitude shout, **Salvation belongs to our God who sits on the throne, and to the Lamb**. Then, the angels responded, **Amen, blessing and glory and wisdom, thanksgiving and honor and power and might be to our God forever and ever, Amen**.

7:11-12

When these Tribulation saints began to glorify Christ, the angels joined them in their worship. However, the angels couldn't cry *salvation* because it is not available to them. But they spoke wonderful words of adoration. The only way angels can experience the wonderful grace and mercy of God, by the way, is by observing it in the Lord's Redeemed. As you have it in *Ephesians 2:6-7,*
   ...and raised us up together, and made us sit together in the heavenly places in Christ Jesus, **that in the ages to come he might**

show the exceeding riches of his grace in his kindness toward us in Christ Jesus.

In eternity, from age to age, we believers in Christ will be on display as trophies of God's mercy and grace before all his angels and all other created beings. Here in chapter 7, we find a whole *multitude* of these trophies. They have come out of the *great tribulation* and arrived in Heaven to the great amazement and delight of the angels. Jesus said,

...joy shall be in heaven over one sinner that repenteth... Luke 15:7

7:13-14

At this point, an *elder* stepped up to John and asked him a question. *Can you identify who these people are, John?* His question was put to John to accentuate the uniqueness of this particular group of God's saints. John answered that he didn't know. This, in itself, is evidence that they are not the Church since John, an Apostle and elder of the Church, certainly would have recognized his own group. The *elder* then went on to explain to John that these were a brand new category of saint. They are Tribulation Saints ... who have *come out of the great tribulation* and have *washed their robes and made them white in the blood of the Lamb*. In respect to the fact that they have been washed in the blood of the Lamb, they certainly have that in common with the Church. However, there are some differences between them and the Church, as it was described back in chapter 5. Here is a comparison:

Tribulation Saints (chapter 7)	Church Saints (chapter 5)
• ...wear *white robes*	wear *white raiment*
• ...hold *palms*	hold *harps and vials of prayers*
• ...are uncrowned	wear *crowns*
• ...stand before the throne	are seated on *thrones*
• ...cry, *Salvation to God and His Lamb*	sing, *Worthy is the Lamb who ... has redeemed us*

Again, the thing that they have in common with the Church is they ***have washed their robes and made them white in the blood of the Lamb***. Dr. McGee points out that normally blood stains things, but the blood of Jesus does just the opposite. It washes and removes stains. Regardless of whether one is a Tribulation saint or a Church saint or an Old Testament saint, all who have come to God by faith have been washed from their sins by means of the cleansing blood of Jesus Christ, provided for us all at the cross. As we had it back in *Revelation 1:5*,

*...and from Jesus Christ, the faithful witness, the firstborn from the dead, and the ruler over the kings of the earth. To him who loved us and **washed us from our sins in his own blood**...*

I once heard of a denomination that was so offended by talk about the blood of Christ that they authorized all references to blood to be removed from their hymns and literature. Unsaved people hate the concept of blood atonement for their sins. It offends them. I think that is because they hate the thought that they are sinners at all. However, men and women cannot change what they are by simply denying it. As you have it in *Jeremiah 13:23*,

*Can the Ethiopian **change** his skin or the leopard its spots? Then may you also do good who are accustomed to do evil.*

There is no remedy for the stain of sin in the life of a human being other than the shed blood of the Lord Jesus Christ. It is his blood that washes away the sin-stains that stand between a sinner and Holy God. It alone is sufficient to cleanse and make someone whole again. As you have it in *Ephesians.1:7*,

*In him **we have redemption through his blood**, the forgiveness of sins, according to the riches of his grace...*

Praise God for the cleansing blood of our dear Savior, Jesus Christ! Amen?

7:15-17

Now, let's look for a moment at the position these Tribulation saints enjoy in Heaven. Notice that they have been given a place, a job, a security and a fellowship. Let's break it down.

They are *before the throne of God*. Now that's the **place** to be, brother! They were truly home.

They *serve him night and day*. Now, that's a **job** worth having! Heaven is not a place of inactivity and boredom, by the way. It is a place of real, effective and profitable service to God.

They are promised they will suffer no more *hunger*, no more *thirst* and no more *heat*. Now, that's real **security**! We have seen the horrible conditions that will prevail during the first half of the Tribulation that will come about because of the first five Seal judgments, but the second half of the Tribulation will be far worse. These saints will have come out of that later time period. But, when they get to Heaven, they will never again experience the horrible things that they endured down on Earth. There, they will be protected forever. Suffering, for these Tribulation saints in Heaven, will forever be a thing of the past.

Their ever present and caring Shepherd, the Lamb himself, will ever be at their side. Now ... that's **fellowship**, brother. It doesn't get any better than that! Never again will they be separated from the physical presence of their Shepherd and his tender care. It says here that he himself will always be present to *feed* them and to *lead them to fountains of living waters*. This reminds me of that wonderful promise to them in Isaiah,

He shall feed his flock like a shepherd: he shall gather the lambs with his arm, and carry them in his bosom, and shall gently lead those that are with young. Isaiah 40:11 (KJV)

These are the saints that will come out of the Great Tribulation. They are yet to be. Doubtless, a vast number of them will have been won to Christ by the 144,000. How gracious and wise is our great God. Long after the Church will have been taken from the earth, the Lamb of God will still be calling out a people for his name's sake. Amazing plan. Amazing love. Amazing grace, aye?

REVELATION 8 - 9

THE TRUMPET JUDGMENTS BEGIN

The interlude between the sixth and seventh Seal is now over. Chapter 8 opens with the breaking of the seventh Seal. This Seal introduces and commences the Trumpet Judgments. Time-wise, these judgments cover all of the rest of Earth's history. The events of the first five Seals took place during the first three and a half years of the Tribulation. They were indirect judgments and lead up to the Great Tribulation (the last three and a half years of the Tribulation). Beginning with the sixth Seal, God began to pour out direct judgments on the earth and we arrived at the beginning of the Great Tribulation. The Trumpets will complete God's direct judgments on the earth and they will be increasingly severe and punishing.

The Trumpet judgments are the epitome of God's supernatural interventions on Earth. By means of these judgments, God will put down the wicked and put all enemies under the feet of his Son while, at the same time, he extracts out of Satan's dark kingdom all the remaining souls who will respond to his gracious gift of salvation. So, the breaking of the seventh Seal is a very pivotal point in earth's history indeed. When the Trumpets it unleashes have run their course, Satan and his dark kingdom will have been eradicated and God great offer of salvation will be complete. *Psalm 46,* speaks of these coming judgments in graphic terms:

God is our refuge and strength, a very present help in trouble. **Therefore we will not fear, even though the earth be removed, and though the mountains be carried into the midst of the sea; though its waters roar and be troubled, though the mountains shake with its swelling**. *Selah. There is a river whose streams shall make glad the city of God, the holy place of the tabernacle of the Most High. God is in the midst of her, she shall not be moved; God shall help her, just at the break of dawn. The nations raged, the kingdoms were moved;* **he uttered his voice, the earth melted**. *The LORD of hosts is with us; the*

Strange Work

God of Jacob is our refuge. Selah. **Come, behold the works of the LORD, who has made desolations in the earth**. *He makes wars cease to the end of the earth; he breaks the bow and cuts the spear in two; he burns the chariot in the fire.* **'Be still, and know that I am God; I will be exalted among the nations, I will be exalted in the earth!'** *The LORD of hosts is with us; The God of Jacob is our refuge. Selah*

Rev. 8:1-5

When he opened the seventh seal, *there was* **silence in heaven for about half an hour**. *And* **I saw the seven angels** *who stand before God, and to them were given* **seven trumpets**. *Then another angel, having a* **golden censer**, *came and stood at the altar. He was given much* **incense**, *that he should offer it with the* **prayers** *of all the saints upon the* **golden altar** *which was before the throne. And the smoke of the incense, with the prayers of the saints, ascended before God from the angel's hand. Then the angel took the censer, filled it with fire from the altar, and threw it to the earth. And there were noises, thunderings, lightnings, and an earthquake.*

8:1-2

When the seventh Seal was broken, I suspect that John, as well as all of the rest of Heaven, were caught flat footed by what happened next. This being the last Seal, they no doubt expected something immediate and spectacular to occur. What actually happened though was ... nothing at all. John says, **there was silence in heaven for about half an hour**. Now, so far in the book of Revelation, you may have noticed that Heaven isn't exactly a quiet place. It is filled with activity and sound. We have heard the voices of people and angels, living creatures and awesome voices from God, his throne and from Christ. Back in chapter 5, we read that the Living Creatures there, never ceased to cry **Holy, Holy, Holy, night and day**. Heaven is filled with noise, praise, voices, thunders, singing and, no doubt, laughter as well. But, when the Lamb broke the seventh Seal from off his scroll, everything and everyone in Heaven became absolutely quiet. All activity and noise ceased. There was utter **silence**. Why will that be, do you think? I believe it is the calm before the storm. In light of our Lord's long-suffering, gracious and merciful character, this great pause before he commences his final and ultimate judgments on Earth is both understandable and predictable. This great silence will occur simply because he whose mercy endures forever, will be demonstrating, one last time, his great reluctance to pour out his righteous and long overdue judgments on mankind. *Lamentations 3:33-34,* says,

*...For he does not afflict **willingly**, nor grieve the children of men. To crush under one's feet all the prisoners of the earth...*

Peter says,

*The Lord is not slack concerning his promise, as some count slackness, but is **long-suffering** toward us, not willing that any should perish but that all should come to repentance. Second Peter 3:9*

However, although God is a loving, long-suffering and merciful God ... make no mistake about it ... the day will come when he will act and ***crush*** under his nail scarred ***feet all the prisoners of the earth*** (Lamentations 3:34). Here in our text, that day has now arrived ... the day when Almighty God will arise and deal with blasphemous and rebellious mankind who has so persistently spurned his Son and polluted the earth with all manner of evil. Over and over again, both in his Word and through the preaching of his servants, the Lord has warned the wicked that a day of reckoning will come. Now it has. **This is the beginning of God's *strange work*** (Isaiah 28:21).

Our text says that the ***silence in Heaven*** lasted for thirty minutes. That is not very long, actually. Yet, thirty minutes of total silence on such an august occasion and in the presence of such an innumerable host of beings will no doubt seem like an eternity. Surely, the air will be electric with anticipation and foreboding as all wait to see what God is about to do. Surely, the silence will be so palpable that one could cut it with a knife. One can almost hear the angels thinking ... *What will God do to those who have spurned his love and counted the sacrifice of his Son to be of no consequence?* All must wait. All is silent ... for God Almighty is about to arise and ***shake terribly the earth*** (Isaiah 2:21b).

Finally, something began to happen. John says, *I saw seven angels stand before God*. The Greek word translated *before* here is the word, ἐνώπιον *(enopion)*. I believe this word is emphasizing a special class of angelic beings who are associated with the throne of the Almighty. Its root meaning is to "dwell with" or "camp out with." So, I believe these particular angels are unique. They are Angels of the Presence. Gabriel is such an angel. When he rebuked Zechariah for not believing his message, he said with incredulity,

*I am Gabriel, who **stands in the presence** of God, and was sent to speak to you and bring you these glad tidings. Luke 1:19*

We can just about read Gabriel's mind by that statement. He was thinking, *How could anyone not believe the word of an Angel of the Presence*? I believe the seven angels in our text here are of that elite group. This passage is another indication of their continuous presence before the Father. They are the same **seven spirits** who greeted us back in chapter one, by the way, and also the same angels who were burning before the throne in chapter 5. John says they were given **seven trumpets**.

8:3-4

Following the distribution of the **seven trumpets** ... **another angel, having a golden censer, came and stood at the altar**. Now, it is important to keep in mind that there are two altars in this scene. The brazen altar was the altar where sacrifices were laid and burned. It was located just outside the door of the Holy Place out in the courtyard. We know that this angel was standing at that altar because he took *fire* from it. The fire on the brazen altar was kept burning twenty-four hours a day. John saw the angel dip his golden censer into the fire and then take it inside the Holy Place. Twice daily, priests at the temple on earth took fire from the brazen altar of sacrifice and took it inside the Holy Place to the little four horned golden altar located just in front of the veil before the Holy of Holies. There, they mixed the fire with incense on the little golden altar before the Lord. Here, however, you will notice that an additional ingredient is said to be mixed in. Our text says that the angel mingled the fire and incense with **the prayers of all the saints** and, we read, **the smoke of the incense, with the prayers of the saints, ascended before God from the angel's hand**. This will be an event pregnant with significance on the day when it actually occurs. *Psalm 141:2*, says,

*Let my **prayer** be set before you as **incense**, the lifting up of my hands as the evening sacrifice.*

The mingling in of the ***prayers of all the saints*** with the ***incense*** indicates that God's final Trumpet judgments will come about in answer to the prayers of all of God's people from all time. Over the centuries, countless prayers have been sent up to God by his people … prayers calling for deliverance, help, justice, vindication, intervention and vengeance. And, as with all yet unanswered prayers from the beginning of human history, they have not gone unnoticed nor been forgotten by God. Many of these prayers are imprecatory prayers (prayers calling for judgment). The cries of the martyrs under the altar, back at the breaking of the fifth Seal, were imprecatory prayers. They cried, ***How long O Lord, Holy and True, until you judge and avenge our blood on those who dwell on the earth?*** (6:10) There have been many prayers to God that were like this down through the ages. Some of them are found in the Psalms. Here is an example of one from King David.

*For the sin of their mouth and the words of their lips, **let them even be taken in their pride**, and for the cursing and lying which they speak. **Consume them in wrath**, consume them, that they may not be; and let them know that God rules in Jacob to the ends of the earth. Selah. Psalm 59:12-13*

All such prayers, along with countless others, will one day rise up afresh before God … just prior to the blowing of the first Trumpet.

8:5

As John continued to watch, the angel with the fire emerged from the Holy Place with his now empty censer and John saw him approach the brazen altar. Arriving there, once again the angel dipped his censor into its fiery coals. This time, however, he suddenly and unexpectedly turned and ***threw*** the fiery coals down upon the earth. This is striking symbolism. The brazen altar was the place of sacrifice, you see … an altar where, down through ancient Jewish history, continuous offerings for sin had been slain and burned. Day after day, over and over again, each of these sacrifices pictured the sacrifice of God's Lamb/Son who would one day come and offer himself, once and for all, for the sins of the whole world. The significance of the angel's casting fire down to the earth from **that** particular altar is pregnant with significant. Earth-dwellers of that day will have been continuously rejecting Christ's sacrifice for them on the cross. Now, there is nothing left but to experience the fiery judgment of God for their stubborn rejection. Further, their punishment must come at the hands of that very same Lamb that was sacrificed for them in the first place!

After the smoke of the prayers of all the saints goes up, the fire of God's judgments will begin to come down upon the earth. In concurrence with the casting of fire down to earth by the angel ... there was also *thunderings*, flashes of *lightening* and ominous *noises* (should read *voices*) from God's throne and, down on Earth, there was an *earthquake*. You will remember this is also what occurred at God's throne just prior to the Seal judgments (4:5). It reoccurs here, just before the Trumpet judgments begin. [Note: The NKJV translates the word, φωναὶ (*phonai*) as *noises*, when it should have been rendered *voices*. It is the same word that was translated *voices* back in 4:5 in the same context.]

THE FIRST TRUMPET SOUNDS ...

HAIL AND FIRE MINGLED WITH BLOOD COVER THE EARTH

Rev. 8:6-7

*So the seven angels who had the seven trumpets prepared themselves to sound. **The first angel sounded**: and **hail and fire** followed, **mingled with blood**, and they were thrown to the earth. [**Nu** adds "and a third of the earth was burned up,"] and a third of the trees were burned up, and all green grass was burned up.*

8:6

Our text says the seven angels with the seven trumpets **prepared themselves to sound**. I have tried to picture that. What kind of preparations did John see? Practicing their notes? Cleaning their instruments? Arranging who would go first, second? Just asking ... I can't say as I know. Getting back to business here, there is a very important prophecy in Micah that we should look at before we examine these judgments. Micah said,

*As in the days when you came out of the land of Egypt, I will show them wonders. The **nations shall see and be ashamed** of all their might; they shall put their hand over their mouth; their ears shall be deaf. They shall lick the dust like a serpent; they shall crawl from their holes like snakes of the earth. **They shall be afraid of the LORD our God**, and shall fear **because of you**. Micah 7:15-17*

This prophecy relates directly to the days of the Trumpet judgments and tells us why they will parallel the plagues that God sent upon the Egyptians in Moses' day. Wonders are scheduled for the earth ... wonders chosen specifically by God to be of the same nature as those that occurred when Israel was delivered from the hand of the Egyptians ... wonders that were designed specifically to remind the nations of God's love for, and special relationship to, his chosen people, the Jews.

Let's step aside again. May I say to you, if you don't have a problem believing the literal historic and supernatural plagues of the Exodus, you are not likely to have a problem believing the literalness of the plagues of the Trumpet judgments we are about to see. Many have tried to explain both away, however. Not too long ago, there was a program on PBS trying to explain away the literal miracles of the Bible. This is the common approach by the world to the miracles that God has performed in history. As a youth at a certain church camp, I remember being ridiculed by two preachers for believing that *Jonah was swallowed by a whale*! *Ha! Ha*! They then instructed us that this biblical story was just a myth. Not only did these skeptics not believe in the historic miracles of the Bible, but they were ignorant of the Bible's presentation of them as well. The Bible says, **Now God had prepared a great fish to swallow Jonah** (Jonah 1:17) ... not a *whale*, as those two Biblical illiterates assumed. I can only imagine what they might say about the prophecies of which we are about to read. J.B. Smith, one of the great Bible expositors of yesteryear, commenting on these miraculous judgments, warned, **One needs to be cautious how he regards the miracles in unfulfilled passages of divine prophecy** *lest he undermine his own faith in the miracles of divine history*. Hear, hear!

8:7

When the first angel blew his trumpet, once again **hail and fire** fell upon Earth ... just as it had done in the days of old during Moses time. However, this time it was far more severe than its ancient counterpart in Egypt. This time, it was worldwide and, in addition, it spattered Earth-dwellers with **blood**. How frightening that will be when it comes. Also, it destroyed a third of all the trees and grasses on Earth. Once again, it will be very difficult for men to separate this event from the supernatural. It will be another slap in the face to mankind's perceived understanding of nature. This judgment is alluded to in other scriptures as well. *Psalm 11:6*, says,

Upon the wicked he will rain coals; *Fire and brimstone and a burning wind shall be the portion of their cup.*

Psalm 140:10, says,

Let burning coals fall *upon them; let them be cast into the fire, into deep pits, that they rise not up again.*

Joel prophesied about the effect that this judgment will have on **cattle** in that day, saying,

How do the beasts groan! the herds of cattle are perplexed, *because they have no pasture; yea, the flocks of sheep are made desolate. O Lord, to thee will I cry: for* **the fire hath devoured the pastures of the wilderness, and the flame hath burned all the trees of the field**. *The beasts of the field cry also unto thee ... Joel 1:18-20a*

The first Trumpet judgment will be the beginning of an environmentalist's nightmare on Earth. However, we need to understand that God has no great concern for his creation when man, for whom it was created and who is the crown of that creation, is persisting in willful rebellion against him. To care about the creation when this judgment is occurring would be analogous to one's son being killed while riding a bike and then being concerned about the bike. Make no mistake about it, God will not give a rat's eyebrow for all the forests and grasses of Earth if, by means of burning them, just one man or woman might be saved. Notice, however, that no human being was killed by the first Trumpet judgment. It is an alarm.

Someone has said, *God always sounds an alarm before he judges*. A **third** of the forests and grasses will perish, but only a third. God will still be exercising his restraint and long-suffering, you see. The God of all mercy is measured in his judgments and, even at this late hour, will still be waiting for men and women to turn to his Son and be saved. This first Trumpet parallels the seventh plague of Egypt found in *Exodus 9:23*,

*And Moses stretched out his rod toward heaven; and the LORD sent thunder and **hail**, and **fire** darted to the ground. And the LORD rained hail on the land of Egypt.*

THE SECOND TRUMPET SOUNDS ...

A MOUNTAINOUS FIERY OBJECT PLUNGES INTO THE SEA

Rev. 8:8-9

*Then the second angel sounded: And **something like a great mountain** burning with fire was thrown into the sea, and **a third of the sea became blood**. And **a third of the living creatures in the sea died**, and **a third of the ships were destroyed**.*

If the first Trumpet was an alarm, the second will come as disaster alert! You may have seen Hollywood's movie, *Deep Impact*. It is the fictional story of a giant comet's impact on Earth. If you saw that movie, you will have seen a graphic depiction of something that is strikingly similar to this future event and the devastation that will result from it. Unlike Hollywood's film, however, a comet will not cause this disaster. The description here is more in keeping with the impact of an asteroid accompanied by added supernatural effects. Notice that it is said that this object was ***thrown into the sea***. What an **impact** that will make when it strikes the earth in that day. How awesome it will be when it comes. Yet, again, notice the thirds. God limits the destruction caused by this flung mountain of fire.

As a result, a ***third*** of the world's ***ships*** will go down to *Davie Jones Locker*. Doubtless, this will be due to the giant tsunamis which such a hurled object will generate. A third of all sea life will perish as well and a third of the sea will be literally turned to blood. Again, these thirds continue to speak of the mercy and longsuffering of God in that day. Now, the question arises, is this real blood? Again, my mind goes back to those two pseudo-ministers I encountered at camp in my youth. I recall that they also spent a good deal of time attacking the blood that accompanied Moses' first plague on Egypt. The Bible says the waters of the Nile were turned to blood. They said that was absurd. They said that, *Probably, a volcano erupted up-river and red mud came down making the waters of the Nile just look like blood.* May I say to you, either you believe what Scripture says or you don't. As far as I'm concerned, if the Bible says that it was **blood**, it was **blood**. When the judgment of the second Trumpet comes, it will parallel the first plague in Egypt in *Exodus 7:20-21,*

*And Moses and Aaron did so, just as the LORD commanded. So he lifted up the rod and struck the waters that were in the river, in the sight of Pharaoh and in the sight of his servants. And all the waters that were in the river were **turned to blood**. The **fish that were in the river died**, the river stank, and the Egyptians could not drink the water of the river. So **there was blood throughout all the land of Egypt**.*

THE THIRD TRUMPET SOUNDS ...

EARTH'S FRESH WATERS ARE CONTAMINATED

Rev. 8:10-11

*Then the **third angel sounded**: And a **great star** fell from heaven, burning like a torch, and it **fell on a third of the rivers and on the springs of water**. The name of the star is **Wormwood**. A third of the waters became wormwood, and **many men died** from the water, because it was made bitter.*

8:10-11

You will remember that, during the Exodus, God changed bitter water to sweet at Marah (Exodus 15:22-25) so that his people might have water to drink. Here, the opposite occurs. He will change sweet water to bitter by means of a ***great star***. John saw it fall and strike the fresh waters of the earth. He was told the star's name was ***Wormwood***. This is a significant name in Scripture and it helps us to understand God's reason behind this judgment. In the Old Testament, ***wormwood*** is a word that is associated with idolatry. For example, we read in *Deuteronomy 29:18*,

*...so that there may not be among you man or woman or family or tribe, whose heart **turns away today from the LORD our God, to go and serve the gods of these nations**, and that there may not be among you **a root bearing bitterness or wormwood**...*

Wormwood is also a word used to describe man's poor judgment (Amos 5:7) as well as calamities and sorrow (Jeremiah 9:15; 18:15). Putting the pieces of the puzzle together, the name of this ***great star*** suggests that the calamity and sorrow that will result it has come about because of man's poor choices in choosing to worship idols rather than the true and living God. It also will be in retribution for all the injustice, sorrow and pain that man's idolatry and bogus religions have inflicted on the world. The blowing of the third Trumpet will initiate the most severe judgment yet, and it will be the first to initiate loss of human life. John says ***many men died from the water***. This third Trumpet is also a parallel of the first plague in Exodus.

THE FOURTH TRUMPET SOUNDS ...

A THIRD OF DAY AND NIGHT FALLS INTO UTTER DARKNESS

Rev. 8:12

*Then the **fourth angel sounded**: And a third of the sun was struck, a third of the moon, and a third of the stars, so that a third of them were **darkened**. A **third of the day** did not shine, and likewise the **night**.*

When the fourth angel blew his trumpet, Earth's sources of light in the heavens were turned off and utter ***darkness*** came upon the earth for a ***third*** of each day and night. I believe God will send this plague to give lost men and women a taste of what it will be like to be eternally separated from him in the Lake of Fire. Jesus said,

*For to everyone who has, more will be given, and he will have abundance; but from him who does not have, even what he has will be taken away. And cast the unprofitable servant into the **outer darkness**. There will be weeping and gnashing of teeth. Matthew 25:29-30*

May we step aside here for a moment? Contrary to popular opinion, the Lake of Fire is a place of utter isolation and darkness. Such darkness is a fearful thing in itself. When I was a youngster, my parents and I went on an excursion to the famous Carlsbad Caverns in southeastern New Mexico. After we hiked down into the cave, the tour guide sat us all down and informed us that he was going to turn out the lights so we could experience absolute darkness. He then turned out the lights. Immediately, groans began to be heard. The darkness could almost be felt. He instructed us to hold our hands before our faces and see what we could see. We could see nothing. It was as if we had all gone blind. It was very sobering and we were all greatly relieved when the lights came back on.

On another occasion, my family and I were out camping at Wall Lake in the Gila National Forest (pronounced *hee la*). I awoke in the middle of the night to discover that the moon had gone down but, to my delight and amazement, I found that the stars themselves were flooding the camp with soft light. Being a city dweller, that was something I hadn't experienced before. During the judgment of the fourth Trumpet, all light from heavenly bodies will be quenched for a third of the nights and a third of the days and that will be a very long time, brother! For four hours during the day and four hours during the night, men will be confronted with absolute darkness, vividly demonstrating the condition their souls will experience in an eternity without Christ. How terrifying that will be can only be imagined. We are not told how many days this judgment will last but, if it lasted for very many ... apart from divine intervention ... the Earth would freeze. This judgment parallels the ninth plague of Exodus.

*Then the LORD said to Moses, 'Stretch out your hand toward heaven, that there may be **darkness** over the land of Egypt, **darkness which may even be felt**.' So Moses stretched out his hand toward*

heaven, and there was thick darkness in all the land of Egypt three days. Exodus 10:22

Both Isaiah and Jesus predicted this coming judgment.

*For **the stars of heaven and their constellations will not give their light**; **the sun will be darkened in its going forth, and the moon will not cause its light to shine**. Isaiah 13:10*

*And there will be **signs in the sun, in the moon, and in the stars**; and on the earth distress of nations, with perplexity, the sea and the waves roaring; men's hearts failing them from **fear** and the expectation of those things which are coming on the earth, for the powers of heaven will be shaken.* [Jesus' words] *Luke 21:25-26*

THE ANGEL WITH THE THREE WOES

Rev. 8:13

And I looked, and I heard an **[NU replaces *"angel"* with *"eagle"*]** *flying through the midst of heaven, saying with a loud voice, 'Woe, woe, woe to the inhabitants of the earth, because of the remaining **blasts of the trumpet of the three angels who are about to sound!'***

8:13

Before the fifth Trumpet sounded, John saw a prepared *eagle* go forth to circumvent the earth and cry out a fearful message. Its bone-chilling warning was, ***Woe, woe, woe to the inhabitants of the earth, because of the remaining blasts of the trumpet of the three angels who are about to sound!*** Lange, in his commentary, pictures this as a spirit being that soars at great altitude so that it is visible to the far meridian of Earth. However, I take it for what it says. *A talking eagle*, you ask? Exactly. God sent a message to Balaam by the mouth of a jackass, did he not (Numbers 22:28)? God can use whatever instrument he chooses to get his Word out. What language will the *eagle* speak? We are not told. But, doubtless, it will be universally understood. The Greek words for *woe* here are Οὐαὶ οὐαὶ οὐαὶ *(Owiiiiiii! ... Owiiiiiii! ... Owiiiiiii!)*. The eagle's cry will pierce the skies with this ominous onomatopoeia ... followed by its sobering prophetic words. No doubt, this will impart quite a jolt to Earth-dwellers as they see and hear this macabre phenomenon. Will anyone give heed to his cry? I believe they will. After all, this eagle will be speaking the Word of God and *faith comes by hearing and hearing by the Word of God* (Rom. 10:17).

The final three Trumpet judgments to which God's prepared eagle will be referring to are called *woes* because they will bring unprecedented ruin to the earth and to its remaining rebellious peoples. The fifth Trumpet will be the first woe, the sixth will be the second woe and the seventh will be the third and final woe. Dr. McGee points out that there are over six hundred warnings about Hell in the Bible. He says, *If you were driving your car down the road and you read over six hundred signs that said, 'TURN BACK, THIS ROAD LEADS TO DESTRUCTION', would you keep on going down that road? Could you blame someone else or sue the Highway Department if you suddenly drove off a cliff?* Talk about no excuse! Earth-dwellers of this future day will have more opportunities to be saved and avoid disaster than all the other generations of human history combined. However, as we will shortly see, multitudes will simply harden their hearts the more and stiffen their necks the more in adamant unbelief at God's merciful warnings. *Proverbs 29:1*, will be fulfilled in spades in that day on those who obstinately continue to refuse the grace of God that is being offered to them...

He who is often rebuked, and **hardens his neck***, will* **suddenly be destroyed***, and that without remedy.*

THE FIFTH TRUMPET (FIRST WOE)

DEMON LOCUSTS ARE RELEASED FROM THE ABYSS

Rev. 9:1-12

Then **the fifth angel sounded***: And* **I saw a star fallen from heaven to the earth. To him was given the key to the bottomless pit***. And he opened the* **bottomless pit***, and smoke arose out of the pit like* *the smoke of a great furnace. So the sun and the air were darkened because of the smoke of the pit. Then out of the smoke **locusts** came upon the earth. And **to them was given power, as the scorpions of the earth have power**. They were commanded not to harm the grass of the earth, or any green thing, or any tree, but only those men who do not have the seal of God on their foreheads. And **they were not given authority to kill them, but to torment them** for **five months**. Their torment was like the torment of a scorpion when it strikes a man. **In those days men will seek death and will not find it**; they will desire to die, and death will flee from them. **The shape of the locusts was like horses prepared for battle**. On their heads were **crowns** of something like gold, and their faces were like the **faces of men**. They had hair like **women's hair**, and their teeth were **like lions' teeth**. And they had **breastplates** like breastplates of iron, and the **sound of their wings** was like the sound of chariots with many horses running into battle. They had **tails like scorpions**, and there were stings in their tails. Their power was to hurt men five months. And they had as **king over them** the angel of the bottomless pit, whose name in Hebrew is **Abaddon**, but in Greek he has the name **Apollyon**. **One woe is past**. Behold, still two more woes are coming after these things.*

9:1

When the fifth angel blew his Trumpet, the first *woe* commenced down on Earth. John says he saw a ***star fallen from heaven***. This symbol refers to a person. We know that because of the personal pronouns *he* and *him* that are used here. As we have already discussed, a ***star*** is sometimes used in the Bible to designate an angel. I believe that to be the case here. But who is this angel? There is a hint to his identity in the tense of the Greek word, ***fallen***, that is used here. It is in the present tense which denotes an action that was completed in the past but whose effect continues on into the present. In other words this ***star*** has ***fallen***, is ***fallen***, and always will be ***fallen***. Jesus said,

*I saw Satan **fall** like lightning from heaven. Luke 10:18b*

This ***fallen*** angel is Satan himself. At the sounding of the fifth Trumpet, he will be given the ***key to the bottomless pit*** to go down and release a multitude of other fallen angels (demonic beings) who have long been imprisoned there. The Greek word translated ***bottomless pit*** here is, ἀβύσσου (*aboussoo*), from which we get our English word *abyss*. This is the first of seven mentions of the Abyss in Revelation. We learn from Luke 8, Jude 6 and Second Peter 2, that the Abyss is the temporary holding place of a certain class of fallen angel. Based on Peter's statement in Second Peter 2, I believe that the demons who are loose on Earth today are a different group. Nevertheless, all of them have a horror and an aversion to the Abyss. We see that in Christ's encounter with some of them in Luke 8:31. There, the demons that he cast out of the wild man of Gadara **begged him that he would not command them to go out into the abyss**. Consider these scriptures also.

For if God did not spare the angels who sinned, but cast them down to hell and delivered them into **chains of darkness**, *to be reserved for judgment... Second Peter 2:4*

And the angels who did not keep their proper domain, but left their own abode, **he has reserved in everlasting chains under darkness** *for the judgment of the great day. Jude 6*

The Abyss is for real. Apparently, it is located somewhere in the bowels of the earth. At the sounding of the fifth Trumpet, Satan will be allowed to set loose a certain number of these long incarcerated spirits who will come forth aching for action and yearning to do Satan's bidding.

9:2-3

John says that when the Abyss was opened **the sun and the air were darkened because of the smoke of the pit.** I witnessed the eruption of Mount Saint Helens in the state of Washington in 1980. As its ash and gasses exploded thousands of feet upwards into the atmosphere, I had the creepy feeling that the Abyss had been opened. How utterly awesome it will be when it actually occurs one day. The fifth Trumpet will be a terrifying and severe plague, indeed. Notice that the vegetation will be exempt whereas, in its parallel, the locust plague of Exodus 10, they ate all of the vegetation. These demons, when they come, will deal a much heavier blow than the locusts the Egyptians had to contend with in Moses' day. The fact that they are said to have been given authority to hurt men implies that these cruel creatures will come with a built-in desire to torture mankind.

Again, let's step aside for a moment. The question arises ... *Why would Satan and his fallen angels help God carry out his judgments?* The answer, I believe, lies in the fact that Satan and his demons actually hate mankind. I think that is because man is made in the image of God as well as the fact that man has been the object of God's love and purpose throughout history. This is more than sufficient cause for Satan and his demons' hatred and envy of man. Add to that the fact that every individual human being has the potential, through faith in Christ, to be exalted to the very right hand of God on High (Ephesians1) and that really stirs up the animosity of Satan and his demons. Frankly, Satan and his crowd would be happy to see mankind obliterated. During the days of the fifth Trumpet, however, they will have to settle for mere infliction of suffering on men, probably little realizing that by doing so, God will be using them for his own purposes. The judgment of the fifth Trumpet is also prophesied so specifically in *Joel 2:1-11,*

Blow the trumpet in Zion, And sound an **alarm** *in My holy mountain! Let all the inhabitants of the land tremble; for* **the day of the LORD is coming***, for it is at hand: a day of darkness and gloominess, a day of clouds and thick darkness, like the morning clouds spread over the mountains.* **A people come, great and strong, the like of whom has never been; nor will there ever be any such after them***, even for many successive generations. A fire devours before them, and behind them a flame burns; the land is like the Garden of Eden before them, and behind them a desolate wilderness; surely nothing shall escape them. Their appearance is like the appearance of* **horses***; and like swift steeds, so they run. With a* **noise** *like chariots over mountaintops they leap, like the noise of a flaming fire that devours the stubble, like a strong people set in* **battle array***.* **Before them the people writhe in pain***; all faces are drained of color. They run like mighty men, they climb the wall like men of war;* **every one marches in formation, and they do not break ranks.** *They do not push one another; every one marches in his own column. Though they lunge between the weapons, they are not cut down. They run to and fro in the city,* **they run on the wall; they climb into the houses, they enter at the windows like a thief.** *The earth quakes before them, the heavens tremble; the sun and moon grow dark, and the stars diminish* *their brightness. The LORD gives voice before his army, for his camp is very great; for strong is the One who executes his word. For* **the day of the LORD is great and very terrible; who can endure it***?*

Many prophecies in the Bible have more than one fulfillment. This prophecy is a good example of a prophecy that has a double fulfillment. One fulfillment is usually a **near fulfillment** and the other is **far**. Although the prophet Joel was describing a local locust plague that would come upon Israel in his own day (the **near** fulfillment), his words far exceeded what took place at that time. So, they also referred to a second fulfillment that will occur at the time of the fifth Trumpet (the **far** fulfillment).

9:4

Returning to our text, notice it says here that the 144,000 were exempt from this plague because of God's protective seal on their foreheads. This is important information in that it clues us in to the fact that all of the 144,000 will still be alive during the days of the fifth Trumpet which is well into the Great Tribulation.

9:5-6

John continues, ***And they were not given authority to kill them, but to torment them for five months, their torment was like the torment of a scorpion when it strikes a man****.* We cannot be certain whether these demonic beings will be visible or not, but they certainly will be felt. Joel prophesied they will ***lunge between the weapons, they are not cut down.*** People will attempt to defend themselves from these demonic creatures but ... to no avail.

He continues ... ***In those days, men will seek death and will not find it; they will desire to die, and death will flee from them.*** For five months, men will seek to die because of this plague but they will not be allowed to do so. A shocking statement, is it not? Just how they will be prevented from dying we are not told. Apparently, those who attempt suicide will only add to their miseries. Men often brag that they are the captains of their own fate. I am reminded of that popular and smug song, *I Did It My Way*! At the judgment of the fifth Trumpet, God will call mankind on that boast. At that time, men and women will not even be able to kill themselves. Why do you think

God will not allow people to die during those days? Would it surprise you if it was because of his mercy? If people were allowed to kill themselves, they would simply be transferring themselves into a far greater misery in Hell than they were experiencing under the fifth Trumpet ... and that misery would last forever.

Let me add a comment here. States and countries that have legalized euthanasia are inflicting a great tragedy on people. How sad that those who think they are being kind by providing relief from suffering are, in fact, multiplying their victim's awful suffering a thousand fold (if they are unsaved folks) by sending them on to a Christless eternity in the Lake of Fire. If they had not prematurely taken their lives ... who knows if they might have been saved? The judgment of the fifth Trumpet is aimed at remedy of life. No one will be allowed to die during its days.

9:7-10

Before we leave this passage, it would be profitable to take a look at the description here of these demonic tormentors. They stand before us here, in all of their strutting, proud and monstrous demeanor. Remember, however, they are actually spirits (fallen angels). As spirit beings, like their demon comrades today, they are normally invisible. However, if they actually manifest themselves in that day as they are described here, they will greatly add to men's terrors. All eight aspects of their visible appearance seem to point to self design and smack of unmitigated pride. John says:

...their shapes were **like horses prepared for battle**. By this guise, they flaunt their perceived prowess, power and speed.

...upon their heads were **crowns of something like gold**. The Greek word here for *crowns* is στέφανοι (*stephanoi*). This is the word for a victor's crown. Satan's demons prefer this crown. It is the same one that Satan's Antichrist was wearing at the first Seal judgment (6:2). Why do they desire a victor's crown? Well, I believe it has to do with the fact that they all have that something in them that wants to be better than Christ. When we get to chapter 14, we will see that Christ wears this crown. He is the only one who is truly worthy to wear it, by the way. He is the great Victor. He is the one who is the victor over Satan, sin, the world and even death itself. These demons declare themselves to be victors, but as Dr. McGee comments, *they are losers*. Our text says their ***crowns*** are not even made of real gold! These reprobates possess no real wealth either!

...their faces are the ***faces of men***. They probably present themselves with the faces of men to attempt to portray intelligence but, if they are so smart, why did they rebel against God in the first place?

...they have ***hair like women's hair***. This appears to be a vain attempt at beauty, but they are stupidly unaware of how grotesque they really appear.

...their ***teeth were like lion's teeth***. With their teeth they present themselves as strong and ferocious, but they have no power or strength other than what has been given them.

...they wear breastplates ***like breastplates of iron***. As such, they masquerade as invincible, but the day will soon arrive when one little word will destroy them all.

...*the sound of their wings was like the sound of chariots with many horses running to battle*. With the noise of their wings, this mob will strike terror into the hearts of men. My son, Dave, loves to visit a spot in Mexico where all the Monarch butterflies migrate. He says there are so many millions of them that the air is filled with the constant whooshing of their wings and their combined weight often breaks limbs from off the trees! Isn't that amazing? These fellows, however, will be no butterflies and the roaring sound of their wings will be horrifying.

...they have ***tails like scorpions***. Their tails are their diabolic instruments of torture. Someone has said, *A camel is a race horse put together by a committee!* I can't help but think of that jocular truism here. Surely these demons must have concocted their own appearance by committee. No doubt they will be very proud of the result, scarcely realizing what monstrosities they actually are.

9:11

By the way, I do not believe you can find a clearer picture of our enemy, Satan, than is described to us here in Revelation 9. He hurts simply because it is his depraved nature to do so. The destruction and torment of human beings is his sheer, perverted pleasure. In verse 11, he is called the Destroyer ... both in Hebrew (***Abaddon***) and in Greek (***Apollyon***). That just about says it all.

THE SIXTH TRUMPET (THE SECOND WOE) SOUNDS ...

A SECOND DEMONIC INVASION COMMENCES

Rev. 9:13-16

*Then **the sixth angel sounded**: And I heard a **voice** from the four horns of the **golden altar** which is before God, saying to the sixth angel who had the trumpet, '**Release the four angels who are bound** at the great river Euphrates'. So the four angels, who had been prepared for the hour and day and month and year, **were released to kill a third of mankind**. Now the number of the army of the horsemen was **two hundred million**; I heard the number of them.*

Before we go on, let's remind ourselves of two important things that will be happening on Earth during the days of these final judgments. First, God will be continuing to seek the redemption of all who will call upon his Son and be saved. And, at the same time, he will be steadily and increasingly upping the ante on the wicked by pouring out more and more severe wrath upon them. As you have it in *Psalm 94:23,*

He has brought on them their own iniquity, and shall cut them off in their own wickedness; ***The LORD our God shall cut them off****.*

And again, in *Psalm 37:10-11,*

For yet a little while and the wicked shall be no more*; indeed, you will look carefully for his place, but it shall be no more. But **the meek shall inherit the earth**, and shall delight themselves in the abundance of peace.*

When John heard the sixth Trumpet sound, immediately he heard a voice speak from the ***four horns*** of the ***golden altar***. This is the little altar that was inside the Holy Place. It was where the angel mixed the prayers of the saints with incense and offered them up to God back in 8:3. This altar is a square box in design and it has upward hooked horns at each of its four corners. In Old Testament times, once a year on the Great Day of Atonement, the blood of a sacrificial lamb was applied to each of these horns by the High Priest for the sins of the people. Year after year, this pictured God's coming mercy through the blood of his provided Lamb, Jesus Christ. The fact that the *voice* that initiated the judgment of the sixth Trumpet called out from these *horns* indicates that the voice itself was that of the blood of Christ. At that time, most Earth-dwellers will still be adamantly rejecting the blood of God's Lamb and thereby cementing their fate at the hands of the very One who loved them and died to set them free. As you have it in *Hebrews 10:26-27*,

For if we sin willfully after we have received the knowledge of the truth, there no longer remains a sacrifice for sins, **but a certain fearful expectation of judgment***, and fiery indignation which will devour the adversaries.*

The *voice* that spoke from the *horns* of the *golden altar* said, *Release the four angels who are bound at the great river Euphrates*. Who might they be? Well, let's see what we can glean about them from the text:

It says they were *bound*. This is a strong indication that they are of the demon crowd. Only spirits that have rebelled against God in the past are said to be incarcerated in the Scriptures.

Then, it says they were *prepared for* this judgment. The present perfect participle in the Greek here indicates that they were prepared in the past and are, at this very moment, waiting to be loosed.

Next, it says they were *at the great river Euphrates*. This river is in the Mesopotamian Valley. It separates the far-east from the land of Palestine running from Turkey and Syria in the north down through Iraq to the Persian Gulf. American troops fought their way across this river several times in the war to liberate Iraq. It was in this very geographical area that sin was first known in the Garden of Eden. The first great judgment of mankind also fell here in the days of Noah when God destroyed the original world and its inhabitants by water (Genesis 6).The first counterfeit religion was born here when, at Babylon, Nebuchadnezzar set up an image of himself and demanded all his subjects must worship it. The great enemies of God's people, the

Babylonians, Syrians, Assyrians ... the Medes, the modern day Iranians and countless others have all flourished in this valley. It is at this river, so filled with the history of rebellion and sin, that four great evil principalities of the spirit-world are presently waiting ... chained there ... until the day of their release.

Then, it says they were prepared *for the hour and day and month and year*. The construction of these words in the Greek, with the absence of the article, indicates that it is not speaking about separate periods of time but rather an exact point in time. These evil principalities are waiting for the exact year, month, day and hour of the sounding of the sixth Trumpet that will release them from their chains.

Finally, it says they were released *to kill a third of mankind*. The sounding of the sixth Trumpet will precipitate a second outpouring of demonic beings upon the earth. John says he heard the number of them ... two hundred million strong. The sixth Trumpet was aptly named the second *woe*, back in 8:13. It will be the severest judgment yet of the Great Tribulation.

Rev. 9:17-19

*And thus I saw the **horses** in the vision: **those who sat on them had breastplates** of fiery red, hyacinth blue, and sulfer yellow; and the heads of the horses were like the heads of lions; and out of their mouths came fire, smoke, and brimstone. **By these three plagues a third of mankind was killed**; by the fire and the smoke and the brimstone which came out of their mouths. For* **[NU omits *"their"*]** *the power* **[NU adds *"of the horses"*]** *is in their mouth and in their tails; for their tails are like serpents, having heads and with them they do harm.*

The outpouring of demonic beings from the now unlocked Abyss will be led by the four fallen principalities out of the Euphrates River. This time around, however, the result will be far more devastating than the previous release of demons. These four will go forth with the authority to kill a *third* of all humanity on Earth. You will remember that a quarter of Earth's population perished at the breaking of the fourth Seal back in 6:8. After the sixth Trumpet has run its course, over half of the world's population will have perished.

Let's look at John's description of these two hundred million demons for a minute. He saw them come forth as mounted riders with armored **breastplates** which were **fiery red**, **hyacinth blue**, and **sulfur yellow**. These colors seem to reflect their fiery origin from out of the Abyss. Their horses' heads were **like the heads of lions** and their tails **like serpents, having heads; and with them they do harm**. When they come, in that day, they will come murdering and tormenting with a vengeance. Many have attempted to water this passage down. Some, using Augustine's allegorical method of interpretation, have said this is actually a picture of World War III with its armies and tanks and helicopters. The human heart has a very difficult time accepting that such a literal judgment could, or would, be sent from God on mankind. Yet, the Scripture says,

The LORD has made all for himself, yes, even the wicked for the day of doom. Proverbs 16:4

Again, the difficulty with Revelation is not so much in interpreting it as it is in believing it. Dr. Newel says of this Sixth Trumpet ... *believe and you scarcely need comment*. This judgment will parallel the tenth plague in Exodus.

And it came to pass at midnight that the LORD struck all the firstborn in the land of Egypt, from the firstborn of Pharaoh who sat on his throne to the firstborn of the captive who was in the dungeon, and all the firstborn of livestock. So Pharaoh rose in the night, he, all his servants, and all the Egyptians; and there was a great cry in Egypt, for there was not a house where there was not one dead. Exodus 12:29-30

Rev. 9:20-21

But the rest of mankind, who were not killed by these plagues, **did not repent** of the works of their hands, that they should not worship demons, and idols of gold, silver, brass, stone, and wood, which can neither see nor hear nor walk. And they did not repent of their **murders** or their [**NU changes "sorceries" to "drugs"**] or their **sexual immorality** or their **thefts**.

This certainly tags down the hardness of heart that will be the hallmark of the people who are left on Earth during the closing days of the Great Tribulation. It is significant that their sins read like today's newspaper. This is yet another indicator that you and I are living very close to the days being described here.

John says they **did not repent.** Again, this demonstrates that God's purpose, even at this very late hour, is still aimed at remedy of life. It will still be his desire that men and women repent and turn to his Christ for salvation. But, they will not. They are all in the same boat now. Our text says ... **But the rest of mankind ... did not repent**... This statement includes all the remaining Jews who have not turned to Christ at that late hour. *Ezekiel 33:11*, comes to my mind...

Say to them, 'As I live,' says the Lord GOD, **'I have no pleasure in the death of the wicked, but that the wicked turn from his way and live**. *Turn, turn from your evil ways! For why should you die, O house of Israel?'*

Though unheeded, God will still be reaching out to wicked Israelites during those final days.

Now, although they are not mentioned here, I believe that most of the 144,000 will no longer be alive on Earth at this time. I say that because the single most important factor in the changing of a human heart is the Word of God. But our text says that the men who were left **did not repent**. This is a strong indicator to me that the Word of God is no longer being preached. Miracles, signs and even direct interventions by God cannot change one human heart. Those things may get people's attention, but there must be hearing of the Word of God in order for lives to be changed. Salvation cannot and does not take place apart from the Word of God. As you have it in *Romans 10:13-14*,

For, 'whoever calls on the name of the LORD shall be saved.' How then shall they call on him in whom they have not believed? And how shall they believe in him of whom they have not heard? And **how shall they hear without a preacher**?

And again, in *First Peter 1:23*,

Being **born again**, *not of corruptible seed, but of incorruptible,* **by the word of God**, *with liveth and abideth forever.* (KJV)

The fact that, after the sixth Trumpet, those who were left did not repent, leads me to believe they have killed off most, if not all, of the 144,000, along with most of the others who were preaching the Word of God to them. And, by doing so, they have unwittingly sealed their own fate. Now, let's look briefly at this list of sins which these Earth-dwellers will be so doggedly refusing to turn away from. It says:

...they **worship demons** and **idols**. This is mankind's oldest and most common sin. First Corinthians 10:19-20, informs us that demon and idol worship are synonymous. It is very prevalent in our day. In India alone, there are an estimated one hundred million plus idols associated with the Hindu religion alone. *Romans 1:22-24*, says,

Professing to be wise, they became fools, and changed the glory of the incorruptible God into an image made like corruptible man; and birds and four-footed animals and creeping things. Therefore, God also gave them up to uncleanness, in the lusts of their hearts, to dishonor their bodies among themselves.

...they refuse to turn from their **murders**. Romans 1, says when men walk away from God, he turns them over to their own evil devices. These devices are enumerated in that chapter and you will find murder is one of them (Romans 1:29). Today's news media is swamped with reports of the murders that are rising like a flood in our day. I give you Chicago for example. This is another indicator of the lateness of the hour in which we are living.

...they refuse to repent of their **drugs**. This Greek word is very interesting. The word is φαρμάκων **(*farmakon*)**. It is the word from which we get our word *pharmacy*. Until recently, it seemed completely illogical to translators of the Bible to translate this word **drugs**, although it is the word's primary meaning. So they translated it **sorceries**. The NIV translates it **magic arts**. However, here at the beginning of the 21st century, it has become quite apparent that the Spirit of God meant exactly what he said! NU's correction in the text is right on. The Spirit said, **drugs**, and he meant **drugs**. Drug abuse is behind much of the crime and lawlessness in the world today and it is a skyrocketing problem around the globe. It has become such a problem in our country that it has caused drug wars in Mexico that are so violent that our state department has feared a total collapse of the Mexican government. It is reported that, in the last few years, nearly fifty thousand people have been murdered over drugs in Mexico alone. Colorado and Washington recently legalized marijuana in order to raise tax revenue by the sale of same. In the days of the blowing of the sixth Trumpet, the Bible says that drugs will be a major problem. And, as far as God is concerned, he will demand that men repent of them. From the looks of it, I would say that day is just around the corner, wouldn't you?

...they refused to repent of their *sexual immorality*. The tremendous increase today in sexual immorality and our society's unwholesome fixation on sex is another indicator of the lateness of the hour. Television, advertising and education is obsessed with sex, sex and more sex. It is alarming how sexual immorality has permeated our country and even our churches in the last decade. Premarital sex and homosexuality has become such accepted norms that both are now actually being taught in public schools at the earliest ages. Right now, laws are being formulated and passed that forbid even speaking out against sexual immorality. A few years back, when I lived in Oregon, I voted on a measure that would forbid promoting homosexuality in the public schools of Oregon. It lost. The airwaves were full of teachers and administrators opposing it. They wanted it taught. The Portland, Oregon school system attempted to ban the Boy Scouts from their campuses because that organization took a stand against homosexuals in positions of leadership. In another instance, one of Portland's police chiefs was found to have taken a stand against homosexuality in a speech at a Christian peace officers conference nearly ten year previously. Upon uncovering that information, immediately a campaign was launched against him to have him fired. Ordination of homosexuals to the ministry is approved and practiced in more and more main line denominations today. Pornography is on every corner and, in the last few years, it has spread into homes across America and the world via the Internet. As a pastor, I frequently encountered Christians who were unashamedly shacking up together. They insisted there was nothing wrong with it. Churches today are filled with people who blatantly give themselves to all manner of sexual immorality. This last wicked generation, of which we are reading, will refuse to repent of their sexual immorality ... just as our generation is doing now.

...they refused to repent of their ***thefts***. Nothing speaks louder of one's self-absorption than stealing from one's neighbor. My daughter told me that if she wanted to get rid of anything in her neighborhood, all she had to do was to leave it out on the front porch. She said she had an old rug they didn't want to pay the garbage men to haul off, so they just put it out on the porch, and sure enough, in short order, it disappeared. Stealing is rampant in America today. Consumers pay billions of dollars in added costs for goods so that stores can be compensated for their shoplifting loses. Don't you think we are very close to these very dark days that are being prophesied here in Revelation?

Well, there we have it. The ***second woe*** (the sixth Trumpet), is past. It will result in the death of one third of earth's remaining sin-hardened peoples. And, those who are left will be adamantly refusing to turn from their wickedness. One ***woe*** is yet to come.

REVELATION 10 - 11:14

THE INTERLUDE BETWEEN THE 6TH AND 7TH TRUMPET

We come now to **the second interlude** in the book of Revelation. Just as there was an interlude between the sixth and seventh Seals, this is **the interlude between the sixth and seventh Trumpets**. These interludes are given to fill us in on many additional and pertinent pieces of information before the text continues on with the linear action of the ongoing judgments of the Tribulation. During the interlude between the sixth and seventh Seals (chapter 7), we were introduced to the 144,000 and an innumerable multitude of Tribulation Saints. Here in this second interlude, we will be introduced to several things, namely:

1. Three crucial **personalities** of that future day.

2. The fulfillment of *the mystery of God* on Earth.

3. A strategic and all important Jewish *temple* at Jerusalem that will play a key role during the Great Tribulation.

Here in chapter 10, we will be introduced to one of these personalities as well as the concept of the *mystery of God* as it applies to these final days of world history that we are studying.

Rev. 10:1-4

*I saw still **another mighty angel** coming down from heaven, clothed with a cloud. And a **rainbow** was on his head, **his face was like the sun**, and his **feet like pillars of fire**. He had a little **book** open in his hand. And he set his right foot on the **sea** and his left foot on the*

Strange Work

*land, and cried with a loud voice, as when a lion roars. When he cried out, **seven thunders uttered their voices**.* *Now when the seven thunders* **[NU changes** *"uttered their voices"* **to** *"sounded"*] *I was about to write; but I heard a voice from heaven saying,* **[NU omits** *"to me"*] *'Seal up the things which the seven thunders uttered, and **do not write them**.'*

10:1

From a literary point of view, someone has said, *No greater scene, no more riveting passage or personage, no more majestic event is found written in ancient literature than the Mighty Angel of Revelation ten.* That certainly is true. Let's look at him and see if we can determine his identity. The description that is presented to us here is an awesome one indeed. We read:

...he was **clothed with a cloud**. I take this to be a reference to the *Shekinah* (glory) of God (see page 12 ... Revelation :1:7).

...a **rainbow was on his head**. Rainbows are God's designated sign of the Noahic Covenant (Gen. 9:12-17). Wherever a rainbow is found, it that speaks to God of his covenant with Noah never to destroy the Earth again with water. Not, mind you, that God needs any reminders. But, he has chosen to have that sign before him at all times. That's why one is around his throne. There are literally thousands of rainbows on the Earth that are visible to God at any one point in time. God is a covenant making and keeping God. His Word is his bond.

...his face **was like the sun**. He possessed great glory. You will remember that Jesus was seen having such resplendence, back in chapter one, where we read, **and his countenance was as the sun shining in his strength**.

...his feet and legs burned **like pillars of fire**. This too is a parallel to the description of Christ back in 1:15, which spoke of the fact that he was the one who will carry out all of the judgments of God.

...his **voice** was **as when a lion roars**. His voice added great authority to his overall demeanor. When he spoke, people and spirits listened.

...in his **hand** he held the now opened scroll from chapter 5. The scroll was a **little book** now since the majority of events that were written in it had already been revealed. However, there was still more to come. The actual number of events that will yet take place after the blowing of the seventh Trumpet are relatively few, however. Time-wise, here in chapter ten, we are very close to the end of the Great Tribulation, perhaps within mere days or even hours of Christ's Second Coming.

If John had not specifically called this amazing personage *another strong angel*, who would you have taken him to be? Jesus, am I right? And, that is a very common interpretation. However, this is not Christ for several reasons which we will shortly see. But, if he is not Christ, who is he? I believe this to be a very unique and special archangel of God. In fact, he is the only archangel who is named in the Bible. His name is Michael. His name means, *who is like God*. This explains his appearance, does it not? If you and I were to see the archangel, Michael, we would think we were looking at God himself! He truly must be a sight to behold and a personality extraordinaire. Apparently, God created him specifically to visibly reflect many of his own attributes. Michael is also found in the following scriptures:

*Yet **Michael the archangel**, in contending with the devil, when he disputed about the body of Moses, dared not bring against him a reviling accusation, but said, The Lord rebuke you! Jude 9*

*At that time **Michael** shall **stand up**, **The great prince who stands watch over the sons of your people**; and there shall be a time of **trouble**, such as never was since there was a nation, even to that time. And at that time your people shall be delivered, everyone who is found written in the book. Daniel 12:1*

Notice that, in the Daniel prophecy, it clearly says that Michael will play a key role in relation to Israel during the Great Tribulation. It specifically says that Michael will intervene on behalf of the Jews during *a time of trouble such as never was since there was a nation*. Also, it predicts, *at that time your people shall be delivered.* So, Michael will be instrumental in the help of the Jewish people during the Great Tribulation. He will do battle for them in the spiritual realm and be a key element in their help and preservation. We will get more details about this standing up for the Jews when we get to chapter 12. There, we find that it is Michael who will ultimately toss Satan out of Heaven.

10:2-4

What a scene John saw here in relation to this mighty archangel of God. Back in chapter 4, John was told to *come up here and I will show*

you things that must be hereafter. This event, beloved, is one of those ***things***. What we are reading about here, that John witnessed, will actually occur in history one day. I believe you and I will actually see this event for ourselves, when Michael **stands up** (Dan. 12:1), thunders his powerful proclamation and then, sets out on his mission to help the Jews, down on the earth.

As John continued to watch, the mighty angel took a huge stance, planting one great foot on the land and the other on the sea. In his left hand, was the **little book** that was given to Christ back in chapter 5. You will remember that it contained the complete program of just exactly how Christ's kingdom and eternal dominion would come about on the Earth. What a scene! Clutching this great document in his left hand and lifting his right up to Heaven above ... like a mighty conqueror ... he let out a lion-like roar! It was a battle cry. It was like a trumpet sounding a cavalry charge. And immediately his cry was answered by **seven thunders** from Heaven above. In reality, this was the voice of God. The term, **seven thunders**, is an ancient Jewish idiom for the "voice of God." The scholar and grammarian, Vincent, says that the Jews spoke of thunder as the *seven voices of God.* John was about to write what the **seven thunders** said, when another voice said, ***Seal up the things which the seven thunders uttered, and do not write them.***

Why do you suppose John was told not to write God's response to his mighty angel's cry? Well, God always has the right to be God, does he not? With him there will always be mysteries and unrevealed things. This is a reminder of that reality. I believe we will continue to encounter mysteries from and about God throughout eternity. The main thing though is that we trust him even when he does not see fit to reveal all that we would like to know. In those times, when we do not have all the answers, by faith we must simply lean on him though our finite minds may not grasp his purposes. Some time ago, I read that a wonderful Christian leader and educator that I highly respect had been diagnosed with Parkinson's disease. My first reaction was to ask, *Why, Lord? Why that dear saint, of all people*? And, you know, God didn't answer. That was because, frankly, it was none of my business. God will be God. My assignment is to trust him, not to understand everything he does or allows. His secrets are his glory and our opportunity to exercise faith. As you have it in *Proverbs 25:2a*:

*It is the glory of God to **conceal a matter**...*

Rev. 10:5-7

The angel whom I saw standing on the sea and on the land raised up his **[NU: adds *"right"*]** *hand to heaven and swore by him who lives forever and ever, who created heaven and the things that are in it, the earth and the things that are in it, and the sea and the things that are in it, that there should be **delay no longer**, but **in the days of the sounding of the seventh angel**, when he is about to sound, **the mystery of God would be finished**, as he declared to his servants the prophets.*

Next, the mighty angel *swore by him who lives forever and ever, who created heaven and the things that are in it, the earth and the things that are in it, and the sea and the things that are in it*. Make no mistake about it, Michael's oath was grounded on the Person of the Lord Jesus Christ. God's unique Son is the one who *lives forever and ever* and who created heaven and Earth. As we had it back in 1:18:

*I am he who **lives**, and was dead, and **behold I am alive forevermore**. Amen.*

Speaking of Christ as the Creator, *Colossians 1:16* says,

*For by him all things were **created** that are in **heaven** and that are on **earth**, visible and invisible, whether thrones or dominions or principalities or powers. **All things were created through him** and for him.*

And again, in *John 1:3*,

*All things were **made** through him, and without him nothing was made that was made.*

And, as you have it in *Hebrews 1:1-3*,

*God, who at various times and in various ways spoke in time past to the fathers by the prophets, has in these last days spoken to us by his Son, whom he has appointed heir of all things, **through whom also he made the worlds**; who being the brightness of his glory and the express image of his person, and upholding all things by the word of his power, when he had by himself purged our sins, sat down at the right hand of the Majesty on high...*

So, the mighty angel swore his dramatic oath in Jesus name. In His matchless name, the angel swore that *there should be delay no longer, but in the days of the sounding of the seventh angel, when he is about to sound, the mystery of God would be finished*. Now, it is very important here to get the translation straight. The problem lies in the phrase, *about to sound*. The King James Version correctly renders it, *when he shall begin to sound*. Grammatically, it could be rendered either way, but it is clear from the whole of Scripture that the *mystery of God* will not be *finished* before, nor during, the days when the seventh angel is blowing his trumpet. Rather, it will be completed **after** this all important seventh Trumpet ceases to sound. In point of time, *the mystery of God* will not be completed for over a thousand years after the seventh angel blows his Trumpet. I will address that further in a bit. Now, just exactly what is *the mystery of God*? Let's look to the Scripture for the answer. Consider the following scriptures:

Ephesians 3:3-5

*...by revelation he made known unto me **the mystery** (as I have briefly written already, by which, when you read, you may understand my knowledge in the mystery of Christ), which in other ages was not made known to the sons of men, as it has now been revealed by the Spirit to his holy apostles and prophets.*

Isaiah 25:6-7, says,

And in this mountain [Zion, at Jerusalem] *shall the Lord of hosts make unto all people a feast of fat things of wines on the lees, of fat things full of marrow, of wines on the lees well refined. And **he will destroy in this mountain the face of the covering cast over all people, and the veil that is spread over all nations**.*

The *mystery of God*, to which the angel was referring then, is Christ Jesus himself and refers to just who Jesus truly is. After the *days of the sounding of the seventh angel*, the God-Man will no longer be a *mystery*. By the end of those *days*, there will no longer be any question in all of God's wide universe, or any other realm, about the person of the Lord Jesus Christ. Presently, Jesus is a *mystery* to the vast majority of people in our world. Even here in gospel saturated America, his person remains a mystery to most people. At his Second Coming when *every eye will see him*, the mystery of Christ will be cleared up for all who are living at that point in time. After that, however, subsequent generations will have their enlightenment as they *feast* (Isaiah 26:6-7 above) with Christ at Jerusalem. But, *the mystery of God* will, even then, not be *complete* until all men of all time understand who Jesus is. This will not come about until the end of the Millennium. The Millennium itself falls under the seventh Trumpet. After the final battle of Gog and Magog, at the end of the Millennium (Rev. 20:8), this mighty angel's prophecy will reach its ultimate fulfillment. What a wonderful day that will be, when the *mystery of God* is cleared up once and for all and for all time. Then the words of *Philippians 2:9b-11*, will find their ultimate fulfillment.

...*that at the name of Jesus every knee should bow, of those in heaven, and of those on earth, and of those under the earth, and that every tongue should confess that Jesus Christ is Lord, to the glory of God the Father.*

Rev. 10:8-11

Then the voice which I heard from heaven spoke to me again and said, **'Go, take the little book** *which is open in the hand of the angel who stands on the sea and on the earth.' So I went to the angel and said to him, 'Give me the little book.' And he said to me,* **'Take and eat it***; and it will make your stomach **bitter**, but it will be as sweet as **honey** in your mouth.' Then I took the little book out of the angel's hand and ate it, and it was as sweet as honey in my mouth. But when I had eaten it, my stomach became bitter. And* **[NU omits "he" and adds "they"]** *said to me,* **'You must prophesy again about many peoples, nations, tongues, and kings.'**

John was told to approach the mighty angel and take the little book from his hand. When he obeyed, the angel told him to **take and eat it**. This is a familiar symbolism in the Bible. It meant that what remained of the little book was now to become the rest of the subject matter of John's writing and preaching. This remainder of Christ's scroll contained all the rest of the program of God for Christ and his kingdom. Though much of it had already been revealed, there was still more to be looked at. This same symbolism is found in Ezekiel. There we read,

*Now when I looked, **there was a hand stretched out to me**; and **behold, a scroll of a book** was in it. Ezekiel 2:9*

*Moreover he said to me, 'Son of man, **eat** what you find; **eat this scroll**, and go, speak to the house of Israel. So I **opened my mouth**, and he caused me to eat that scroll. And he said to me, 'Son of man, feed your belly, and fill your stomach with this scroll that I give you.' **So I ate**, and it was in my mouth like **honey** in sweetness. Then he said to me: 'Son of man, go to the house of Israel and speak with my words to them'. Ezekiel 3:1-4*

*So the Spirit lifted me up and took me away, and **I went in bitterness**, in the heat of my spirit; but the hand of the LORD was strong upon me. Ezekiel 3:14*

Like Ezekiel, when eating the scroll, John found it was *sweet* to his tongue but became *bitter* in his stomach. In Ezekiel's case, this was because the words in the book he ate contained both blessings (sweet), and curses (bitter), grace (sweetness) and judgment (bitterness) concerning Israel. The scope is much broader with Christ's **little book**, however. It contained both blessings and curses upon the whole world. John would find them to be both *bitter* and *sweet* to think and speak about. Nevertheless, he was told he must tell them to **many peoples, nations, tongues and kings**. This is why, when we read the book of Revelation, it is sometimes very sweet to us and, at other times very bitter as well.

The vision ends with both the archangel and the Father saying, in effect, ***John, you've got your work cut out for you. You must tell the rest of the story. You must get this Word out to many people***. Way down here, some twenty odd centuries later, we realize this included us, dear reader. The Apostle John got those bittersweet words out, didn't he!? Now it is up to us to get them out as well. Let me share something else here before we move on. Both John and Ezekiel symbolically ate God's Word. The Word of God is something to be experienced, brother and sister. Have you been experiencing it ... eating it up? If not, you're missing out on God's best for you. Jeremiah said,

*Your words were found, and I **ate** them, and **your word was to me the joy and rejoicing of my heart**; for I am called by your name, O LORD God of hosts. Jeremiah 15:16*

Psalm 119:103, says,

*How **sweet** are your words to my taste, sweeter than **honey** to my mouth!*

I am convinced that the greatest need of God's people in the world today is that they be systematically and regularly partaking of the Word of God. Do you read your Bible? Do you feast daily on the Word of Christ? Do you allow it to ***dwell*** down ***in you richly*** (Col. 3:16)? By doing so, you are sitting at Jesus' feet, you know. Therein lies salvation, victory over sin, wisdom, knowledge, fellowship with God, evangelism, the filling of the Holy Spirit and much more. None of these things, however, can be acquired apart from the regular intake of the Word of God. You and I, like John and Ezekiel, need to be assimilating the Word of God so it can work its life-changing power in and through us. There was a fellow, where I once worked, who gave his heart to Christ. The striking thing though, was that he immediately began to devour the Bible like no one I had ever known before. In six short months he had read the entire Bible through and many of its books several times over. Needless to say, his love for the Savior was remarkable and his testimony for Christ was powerful and without reservation. Is it any wonder the Spirit of God began to use him in the lives of other people? There are no shortcuts, beloved. Read the Word.

*...like newborn babes, **long** for the pure milk of the **Word**, that by it you may grow in respect to salvation... First Peter 2:2* (NAS)

*Let the word of Christ **dwell in you** richly in all wisdom... Colossians 3:16a* (KJV)

*If ye abide in me, and **my words abide in you**, ye shall ask what ye will, and it shall be done unto you. Herein is my Father glorified, that ye bear much fruit; so shall ye be my disciples. John 15:7-8* (KJV)

We continue here in chapter 11, with the interlude between the sixth and seventh Trumpets and we will be given three more crucial pieces of information before we return to the ongoing events of the Great Tribulation. We will learn that during the days of the Great Tribulation:

1. A Jewish ***temple*** will be located at Jerusalem.

2. Two men will appear on the earth who will be incredible *witnesses* for Christ.
3. A *beast* will reign over all the earth who is Antichrist.

Before we look at this passage, let me share a thought or two about this future *temple* at Jerusalem. For the past nineteen hundred plus years, the Jewish people have had no home or national identity in their Biblical homeland. Only in my generation have they stepped back out upon the world stage as a nation. In 1948, when I was eight years old, they achieved that status. Since that momentous year, many Jews have returned to the homeland of their fathers. It has been intriguing to watch, to say the least. Furthermore, after the Six Day War, they captured and now control their ancient capital of Jerusalem. However, prophetically speaking, there are still many pieces of the puzzle that are still missing. One major piece is the temple. It must be rebuilt at Jerusalem in order to fulfill many prophecies concerning the last days. However, one of Islam's holy places, the Dome of the Rock, stands squarely on the site where the Jews' ancient temple once stood and where the Jews' new temple must be rebuilt. That is a problem. Therefore, the temple mount continues to be a major source of friction between the Jews and the followers of Islam. Orthodox Jews still hope and plan to build their temple there. As far back as 1967, a group of American Jews placed an ad in the Washington Post soliciting donations to purchase building materials for this temple. Not long ago, on the Internet, I found multiple web sites dealing with the rebuilding of the Jew's temple at Jerusalem. It is a current affairs issue today. Malachi, prophesying the Second Coming of Messiah, said,

*Behold, I send my messenger, and he will prepare the way before me. And the Lord, whom you seek, will suddenly come to **his temple**, even the Messenger of the covenant, in whom you delight. Behold, he is coming, Says the LORD of hosts. But who can endure the day of his coming? And who can stand when he appears? For he is like a refiner's fire and like launderer's soap. He will sit as a refiner and a purifier of silver; he will purify the sons of Levi, and purge them as gold and silver, that they may **offer to the LORD an offering** in righteousness. Malachi 3:1-3*

Daniel, speaking of Antichrist's wheeling and dealings during the Tribulation, said,

*But in the middle of the week **he shall bring an end to sacrifice and offering**. And on the wing of abominations shall be one who makes desolate, even until the consummation, which is determined, is poured out on the desolate. Daniel 9:27*

Jesus, speaking of this very prophecy, said that this **abomination** would take place in the Holy of Holies, ναοῦ (*naou* from *naos*), the holiest inner sanctum of the *temple* saying,

*Therefore when you see the 'abomination of desolation,' spoken of by Daniel the prophet, standing in the **holy place** [**naos**] (whoever reads, let him understand), then let those who are in Judea flee to the mountains. Matthew 24:15-16*

There are a good many things to study in the above sited scriptures concerning the temple but first, let's talk about their time periods for a minute. Daniel's prophecy above spoke of a *week* and *the middle of the week* during which Antichrist would make and then break a covenant with the Jews. When this occurs, Daniel said Antichrist will cause the *sacrifice and offering* to *cease*. The weeks that Daniel is speaking of have been proven by Biblical scholars to be prophetic weeks of years. That is, each one of Daniel's weeks actually equal a time period of seven years. *The middle of the week* then would mean three and a half years into it. See Appendix B for a more detailed discussion of this. Also, I refer you to Sir Robert Anderson's book, **The Coming Prince**, for the classic work on these prophetic years. When the prophecy from Daniel 9 is carefully analyzed, we glean the following facts:

...When Antichrist, who both Daniel and Jesus said would bring about **the abomination of desolation**, begins his rise to power, amongst his first official acts as world dictator will be to enter into a seven year treaty with the Jewish people (*he shall confirm a covenant with many for one week*). A key part of that treaty will very likely grant the Jewish people the right to rebuild their temple on its original site, removing the Dome of the Rock. This future temple at Jerusalem will be the fourth on that site. The first three were:

Solomon's Temple... destroyed by Nebuchadnezzar in 586 BC

Ezra's Temple ... completed on March 12, 515 BC (Ezra 6:15)

Herod's Temple ... Ezra's temple was remodeled and expanded during Jesus' lifetime and subsequently destroyed by the Romans in AD 70. There has been no temple at Jerusalem since that time.

...At the mid-point of Antichrist's seven year covenant with the Jews, he will break his treaty and seize their temple at Jerusalem. Then, he will institute the worship of himself at the Jew's temple. Emperor Worship will once again be instituted on Earth, following the ancient practice of the Roman Caesars who were before him. *Second Thessalonians 2:3-4* speaks of this:

*Let no one deceive you by any means; for that day will not come unless the falling away comes first, and the man of sin is revealed, the son of perdition, who opposes and **exalts himself above all that is called God** or that is worshiped, **so that he sits as God in the temple of God**, showing himself that **he is God**.*

Jesus forewarned the Jews that this day would come when Antichrist would break his treaty with them saying,

*...when you see the abomination of desolation **standing in the holy place** spoken of by Daniel the prophet, let those who are in Judea flee to the mountains. Matthew 24:15-16*

When Antichrist breaks his covenant with the Jews, like Hitler before him, he will then begin a systematic attempt to exterminate them. That's why Jesus warned them that, when they saw these things come to pass, they were not to waste any time getting out of town. The point is, there will be a temple at Jerusalem during the Great Tribulation so that all these things can be fulfilled.

Rev. 11:1-2

*Then I was given a reed like a **measuring rod**. And the angel stood, saying, 'Rise and measure the **temple of God**, the altar, and those who worship there. But **leave out the court** which is outside the temple, and do not measure it, for it has been given to the Gentiles. And they will tread the holy city underfoot for **forty-two months**.'*

Now, let's look at this passage. You will remember, in chapter 10, John's vision of the **mighty angel** took place down on Earth. He is still down on the earth here. He saw a **temple** and was told to **measure the temple of God, the altar, and those who worship there.** There are two important things to note here:

First, this *temple* is real. The command to measure it emphasizes the reality of that temple in that future day. It is something you can lay a line to.

Second, it belongs to God, as does the altar and all *those who worship there* (the Jews). Measuring is an act of ownership. The temple, the altar and the Jews who worship there in that future day belong to God. They are his possessions and the Jews are his chosen covenant people. However, the angel instructs that the outer *court* of the temple is not to be measured because *it has been given to the Gentiles and they will tread the holy city underfoot for forty-two months* (three and a half years). The outer court was called the Court of the Gentiles in Jesus' day because that was as far as a Gentile was allowed to enter into the temple area. During the three and a half year Great Tribulation, it will still function in that capacity.

When you put the pieces of the puzzle together, it goes something like this. At the beginning of the Tribulation, Antichrist will make a seven year treaty with the Jewish people, allowing them to dwell safely in their homeland and to rebuild and worship unhindered at their temple (Daniel 9:27). However, three and a half years into that treaty, he will break his treaty, turning on the Jews and seizing their temple. Then he will blasphemously establish himself there to be worshipped (Daniel. 9:27; Matthew 24:15-16; 2 Thessalonians 2:3-4). From that day on, Antichrist's worshippers will come from all over the world to stand in the outer *court* of the Gentiles, bringing their gifts and sacrifices to him. That's why the angel told John not to measure it. During those days, that area will not belong to God. This detail is fascinating because, apparently, Antichrist worship at the temple will have the same restrictions as was imposed in the Old Testament on the Jews so that no one but his priests will be allowed to enter the Temple proper. Satan is such a counterfeiter. And, so will his man, Antichrist, be! I suspect that only the False Prophet, acting as High Priest, will be able to enter into the Holy of Holies where the *abomination of desolation* (Antichrist's image?) will sit (Matthew 24:15). So, **the temple at Jerusalem is a key ingredient** in the outworking of the events of the last days. It will serve as:

...A Jewish place of worship during the first half of the Tribulation

...A possession for Antichrist to seize for his own at the middle of the Tribulation

...The center for Antichrist worship during the last three and a half years (the Great Tribulation)

...The temple to which Jesus will return at his Second Coming. After setting foot on the Mount of Olives, our Lord will enter Jerusalem through the Eastern Gate *suddenly* coming to his temple as prophesied in Malachi 3:1. This was foreshadowed, by the way, when he rode the donkey colt into that city on Palm Sunday some two thousand years ago. Do you remember where he went? He went directly to Herod's temple and unexpectedly pounced upon the thieves there! Having made himself a whip, he cleaned the place out crying,

It is written, 'my house is the house of prayer,' but you have made it a den of thieves! Luke 19:46

These truths are very exciting. You and I are very likely living at the very edge of the fulfillment of these prophecies. There is such a stirring of the Jews in the land of Palestine today and there is such tension over Jerusalem and the Temple Mount there. Thousands of Jews gather daily there for prayer at the Wailing Wall (all that is left of Solomon's temple). Tensions with their enemies continue to escalate over that all-important city and temple site. Never has the Church seen such exciting signs that the close of the age is drawing to its conclusion!

Rev. 11:3-6

*And I will give power to my **two witnesses**, and they will prophesy **one thousand two hundred and sixty days**, clothed in sackcloth. These are the two olive trees and the two lampstands standing before the* **[NU changes "God" to "Lord"]** *of the earth.* ***And if anyone wants to harm them, fire proceeds from their mouth and devours their enemies****. And if anyone wants to harm them, he must be killed in this manner. These have power to shut heaven, so that no rain falls in the days of their prophecy; and they have power over waters to turn them to blood, and **to strike the earth with all plagues, as often as they desire**.*

11:3

The Old Testament prophets foretold that Messiah would have two forerunners. Because only one is specifically named in Scripture, the Jews only recognize one. The forerunner that the Scripture names, is Elijah. As you have it in *Malachi 4:5-6*:

Behold, I will send you **Elijah** *the prophet* **before the coming of the great and dreadful day of the LORD**. *And he will turn the hearts of the fathers to the children, and the hearts of the children to their fathers, lest I come and strike the earth with a curse.*

Orthodox Jews still look for Elijah to appear. Every year, they symbolically set a place for him at their tables during Passover. Elijah will indeed be sent to Earth, just as Malachi prophesied, **before the great and dreadful day of the Lord** (the Great Tribulation).

The second prophesied forerunner of Christ appeared on the scene at his first coming. He was John the Baptist. When the Pharisees asked him who he was, he replied that he was the one of whom Isaiah spoke when he said,

The voice of one crying in the wilderness: *'Prepare the way of the LORD; make straight in the desert a highway for our God.' Isaiah 40:3*

It is important to note that Jesus also tied John the Baptist to Malachi's prophecy of his Second Coming. In *Luke 7:27,* he said, concerning John,

This is **he** *of whom it is* **written**: *'Behold, I send my messenger before your face, who will prepare your way before you…' Malachi 3:1a*

Jesus stopped his quote right in the middle of the verse. The rest of that verse, however, is of weighty import because it goes on to say, **and the Lord, whom you seek, shall suddenly come to his Temple.** These words refer to the time of the end of the Great Tribulation when Christ will return to his temple and begin his earthly reign. It seems to me, this is strong evidence that one of the two witnesses here in Revelation 11 is John the Baptist. It also seems logical that both of the two witnesses in Revelation 11 would be Messiah's two prophesied forerunners, Elijah and John the Baptist. Luke 1:17 also links these two prophets together. I believe that both of these powerful prophets will be on the scene during the three and a half year Great Tribulation, just prior to the Lord's Second Coming. When they appear, what a dynamic duo these two forerunners of the Messiah will make, aye? Let's look a bit closer at them.

In verse three, it says, ***and I will give power to my two witnesses, and they shall prophesy***. Clearly, they will be preaching in that day. Both Malachi and Isaiah confirm that the Messiah's forerunners will be preachers. Our text says they will prophesy for ***one thousand two hundred and sixty days*** (three and a half years), clothed in sackcloth. Sackcloth is the ancient Jewish clothing worn for mourning. There are many good reasons why these two witnesses will dress that way. I can think of a half dozen off the top of my head. They will dress in sackcloth because:

…Thousands of believing Jews and Gentiles will be suffering and dying daily for their faith in Christ.

…Countless other Jews and Gentiles will be perishing from off the earth to go off into a Christless eternity.

…A great number of Jews (2/3rds) will be stubbornly refusing the two witnesses' preaching and be continuing on in their obstinate refusal to believe in Christ.

…Satan's deceptions and distortions will be everywhere.

…Immorality and sin will be rampant.

…And last, but most importantly, Antichrist will sit in the Jew's temple … being worshipped there.

Sackcloth will be very appropriate attire under such conditions as these, wouldn't you say?

11:4-6

John continues … ***They are the two olive trees and the two lampstands standing before the Lord of the earth***. This is a direct reference to the symbolism of Zechariah 4. That passage refers to Joshua and Zerubbabel, two Spirit filled servants of God in their day. The meaning is identical here. This is simply saying the ***two witnesses*** will be Spirit filled men as well. Remarkably, the Bible says that John the Baptist was filled with the Holy Spirit from his mother, Elizabeth's, womb (Luke1:15). And, Elijah was so Spirit filled that when his successor, Elisha, asked for a double portion of his Spirit …

Elijah told him that he didn't know if that was possible (2 Kings 2:9-10)! These two men were mighty Spirit filled servants of God in the past and so, I believe, they will be again ... during the dark days of the Great Tribulation.

Notice here, what raw supernatural power they will possess. The text says, ***And if anyone wants to harm them, fire proceeds from their mouth and devours their enemies***. Literally? Yes, they will be formidable and invulnerable witnesses indeed. I suspect there will be precious few attempts made on their lives, however, after their enemies get a taste of the fiery consequences of such attempts! Elijah, by the way, called down fire from heaven on his enemies when King Ahab tried to arrest him. Do you remember that? We read about it in *Second Kings 1:9-10*:

*Then the king sent to him a captain of fifty with his fifty men. So he went up to him; and there he was, sitting on the top of a hill. And he spoke to him: 'Man of God, the king has said, Come down!' So Elijah answered and said to the captain of fifty, **'If I am a man of God, then let fire come down from heaven and consume you and your fifty men.' And fire came down from heaven and consumed him and his fifty**.*

Elijah was not easily arrested back then ... nor will he or John the Baptist be, in the days of their testimony during the Great Tribulation. Also, notice it says that these two witnesses will have power to ***shut heaven, so that no rain falls in the days of their prophecy***. That is something that Elijah also did in the past. Further, it says they will have power ***over the waters to turn them to blood*** and to ***strike the earth with all plagues as often as they desire***. Boy, are they going to be thorns in the side of Antichrist and his followers. Some take this last statement as grounds for assuming the other witness is Moses because he too used such plagues. But, personally, I believe the evidence that he is John the Baptist is far more weighty and compelling. Herod had a great fear that John the Baptist would come back from the grave, by the way (Matthew 14:1-2). And, I am confident, so he shall.

Rev. 11:7-14

*When they finish their testimony, the **beast that ascends out of the bottomless pit** will make war against them, overcome them, and kill them. And their dead bodies will lie in the street of **the great city which spiritually is called Sodom and Egypt,** where also [**NU changes "our"**] **their Lord was crucified**. Then those from the peoples, tribes, tongues, and nations will see their dead bodies three-and-a-half days, and not allow their dead bodies to be put into graves. And those who dwell on the earth will **rejoice** over them, make merry, and send gifts to one another, because these two prophets tormented those who dwell on the earth. Now **after the three-and-a-half days the breath of life from God entered them, and they stood on their feet**, and great **fear** fell on those who saw them. And they heard a loud voice from heaven saying to them, 'Come up here.' And they ascended to heaven in a cloud, and their enemies saw them. In the same hour there was a great earthquake, and a tenth of the city fell. In the earthquake seven thousand people were killed, and the rest were afraid and gave glory to the God of heaven. The second woe is past. Behold, the third woe is coming quickly.*

11:7-10

We come now to a third personality to be introduced to us here in Revelation 11. This is the first of thirty-six references to **the beast** in Revelation. It is one of the names for Antichrist. We haven't encountered him under this name in Scripture before. However, this name will be used extensively to refer to him from here on. Our text says that he **ascends out of the bottomless pit**. I believe this refers to his miraculous resurrection which we will look at when we get to Revelation 13.

Second Thessalonians 2, clearly tells us Antichrist will be a man. At this point, it would be helpful to read some of the several scriptures that refer to this fellow. They are as follows:

He shall speak pompous words against the Most High, *shall* **persecute the saints of the Most High**, *and shall intend to change times and law. Then the saints shall be given into his hand for a time and times and half a time.* [three and a half years] *But the court shall* *be seated, and **they*** [I take this to be a reference to the Trinity] *shall take away his dominion, to consume and destroy it forever. Daniel 7:25-26*

*And forces shall be mustered by him, and they shall defile the sanctuary fortress; then they shall **take away the daily sacrifices**, and **place there the abomination of desolation**. Those who do wickedly against the covenant he shall corrupt with flattery; but the people who know their God shall be strong, and carry out great exploits. **And those of the people who understand*** [I take this to be the 144,000 and others] ***shall instruct many**; yet for many days they shall fall by sword and flame, by captivity and plundering. Now when they fall, they shall be aided with a little help; but many shall join with them by intrigue. And some of those of understanding shall fall, to **refine** them, **purify** them, and make them white, until the time of the end; because it is still for the appointed time. Then the **king** shall do according to his own will: **he shall exalt and magnify himself above every god**, shall **speak blasphemies against the God of gods**, and shall prosper till the wrath has been accomplished; for what has been determined shall be done. He shall regard neither the God of his fathers nor the desire of women, nor regard any god; for he **shall exalt himself above them all**. But in their place he shall honor a **god** of fortresses;* [I take this "god" to be Satan] *and a god which his fathers did not know he shall honor with gold and silver, with precious stones and pleasant things. Thus he shall act against the strongest fortresses with a foreign god, which he shall acknowledge, and advance its glory; and he shall cause them to rule over many, and divide the land for gain. Daniel 11:31-39*

*Let no one deceive you by any means; for that day will not come unless the falling away comes first, and **the man of sin is revealed**, the son of perdition, **who opposes and exalts himself above all that is called God or that is worshipped, so that he sits as God in the temple of God, showing himself that he is God**. Second Thessalonians 2:3-4*

*And then **the lawless one** will be revealed, whom the Lord will consume with the breath of his mouth and destroy with the brightness of his coming. **The coming of the lawless one is according to the working of Satan, with all power, signs, and lying wonders, and with all unrighteous deception among those who perish**, because they did* *not receive the love of the truth, that they might be saved. Second Thessalonians 2:8-10*

*Little children, it is the last hour; and as you have heard that the **Antichrist** is coming, even now many antichrists have come, by which we know that it is the last hour. First John 2:18*

Returning to our text, we read that when the **two witnesses** finished their testimony the **beast will make war against them, overcome them and kill them**. Verse eight tells us this will occur at Jerusalem. The phrase, **where also their Lord was crucified,** tags down that location as the place of their deaths. It goes on to say that Jerusalem, during those future dark days, is spiritually **called Sodom and Egypt**. She is called **Sodom** because of the sin and perversions that will exist in her during Antichrist's reign. And, she is called **Egypt** because of her persecution of God's people, the Jews, just as they experienced when in bondage in Egypt so long ago. Now, this is not the first time that Jerusalem has been called Sodom. Isaiah also called her that:

*Hear the word of the LORD, you rulers of **Sodom**; Give ear to the law of our God, you people of Gomorra... Isaiah 1:10*

After Christ's **two witnesses** are slain by Antichrist, our text says their dead bodies will lie in the street of Jerusalem for three and a half days, precipitating a worldwide celebration and viewing of their bodies. This is further evidence of how ripe for judgment the Earth will be in that day. The three and a half days they will be dead corresponds to the three and a half years of their ministry. However, their down time will only be a moment compared to duration of their great ministry. Someone has called this worldwide celebration, *The Devil's Christmas.*

11:11-13

John continues ... **Now after the three and a half days, the breath of life from God entered them and they stood on their feet**. Won't that be something!? Then, when they were taken up to heaven, John says, **and their enemies saw them**. You know, for the past nineteen hundred plus years no one has been able to make heads or tails of just how the entire world could simultaneously look upon these two dead bodies and then observe them ascend up into Heaven. So, for centuries men chalked this prophecy up to just another inaccuracy in the Bible. They said it was physically impossible for all the enemies of God's two witnesses to simultaneously view their dead bodies much less their ascension. With the advent of satellite television and the Internet, however, the how of it has become clear. This is another piece of evidence as to just how close we may be to these actual events. I believe Christ's *two witnesses* will be raised from the dead and ascend into Heaven right in front of a viewing audience of billions! Can you picture it? I can almost hear someone at one of Satan's cocktail parties yell, *Hey look*!!! Then, as all eyes will turn to their TVs, laptops, iPads, cell phones and such like ... there ... where once two dead and mutilated bodies were lying ... they will be seen standing on their feet again. I think I heard a glass break!

Once again, John heard a voice from heaven call out those three special words, *Come up here*, and Christ's *two witnesses* were out of there! Our text says, *great fear fell on those who saw them*. Celebration will turn to horror and then a great earthquake will strike the city called *Sodom* and *Egypt*. Our text says that seven thousand will perish and a tenth part of the city will be knocked to rubble in retaliation for the atrocities Jerusalem had inflicted on the Lord's two witnesses ... no doubt, all right in front of the media of the entire world. Because of the unprecedented nature of these things, our text says that even the ungodly at that time will, in their own impulsive way, *give glory to the God of heaven*.

11:14

In conclusion, our text says the *second woe* (begun by the sixth Trumpet back in 9:12-13) is past and the *third woe* is coming quickly. This also clues us that we have come to the end of the second interlude and will now be returning to the linear action of the Great Tribulation.

REVELATION 11:15 - 19

THE SEVENTH TRUMPET SIGNALS THE BEGINNING OF THE END

We return now to the linear action of the Great Tribulation. The interlude between the sixth and seventh Trumpets is past and we have arrived at what, unquestionably, will be the most epic and dramatic turn in end-time world history ... namely, the sounding of the Seventh Trumpet. Back in chapter 10, the ***mighty angel*** said that in the ***days*** of the sounding of the seventh Trumpet there would be no further delay... but, in those days, he said, ***the mystery of God*** (referring to who the Lord Jesus Christ really is) will be ***finished, as he has declared to his servants, the prophets***. For example, as we have it in *Isaiah 25:6-7*,

The LORD of hosts will prepare a lavish banquet for all peoples on this mountain; A banquet of aged wine, choice pieces with marrow, And refined, aged wine. And on this mountain ***He will swallow up the covering which is over all peoples, even the veil which is stretched over all nations***.

At that point in time, all of Heaven will have been holding its breath for the momentous event of the sounding of the seventh Trumpet for its blast will be the sound of ultimate victory! The seventh trumpet signals that the time for the personal intervention by the Lord Jesus Christ, himself, has now come. The blowing of the seventh Trumpet will begin an unstoppable and methodical march of God to set all things straight in Heaven and Earth, culminating in the complete and irrefutable revelation of who Jesus Christ truly is. When the seventh angel blows his trumpet, Heaven is going to go wild.

Now, let's remind ourselves of the exact timing of this event and what will immediately follow it. Time-wise, the seventh Trumpet will be blown at the very end of the Great Tribulation ... within a matter of days, if not hours, of the Second Coming of the Lord Jesus Christ. Immediately upon the blowing of the seventh Trumpet, Christ's Bowl judgments will be poured out upon the earth in rapid, staccato procession ... like the grand finale of a giant fireworks display. Then, Christ will descend to Earth, dispose of his enemies, enter his temple at Jerusalem and begin his millennial (1000 year) reign here.

Now, it is also important to realize that, from a human standpoint, the days of the seventh Trumpet will encompass a considerable segment of time. Many historic events and the things that are related to them fall under ***the days of the voice of the seventh angel*** (10:7). In order to be clear, let's list them. The ***days*** of the seventh Trumpet will include:

...all of the seven Bowl Judgments

...the complete destruction of Antichrist's capitol, economic, political and religious system

...the annihilation of Antichrist's armies at the battle of Armageddon

...the casting of Antichrist and his False Prophet into the Lake of Fire

...the Second Coming of Christ

...the resurrection and restoration of Israel to their land

...the judgment of the nations

...the one thousand year reign of Christ on Earth

...the final battle of Gog and Magog at the end of the Millennium

...the consignment of Satan to the Lake of Fire

...the resurrection and judgment of all wicked people at the Great White Throne judgment

THE SOUNDING OF THE SEVENTH TRUMPET

Rev. 11:15-19

Then the seventh angel sounded: *and there were loud voices in heaven, saying, 'The* **[NU changes "kingdoms" to the singular here] kingdom of this world has become the kingdom of our Lord and of his Christ, and he shall reign forever and ever!'** *And the twenty-four elders who sat before God on their thrones fell on their faces and* *worshipped God, saying: 'We give you thanks, O Lord God Almighty, The One who is and who was* **[NU omits *"and who is to come"*]** *Because you have taken your great power and reigned.' The nations were angry, and* **your wrath has come, and the time of the dead, that they should be judged, and that you should reward your servants the prophets and the saints**, *and those who fear your name, small and great,* **and should destroy those who destroy the earth**. *Then the temple of God was opened in heaven, and the* **ark of his covenant was seen** *in his temple. And there were lightnings, noises, thunderings, an earthquake, and great hail.*

11:15

When the seventh angel blew his trumpet, pandemonium broke out in Heaven. This was the trumpet that everyone had been waiting for. From this time on, all of God's created intelligences would be able to see the end. The cries of God's saints for intervention, going back to the beginning of time, will now be answered. Here are a couple of those cries from the Psalms:

Arise, **O LORD**, *in thine anger, lift up thyself because of the rage of mine enemies: and awake for me to the judgment that thou hast commanded. Psalm 7:6*

Arise, **O LORD**; *let not man prevail: let the heathen be judged in thy sight. Psalm 9:19*

So, when the seventh angel blew his trumpet, John heard a great jubilation break out in Heaven ... a cacophony of voices ... the like of which, I suspect, had never before been heard there. The air became filled with cries saying, **The kingdom of this world has become the kingdom of our Lord and of his Christ, and he shall reign forever and ever**. The NASV correctly translates the word **kingdom** here in the singular. Both of these words, **kingdom** and *is become* are in the singular. Dr. McGee points out that you and I view this world as divided into little territories of nations with new ones being formed and old ones being deleted or changed from time to time. So, he says, we draw and redraw our little lines on our maps to distinguish their boundaries. But God sees the world as it truly is ... just one dark kingdom ... ruled over by the Prince of Darkness. In Matthew 4:8-9, we read that Satan took Jesus up on a high mountain and offered him all the kingdoms of the world ... provided that Jesus would fall down and worship him. It was a legitimate offer. They were his to give. If this were not so, it would not have been a temptation. Second Corinthians 4:4, calls Satan **the god of this world**. Sin and selfishness, sickness and savagery, death and spiritual darkness, blindness and rebellion, war and graveyards are all hallmarks of this god's **kingdom.** McGee further comments, *God sees Satan's slaves plodding like zombies to fill up the cemeteries.* The sounding of the seventh Trumpet is the beginning of the end to all of this! From that precise point in time, Satan's kingdom will be systematically dismantled by the King of kings and Lord of lords. Hallelujah, indeed!

11:16-18

The twenty-four elders entered into to this jubilation as well and John heard them say, **We give you thanks, O Lord God Almighty, the one who is and who was because you have taken your great power and reigned. The nations were angry, and your wrath has come, and the time of the dead, that they should be judged, and that you should reward your servants the prophets and the saints, and those who fear your name, small and great, and should destroy those who destroy the earth**. These words of praise by the leaders of the Church are the **key** to defining the wide range of time that the ***days*** of the seventh Trumpet encompass. Let's break their declaration down. They proclaim:

...**We give you thanks ... because you have taken your great power and reigned**. When the seventh Angel sounds, God and his Christ truly will have begun to exercise their great power to intervene upon the Earth. From that exact moment on, Satan's grip on this world will begin to slip and his kingdom will begin to unravel.

...**The nations were angry and your wrath has come**. The anger of the nations will have been building throughout the Great Tribulation. Now, God's hot wrath will begin to rain down upon them by means of the Bowl judgments and then reach its apex at the battle of Armageddon. At that battle, all the nations of the earth will be gathered together to experience firsthand the wrath of God's Almighty Lamb.

...And the time of the dead [has come] *that they should be judged*. The judgment of the dead from all time will be set in motion by the blowing of the seventh Trumpet (though not all at one time, nor all on the same day). Jesus said,

*Do not marvel at this; for **the hour is coming** in which **all who are in the graves will hear his voice** [Christ's voice] and come forth; those who have done good, to the resurrection of life, and those who have done evil, to the resurrection of condemnation. John 5:28-29*

...And that you should reward your servants the prophets and the saints. Bear in mind that judgment and rewards are two very different issues in the plan of God. Rewards will be given for faithfulness and fruitfulness. The elders speak here of two different groups who are scheduled for rewards during the *days of the seventh Trumpet*. The Church is not one of them, by the way. She will have already been rewarded, as we noted back in 4:4. The people who the elders are referring to here are Old Testament *prophets* and *saints*. They will receive their rewards after their resurrection at the end of the Great Tribulation. They include such people as Adam and Eve, Enoch, Jonah, Ruth, Hannah, David, Isaiah, Jeremiah, Ezekiel, Hosea, Elijah, Elisha and John the Baptist, the greatest of the Old Testament prophets (Matthew 11:7-11). *Daniel 12:2,* is a key scripture here...

*And many of those who **sleep** in the dust of the earth shall **awake**, some to everlasting life, some to shame and everlasting contempt. Those who are wise shall shine like the brightness of the firmament, and those who turn many to righteousness like the stars forever and ever.*

[Note: Yet another group of saints, the Tribulation saints, will also be resurrected and rewarded at the end of the Great Tribulation. I believe that this is implied in Daniel 12:2. Logic also dictates this and it is my opinion that it will occur in conjunction with the resurrection of Israel and the Old Testament saints.]

...And [you] *should destroy those who destroy the earth*. In conclusion, the elders testify that during the days of the blowing of the seventh Trumpet, Christ will destroy all *those who destroy the earth*. Destruction of the Earth is one of the wanton hallmarks of the wicked. A modern day example that comes to mind was when Saddam Hussein ordered his troops to torch hundreds of oil wells in Kuwait and dump

millions of gallons of oil into the Persian Gulf. The resulting devastation was horrendous and its effects will last for generations. From the beginning of time, wicked men have been destroying God's beautiful Earth, both individually and collectively. Their self-centered, reckless and *devil may care* attitude toward God's creation is witnessed on a daily basis in our world and is well documented in both ancient and modern history.

Think about this for a minute. God placed man over the earth to care for, manage and preserve it. In *Genesis 1:26*, we read,

*And God said, let us make man in our image, after our likeness: and let them have **dominion** over the fish of the sea, and over the fowl of the air, and over the cattle, **and over all the earth**, and over every creeping thing that creepeth upon the earth.* (KJV)

But, when sin entered in, man became Earth's destroyer instead of its keeper. Jesus said,

*The Son of Man will send out his angels, and they will gather **out of his kingdom** all things that **offend**, and those who **practice lawlessness,** and will cast them into the furnace of fire. There will be wailing and gnashing of teeth. Matthew 13:41-42*

For all the destroyers of the earth then, there is a payday coming. It will take place during the days of the blowing of the seventh Trumpet. The elders joyfully confessed that all these things were set in motion when the seventh angel sounded his Trumpet. Truly, on that day, the kingdom of this world will indeed have become *the kingdom of our Lord and his Christ*. When the seventh trumpet sounds, it's a done deal! The process of putting all enemies under the feet of the Son of God will have begun and will be relentlessly executed all the way down to its conclusion at the Great White Throne judgment (Rev. 20).

11:19

At the close of this great and joyous scene **the temple of God was opened in heaven and the ark of his covenant was seen.** Keep in mind that God's **temple** in Heaven is the real one of which the tabernacle of Moses in the wilderness, as well as the later temples of Solomon, Ezra, Herod, and the temple of the Tribulation are mere shadows. Immediately following the jubilation that will erupt at the blowing of the seventh Trumpet, Heaven's temple will once again be opened and men down on Earth will once again be able to see up into Heaven (6:14-17). This time, however, they will be staring directly into the Holy of Holies and will be able to see the **ark of his covenant** there. The *ark* is a distinctly Jewish piece of furniture, by the way. Therefore, I believe this event will be especially aimed at the unbelieving Jews who are still alive on earth at that very late hour. This whole amazing event will answer the prayer of *Psalm 132:8-9*,

*Arise, O LORD, to your resting place, you and the **ark** of your strength. Let your **priests** be clothed with righteousness, and let your **saints** shout for joy.*

The lid of the ark was called the **mercy seat**. It was made of solid gold and included two golden cherubim with their wings extended over it. Inside the ark were the stone tablets written on by the finger of God (Exodus 40:20), Aaron's rod that budded (Numbers 17:8-11), and a bowl of manna from the wilderness wanderings of the people of Israel (Exodus 16:33-34). Of all the furniture in the Temple, the **ark** speaks the loudest of the fact that God is in covenant relationship with his chosen people, the Jews. When the ark becomes visible from Heaven, time will be running out for those remaining Jews who are still persisting in their unbelief down on Earth. This visual display will be a powerful appeal to them. In essence, God will be saying, *I haven't forgotten who you are and all my covenants with you. Have you forgotten me and your covenant with me? The Mercy Seat is still open. Won't you come?* God's great love for his ancient covenant people is incredible. As we have it in *Romans 11:28-29,*

As concerning the gospel, they [the Jews] *are enemies for your sakes: but as touching the election, they are beloved for the father's sakes. For the gifts and calling of God are without repentance* [irrevocable].

REVELATION 12

THE WOMAN AND THE DRAGON

Allow me to reiterate, if I may ... as far as timing is concerned, when the seventh Trumpet is blown the seven Bowl judgments will immediately commence on Earth in rapid-fire succession. These judgments will take place in a matter of days or possibly even hours and culminate in the Second Coming of the Lord Jesus Christ. However, since we readers of Revelation will be given a good deal more information before we actually come to the description of those events ... it will seem like a much longer period of time than it actually will take when it occurs. Keep this in mind as we come now to **the third interlude** here in the book of Revelation. This is **the interlude between the blowing of the seventh Trumpet and the pouring out of the first Bowl judgment**. It will take up all of chapters 12 and 13. In these pages, our Lord will enlighten us concerning many of the events, conditions, peoples and politics that will exist on Earth during the Great Tribulation. Also, this section will go a long way in helping us to understand why God will strike Earth-dwellers with such a clinched fist during those final climatic hours of secular world history and Gentile dominion over the earth.

Rev. 12:15

Now a great **sign** appeared in heaven: a **woman** clothed with the sun, with the moon under her feet, and on her head a garland of twelve stars. Then being with child, she cried out in labor and in pain to give birth. And another **sign** appeared in heaven: behold, a great, fiery **red dragon** having seven heads and ten horns, and seven diadems on his **heads.** His **tail** drew **a third of the stars** of heaven and threw them to the earth. And the dragon stood before the woman who was ready to give birth, **to devour her Child** as soon as it was born. **She bore a** *male Child who was to **rule** all nations with a **rod of iron**. And her Child was caught up to God and his throne.*

12:12

What awesome visages greeted John's eyes in this new vision! First, a resplendently dressed pregnant woman appeared who was in the throes of childbirth. Then, ominously, a terrible many-headed **red dragon** appeared and murderously positioned itself before the woman **to devour her Child as soon as it was born**. The repeated word, **sign**, here, tells us that these are symbolic representations. Careful analysis will make their significance clear. Let's look at them.

...The **woman.** There is something vaguely familiar about her. Oh yes, some of the same elements in her makeup are also found in Joseph's dream in *Genesis 37:9-10*. There, we read,

*Then he dreamed still another dream and told it to his brothers, and said, 'Look, I have dreamed another dream. And this time, the **sun**, the **moon**, and the **eleven stars** bowed down to me.' So he told it to his father and his brothers; and his father rebuked him and said to him, 'What is this dream that you have dreamed? Shall your mother and I and your brothers indeed come to bow down to the earth before you?'*

The **woman** was **clothed with the sun, with the moon under her feet, and on her head a garland of twelve stars**. These are the same three elements Joseph saw in his dream. He saw **the sun, the moon, and the eleven stars** bowing down before him. It was clear to Joseph's family that the **sun** represented Jacob; the **moon** represented their mother, Rachel, and the **eleven stars**, Joseph's eleven brothers. They were all greatly incensed by Joseph's dream.

Later, God changed Jacob's name to Israel and his sons become the twelve tribes of Israel. The Apostle Paul, speaking about the descendants of Israel, says in *Romans 9:3-5*,

*For I could wish that I myself were accursed from Christ for my brethren, my countrymen according to the flesh, who are **Israelites**, to whom pertain the adoption, the glory, the covenants, the giving of the law, the service of God, and the promises; of whom are the fathers and **from whom, according to the flesh, Christ came**, who is over all, the eternally blessed God. Amen.*

The ***woman*** ... ***sign*** that John saw is clearly symbolic of the nation of Israel from whom, Paul says, ***Christ came***.

12:3-4

...The ***dragon***. What a fearsome and murderous specter the ***fiery red dragon*** with ***seven heads*** and ***ten horns*** presented to John's eyes. As he watched it, its gigantic tail thrashed across the skies and drew ***a third of the stars of Heaven and threw them to the earth***. Then, the awful thing halted menacingly before the woman. Its evil intent was obvious. It was awaiting the birth of the woman's child in order to gobble it up as soon as it was born! The ***dragon*** ... ***sign*** represents Satan. Verse nine identifies him as such, by name. Let's consider some of the elements of his symbol and see if we can discern what they might allude to.

    a. He is ***red.*** I believe this speaks of his bloody and murderous nature. Our Lord says of him in *John 8:44b*,

       He was a murderer from the beginning, *and does not stand in the truth, because there is no truth in him. When he speaks a lie, he speaks from his own resources, for he is a liar and the father of it.*

    b. He has ***seven heads.*** Like many other monsters of ancient mythology, this probably speaks of Satan's perceived indestructibility. It would be a formidable task to kill a seven-headed monster such as this.

    c. He has ***ten horns.*** His ten horns speak of his perceived power. I say *perceived* because, although he is very powerful indeed, his power is not as great as he thinks. As we have noted before, ***horns*** are often used as a symbol of power in the Scripture. The Lamb, back in chapter 5, had ***seven horns***, a symbol for total or complete power. Satan's symbol here, having ***ten horns***, is an indication that he views himself as stronger than the Lamb.

    d. He dragged a third of the ***stars of heaven*** down to Earth with his ***tail***. As previously noted, stars are sometimes used as symbols for angels in the Bible. I believe that to be the case here. We know from the Scripture that Lucifer was not the only angel that fell (First Peter 3:18-20). The *stars*, which the dragon flung down to the earth, no doubt refer to the angels who Satan caused to fall along with him. We refer to them as *demons* today. And, by the way, a *third* of the angels of Heaven is no small number, for God's angels are said to be innumerable (Hebrews 12:22).

e. He positioned himself before the *woman* to gobble up the *male child as soon as it was born.* This is an obvious allusion to Satan's attempt in history to kill the baby Jesus. An account of it is found in *Matthew 2:16,*

Then Herod, when he saw that he was deceived by the wise men, was exceedingly angry; and he sent forth and **put to death all the male children who were in Bethlehem and in all its districts, from two years old and under**, *according to the time which he had determined from the wise men.*

No mistake about it, Satan was the one behind King Herod in that awful incident.

May we step aside again here for a minute? Satan has been trying to stop Christ from coming into our world ever since the Garden of Eden. After the fall, the Lord said to Satan,

And I will put enmity between **you** *and the woman, and between your seed and her* **Seed***; he shall* **bruise** *your head, and you shall bruise his heel. Genesis 3:15*

Christ is the promised *Seed* that the Lord was referring to there. I take it that Satan's *seed* refers to his demons as well as to all unregenerate human beings that are currently under his control. People who don't know the Lord belong to Satan, just as the fallen angels do. They are his property and confederates and he uses them as he pleases. So, in a very real sense, they are all Satan's *seed*. As Jesus put it to the Pharisees in John 8,

You are of **your father the devil***, and the lusts of your father you will do. John 8:44a*

Paul, speaking of lost and unsaved people, said,

*And **that they may recover themselves out of the snare of the devil**, who are taken captive by him at his will. Second Timothy 2:26* (KJV)

Jesus, commissioning Paul, said that he was sending him forth with the gospel...

*To open their eyes, and to turn them from darkness to light, and **from the power of Satan** unto God, that they may receive forgiveness of sins, and inheritance among them which are sanctified by faith that is in me. Acts 26:18* (KJV)

The Hebrew word translated **bruise** in Genesis 3:15, actually means *to crush*. Crush a serpent's head and its death is assured. God's words to Satan were unmistakable. *Someday the **Seed** of the woman will come and he will kill you*. Doubtless, this made Satan sweat. No one can fully understand biblical or even secular history until they understand how its events are related to Satan's attempts to stop the promised **Seed** from coming into the world.

Shortly after this prophecy was spoken, Satan moved Cain to kill Abel in order to keep the **Seed** from coming ... but God raised up Seth. During the time of the great Flood, I believe it was Satan who moved all of mankind to become so wicked that God would have to destroy them and thereby nullify the coming of the **Seed of the woman** ... but God raised up Noah. When Abraham arrived upon the scene, God made a covenant with him saying, **in your seed shall all the nations of the world be blessed** (Genesis 22:18). From that time on, the **Seed** became embedded in a specific line of the descendants of Abraham. So, Satan began to attack that line and moved Esau to say, *I will slay my brother Jacob* ... through whom the Seed was to come ... (Genesis 27:41) ... but Rebekah sent Jacob away to Laban's house.

In the days of the kings of Israel, God further defined the **Seed's** coming when he pronounced it would come from the royal line of the **seed of David** (Second Samuel 7:12). The history of the aftermath of this new defining of line of the **Seed** can be read in First and Second Kings and First and Second Chronicles, as well as several other places in the Old Testament. These books are replete with accounts of Satan's onslaughts on the royal line. Take for example, the account of wicked Queen Atheliah in Second Kings 11. When her son, king Ahaziah, died, she seized the throne and immediately set about to exterminate all of the royal seed so that she alone would sit on the throne of Israel. She almost made a complete job of it too, having murdered, she thought, all of her grandchildren. But God had seen to it that she missed one. While Atheliah was busy exterminating all of the royal seed, Jehoshiba whisked away little baby Joash and his nurse and brought them to Jehoiada, the priest, for protection in the temple. For six years God's whole purpose in the promised *Seed* rested in the life of that one sole little boy. Then, when Joash was seven years old, Jehoiada set him on the throne as the boy-king of Israel and had wicked, Satan instigated Atheliah, put to the sword. And, once again, the promised *Seed* was secured and preserved.

Finally ... Satan not being able to stop it ... the **Seed of the woman** came to Earth. As you have it in *Galatians 4:4*,

But when the fullness of the time had come, **God sent forth his Son, born of a woman***, born under the law...*

Now, Satan was faced with the *Seed* Himself. He had arrived. Immediately, he moved Herod to destroy the child, but the plan failed. Being warned in a dream, Joseph fled with the infant into Egypt (Matthew 2:13-14). All through Christ's life on Earth, Satan continued to plot to kill him. Finally, by means of Jewish and Roman leaders, the *Seed* was nailed to a Roman cross. Satan's laughter must have echoed throughout the universe! At long last, he thought, he had succeeded in destroying the promised *Seed*! He had killed the one who God had said would kill him ... and the prophecy of Genesis 3:15, had been nullified. What Satan didn't know, however, was that it was in the sovereign plan of God that his Son die on the cross. Jesus had come specifically to lay down his life as a sacrifice for the sins of the whole world (First John 2:2). Then, after having satisfied God's righteous demands, the *Seed* arose from the dead.

O the depth of the riches both of the wisdom and knowledge of God! How unsearchable are his judgments, and his ways past finding out. Romans 8:33

What a shock it must have been when Satan realized that he had not only lost again but now, he had been set up to lose scores of his slaves as well! As you have it in *Hebrews 2:14-15*,

Inasmuch then as the children have partaken of flesh and blood, He Himself likewise shared in the same, that through death **He might destroy**

him who had the power of death, that is, the devil, *and release those who through fear of death were all their lifetime subject to **bondage***.

Ha! Because of our Savior's death on the cross, a Door was now open for the captives to be set free (Jn. 10:9)! By faith in Christ, Satan would no longer be master ... and **death**, which brought so much fear to us all, had lost its sting. Nevertheless, ever since that wonderful resurrection morning, Satan still pursues his dogged opposition to the ***Seed***. Now, however, he concentrates on anything and anyone who has anything to do with Christ as he stalks the Earth ***seeking whom he may devour*** (First Peter 5:8b). Today, Satan continues to scratch and claw for every advantage to thwart the ***Seed's*** people and Christ's purposes ... and especially his coming to Earth again one day. But, Satan is a loser and an already defeated foe. He lost in Eden and he has lost over and over again down through history in his opposition to God's ***Seed***. He lost big time at the cross and he is losing today. Jesus said, ***I will build my church and the gates of hell shall not prevail against it.*** Inexorably, Jesus Christ is now systematically ransacking Satan's kingdom and calling out of it a people for his name's sake.

We are given this history lesson here in Revelation 12, to remind us of the great struggle that has gone on, and continues to go on, concerning the ***Seed*** of the woman. The struggle will greatly intensify during the dark days of the Great Tribulation. At that time, Satan will pull out all the stops to attempt to hold on to what is his and to oppose the ***Seed***. He will seek to exterminate anyone and everyone who has anything to do with Christ and, ultimately, will make war with the Lamb Himself at his Second Coming. But, as the saying goes ... *The bigger they are, the harder they fall*!

12:5

...The ***male Child***. John says, ***She bore a male child ... who was to rule all nations with a rod of iron***. This universal rule with a ***rod of iron*** is an unmistakable allusion to the prophecy of the Son in *Psalm 2:7-9,*

*I will declare the **decree**: The LORD has said to me, 'you are my **Son**, today I have begotten you. Ask of me, and **I will give you the nations for your inheritance**, and the ends of the earth for your* *possession. You shall break them with **a rod of iron**; you shall dash them to pieces like a potter's vessel.'*

Clearly, the **male Child** represents Christ**.** As John continued to watch the awesome drama unfold, the **male Child** was indeed born but, before the dragon could gobble him up, he **was caught up unto God and to his throne**. This is an obvious reference to Christ's ascension and exaltation to the right hand of God. As you have it in Acts 1:9,

*...And when he had spoken these things, while they beheld, **he was taken up**; and a cloud received him out of their sight.* (KJV)

And, in *Hebrews 1:3,* we read,

*...and when he had by himself purged us from our sins, **he sat down at the right hand of the Majesty on High***...

Rev. 12:6

*Then the woman **fled** into the wilderness, **where she has a place prepared by God**, that they should **feed** her there one thousand two hundred and sixty days* [three and a half years].

When Antichrist breaks his treaty with the Jews, and seizes their temple at the middle of the Tribulation, Jesus forewarned his covenant people, the Jews, to immediately *flee* out of Jerusalem saying,

*Therefore when you see the 'abomination of desolation,' spoken of by Daniel the prophet, standing in the holy place (whoever reads, let him understand), then let those who are in Judea **flee to the mountains**... Matthew 24:15-16*

When this event actually occurs in real time, our text says that those who obey Christ's words to flee will ultimately come to ***a place prepared by God***. We read here ... **Then the woman fled into the wilderness where she has a place prepared by God.** God will make a place of refuge in the wilderness for his covenant people who obey him and make it out of Jerusalem on that awful day when Antichrist breaks his treaty, seizes their temple and attempts to destroy them all. How will God protect them there? Let me assure you, he will have no problem on that score. Do you remember how Jesus escaped from the mob at Nazareth? They were hellbent on throwing him off a cliff (another instance, by the way, of Satan's attempt to destroy the ***Seed***). But, Jesus simply walked right through them, did he not (Luke 4:28-30)? With God, such things are a piece of cake.

Our passage goes on to read, ***that they should feed her there one thousand two hundred and sixty days*** (three and a half years). Who do you suppose ***they*** are who will be doing the feeding at that time? Also, what do you suppose ***they*** will feed those Jews for three and a half years? Would it surprise you to learn that these Jews will be fed with ***manna***? That is the implication here. I believe this word, ***they***, refers to angels who will daily feed these Jews, just as they fed their ancient counterparts out there in that same wilderness in Moses' day. One day, soon, the Jewish people will dine once again on ***angel's food*** (Psalm 78:25).

One more thing here ... do you remember from our discussion that we talked about the fact that the Jews of the Tribulation would be saved by direct confrontation, like the Apostle Paul was saved before them? Although that will be the method of many of the Jews' salvation during the Tribulation, no doubt they will not all be saved at the same time or at the same place. For example, I believe that many will be saved through the confrontation of the sixth Seal. I put the 144,000 in that group. However, these who flee from Satan here in Revelation 12, are yet another group of Jews. They are **Judean Jews** who will have been living in and around Jerusalem and worshipping at their rebuilt temple there. They too will have just experienced the trauma of the sixth Seal but ... to compound that awful experience ... as soon as the skies have been zipped up again, they will find the invading Antichrist on their doorstep who will seize Jerusalem and their temple! Those Jews who are wise ... will immediately flee out of there for their lives. They will have been prospering under Antichrist's protection and blessing. Under his treaty of protection, for three and a half years they will have had peace ... but, on that day, they will experience his treachery as prophesied in Daniel 7, and warned against by Jesus in Matthew 25. And, those who flee ***to the mountains***, as Jesus instructed, will ultimately arrive at the place of refuge. But, upon their arrival, boy will they be in for a shock. The Lord Jesus Christ, their God and Messiah, will be waiting for them there! And, then, he himself will save them by direct confrontation! As you have it in *Ezekiel 20:35-38*,

*'And **I will bring you into the wilderness** of the peoples, and there **I will plead my case with you face to face**. Just as I pleaded My case with your fathers in the wilderness of the land of Egypt, so I will plead my case with you,' says the Lord GOD. '**I will make you pass under the rod**, and I will bring you into the bond of **the covenant**;* [I take this to refer to the New Covenant] *I will purge the rebels from among you, and those who transgress against me; I will bring them out of the country where they dwell, but they shall not enter the land of Israel. **Then you will know that I am the LORD**.'*

What an amazing prophecy, aye? Wouldn't you like to be a fly on the wall when that confrontation takes place?

Rev. 12:7-12

*And **war** broke out in heaven: Michael and his angels fought with the dragon; **and the dragon and his angels fought, but they did not prevail, nor was a place found for them in heaven any longer**. So the great dragon was cast out, that serpent of old, called the Devil and Satan, who deceives the whole world; he was cast to the earth, **and his angels were cast out with him**. Then I heard a loud voice saying in heaven, "Now salvation, and strength, and the kingdom of our God, and the power of his Christ have come, for the **accuser** of our brethren, **who accused them before our God day and night, has been cast down**. And they overcame him by the blood of the Lamb and by the word of their testimony, and they did not love their lives to the death. Therefore rejoice, O heavens, and you who dwell in them! **Woe to the inhabitants of the earth and the sea! For the devil has come down to you, having great wrath, because he knows that he has a short time**.*

12:7-9

As I have said previously, I am persuaded that the events in Revelation are given to us in the exact chronological order in which they will actually occur in history. This passage adds further weight to that hypothesis because, right here in the middle of the story of these fleeing Judean Jews, it's as if the phone rings and we readers are suddenly summoned back up to Heaven. Why? Because, at that same exact point in time, something extremely significant will also be happening up there. A parallel crisis will have begun in Heaven. As God's people, the Jews, are fleeing for their lives down below, God Almighty is going to make his own move on Satan up above ... to *cast him permanently out* of Heaven. Again, may I say to you, my how God loves his covenant people. Because of their awful plight at, Satan backed, Antichrist's hands down on Earth ... God will retaliate *tit for tat* against Satan in Heaven above.

Now, it is important to understand that Satan and his demons presently have access to Heaven. We read in our passage here that, up there, they constantly accuse the **brethren before our God day and night**. Right this very moment, up in Heaven, Satan and his demons are hard at work tattling on the people of God and laying out endless accusations against them. Did you know that your name is being brought up before God in Heaven by demons, dear saint? Our sins, our defeats, our weaknesses, our falters and our failures (and who knows what else) are constantly being presented before God by Satan's crowd. Don't think he doesn't watch us. But thanks be to God, we have an *Advocate*, Jesus the Righteous One, who stands up for us! As we have it in *First John 2:1*,

*My little children, these things I write to you, so that you may not sin. And if anyone sins, we have an **Advocate** with the Father, Jesus Christ the righteous.*

And, again in *Hebrews 7:25-26*,

*Therefore He is also able to save to the uttermost those who come to God through him, since he always lives to make **intercession** for them. For such a **High Priest** was fitting for us, who is holy, harmless, undefiled, separate from sinners, and has become higher than the heavens...*

Satan has access to Heaven today, just as he has had throughout history. Job's story is more than ample proof of that fact. We learn here from Rev.12:9-10, however, that there is a day coming when our God will no longer tolerate his presence, nor his scurrilous accusations, in Heaven any more. There will come a day when he and his are going to be tossed bodily out of Heaven. Our text says this will precipitate *war in Heaven*. When the Judean Jews are fleeing Satan's man on Earth, Satan will suddenly find himself in hand to hand combat in Heaven above with God's archangel, Michael. Can we even imagine such a thing?

I picture it unfolding something like this. God ... observing his people fleeing from Antichrist down on Earth ... suddenly says to Michael, *Throw Satan out*. Satan says, *What!* God says, *Michael, throw him out, and all of his demons with him*. Satan says, *Michael????... you must be kidding ... why, I'm so much greater than Michael that he didn't dare even to make an accusation against me when we disputed over Moses' body ... remember that*?!! (Jude 9) *Michael will never see the day he can take me! I was above him from the beginning. I'm Lucifer, Son of the Morning!* What a scene that will be, brothers and sisters, and you and I are going to be there to witness it, by the way. It says here that *war broke out in Heaven*. Hot battle raged for every inch of ground, but Michael (*who is like God*) will live up to his name on that day. He will prove to be more of a match than Satan had bargained for. The war continued, our text says, until no *place* was *found for them in Heaven any longer*. Apparently, Satan and his demons will seek to retain a foothold in every nook and cranny of Heaven, but to no avail. Their whole sorry lot will be forcibly evicted!

So the great dragon was cast out, that serpent of old, called the Devil, and Satan, who deceives the whole world; he was cast to the earth and his angels were cast out with him. Satan has always thought of himself as greater than all the angelic beings and, incredibly, even above God himself. It is going to be quite a shock when he discovers that he's not even Michael's equal when, at that great Archangel's hand, he is unceremoniously tossed out of Heaven! Isaiah called it right when he said,

How you are fallen from heaven, ***O Lucifer, son of the morning!*** *How you are cut down to the ground, you who weakened the nations! For you have said in your heart:* ***'I will ascend into heaven, I will exalt my throne above the stars of God****; I will also sit on the mount of the congregation on the farthest sides of the north; I will ascend above the* *heights of the clouds, **I will be like the Most High**.' Yet you shall be brought down to Sheol, to the lowest depths of the Pit. Isaiah 14:12-15*

12:10-12

Immediately upon Satan's expulsion from Heaven, John heard a loud voice saying, ***Now salvation, and strength, and the kingdom of our God, and the power of His Christ has come, for the accuser of our brethren, who accused them before our God day and night, has been cast down.*** This cleansing of Heaven will be a giant step in the establishment of Christ's dominion over all. At the expulsion of Satan from Heaven, Christ's train will have truly left the station and will be continuing on its unstoppable course to victory. A great celebration commenced. The voice continued:

... ***and they overcame him by the blood of the Lamb.*** Satan's accusations cannot and will not stand in the face of Jesus' shed blood on the behalf of his saints. They all have been washed in the blood of the Lamb, you see. Regardless of what anyone has to say about a true child of God, as far as God is concerned they have all been made perfect in Christ. As you have it in *Ephesians 5:26-27,*

*That he might sanctify and cleanse it with the **washing** of water by the **word**, that he might present it to himself a glorious church, not having spot, or wrinkle, or any such thing; but that it should be holy and **without blemish**.* (KJV)

...***and by the word of their testimony.*** Satan's accusation cannot and will not stand in light of the words of the saint's verbal testimonies either. Their confession of Christ sets them apart from all accusations. As you have it in *Romans 10:9-10,*

...that if you confess with your mouth the Lord Jesus and believe in your heart that God has raised Him from the dead, you will be saved. For with the heart one believes unto righteousness, and with the mouth confession is made unto salvation.

And again, in *Romans 8:33-34,*

*Who shall lay **anything** to the charge of God's elect? It is God that **justifieth**. Who is he that condemneth? It is Christ that died, yea rather, that is risen again, who is even at the right hand of God, who also maketh intercession for us.*

...and they did not love their lives to the death. Nor could Satan's accusations stand in light of the perseverance of the saints. As Satan already knows, and all other intelligent beings will one day know, a true child of God just will not quit!

Then John heard a loud voice say, *Woe to the inhabitants of the earth and the sea! For the Devil has come down to you, having great wrath, because he knows that he has a short time*. You can bet that, after this event has taken place, Satan will be livid. John's attention was now drawn back to Earth where the Judean Jews were still fleeing for their lives. Down there, Satan, filled with wrath from being tossed out of Heaven, had just arrived. That will not bode well for the Jewish people.

Rev. 12:13-17

Now when the dragon saw that he had been cast to the earth, ***he persecuted the woman who gave birth to the male Child****. But the woman was given two* ***wings of a great eagle****, that she might fly into the* ***wilderness to her place****, where she is nourished for* ***a time and times and half a time****,* [Hebrew idiom for three and a half years] *from the presence of the serpent. So the serpent spewed* ***water*** *out of his mouth like a* ***flood*** *after the woman,* ***that he might cause her to be carried away by the flood****. But the earth helped the woman, and* ***the earth opened its mouth and swallowed up the flood*** *which the dragon had spewed out of his mouth. And the dragon was enraged with the woman, and he went to make* ***war*** *with the* ***rest*** *of her offspring,* ***who keep the commandments of God and have the testimony of Jesus*** [NU omits "Christ"].

12:13-14

When Satan arrived on Earth, still licking his wounds from being expelled from Heaven, our text says he came down with great anger toward Israel. We read, *when the dragon saw that he had been cast to the earth, he persecuted the woman who gave birth to the male Child*. At that time, Satan will throw his full weight behind Antichrist's forces as they pursue the Judean Jews who are fleeing out of Jerusalem. But, *the woman was given two wings of a great eagle, that she might fly into the wilderness to her place, where she is nourished for a time and times and half a time from the face of the serpent.* When it says here that these Jews were given *the wings of a great eagle*, it is doubtless referring to the supernatural assistance of their great God. *Isaiah 40:31,* comes to mind, does it not?

But they that wait upon the Lord shall renew their strength; **they shall mount up with wings as eagles**; *they shall* **run** *and not be weary; and they shall* **walk**, *and not faint.*

Although this passage from Isaiah is speaking figuratively, it has, in fact, been fulfilled literally on several occasions. For example, when Elijah tirelessly out-ran Ahab's galloping chariot all the way from Mount Carmel to Jezreel, a distance of around thirty miles (First Kings18:46). And again, we saw it in the life of Sampson (Judges 14-16) as well. Apparently, there will be a similar literal fulfillment of Isaiah 40:31, when God helps Israel flee from Antichrist in that future day. The implication is that they will be given supernatural speed and agility in the day of their escape. Israel will have *two wings of a great eagle* in that day ... a direct illusion to their great God's assistance in allowing them to escape. Truly, as you have it in *Romans 8:31b,*

If God be for us, who can be against?

12:15-16

In a way, I envy these fleeing Jews of that future day. They are in for an incredible experience of deliverance by the great, omnipotent, delivering hand of their God. And, it will come about in the same manner that Moses and the ancient Israelites, who fled before Pharaoh before them, experienced. For, just as it was with those ancient counterparts, once again there will be a pursuing enemy behind (Antichrist and his armies) and a seemingly insurmountable water obstacle before them (the flooding Jordan River) which will appear to seal their doom. As the Red Sea blocked ancient Israel's way to safety, during the Exodus, a supernatural *flood* from Satan will confront the fleeing Judean Jews of the Great Tribulation. I believe that *Daniel 9:26,* also speaks of this flood,

And after the sixty-two weeks Messiah shall be cut off, but not for himself; and the people of the ***prince who is to come*** *[Antichrist] shall destroy the city and the sanctuary. The end of it* [the entire event of

Antichrist's seizing of the temple and subsequent pursuit of the fleeing Jews] *shall be with a **flood**, and till the end of the **war*** [at Armageddon] *desolations are determined.*

God's people will have to cross the Jordan River to reach the place of safety in the wilderness beyond. Satan, knowing this, will supernaturally cause a tremendous flood at the river to stop them and to hold them there so that Antichrist's armies can destroy them on its banks. Most likely, he will cause a torrential rain in the terrain above where they will be attempting to cross. I suspect that it will be like no other flood that the Jordan basin has ever experienced. We can only imagine how terrifying that will be to those who are fleeing for their lives from Antichrist's soldiers. But God, (I love that phrase, don't you?) ... but God ... the same God who divided the Red Sea of old and delivered his people from Pharaoh, will intervene once again. Our text says, **But the earth helped the woman, and the earth opened its mouth and swallowed up the flood.** An earthquake ... the earth cracked open ... and Satan's flood went cascading down into the bowels of the earth as God's people, once again, crossed over an impassable water barrier on dry ground! Wouldn't you love to be there to see it!? At that time, that great promise of *Isaiah 43:1-3a*, will be literally fulfilled,

But now, thus says the LORD, who created you, O Jacob, and he who formed you, O Israel: 'Fear not, for I have redeemed you; I have called you by your name; you are mine. **When you pass through the waters, I will be with you; and through the rivers, they shall not overflow you.** *When you walk through the fire, you shall not be burned, nor shall the flame scorch you.* **For I am the LORD your God, The Holy One of Israel, your Savior**...'

Also, the prophecy of *Psalm 124*, will likewise be literally fulfilled on that day,

If it had not been the LORD *who was on our side, Let Israel now say; 'If it had not been the LORD who was on our side, when men rose up against us, then they would have swallowed us alive, when their wrath was kindled against us; then* **the waters would have overwhelmed us, the stream would have gone over our soul***; Then* **the swollen waters would have gone over our soul***. Blessed be the LORD, who has not given us as prey to their teeth. Our soul has escaped as a bird from the* *snare of the fowlers; The snare is broken, and **we have escaped**. Our help is in the name of the LORD, who made heaven and earth.'*

Isn't our God, his power, his faithfulness and his Word amazing!?

12:17

Once again, Satan will be forced to turn away in defeat. But, as he goes, he will be vowing bloody war on the rest of the people of God. Our text says he will go to **make war with the rest of her offspring, who keep the commandments of God and have the testimony of Jesus Christ**. After these humiliating defeats, Satan will turn away in rage and go after the remainder of the Jews who know Christ, which includes the 144,000. This, I believe, will begin the days of the systematic slaughter of the people of God on Earth. Thus, the chapter ends.

We have been given a great deal of important information here. Our Lord has given us a panoramic view of his purpose for the Jew from the time when he, himself, came into our world ... through them ... and then all the way down to their future flight out of Jerusalem during the opening days of the Great Tribulation. We have read about two key players in the coming Great Tribulation: Satan and the Jews. We have learned about two key events: the fleeing of the Jews from Antichrist and the expulsion of Satan from Heaven. These characters and events, rightly understood, add greatly to our understanding of the Great Tribulation. This chapter also adds further weight to the proposition that the entire Tribulation period is primarily about God's program for his covenant people, the Jews. It is designed to refine and purify them and set the stage for their God and Savior to deliver them ... once and for all for his name's sake.

REVELATION 13

THE ANTICHRIST AND HIS FALSE PROPHET

Rev. 13:12

Then **[NU changes "I" to "he"]** *stood on the sand of the sea. And I saw a beast rising up out of the sea, having* **seven heads and ten horns**, *and on his horns* **ten crowns**, *and on his heads a blasphemous name. Now the beast, which I saw was like a* **leopard**, *his feet were like the feet of a* **bear**, *and his mouth like the mouth of a* **lion**. **The dragon gave him his power, his throne, and great authority**...

THE BEAST WHO ARISES OUT OF THE SEA

We are still in **the third interlude** here in chapters 12 and 13. Chapter 13 is a new vision, but the scene is still down on the earth. I must admit that NU's correction of the text threw me a bit of a curve at first. I had always assumed that it was John who was standing on the seashore when he saw this vision but the better reading here is not *I* but *he*, referring back to Satan in chapter 12. So, the last verse in chapter 12, combined with the first verse of chapter 13, reads,

And the **dragon** *was enraged with the woman, and he went to make war with the rest of her offspring, who keep the commandments of God and have the testimony of Jesus. Then* **he** *stood on the sand of the sea... Revelation 12:17-13:1a*

So, it was Satan who John saw standing on the seashore. Then, as John watched, slowly, ten horns with ten crowns upon them began to rise up from the sea. Eventually, seven grotesque heads were exposed from which the ten horns protruded. Furthermore, each dripping head was emblazoned with its own **blasphemous name**. Finally, the entire beast came wading out to Satan like a great Frankensteinian monster coming home to its master. In appearance, its body was like a **leopard**, its feet like a **bear**, and its mouth was like a **lion**. If you are a student of the prophet Daniel, you will sense that there is something quite familiar about this beast because each of the animals that make up its body, are also found in Daniel 7. There, using the imagery of four different beasts, God revealed to Daniel that, in the future, four great world dominating empires would arise upon the Earth. Daniel described them as follows:

The first was *like a lion*. It was explained to Daniel that the lion represented the Babylonian Empire under which he was living at the time having been taken there as a captive by Nebuchadnezzar.

The second was *like a bear*. It represented the Medo-Persian Empire that followed Babylon. Daniel lived during the reign of that empire as well.

The third was *like a leopard*. In retrospect, we know that it symbolized the next empire to step out on the stage of world history. That would be the Grecian Empire.

The fourth beast, Daniel said, was *dreadful and terrible*. It symbolized the fourth empire that would come … the Roman Empire … in **both** of its future stages. The first stage began a couple hundred years before, and then continued well past, Jesus' day. But, Daniel's vision of that beast included its second stage as well … when it will be resurrected again during the last days of the Tribulation. In Daniel's vision, this second stage was symbolized by the beast's *ten horns* along with its *little horn* that Daniel saw. So, the prophecy of Daniel 7, not only foretold the rise of the Roman Empire but it also prophesied that it would **reappear** on Earth in the last days. This second stage of the Roman Empire is very important to our study here in Revelation.

The beast that John saw rise up out of the sea and come to Satan … is a composite of all four of the beasts in Daniel's vision. The significance of its composite nature is that this last world-dominating kingdom will contain elements of all four of the great and dominating Gentile empires that preceded it. As such, it will be the epitome of Gentile reign on Earth. This is the **political/governmental** side of the *beast* symbol here in Revelation 13. However, we will discover that it represents even more than that. It also represents a person. This second meaning of the symbol is its **personality/dictator** side. Let's break it down. The *beast*, John saw:

…came out of the Mediterranean *sea*. This is an indicator that Antichrist and his ten-king federation will arise out of the European Theater of the old Roman Empire.

... had ***ten horns*** and ***ten crowns***. We learn from Daniel 7, that in the second stage of the Roman Empire (when it manifests itself again during the days of the Tribulation), it will arise out of a ten king confederation. We also learn from Daniel 7, that ***seven*** of those kings will come on board with Antichrist ... voluntarily, but ***three*** others will have been uprooted by him and be replaced by other kings. After those initial adjustments, the ten kings will rule with and under Antichrist during this last phase of the revived Roman Empire. The beast's ***ten horns*** here in Revelation 13, represent the same kings as found in Daniel's vision. They are also found in Revelation 17. For comparison, here is a look at these kings in the Daniel 7, and Revelation 17, passages:

__The ten horns are ten kings__ who shall __arise from this kingdom__. And __another__ shall rise after them; he shall be different from the first ones, and __shall subdue three kings__. He shall speak pompous words against the Most High, shall persecute the saints of the Most High, and shall intend to change times and law. Then the saints shall be given into his hand for a time and times and half a time. Daniel 7:24-25

__The ten horns__ which you saw are __ten kings__ who have received no kingdom as yet, but they receive authority for __one hour as kings with the beast__. Revelation 17:12

So, the Bible prophesies, both in Daniel and also here in Revelation, that Antichrist's kingdom will consist of a ten king confederation that will arise out of the ancient Roman Empire. Dr. McGee observes that the Roman Empire was never really destroyed or conquered but, rather, simply disintegrated and elements of it still survive today in the laws, customs and peoples of Europe. The Bible predicts that, in the last days, out of those peoples ... it will rise again in the form of a ten king confederation headed up by Antichrist.

...had ***seven heads***. We learn from Revelation chapter 17, the seven heads of this beast represent yet another set of kings. They represent seven, long dead and ancient rulers of the original Roman Empire. They were men whose personalities and lives were pictures or **types** of the yet future Antichrist who was yet to come. As you have it there in Revelation 17,

There are __also seven kings__. Five have fallen, one is, and the other has not yet come. And when he comes, he must continue a short

time. The beast that was, and is not, is himself also the eighth, and is of the seven, and is going to perdition. Revelation 17:10-11

So, to sum up, the beast's **ten horns** represent a last-days confederation of ten kings who will rule with Antichrist, but its **seven heads** represent seven ancient Roman Caesars that once ruled over the ancient Roman Empire who were types (or pictures) of the coming Antichrist. Their twisted characters and blasphemous actions, you see, epitomized and remind us of him. We will discuss the identity of these seven Caesars when we get to chapter 17. This is all part of the **political/governmental** side of this **beast** symbol that John saw.

Now, let's look at the other side of this symbol because, remember, the **beast** also represents a **person**. This is the **personality/dictator** side of the symbol. Notice that the beast becomes personalized in the last phrase of verse two where the text says, **The dragon gave him his power, his throne, and great authority.** The personal pronouns here tell us this is also speaking about a person and that Satan will grant him great supernatural powers. In Matthew 24, Jesus predicted that the days of the Great Tribulation will be days when there will be incredible displays of supernatural power. I might add, that will be both from God's side of the equation as well as Satan's. Our text here says that Satan will give his power to Antichrist. The implication of that is no small matter. Satan has great supernatural powers. He wiped out Job's servants, his house and his children using fire from heaven and a tornado (Job 1:16-19). What would such supernatural weapons do to any human military, even that of the United States? Later in this chapter, we will read that the False Prophet will be able to call down fire from heaven. What could such a weapon do to an aircraft carrier, a tank or ground troops? Make no mistake about it, when this day comes ... when Satan has given his power over to Antichrist ... the military might of any nation will not stand a chance against him. No wonder the people of Earth will say, **Who is able to make war with him?** (13:4b)

Now, both in the Old and New Testaments, the Bible predicts that one day a man will come who will be the near embodiment of Satan himself. If Satan could become incarnate and make himself into a human being, I believe that he would. He's that anxious to be like the Most High. But since he can't, he plans to copycat, as near as possible, what God has done. Satan too will have his man! One of the names of Satan's man in the Bible is Antichrist. As you have it in *First John 2:18*,

Little children, it is the last hour; and as you have heard that the **Antichrist** *is coming, even now many antichrists have come, by which we know that it is the last hour.*

Antichrist is the **personality/dictator** side of this ferocious beast symbol that John saw. He will step out on the stage of human history to rule the world during the dark days of the Great Tribulation. Daniel prophesied,

And in the latter time of their kingdom, when the transgressors have reached their fullness, **a king shall arise**, *having fierce features, who understands sinister schemes.* **His power shall be mighty, but not by his own power**; *he shall destroy fearfully, and shall prosper and thrive; he shall destroy the mighty, and also the holy people. Through his cunning he shall cause deceit to prosper under his* **rule**; *and he shall exalt himself in his heart. He shall destroy many in their prosperity. He shall even rise against the Prince of princes* (Jesus); *but he shall be broken without human means. Daniel 8:23-28*

Dr. Criswell says of him, *All the glories of the kingdoms of earth will reside in Antichrist reign. He will be like a Nebuchadnezzar, a Tiglath-Pilizer, a Shalmanezer, a Julius Caesar, an Alexander the Great, a Napoleon, a Frederick the Great, and a Charlemagne all wrapped into one. He is Satan's masterpiece.*

So, to conclude, it is very important to remember that the symbol of this ***beast*** from the ***sea*** is a complex one. That is, there is more than one thing that it symbolizes. It is a symbol of both Antichrist's political kingdom as well as Antichrist himself.

Rev. 13:3-4

And I saw **one of his heads** *as if it had been mortally wounded, and his deadly wound was healed. And all the world marveled and followed the beast. So they* **worshipped the dragon** *who gave authority to the beast; and* *they **worshipped the beast**, saying, 'Who is like the beast? Who is able to make **war** with him?'*

Because of the personal pronouns used here, we know that these verses are continuing to give us information about the personality/dictator side of the beast symbol ... Antichrist, himself. John says that **one of his heads** was **mortally wounded**. John saw that the beast had received a death blow to one of its heads ... which should have killed it ... but, he says, the **deadly wound was healed**. Because of this miraculous recovery, **the world marveled and followed after the beast** and they **worshipped** both the **dragon who gave authority to the beast** and the **beast**. *Second Thessalonians 2:3-8,* also speaks of the Antichrist worship that will come about in that future day.

*Let no one deceive you by any means; for that day will not come unless the falling away comes first, and the **man of sin is revealed**, **the son of perdition**, who opposes and **exalts himself above all that is called God or that is worshipped, so that he sits as God in the temple of God, showing himself that he is God**. Do you not remember that when I was still with you I told you these things? And now you know what is restraining, that he may be revealed in his own time. For the mystery of lawlessness is already at work; only he who now restrains will do so until he is taken out of the way. And then **the lawless one will be revealed**, whom the Lord will consume with the breath of his mouth and destroy with the brightness of his coming.*

My, how the peoples of the world will fall in line when they see the miraculous healing of Antichrist's mortal wound! There is a very important principle here that I would like to address ... so, let's step aside for a moment. Beloved, **there is great danger in building one's theology on experience rather than on the Word of God**. It is very dangerous to build what one believes on what one sees and/or experiences ... rather than upon what one reads in the objective Word of God. Satan is a liar, a deceiver and a counterfeit. The world is full of his tricksters and deceivers. Sadly, many people, and even some of the saints of God, readily receive and believe what they see and experience over what they read in their Bibles. *Second Corinthians 11:13-15,* warns,

*For such are false apostles, deceitful workers, transforming themselves into apostles of Christ. And no wonder! For **Satan himself transforms himself into an angel of light**. Therefore it is no great thing if*

*his **ministers** also transform themselves into ministers of righteousness, whose end will be according to their works.*

Our text here says that the world will worship both Satan ***and*** his puppet, Antichrist, because of what they see. They will all fall in line because of Antichrist's miracle over death, his amazing power and his military prowess. Daniel noted this militaristic relationship of Antichrist saying,

*He shall regard neither **the God of his fathers** nor **the desire of women**, nor regard any god; for he shall exalt himself above them all. But in their place he shall **honor a god of fortresses**; and a god which his fathers did not know he shall honor with gold and silver, with precious stones and pleasant things. Daniel 11:37-38*

I have been thinking on the above prophecy in light of recent world events. Not long ago, I listened to a Moslem convert to Christianity who was interviewed on Fox News. He grew up in the Muslim religion and was taught from infancy that he was to hate his enemies. He went on to say that Islam teaches that their enemies are the *infidels*, especially Jews and Christians. He also said that the Moslem religion is a *religion of domination* and that Allah, its god, is a god of *might and valor*. Since the bombing of the World Trade Centers, and subsequent other attacks by Islamic extremists, it is becoming more and more clear how Antichrist might very much be attracted to such a religion and its warlike god and, hence, may initially be a Moslem. This would further explain why, when he suddenly ascends to power at the beginning of the Tribulation, he will be in a position to make a treaty with Israel (Dan. 9:27). All around the world, the ancient conflict between Islam and Israel continues to rage as Islamists continue their ceaseless attacks on Israel. They are bound and determined to annihilate it from the face of the earth. What amazing times we live in. The prophecies of the Bible are becoming more and more relevant and understandable every day.

Rev. 13:5-10

*And he was given a **mouth** speaking **great things** and **blasphemies**, and he was given authority to continue for **forty-two months** [three and a half years]. Then he opened his mouth in*

blasphemy against God, *to blaspheme his name, his tabernacle, and those who dwell in heaven.* ***It was granted to him to make war with the saints*** *and to* ***overcome*** *them. And* ***authority was given him over every tribe,*** *[NU adds "and people, tongue, and nation"]. All who dwell on the earth will worship him, whose names have not been written in the Book of Life of the Lamb slain from the foundation of the world. If anyone has an ear, let him hear. He who* ***leads into captivity*** *shall go into captivity;* ***he who kills with the sword*** *must be killed with the sword. Here is the patience and the faith of the saints.*

13:5

We continue here with the personality/dictator side of the beast symbol (the description of Antichrist himself):

First, John says ... ***And he was given a mouth speaking great things***. Antichrist will be a mesmerizing orator. It is said that Hitler was a formidable speaker and that he could sway an audience to believe just about anything. I believe that was because he himself had the spirit of Antichrist. But the world has yet to see anything like the oratory skills that the ***beast*** will possess. He will be a Winston Churchill, a Disraeli and an Adolph Hitler all rolled into one. *Daniel 7:8,* also alludes to Antichrist's oratory prowess,

I was considering the horns, and there was another horn, a little one, coming up among them, before whom three of the first horns were plucked out by the roots. And there, in this horn, were eyes like the eyes of a man, ***and a mouth speaking pompous words***.

13:6

Second, John says he will speak ***blasphemies***. *Daniel 7:25,* agrees,

He shall speak pompous words against the Most High, *shall persecute the saints of the Most High, and shall intend to change times and law. Then* ***the saints shall be given into his hand*** *for a time and times and half a time* [three and a half years].

13:7

Third, John says ... *It was granted to him to make war with the saints and to overcome them*. This too is in agreement with Daniel 7:25, quoted above. From these scriptures we understand how difficult it will be to be a believer during the Great Tribulation. In that day, to follow Christ will be a virtual death sentence. You will remember from chapter 12, after Satan was ejected from Heaven, he came down to Earth in great wrath. No longer able to *accuse* the saints in Heaven, he will energize his Antichrist to launch a campaign to eradicate them from off the earth. My, how Satan hates God's children! When his man reigns supreme, he will ride roughshod over them and they will *be given into his hand*. Jesus spoke of this as well,

You will be betrayed even by parents and brothers, relatives and friends; ***and they will put some of you to death*** *and you will be hated by all for my name's sake. But not a hair of your head shall be lost. By your* ***patience*** *possess your souls. Luke 21:16-19*

13:8-9

Fourth, he says ... *All who are living on the earth will worship him*. The vast majority of the peoples of the world will one day worship Antichrist. However, we also see from our text that there will be those who will refuse to do so, namely, those whose names are found *written in the Book of Life of the Lamb slain from the foundation of the world*. This is Romans 8, and Ephesians 1, territory. The names that are written in the Lamb's Book of Life are his chosen, called and elect ones. It is a book that records all that have responded to Christ by faith and received God's great offer of salvation in his Son. Are you aware that your name is written there, dear saint? Jesus told his disciples,

Nevertheless do not rejoice in this, that the spirits are subject to you, but rather rejoice because ***your names are written in heaven****. Luke 10:20*

It is also mention in Revelation 17:8; 20:12, 15 and 21:27. The Apostle Paul also spoke of it,

And I urge you also, true companion, help these women who labored with me in the gospel, with Clement also, and the rest of my fellow workers, **whose names are in the Book of Life**. *Philippians 4:3*

May I tell you a little story about life and death and the importance of being written in the Lamb's book of life? The morning that I was writing the first draft of this chapter (in fact, right here at this very point in the middle of this sentence), my phone rang. I was a Pastor at the time and I was called away to a youth camp out at Elephant Butte Lake near our church. I was told that a terrible tragedy had occurred and I needed to come right away. As it turned out, two of the young campers who were on a trip with their youth group from Ohio, had just received word that both their parents, who were themselves on vacation in Hawaii, had been killed in a helicopter crash. When I arrived at the camp, their youth leader told me that the parents of these two young people had been wonderful dedicated Christians and had done a marvelous job of raising these two teenagers. Tragic as this was, there was comfort for these young people because they knew for sure that their godly and beloved mom and dad had gone to be with the Lord. Their names had been written in the Lamb's Book of Life, you see. None of us, Christian or non-Christian, know the hour of our departure from this Earth. Are you ready? Is your name written in the ***book of life of the Lamb slain from the foundation of the world***? This is such an important issue that the Lord himself interjects, ***If anyone has an ear, let him hear…***

13:10

Finally, here in verse 10, we have a word that is written specifically to our brothers and sisters who will actually live under the intense persecution of Antichrist. The Holy Spirit speaks words of comfort and assurance to them here saying, **He who leads into captivity shall go into captivity, and he who kills with the sword shall be killed with the sword.** He is saying, *Rest assured, Antichrist and his minions will be dealt with. They will be paid in their own coin*! Many of the Lord's Tribulation Saints will be led away captive in that day to be killed with the sword. The Scripture says, however, Antichrist and all who are his will suffer the same fate. When Peter drew his sword against the mob in the garden of Gethsemane, Jesus said to him,

Put your sword in its place, for all who take the sword will perish by the sword. Matthew 26:52

That is the idea here. Those who have been killing with the sword will themselves soon face the sword. We learn in chapter 19, the sword they will face, however, is the **sword** of the Lord's mouth. Our text continues ... **Herein is the patience and the faith of the saints**. These qualities will be two essentials for a believer in those dark days, **patience** and **faith**, as they wait for the Deliverer to come, knowing for certain that when he appears he will turn the tables on Satan and his darling, Antichrist.

THE BEAST WHO ARISES OUT OF THE EARTH

Rev. 13:11-15

*Then **I saw another beast coming up out of the earth**, and he had two horns like a lamb and spoke like a dragon. And he exercises all the authority of the first beast in his presence, and causes the earth and those who dwell in it to worship the first beast, whose deadly wound was healed. **He performs great signs, so that he even makes fire come down from heaven on the earth in the sight of men**. And he **deceives** those who dwell on the earth by those signs which he was granted to do in the sight of the beast, telling those who dwell on the earth to make an image to the beast **who was wounded by the sword and lived. He was granted power to give breath to the image of the beast**, that the image of the beast should both **speak** and cause as many as would not worship the image of the beast to be killed.*

13:11

We are introduced here to the second important personality who will play a crucial role in Antichrist's kingdom and worship. He too is symbolized by a ***beast***. However, in contrast to the first beast who came up out of the sea ... this beast comes ***up out of the earth***. In 16:13; 19:20 and 20:10, this second beast is called ***the false prophet***. This is a personality that is entirely new to the pages of Scripture. Nowhere else in the Bible has there been so much as a hint about this fellow. He rises up here for the first time in the pages of holy writ. We are given a good deal of information about him. John says:

...I saw another beast coming up out of the earth. The False Prophet will be earthy. All man-oriented false religions are earthy. Carl Marx, the founder of communism said, *Religion is the opiate of the masses*. I agree. One time, I was sharing Christ with a fellow who tried to sidetrack me by saying, *There are millions of Moslems in India. They have a great religion*. I countered, *Religion is man's effort to work his way to Heaven, but the only true way to God is through faith in his Son, Jesus Christ*. I went on to explain, *Christ is not one of man's religions, he is a Person, the Son of the one and only true and living God. Through Christ, God reached down to man and has provided us with a Savior*. The fellow didn't take to that very well. He chose to remain impressed with the many other religions of the world. One day the **beast** from out of the earth, Antichrist's **false prophet**, will head up a new worldwide religion during the days of the Great Tribulation. It will be the religion of Antichrist worship. It will be the epitome of all the false religions that have preceded it ... earthy ... deceptive ... Satanic ... filled with man's ideas, not God's.

...he had two horns like a lamb. The False Prophet will be lamb-like. I interpret this to mean that the False Prophet will be a counterfeit Christ and his worldwide religion will likely be a twisted perversion of Christianity. There is much of that, already, in the world today. The following scriptures warn of it:

*And unless those days were shortened, no flesh would be saved; but for the elect's sake those days will be shortened. Then if anyone says to you, 'Look, here is the Christ!' or 'There!' do not believe it. For **false Christs and false prophets will rise and show great signs and wonders to deceive, if possible, even the elect**... Matthew 24:22-24*

*Let no one deceive you by any means; for that day will not come unless the **falling away comes first**, and the man of sin is revealed, the son of perdition... Second Thessalonians 2:3*

But know this, that in the last days perilous times will come: For men will be lovers of themselves, lovers of money, boasters, proud, blasphemers, disobedient to parents, unthankful, unholy, unloving, unforgiving, slanderers, without self-control, brutal, despisers of good, traitors, headstrong, haughty, lovers of pleasure rather than lovers of

God, **having a form of godliness but denying its power**. *And from such people turn away! Second Timothy 3:1-5*

...**he spoke like a dragon**. When the False Prophet speaks, he will sound like a *dragon*. What comes out of one's mouth is who one truly is, beloved. The False Prophet will present himself to the world as a man of God but what comes out of his mouth will prove him to be a man of Satan. As Jesus put it to the Pharisees in his day,

Brood of vipers! How can you, being evil, speak good things? For **out of the abundance of the heart the mouth speaks**. *A good man out of the good treasure of his heart brings forth good things, and* **an evil man out of the evil treasure brings forth evil thing**... *Matthew 12:34-35*

God's people will know the truth about the *false prophet* by his words.

13:12-14

...***And he exercises all the authority of the first beast ... and causes the earth and those who dwell in it to worship the first beast***. The False Prophet will be the enforcer and promoter of mandatory Antichrist worship. In verses 14 and 15, we learn that he will order ***those who dwell on the earth to make an image*** of the first ***beast*** and will ***be granted the power to give breath to*** it and it will ***cause as many as would not worship the image of the beast to be killed***.

Sound familiar? It should. Satan's murdering in the name of religion has been going on down here for millennia. It will also be the norm when Antichrist's False Prophet steps out upon the scene. However, no doubt it will be more virulent than ever.

...***he... even makes fire to come down from heaven in the sight of men***. Antichrist's False Prophet will be an amazing miracle worker. Verses 13 and 14, tell us that he will work his deceptions by means of signs. *Heads up*, child of God. Always remember that miracles and wonders are never the final word when it comes to verifying truth. They are never to be taken as undisputed proof that what one is seeing, or hearing, is from God. *First John 4:1-3,* says,

Beloved, ***do not believe every spirit****, but* ***test*** *the spirits, whether they are of God; because many* ***false prophets*** *have gone out into the world. By this you know the Spirit of God:* ***every spirit that confesses***

that Jesus Christ has come in the flesh is of God, and every spirit that does not confess that Jesus Christ has come in the flesh is not of God. And this is the spirit of the Antichrist, which you have heard was coming, and is now already in the world.

This scripture tells us how we believers can determine the veracity of an event, a spirit, or a person. Did you catch it? It is the sure fire way to test anyone, be they miracle worker or theologian. Namely, by simply finding out what they believe about the **deity of Jesus Christ**. It was God himself who came into our world and walked among us some two thousand years ago (John 1:1, 14, 18). The question to put to heretics, false prophets, miracle workers and suspicious spirits then ... is, *Do you believe that Jesus was God in the flesh, the Everlasting Father, the Ancient of Days?* If their answer is *No*, then you know that you are talking to a spirit of Antichrist.

The second indispensable thing we can use to test someone is, of course, the Word of God itself. You might call it *the Berean test*. As we have it in *Acts 17:10-11*,

Then the brethren immediately sent Paul and Silas away by night to **Berea**. *When they arrived, they went into the synagogue of the Jews. These were more fair-minded than those in Thessalonica, in that they received the word with all readiness, and* **searched the Scriptures daily to find out whether these things were so**.

A child of God must reject any event, occurrence, thought or teaching that will not hold up under the pure light of the Word of God. I cannot overemphasize the importance of this basic and fundamental principle. The question is ... *Do we judge the Word of God by our experiences or do we judge our experiences by the Word of God?* If we have an experience, hear or see something, or are taught something that does not line up with the Bible ... we must be willing to lay it aside ... no matter how dear it may seem to us and others. The False Prophet of Revelation 13, will be a very powerful miracle and sign-working phony. And, just as many are taken in by such charlatans today, the day will come when the whole world will fall for the False Prophet's miracles and false teaching.

13:15

...he was given power to give breath to the image of the beast that the image of the beast should both speak and cause as many as would not worship the image of the beast that they should be killed. When the False Prophet animates the ***image of the beast***, it will be Daniel 3, all over again. Do you remember the story there about Shadrach, Meshach and Abednego? King Nebuchadnezzar built an image of himself and demanded that at an appointed time each day ... everyone fall down and worship it. Three Hebrew young men refused to do so. Consequently, they were condemned by the king and thrown alive into a superheated, red-hot furnace. Likewise, the False Prophet's ***image*** will be a replica of Antichrist and all mankind will be constrained to worship before it. Our text says that this fearsome thing will be able to ***speak*** and reason and will decree that all who will not worship before it be ***killed***! Amazing. How could that possibly be? Well, most likely, it will be demon animated. Antichrist worship will be formidable indeed in that day ... for it will be Satan's greatest false religion ever.

Rev. 13:16-18

*He causes all, both small and great, rich and poor, free and slave, to receive a **mark** on their right hand or on their foreheads, and that no one may buy or sell except one who has the mark,* [**NU** omits *"or"*] *the name,* [**NU** omits *"of the beast"*] *or the number of his name. Here is wisdom. Let him who has **understanding** calculate the number of the beast, for it is the number of **a man**: His number is **666**.*

13:16-17

In order to do business during the Great Tribulation, people will have to have one of three things ... in one of two places ... on their person. They must have either the ***mark*** of the beast or his ***name*** or the ***number of his name*** ... either on their right hand or on their forehead. No doubt, the "gung-ho" folks will opt for the forehead. You will remember that, back in chapter 7, the 144,000 received the seal of the name of their God on their foreheads. Antichrist and his false prophet will not be outdone. The **mark, the name or the number** of the **beast** will also be available on his followers' foreheads, signifying that he is their god! The mark that the 144,000 bore, however, was to protect them from the judgments of God. The mark the beast's followers will bear will be for the purpose of subjugating and controlling Earth's peoples and for uncovering all who are not in compliance with Antichrist's demands. Someone has said, *Economic oppression is the greatest oppression.* There is a great deal of truth in that. Antichrist and his false prophet will control the world one day in this way. I suspect his coded system will be so absolutely pervasive and popular that there will be little if any black market available to those who oppose him. This will make things very difficult for all who attempt to take a stand against him.

May we step aside here for a moment? Technology exists today that, by means of a computer chip that can be implanted under the skin, one can track a person and pinpoint their exact location at all times. Furthermore, the chip can carry all of one's personal and medical information as well. Companies that have developed this technology suggest that it is going to be a great benefit to mankind. Amongst other things, they say it will be a great help to law enforcement in the apprehension of criminals (if everyone were required to have one, I might add). Until our modern day, such things were unknown and, in fact, inconceivable. But now, down here in the year of our Lord, 2013, for the first time in human history such technology is on the scene. It is coming about, just as the Bible predicted it would.

13:18

This last verse in chapter 13 is written to the believers who will actually be living during those final days of Earth's secular history. It will give them a substantial heads up for spotting the Antichrist. It says that the **number** of Antichrist's **name** will be **666**. This will be just the information that those last-day believers will need in order to pinpoint Antichrist's arrival on the scene in their day. It says here that, at that time, those who have **wisdom** will be able to calculate this number. Webster's Dictionary defines **calculate** as, *to determine by* *mathematical processes*. Perhaps **666** will have to do with Antichrist's name in binary code as currently used by the Internet.

Some time back, I was discussing this number of the name of the Beast, **666**, with my son-in-law while we were watching football. He is a computer systems expert. After a while he said, *Herb, look at this*. He then showed me a chart of the binary code by which all Internet signals are transmitted. Then, he pointed out that the number of single digits that make up the signal for the *www* that designate the *world wide web* adds up to 666! I take this as an indicator that the number of the beast, that has so long been such a mystery, is probably referring to his name in binary code. As it turns out, every time we punch a key on our computers, it sends out an eight digit electrical impulse, made up of negative and positive charges that can be recognized by any other computer anywhere in the world and translated back into the letter or number we originally hit. A typical binary code for one letter looks like this: 00101011. That really peaked my curiosity, so I copied the chart for the binary codes used for each letter of the alphabet. Each sequence of eight electronic impulses has a specific numeric value ... namely: 128, 64, 32, 16, 8, 4, 2, and 1. For example, the code above, 00101011, has a numeric value of: 0, 0, 32, 0, 8, 0, 2 and 1 adding up to a total of 42. The upshot is ... that anyone's name typed over the Internet will have a specific total numeric value when each letter is added together yielding an exact numeric value for that individual's name. The mysterious scripture above, referring to **the number of his name**, may well be referring to its binary code, a reality that has not even existed up until our recent modern day. Here is a sample of the number of the word *Antichrist* in binary code:

(128+64+32+16+8+4+2+1)

A	01000001	64+1=65
N	01101110	64+32+8+4+2=110
T	01110100	64+32+16+4=116
I	01101001	64+32+8+1=105
C	01100011	64+32+2+1=99
H	01101000	64+32+8=104

R	01110010	64+32+16+2=114	
I	01101001	64+32+8+1=105	
S	01110011	64+32+16+2+1=115	
T	01110100	64+32+16+4=116	Total = 1049

Fascinating, is it not? Note, however, the binary code may have to be calculated in relation to some other language other than English ... say Arabic, Greek or Hebrew perhaps?

This brings us to the end of **the third interlude** in the book of Revelation. It began just after the blowing of the seventh Trumpet and takes up all of chapters 12 and 13. In these pages, we have been given a good deal of important information about the peoples, times, and conditions that will exist during the Great Tribulation. We have learned important information about:

...the *woman*, Israel, who gave birth to a *male Child*. She will be forced to flee into the wilderness from Satan's Antichrist one day.

...the *great red dragon*, Satan, who will be evicted from Heaven at the beginning of the Great Tribulation and who, afterwards, will go forth on the Earth seeking to exterminate all of the remaining Jews who believe in Christ.

...the *beast* out of the sea, Antichrist, and his ten king confederation.

...the *beast* out of the earth, the False Prophet, who will promote the worship of Antichrist in that day.

REVELATION 14

HEAVEN'S MOUNT ZION AND THE JUDGMENT OF THE SICKLES

Rev. 14:1-5

Then I looked, and behold, **[NU changes "a"]** *the Lamb standing on* **Mount Zion,** *and with him* **one hundred and forty-four thousand***, having his* **[NU adds "name and his"]** *Father's name written on their foreheads. And I heard a voice from heaven, like the voice of many waters, and like the voice of loud thunder. And I heard the sound of harpists playing their harps. They sang as it were a new song before the throne, before the four living creatures, and the elders; and no one could learn that song except the* **hundred and forty-four thousand** *who were* **redeemed from the earth***. These are the ones who were not defiled with women, for they are* **virgins***. These are the ones who follow the Lamb wherever he goes. These were redeemed from among men, being* **firstfruits** *to God and to the Lamb. And in their mouth was found* **no deceit***, for they are without fault* **[NU omits "before the throne of God"]***.*

14:1-2

We return now to the linear action of the Great Tribulation in time. Keep in mind that the events of which we are about to read will occur in the exact sequence that they are set forth in this chapter. For quite a while now, we have been looking at the dark side of the Great Tribulation. But, here in chapter 14, we come to a shaft of light. Down below, John has been observing Hell on Earth. But now, God takes him back up to Heaven where he once again can see the wondrous glory of God and his Lamb in the midst of his people. In spite of Satan's stranglehold on the earth below, all is well in God's Heaven and God's program is right on track.

Strange Work

In this new vision, John says, ***I looked, and behold, the Lamb standing on Mount Zion***. Now remember, this is the real Mount Zion. In the Greek, with its article, it could be translated ***the Mount Zion***. This Mount Zion is the original of which the one that is down on Earth is just a mere shadow. As you have it in *Hebrews 12:22-23*,

But you have come to Mount Zion and to the city of the living God, the heavenly Jerusalem, to an innumerable company of angels, to the general assembly and church of the firstborn who are registered in heaven, to God the judge of all, to the spirits of just men made perfect...

So, it is at Heaven's ***Mount Zion*** that this scene is set before us. John saw the Lord Jesus standing on that holy mount. Because Christ was seen standing on Mount Zion, and not seated on his throne, clues us that he is once again on the move. Notice that the 144,000 are there as well. We recognize them because they have ***his name and his Father's name written on their foreheads***. You will remember they received that seal back in chapter 7, before they went out into the storm of the Great Tribulation to serve Christ. The fact that we find them up in Heaven now, tells us they have all been martyred. Yet, what a triumphant scene this is! These 144,000 who loved, preached, suffered and died for their Master are now singing to him on Mount Zion. And, their song was at the request of the one whose voice was as the sound ***of many waters***. That, of course, was the voice of the omnipotent Son of God as described to us back in 1:15. As the 144,000 began to sing to their Lord, John says he also heard ***the sound of harpists playing their harps***. Who might these accompanists be? I take it they would be the Church. You will remember that back in chapter 5:8, the elders, who are representatives of the Church, were holding harps. So, I don't feel it is much of a stretch at all to say that you and I are scheduled to take part at this happy occasion by way of manning the instruments.

14:3-5

The 144,000 ***sang, as it were, a new song***. Truly it will be a great privilege for the Church to accompany the ***new song*** of the 144,000 ***before the throne, before the four living creatures, and before the*** *elders* on that future day. Verse three says they sang a song that belonged exclusively to the 144,000.

May we step aside again here for a moment? The Lord loves for his people to sing new songs to him. Repeatedly, in the Psalms, the Lord requests for his people to *sing ... a new song*. New songs come from the heart and God loves that. They cannot be sung by mere rote. Make up a song, dear saint, and sing it to him. Any song, you say? Sure. Go ahead. Any new song will do. It doesn't even have to rhyme if it comes from your heart and he will love it.

Coming back to our text ... here in verse four, we are given a good deal more information about the 144,000 that we were not told back in chapter 7. We read:

...These are the ones who were not defiled with women, for they are virgins. Some people try to explain this statement by saying that it simply means these 144,000 males are pure and single-hearted fellows. However, I see no reason to take it for other than what it says. That is, that they are indeed virgins who have not defiled themselves with women. Now, let me explain what I mean before I get myself into hot water for making such a politically incorrect statement. Think about it for a minute. What kind of women do you think will inhabit the earth during the closing days of the Great Tribulation? They will be ungodly wicked ones, right? Hooking up with one of those gals would, in fact, truly defile a righteous man. All the godly women will, for the most part, have been removed, either by at the Rapture or by being hunted down and killed by Antichrist ... or they will be camped out in the wilderness at the place of refuge. And, believe me, these fellows will be far too busy serving Christ and getting the Word of God out to have time for romance and marriage. Their ministries for Christ will be their dynamic, hectic, dangerous and short-term obsession. They will only be interested in doing their job. Hence, indeed, they will all be virgins to a man. It would be well for us to remember the Apostle Paul's admonition to us believers today along these same lines,

Are you bound to a wife? Do not seek to be loosed. Are you loosed from a wife? ***Do not seek a wife***. *But even if you do marry, you have not sinned; and if a virgin marries, she has not sinned. Nevertheless such will have trouble in the flesh, but I would spare you. But this I say, brethren, the* ***time is short****, so that from now on even* *those who have wives should be as though they had none... First Corinthians 7:27-29*

Each and every one of the 144,000 will have carried out this admonition to the letter. They went out to minister for Christ as **virgins**. They died as virgins. They were single minded in purpose and they didn't allow themselves to become entangled with the wicked women of Antichrist's dark kingdom to which they were preaching. A very wise pastor I once knew, who lived and ministered for Christ well into his nineties, said that over the years of his ministry he had observed that there were three things that remove good men from the ministry ... *pride, money, and women*. The 144,000 will escape all three of these pitfalls. May the Lord multiply their like in the Church today.

*...**These are the ones who follow the Lamb wherever he goes***. The devotion of these fellows to Christ will be on display for all of Heaven to see. They are enamored with their Savior. They follow him around like puppy dogs. Won't that be a wonderful sight, to see such a congregation of Jews adoring their Lord and Messiah? We will see it one day, when we encounter Christ's 144,000 and accompany them in their new song to the Savior.

*...**These were redeemed from among men, being firstfruits to God and to the Lamb***. This word, ***firstfruits***, is a word that speaks of a greater harvest to follow. The fact that these 144,000 are designated ***firstfruits*** means that a much greater harvest of the Jewish people is yet to come. As you have it in *Romans 11:26*,

*And so **all Israel will be saved**, as it is written: 'The **Deliverer** will come **out of Zion**, and he will turn away ungodliness from Jacob...*

*...**And in their mouth was found no deceit***. Deceit means to be crafty, sneaky and disingenuous. These fellows are *true blue*. They embody God's original design for his people to be the righteous people of God. Nathaniel was such a Jew. When Jesus saw Nathaniel coming to him, he said to Philip,

*'Behold, an Israelite **indeed**, in whom is **no deceit**' John 1:47b*

The 144,000 will be a 144,000 Nathaniels! By the way, the company that you and I will keep in Heaven is going to be amazing! What a delight it will be to make the acquaintance of each and every one of these 144,000 men of integrity as we live together with them in eternity.

Let's step aside for a moment. How many of these fellows went out into the Great Tribulation? 144,000. Right? How many do we find standing here on Heaven's Mt. Zion singing to the Lamb? 144,000. Our God certainly is able to keep of his own, is he not!? 144,000 went into the Great Tribulation and 144,000 have arrived safely in Heaven. Jesus keeps his own, beloved. Let's take a minute to look at some of our Lord's great promises to that effect in the Scripture. Job said,

*For he **performs** what is **appointed** for me, and many such things are with him. Job 23:14*

The Psalmist said,

*The LORD will **perfect** that which concerns me; your mercy, O LORD, endures forever; do not forsake the works of your hands. Psalm 138:8*

Jesus said,

*My sheep hear my voice, and I know them, and they follow me. And **I give them eternal life, and they shall never perish; neither shall anyone snatch them out of my hand**. My Father, who has given them to me, is greater than all; and no one is able to snatch them out of my Father's hand. I and my Father are one. John 10:27-30*

The Apostle Paul said,

*In him you also trusted, after you heard the word of truth, the gospel of your salvation; in whom also, **having believed, you were sealed** with the Holy Spirit of promise... Ephesians 1:13*

*...being **confident** of this very thing, that **he who has begun a good work in you will complete it until the day of Jesus Christ**... Philippians 1:6*

*For this reason I also suffer these things; nevertheless I am not ashamed, for I know whom I have believed and **am persuaded that he is able to keep** what I have committed to him until that day. Second Timothy 1:12*

The Apostle Peter, speaking of those who are Christ's, said,

*...who are **kept by the power of God through faith for salvation** ready to be revealed in the last time. First Peter 1:5*

Jude said,

Strange Work

> *Now to him who is able to* **keep you** *from stumbling, and* **to present you faultless before the presence of his glory with exceeding joy**, *to God our Savior, who alone is wise, be glory and majesty, dominion and power, both now and forever. Amen. Jude 24-25*

One hundred forty-four thousand started out down on the Earth and a 144,000 arrived safely home in Heaven and so will you and I, dear child of God. That's because it is God who does the keeping, you see. And, we can take that to the bank. He never loses a single one of his own.

Rev. 14:6-12

> *Then I saw* **another angel** *flying in the midst of heaven,* **having the everlasting gospel to preach to those who dwell on the earth**; *to every nation, tribe, tongue, and people; saying with a loud voice, "Fear God and give glory to him, for the hour of his judgment has come; and worship him who made heaven and earth, the sea and springs of water. And* **another angel** *followed, saying, 'Babylon* **[NU adds "the great is fallen, is fallen," and omits "that great city, because she"] which** *has made all nations drink of the wine of the wrath of her fornication.' Then* **a third angel** *followed them, saying with a loud voice,* **'If anyone worships the beast and his image, and receives his mark on his forehead or on his hand, he himself shall also drink of the wine of the wrath of God**, *which is poured out full strength into the cup of his indignation. He shall be tormented with fire and brimstone in the presence of the holy angels and in the presence of the Lamb. And the smoke of their torment ascends forever and ever; and they have no rest day or night, who worship the beast and his image, and whoever receives the mark of his name. Here is the patience of the saints;* **[NU omits "here are those"]** *who keep the commandments of God and the faith of Jesus.'*

14:6-7

No one who lives through the Great Tribulation will ever be able to accuse God of not giving them a chance. In addition to the testimony of the 144,000 and God's two witnesses, the world in that dark day will also receive the testimony of three separate angels whom

God will send to circumvent the globe and preach to each and every Earth-dweller during the final closing hours of that age. God will send forth one preaching angel, one proclaiming angel and, finally, one warning angel. Let's look at them.

...The first angel John saw flying through the skies (*heaven* here refers to the skies of Earth), had *the everlasting gospel to preach to those who dwell on the earth*. Incredible! In the closing days of the Great Tribulation our gracious and merciful God will send forth his angel to **preach the everlasting gospel** of the Lord Jesus Christ to all Earth-dwellers until every last soul has clearly heard the good news of the salvation that is available to them in Christ Jesus! This has got to be the greatest instance of amazing grace that the world will have ever seen. Truly, as the Psalmist repeatedly exclaims in *Psalm 136*,

His mercy endureth forever... (quoted repeatedly in: 1b,2b,3b,4b,5b,6b,7b,8b,9b,10b,11b,12b,13b,14b,15b,16b,17b,18b,19b 20b,21b,22b,23b,24b,25b,26b)

Now, for millennia, the Church has been involved in carrying out the Lord's commission to *go into all the earth and preach the gospel to every creature* (Matthew 28:19). However, she has never been completely successful. In fact, during some ages the Church has been a complete flop at getting the Word of God out. She has failed in the past and will fail again in the future. Our own generation will fail, as well. We will not get the Word of Christ out to every creature of our own generation. The 144,000 will also take their best shot, even giving their lives for it, but they too will come up short. Ultimately, it's going to take an angel from God to complete the job. I believe it was this very angel with the *loud voice* that Jesus was thinking of when he said,

*And this gospel of the kingdom will be **preached** in all the world as a witness to all the nations, and **then the end will come**. Matthew 24:14*

It will be impossible for men and women **not** to listen when God sends forth his **angel** with the **loud voice** to preach the *everlasting gospel*.

14:8

...The second angel went forth crying, **Babylon the great, is fallen, is fallen**. When Antichrist seizes Jerusalem at the middle of the

Tribulation, there is a good deal of evidence here in Revelation that he will literally change the city's name to **Babylon**. The name, *Jerusalem*, means *city of peace*. *Babylon* is a name derived from the Akkandian, **babilu**. It means **gate of God**. Since Antichrist will declare that he is God, and insist that he be worshipped at the temple at Jerusalem, it makes sense that he would choose the ancient name **Babylon**, the **gate of God**, for the name of his capitol city and center for his blasphemous worship. As we have previously noted, Babylon was the first kingdom to introduce counterfeit religion on Earth under King Nebuchadnezzar, when that ancient king had a statue of himself built and decreed that all his subjects were to bow down and worship it. When Antichrist seizes Jerusalem and renames it *Babylon*, he too will have his statue and require that everyone must fall down and worship it ... epitomizing the long tradition of man-worship in the Kingdom of Darkness which began so long ago at ancient Babylon. However, before Babylon's final demise, Earth-dwellers will be graphically warned of its inevitable destruction by another of God's proclaiming angels. Though the city itself won't literally fall until the pouring out of the seventh Bowl, this angel will circumvent the globe and proclaim it as already fallen. By this bold proclamation, he will be emphasizing the certainty of Babylon's fast approaching destruction which, time wise, will be only hours, or at most, days away. What an amazing warning that will be! This proclaiming angel's ominous and prophetic declaration will, no doubt, place a huge question mark in the minds of Antichrist worshipers in that day. I can almost hear them thinking, *What's he talking about?* Perhaps the Holy Spirit will answer in their hearts, *You know what I'm talking about*! God's proclaiming angel will be speaking the Word of God to them, you see. This warning is in line with the Scripture's statement in *Romans 4:17b*,

...*even God, who quickeneth the dead, and* **calleth those things which be not as though they were**...

14:9-11

...The third angel that went forth, proclaimed, ***If anyone worships the beast and his image, and receives his mark on their foreheads or on his hand, he himself shall also drink of the wine of the wrath of God.*** You can't help but think again here about how gracious and merciful our great God is. During the very last hours of the Great Tribulation, he will still be sending out warnings to men and women in hopes that they will repent and turn to him. *First Timothy 2:4b* says,

...*who desires all men to be saved and to come to the knowledge of the truth.*

Let's look a bit further at the important elements of this final warning by God's angel. He warns,

...*If anyone worships the beast and his image, and receives his mark on his forehead or on his hand, he himself shall also drink of the wine of the wrath of God, which is poured out full strength into the cup of his indignation.* That's telling it like it is, brother ... no holds barred. This angel will loudly declare to every Earth-dweller in that day that those who receive the mark of the Beast will be made to drink of the wrath of God *full strength*. This message, at that late hour, is an indication that people can still be saved and remove the beast's *mark*, by the way. It will still not be too late. However, he warns that those caught with that mark at the appearing of the Lord Jesus Christ will experience God's wrath undiluted, without a drop of mercy and with no way of escape. *Psalm 75:8*, says,

*For in the hand of the LORD there is a **cup**, and the wine is red; it is fully mixed, and he pours it out; surely its dregs shall **all the wicked** of the earth **drain and drink down**.*

...*and he shall be tormented with fire and brimstone.* Jesus told a true story in Luke 16, about a rich man who died and woke up in Hell. The scripture does not say that this was a parable. It is a graphic illustration of what this angel is referring to. The "Hell" that Jesus was referring to is not the Lake of Fire. Rather, it is the temporary holding place of all of the wicked dead. The Lake of Fire, which this angel will be warning of, is the permanent home of the wicked dead. The Bible describes it as a horrible place that is to be avoided at all cost. It was originally created and reserved for Satan and his demons. In chapter 20, we read that *hell* and *death* will be cast into it.

...He further warns that their punishment will be carried out *in the presence of the holy angels and in the presence of the Lamb.* The visibility to the wicked of God's Lamb, accompanied by the presence of his holy angels, will no doubt greatly increase the suffering of the damned. There, in all their naked unrighteousness, they will be fully exposed to the gaze of the Holy One and his holy angels. In Proverbs 8, Christ, speaking as Wisdom incarnate, says,

Blessed is the man who listens to me, watching daily at my gates, waiting at the posts of my doors. For whoever finds me finds life, and obtains favor from the LORD; but he who sins against me wrongs his own soul; ***all those who hate me love death**... Proverbs 8:34-36*

...The angel continued ... ***And the smoke of their torment ascends forever and ever; and they have no rest day or night, who worship the beast and his image, and whoever receives the mark of his name.*** Thus, he will forewarn Earth-dwellers of the eternal nature of the punishment that Antichrist worshippers can expect. Eternal, conscious damnation is not a popular concept today, by the way. It's not in the playbook of political or even ecclesiastical correctness. Yet, Jesus and his Word speak of it openly and specifically. In *Mark 9:43-44,* Jesus said,

If your hand causes you to sin, cut it off. It is better for you to enter into life maimed, rather than having two hands, to go to hell, ***into the fire that shall never be quenched;*** *where* ***'Their worm does not die, and the fire is not quenched.'***

14:12

...The angel concluded his message saying ... ***Here is the patience of the saints; who keep the commandments of God and the faith of Jesus.*** I suspect that this will be a great consolation for those who will be on the receiving end of Antichrist's persecution and murder ... when they hear these words proclaimed from the skies by this awesome angel. They will assure them that their trials are temporary but their tormentors will suffer forever in the Lake of Fire ... and that a dramatic reversal of circumstances is just around the corner. It will only be a matter of time and require only a bit of patience.

Rev. 14:13

Then I heard a voice from heaven saying, **[NU omits *"to me"*]** *'Write: Blessed are the dead who die in the Lord from now on.' 'Yes,' says the Spirit, 'that they may rest from their labors, and their works follow them.'*

In the Psalm 116:15, it is written, **Precious in the eyes of the Lord are the death of his saints**. That is also reflected in these words as well. This exclamation pours out from the heart of God the Father and from the Holy Spirit and is directed at his suffering people who are paying so great a price for believing in his Son during those awful future days of tribulation. Had we been able to actually hear these words as they were spoken, I believe we would have heard great empathy and concern in their inflection as he said, *blessed are the dead who die in the Lord from now on.* This statement from the Father was immediately followed by an *Amen* from the Holy Spirit. I believe that many a suffering Tribulation saint will take comfort in these words as they pour over their Bibles in that day. The Holy Spirit, knowing the good things that await those saints adds ... *that they may rest from their labors, and their works follow them.* Jesus' words in *Luke 6:21-23,* comes to mind here...

Blessed are you who **hunger** *now, for you shall be filled. Blessed are you who* **weep** *now, for you shall laugh. Blessed are you when men* **hate you**, *and when they* **exclude you**, *and* **revile you**, *and* **cast out your name as evil**, *for the Son of Man's sake. Rejoice in that day and leap for joy! For indeed your* **reward** *is great in heaven, for in like manner their fathers did to the prophets.*

May we step aside for a moment and think a bit about the Person of God's Holy Spirit, as He is revealed here?

First, notice that the Holy Spirit is a Person, not an "it." He is the third person of the Trinity. All through the Scriptures, the Spirit is referred to by personal pronouns.

Second, notice that he has a will, intellect and emotions. For example, he can be grieved (Ephesians 4:30). There is no room in Scripture for the notion that the Holy Spirit is any less a person than the Son or the Father. He is no mere force, as many have erroneously taught. Nor is he a mere quantity that someone can get more of ... like pouring water into a glass. You either have Him or you don't (Romans

8:9). His personality is clearly demonstrated here by his words, *'Yes,' says the Spirit, 'that they may rest from their labors, and their works follow them.'* This is a statement from someone who is speaking from their heart. Sadly, there is a great deal of confusion today about the person, work and ministry of the Holy Spirit.

Rev. 14:14-16

*Then I looked, and behold, a white cloud, and on the cloud sat One like the **Son of Man**, having on his head a golden **crown**, and in his hand a sharp sickle. And another angel came out of the temple, crying with a loud voice to him who sat on the cloud, '**Thrust in your sickle and reap**, for the time has come* [**NU omits "For you"**] *to reap, for **the harvest of the earth is ripe**. So he who sat on the cloud thrust in his sickle on the earth, and the earth was reaped.*

We come now to a new vision and it is, perhaps, the most sobering one in the Bible. It answers the question posed in *Hebrews 10:28-29,*

*He that despised **Moses' law** died without mercy under two or three witnesses: of how much sorer **punishment**, suppose ye, shall he be thought worthy, who hath **trodden under foot the Son of God, and hath counted the blood of the covenant** wherewith he was sanctified, an unholy thing, and hath done despite unto the Spirit of grace?* (KJV)

Before we get into it, let's lay a bit of ground work. The harvest of the souls of men can be divided into two broad categories. **The first category is the harvesting of the righteous and the second is the harvesting of the wicked.** These two groups are not harvested together nor will all the individuals in either group be harvested at the exact same point in time. Here, in the last vision of chapter 14, we come to the first batch of the harvest of the wicked. And, since we are back into the linear action of the Great Tribulation, these events described here must take place immediately prior to Christ's literal descent to the earth at the end of the Great Tribulation.

Because of the difficulty this passage presents, many commentators interpret it as merely a preview of the great battle of Armageddon described much later in chapter 19. However, Armageddon does not fit here at all. It would be entirely out of sequence. Everything in this passage points to the fact that this is the harvest of wicked Israel. This harvest will occur immediately following the global warnings of God's three proclaiming angels and just prior to the commencement of the Bowl Judgments. I believe it is set here in stark contrast to the godly 144,000 Jews found just a few verses back. John the Baptist forewarned Israel of this impending judgment saying,

I indeed baptize you with water unto repentance, but He who is coming after me is mightier than I, whose sandals I am not worthy to carry. ***He will baptize you with*** *the Holy Spirit and **fire**. His winnowing fan is in His hand, and **He will thoroughly clean out His threshing floor**, and gather His wheat into the barn; but **He will burn up the chaff with unquenchable fire**. Matthew 3:11-12*

When Christ judges ungodly Israel one day, He will harvest them out of one of two realms. They will either come from the Jews on earth who are still alive at the end of the Great Tribulation or ... as a second source ... they will come from resurrected Israel (Dan. 12:2) ... all Jews from all time all of the way back to the beginning of God's dealings with them as a people. I believe this is what is pictured here in its two phases. In the first part of the vision, John saw, ***One like the Son of Man*** upon ***a white cloud***. This is the same name for Messiah that John used back in 1:13. It is the Old Testament Messianic title for Christ from Daniel 7. No mistake about it, it is Christ who is sitting on the ***white cloud***. His Messianic title is the first evidence that this vision concerns the nation of Israel. Further, he is seen wearing ***a crown*** (singular), which points to the fact that he is functioning here as a king rather than the ***King of kings***. He appears here as the King of Israel who will shortly be placed on the throne of his ancestor, David. The Greek word translated *crown* here is στέφανον (***stephanon***, from ***stephanos***). It is a word that refers to a victor's crown. In sharp contrast to the mocking he received by the Jews at the cross because of his claim to be the King of the Jews ... Jesus, will appear at this time as their indisputable King indeed. By way of contrast, when he comes to judge the whole Earth and to rule the nations, he will be wearing ***many diadems*** (Revelation 19:12).

John says he had a ***sharp sickle*** in his hand. J.B. Smith, an early expositor of Revelation, says that this Greek word, ***sharp***, is used sixteen times in the New Testament and it is always used in a negative and uninviting sense. Sickles are frequently associated with judgment in the Bible. *Joel 3:13-14*, speaking of this very event, says,

*Put in the **sickle**, for the harvest is **ripe**. Come, go down; for the winepress is full, the vats overflow; for their wickedness is great. Multitudes, multitudes in the valley of decision! For the day of the LORD is near in the valley of decision.*

What we are observing here is the fulfillment of that very prophecy. The word, *ripe*, in verse fifteen, is a Greek word that literally means **dried up** or **withered**. It indicates that the recipients of this judgment are long overdue. Now, let's look to see if there is any scriptural basis for the future harvesting of wicked Israelites off the earth and taking them off to judgment. Here, we will need to look at the teachings of Jesus concerning wicked Israel and carefully compare his words from Matthew 13:24-30, 36-42 and 24:37-42.

*Another parable he put forth to them, saying: "The kingdom of heaven is like a man who sowed **good seed** in his field; but while men slept, his **enemy came and sowed tares** among the wheat and went his way. But when the grain had sprouted and produced a crop, then the tares also appeared. So the servants of the owner came and said to him, 'Sir, did you not sow good seed in your field? How then does it have tares? He said to them, 'An enemy has done this.' The servants said to him, **'Do you want us then to go and gather them up?** But he said, **'No, lest while you gather up the tares you also uproot the wheat with them**. Let both grow together **until the harvest**, and at the time of harvest I will say to the reapers, **'First gather together the tares and bind them in bundles to burn them**, but gather the wheat into my barn.' Matthew 13:24-30*

*Then Jesus sent the multitude away and went into the house. And his disciples came to him, saying, 'Explain to us the parable of the tares of the field.' He answered and said to them: 'He who sows the good seed is the **Son of Man**. The field is the world, the good **seeds are the sons of the kingdom,** but the **tares are the sons of the wicked one**. The enemy who sowed them is the devil, **the harvest is the end of the age**, and the **reapers are the angels**. Therefore as the tares are gathered and burned in the fire, so it will be **at the end of this age**. The **Son of Man** will send out his **angels**, and they will gather **out of his kingdom** all things that offend, and those who practice lawlessness,* *and will cast them into the furnace of fire. There will be wailing and gnashing of teeth. Matthew 13:36-42*

But as the days of Noah were, so also will the coming of the Son of Man be. For as in the days before the flood, they were eating and drinking, marrying and giving in marriage, until the day that Noah entered the ark, and did not know until the flood came and took them all away, so also will the coming of the **Son of Man** *be. Then* **two men will be in the field: one will be taken and the other left. Two women will be grinding at the mill: one will be taken and the other left.** *Watch therefore, for you do not know what hour your Lord is coming. Matthew 24:37-42*

The Jews were the people of whom and to whom Jesus was speaking in all three of the passages above. Who did he say would be **taken**? His teaching is clear. It is the unrighteous Jew who will be **taken** and gathered **out** of his Kingdom at the end of the age. They will all find themselves suddenly removed (harvested) from off the earth ... ultimately to be cast ***into the furnace of fire***. It is the godly Jews who will be left on Earth to meet their Messiah at his coming and enter into his kingdom with him. This is a very important concept to get a hold of.

Now, God has been in a continuous covenant relationship with the Jewish people from the days of Abraham. His Mosaic covenant with them, the Law, contained both blessings and curses. For example, in *Deuteronomy 11:26-28*, we read,

Behold, I set before you today a **blessing** *and a* **curse***: the* **blessing***, if you obey the commandments of the LORD your God which I command you today; and the* **curse***, if you do not obey the commandments of the LORD your God, but turn aside from the way which I command you today,* **to go after other gods which you have not known***.*

At the cross, God instituted the New Covenant with his chosen people, the Jew, sealed with the blood of Christ. In the closing days of the Great Tribulation, Christ will resurrect and judge his Jewish people according to whether they were wicked or righteous and in accordance with his covenants with them. Those Israelites who lived their lives under the Old Covenant will be judged by the standards of the Old Covenant. Those who lived their lives under the New Covenant will be judged according to the standards of the New Covenant. As you have it in *Daniel 12:2-3,*

And many of those who sleep in the dust of the earth shall awake*, some to everlasting life,* **some to shame and everlasting contempt***. Those who are wise shall shine like the brightness of the firmament, and those who turn many to righteousness like the stars forever and ever.*

This is the subject of John's vision here of the two sickles. In the first step, Christ, the Judge of Israel, will cut off all the withered fruit from his *vine*, Israel, that remains down on the earth ... differentiating between the ungodly and godly like a gardener hoeing weeds from his garden. This is pictured here when Christ thrusts in his *sickle* upon the earth. Notice that there is no product of that reaping mentioned, just the statement that *the earth was reaped*. I believe this will include both the resurrected Jews ... who will find themselves staring up at Christ as he descends from the sky ... along with all the wicked Jews who are still alive at the end of the Great Tribulation. Together, they will all behold the beginning of Christ's very visible and glorious return. Then, suddenly, they will all be cut down by Christ.

Rev. 14:17-20

Then another angel came out of the temple which is in heaven, he also having a sharp ***sickle****. And another angel came out from the altar, who had power over fire, and he cried with a loud cry to him who had the sharp sickle, saying, 'Thrust in your sharp sickle and* ***gather*** *the* ***clusters*** *of the* ***vine*** *of the earth, for her grapes are fully ripe.' So* ***the angel thrust his sickle into the earth and gathered the vine of the earth, and threw it into the great winepress of the wrath of God****. And* ***the winepress was trampled outside the city****, and* ***blood*** *came out of the winepress, up to the horses' bridles, for one thousand six hundred furlongs.*

This is the second phase of the judgment of unrighteous Jews. It is the *gather* by Christ's angels of the already cut down, dry and rotten *clusters* that Christ has cut off and simply await to be gathered by his angels and taken away to the place of judgment. This second phase of the harvest of wicked Israel will culminate in great carnage.

John saw an angel come out of the temple in Heaven carrying a *sickle*. The fact that he emerges from the temple is a reminder that he has received his orders from within the Holy of Holies itself. All judgment begins with God and is in accordance with his holy character. A second angel from the altar of sacrifice and burnt offering called to the one with the sickle saying, **Thrust in your sharp sickle and gather the clusters of the vine of the earth**. The fact that the second angel calls from the altar of sacrifice reminds us that those who are about to be gathered and taken away to judgment have not responded to their God in faith and have completely rejected the sacrifice of the Lamb of God that was so repeatedly pictured at this altar under the Old Covenant. Notice that the harvest by the angel with the sickle is said to be a *gather* of the *clusters* of the *vine of the earth*. This phrase, *vine of the earth*, adds further weight to the case that what we are looking here is the judgment of unrighteous Israel. The picture of Israel as being God's *vine* is a prominent one in the Old Testament. *Psalm 80:8, 14-15*, says,

You have brought a **vine** out of Egypt; you have cast out the nations, and planted it." "Return, we beseech you, O God of hosts; **look down from heaven and see, and visit this vine** and the vineyard which your right hand has planted, and the branch that You made strong for yourself.

Jeremiah quotes the Lord's speaking to Israel as follows,

Yet I had planted you a noble vine, a seed of highest quality. **How then have you turned before me into the degenerate plant of an alien vine?** Jeremiah 2:21

This is the judgment of **that** *vine* ... specifically, the judgment of its over-ripe *clusters* of its rotten fruit at the end of the Great Tribulation. The cleansing away of these withered, rotten *clusters* will be the final step in the Lord's refining of his covenant people in preparation for his return to deliver them and to fulfill his promise to them of a kingdom on Earth. As you have it in *Zechariah 13:8-9*,

And it shall come to pass, that in all the land, saith the Lord, two parts therein shall be **cut off and die**; but the third shall be **left** therein. And I will bring the third part through the fire, and will refine them as silver is refined, and will try them as gold is tried: they shall *call on my name, and I will hear them: I will say,* **It is my people**: *and they shall say,* **The Lord is my God**. (KJV)

John says the severed **clusters** were cast **into the great winepress of the wrath of God**. As I see it, these things will take place in the following order:

First, all wicked Jews who have ever lived (newly resurrected or currently alive at that time) will observe Christ's Second Coming but will then be immediately cut off by Christ. The Son of Man, seen here as thrusting his cycle over the earth, is probably referring to the exercise of his Word. This is when Jesus' words to Caiaphas will be ultimately fulfilled.

Jesus said to him, 'It is as you said. Nevertheless, I say to you, hereafter **you will see the Son of Man** *sitting at the right hand of the Power, and* **coming on the clouds of heaven**.*' Then the high priest tore his clothes, saying, 'He has spoken blasphemy! What further need do we have of witnesses? Look, now you have heard His blasphemy!' Matthew 26:64-65*

Did you notice that Jesus specifically told Caiaphas that he would see him **coming on the clouds of heaven**? That can only occur at, or at the very beginning of, Christ's Second Coming.

Second, all these wicked Jews will be carried away by Christ's gathering angels ... taken away bodily ... to judgment. As to Caiaphas' case in particular, he will one day be suddenly resurrected ... find himself gazing up at the Son of God in the glory clouds of Heaven ... and then, experience being suddenly cut down and extracted from off the earth by Christ's angels.

Third, we read that the severed **clusters** will be cast **into the great winepress of the wrath of God**. In Luke 17, Jesus said that ungodly Jews would one day be snatched from the earth. That passage has great bearing here. His disciples asked him, **where, Lord?** His answer was clear. Let's read it.

Two men will be in the field: the one will be taken and the other left. And they answered and said to him, **'Where, Lord?**' *So he said to them, 'Wherever the* **body** *is, there the eagles* [vultures] *will be gathered together.' Luke 17:36-37*

Jesus' answer to his disciples as to **where** they would be taken is specific. He said that they would be taken to a place of slaughter where vultures were waiting. Spiros Zodhiates, in his work *The Complete Word Study Dictionary*, defines the Greek word used for **eagles** above as, *An eagle or vulture, a species of rapacious birds represented as preying on dead bodies where some species of vulture is probably intended.* In the book to the Hebrews, the Jews, under their New Covenant, were warned over and over again of the severe judgment that they would receive if they turned away from Christ and spurned the blood of his new covenant with them. As you have it in *Hebrews 2:3*,

*How shall **we** [Jews] **escape** if we neglect so great a salvation, which at the first began to be spoken by the Lord, and was confirmed to us by those who heard him...?*

Following Jesus teaching that ungodly Jews will be caught out of his kingdom and taken away to judgment, it follows that their judgment will take place somewhere other than on Earth. You will recall that this chapter opened at the *city* in Heaven. I take it therefore, because of the context here, that the *city* spoken of in verse twenty is still the Heavenly Jerusalem, not the earthly Jerusalem. Apparently, the judgment of wicked Israel will take place within eyesight of the very city whose gates bear the names of their twelve tribes and that should have been their eternal home. What a terrible judgment that will be. The scene before us truly answers the question as to what punishment should be appropriate for those who have **trampled the Son of God under foot** and **counted the blood of the covenant a common thing** and **insulted the Spirit of grace** (Hebrews 10:29). These wicked Jews will be snatched bodily off the Earth and will then be unceremoniously trampled underfoot by the Son of God in the **winepress of the wrath of God**. I say, *bodily*, because, ultimately, all judgment of all the ungodly will be a bodily judgment. Jesus confirmed this in *Matthew 5:29-30,* when he said,

*And if thy right eye offend thee, pluck it out, and cast it from thee: for it is profitable for thee that **one of thy members should perish, and not that thy whole body should be cast into hell**. And if thy right hand offend thee, cut it off, and cast it from thee: for it is profitable for thee that one of thy members should perish, and not that thy whole **body** should be cast into hell.* (KJV)

Our text says that, as a result, blood ran *up to the horses' bridles* for sixteen hundred furlongs. The picture here is of the notch-like gully that was chiseled below a winepress where the wine would run out as the grapes were pressed. Blood however, will run from this winepress. I expect this trench will be five or so feet deep and run for approximately two hundred miles. To account for that much blood, I did some calculations based on the amount of blood in a human body. This probably is unduly gruesome and graphic, but I felt it was necessary to show the possibility and reliability of these amazing statements in the Word of God. A one foot wide ditch running for two hundred miles at the depth of say, five feet, (the approximate depth of *horses' bridles*) would equal 5260 feet times 200 times 5 times 1 foot. Such a gully would have a capacity of 5,260,000 cubic feet. Rounded to 5,000,000 cubic feet and then multiplied by approximately eight quarts per cubic foot, such an outlet would hold 40,000,000 quarts of liquid. 40,000,000 divided by 6 (assuming approximately six quarts of blood per human body) means that it would take 6.6 million people to produce that volume of blood. More than likely, there will be more people than that in this *winepress of the wrath of God*. The warning from the writer to the Hebrews comes to my mind here, does it not?

It is a fearful thing to fall into the hands of the living God. Hebrews 10:31

I make no apology for this. It is what it is. It is a terrible mistake to assume that God is not a God of judgment.

One last thought ... Daniel 12, says that the resurrection of Israel will occur all at one time and will include both righteous and unrighteous Jews. So, not only will all the unrighteous Jews of all time meet him at the Second Coming (to be cut down and then extracted from off the earth) ... but all the righteous Jews will meet their Messiah at his Second Coming as well (to proceed on in with him into his Kingdom). So, on the positive side, Abraham and Sara, Isaac and Rebekah, Jacob and Leah and Rachel, David and Bathsheba ... and countless other Jews ... will be resurrected to greet their Messiah and enter with him into his Kingdom. In sharp contrast, what a joyous occasion that will be for all of them.

REVELATION 15 - 16

THE POURING OUT OF THE BOWL JUDGMENTS

Rev. 15:1

Then I saw another sign in heaven, great and marvelous: **seven angels having the seven last plagues, for in them the wrath of God is complete**.

This is a new vision. Following the vision of the removal and judgment of unrighteous Jews, John now sees another sign which he says was **great and marvelous**. Seven angels appeared **having the seven last plagues**. These angels will carry out the final series of judgments in the Great Tribulation for **in them**, he says, **the wrath of God is complete**.

Rev. 15:2-4

And I saw something like a sea of glass mingled with fire, and those who have the victory over the beast, over his image **[NU omits "and over his mark"]** *and over the number of his name, standing on the sea of glass, having harps of God. They sing the* **song of Moses**, *the servant of God, and the* **song of the Lamb**, *saying: 'Great and marvelous are your works, Lord God Almighty! Just and true are your ways, O King of the saints! Who shall not fear you, O Lord, and glorify your name? For you alone are holy. For all nations shall come and worship before you, for your judgments have been manifested.'*

Dr. McGee points out that this final outpouring of **the wrath of God** begins in Heaven with a *choir*! And, the choir members are the saints from the Great Tribulation. They have **harps** and they are singing both the **song of Moses** and the **song of the Lamb**. What an amazing group this is! The fact that they possess harps indicates that they are

Church-like, if I may coin a word here, and their songs demonstrate they are made up of both Jews and Gentiles. What a glorious combination and mixture of people these Tribulation saints will be. And, since we find them here in Heaven, it is obvious that they are people who were martyred by Antichrist because of their faith in Christ. Yet, it is said they **have the victory**. How so? Well, they aren't dead, are they!? Nor, are they sad, by any means. In fact, they are singing up a storm! Jesus' words from *John 11:25b-26*, come to mind,

He who believes in me, ***though he may die, he shall live****. And whoever lives and believes in me shall never die. Do you believe this?*

Also, his words from *Matthew 10:28*,

And do not fear those who kill the body but cannot kill the soul. But rather fear Him who is able to destroy both soul and body in hell.

The day these brothers and sisters were put to death on Earth must have seemed the blackest day of their lives. But, immediately afterward, they found themselves in the most joyful, glorious and wonderful place imaginable. Also, they are now present to witnessing their Lord's sending of his seven angels to pour out his final Bowls ***of the wrath of God*** upon the very ones who had put them to death down on Earth. No wonder they are singing. There are several things about these martyrs that are worth noting:

First, they are seen holding the **harps of God**. These are the same instruments of praise that the elders were holding back in chapter 5. At this point in time, these Tribulation Saints will also have been given harps. Like the Church, they too were saved by faith in Jesus Christ and thereby have the right to sing the Song of the Lamb.

Second, they are standing on the fiery and glassy ***sea*** before God's Throne. May I say to you, only people who have acquired the imputed righteousness of Christ will ever be able to stand unharmed on that most holy and fiery ground. If an unredeemed sinner were to attempt to stand there, he would melt like wax in a blast furnace. As you have it in *Psalm1:4-5*,

The ungodly are not so, but are ***like the chaff which the wind drives away****. Therefore the ungodly shall not stand in the judgment,* ***nor sinners in the congregation of the righteous****.*

Third, they are singing **the *song of Moses*** and ***the song of the Lamb.*** They can sing both of these songs because they are a mixed crowd of both Jews and Gentiles. The combination of those two Biblical songs produces a hymn about all that God has ever done for the people he has chosen for himself. The song of Moses is found in Exodus 15 and Deuteronomy 32. The Song of the Lamb, we heard sung back in 5:9-12. The final stanza of these two great songs climaxed with the words, *Great and marvelous are your works, Lord God Almighty! Just and true are your ways, O King of the saints! Who shall not fear you, O Lord, and glorify your name? For you alone are holy. For all nations shall come and worship before you, for your judgments have been manifested.* And all the people said, Amen!

Rev. 15:5-8

After these things I looked, and **[NU omits "behold"]** *the temple of the tabernacle of the testimony in heaven was opened. And* **out of the temple came the seven angels having the seven plagues**, *clothed in pure bright linen, and having their chests girded with golden bands. Then one of the four living creatures gave to the seven angels* **seven golden bowls** *full of the* **wrath of God** *who lives forever and ever. The temple was filled with smoke from the glory of God and from his power, and no* **one was able to enter the temple till the seven plagues of the seven angels were completed.**

Heaven's temple is referred to fifteen times in Revelation. It is the real temple of which all the ones down on Earth were only copies and mere shadows. This is a very Jewish scene here. God is about to pour out his wrath on the earth on behalf of his Jewish people, you see. Make no mistake about it ... the Tribulation is all about *a Deliverer* coming **out of Zion** (Rom. 11:26; Ps. 14:7) to save his covenant people, the Jews. The prophet Zechariah, speaking of that day of reckoning, is very pointed. He says,

For thus says the LORD of hosts: **'He sent me after glory, to the nations which plunder you; for he who touches you touches the apple of his eye**. *For surely I will shake my hand against them, and they shall become spoil for their servants.* **Then you will know that the LORD of hosts has sent me. Sing and rejoice, O daughter of**

Zion! For behold, I am coming and I will dwell in your midst,' says the LORD. *Many nations shall be joined to the LORD in that day, and they shall become my people. And I will dwell in your midst. Then you will know that the LORD of hosts has sent me to you. And the LORD will take possession of Judah as his inheritance in the Holy Land, and will again choose Jerusalem.* **Be silent, all flesh, before the LORD, for he is aroused from his holy habitation***! Zechariah 2:8-13*

In *Genesis 12:3*, the Lord said to Abraham,

I will bless those who bless you, and I will **curse him who curses you***; and in you all the families of the earth shall be blessed.*

Have you been watching the news lately? On every front, Israel continues to be under attack by her enemies. They hate the Jews. Here in our passage, we read that a day in world history will come when God will take vengeance on the enemies of God's people. It will begin shortly after the Rapture of the Church ... reach its peak with his Bowl judgments ... and be capped off by the arrival of the **Deliverer**, the Lord Jesus Christ, who will summarily judge and execute all that remains of the enemies of his chosen people. I repeat, after the Lord takes his Church out of the world, the Tribulation that follows will be primarily about the purifying, saving and delivering of God's covenant chosen people ... the Jews.

Coming back to the text, John saw **seven angels** receive from one of the Living Creatures **seven bowls full of the wrath of God**. These angels are different from the seven angels of the Trumpet judgments. The seven Bowl judgments fall under the seventh Trumpet. After the distribution of the seven final **bowls full of the wrath of God**, we read, **The temple was filled with smoke from the glory of God and from his power, and no one was able to enter the temple till the seven plagues of the seven angels were completed**. During the time when these final judgments are being poured out, God's undivided attention will be upon his wrath. This is why Heaven's temple will be filled with smoke and glory and power ... and no one will be able to enter therein during that time.

THE FIRST BOWL ... PUTRID SORES

Rev. 16:1-2

*Then I heard a loud voice from the temple saying to the seven angels, '**Go and pour out the** [**NU adds "seven bowls"**] **of the wrath of God on the earth**.' So the first went and poured out his bowl upon the earth, and **a foul and loathsome sore** came upon the men who had the mark of the beast and those who worshipped his image.*

I take this **loud voice** to be the voice of Christ Jesus. He is the appointed and sole Judge of all the earth. As Peter told Cornelius in *Acts 10:42*,

*And he commanded us to preach to the people, and to testify that it is he who was **ordained by God to be Judge** of the living and the dead.*

Now, since Christ simply commanded the angels to go and pour out their bowls, it follows that these judgments will occur in rapid succession and without pause. These are the final judgments of the Great Tribulation and the lead in for the Lord's Second Coming.

When the first angel poured out his Bowl, a *foul and loathsome sore came upon the men who had the mark of the beast and those who worshipped his image*. You will remember that the recipients of this judgment were graphically warned by an angel about the dire consequences of receiving Antichrist's mark back in chapter 14. Having ignored his warning, they must now suffer the consequences of their obstinacy. These last plagues continue to parallel those produced through Moses in the Exodus from Egypt. This one parallels the fifth plague on Egypt. As you have it in *Exodus 9:8-10*,

*So the LORD said to Moses and Aaron, 'Take for yourselves handfuls of ashes from a furnace, and let Moses scatter it toward the heavens in the sight of Pharaoh. And it will become fine dust in all the land of Egypt, and it will cause **boils** that break out in **sores** on man and beast throughout all the land of Egypt.' Then they took ashes from the furnace and stood before Pharaoh, and Moses scattered them toward heaven. And they **caused boils** that break out in **sores** on man and beast.*

THE SECOND BOWL

THE SEA TURNED TO BLOOD

Rev. 16:3

Then the **second** *angel poured out his bowl on the* **sea**, *and it became* **blood** *as of a dead man; and* **every living creature in the sea died**.

You will remember that a third of all sea life was destroyed as the result of the second Trumpet judgment (8:8-9). All remaining sea life will be exterminated by the second Bowl judgment. The target of this destruction is tragic. That which God so lavishly created on the fifth day, he will utterly destroy on this day. I can't help but think of how pleased the Lord was on the day that he made all the plethora of sea life for man's pleasure and benefit. We read in *Genesis 1:20-23*,

Then God said, '**Let the waters abound with an abundance of living creatures**, *and let birds fly above the earth across the face of the firmament of the heavens.' So God created great sea creatures and every living thing that moves, with which the waters abounded, according to their kind, and every winged bird according to its kind. And* **God saw that it was good**. *And God blessed them, saying, 'Be fruitful and multiply, and fill the waters in the seas, and let birds multiply on the earth.' So the evening and the morning were the fifth day.*

All remaining sea life will perish at the pouring out of the second Bowl ... all because of man's stubbornness and rebellion.

THE THIRD BOWL

ALL THE FRESH WATER TURNED TO BLOOD

Rev. 16:4-7

Then the **third** *angel poured out his bowl on the* **rivers** *and* **springs of water**, *and they became* **blood**. *And I heard the angel of the waters saying: 'You are righteous,* **[NU omits "O Lord"]** *the One*

who is and who was **[NU adds *"the Holy One"* and omits *"and"*]** *who is to be, because you have judged these things. For* **they have shed the blood of saints and prophets**, *and you have given them blood to drink.* **[NU omits *"For"*]** *It is their just due. And I heard* **[NU omits *"another from"*]** *the altar saying, 'Even so, Lord God Almighty,* **true and righteous are your judgments**.*'*

When the third angel poured out his Bowl, all remaining fresh water on the earth was turned to blood. From that time on, Earth-dwellers will have to drink blood to stay alive. Back in 6:9, at the fifth Seal, the martyrs under the altar cried out to God, **How long, O Lord, holy and true, until you judge and avenge our blood on those who dwell on the earth?** Now, their question is being answered. The day of that vengeance has come. This Bowl is Christ's chosen vindication on behalf of all of his saints and prophets of all time whose blood was shed at the hands of the wicked. His avenging angel cries out ... **You are righteous ... For they have shed the blood of saints and prophets.** Then, the altar itself, that place where so many blood sacrifices for sin had been offered, cries out as well saying, **Even so, Lord God Almighty, true and righteous are your judgments.** By the end of the first three Bowl judgments, all of the waters on Earth will have been turned to blood. This Bowl parallels Moses' first plague.

Thus says the LORD: **'By this you shall know that I am the LORD**. *Behold,* **I will strike the waters which are in the river with the rod that is in my hand, and they shall be turned to blood**. *And the fish that are in the river shall die, the river shall stink, and the Egyptians will loathe to drink the water of the river.' Then the LORD spoke to Moses, 'Say to Aaron, 'Take your rod and stretch out your hand over the waters of Egypt, over their streams, over their rivers, over their ponds, and over all their pools of water, that they may become blood. And there shall be blood throughout all the land of Egypt, both in buckets of wood and pitchers of stone.'" And Moses and Aaron did so, just as the LORD commanded. So he lifted up the rod and struck the waters that were in the river, in the sight of Pharaoh and in the sight of his servants. And all the waters that were in the river were turned to blood. Exodus 7:17-20*

May we step aside here for a moment? All unsaved mankind, as well as everything else on this earth, is scheduled for judgment. *John 3:36,* says,

He who believes in the Son has everlasting life; and he who does not believe the Son shall not see life, but the **wrath** *of God abides on him.*

Second Peter 3:7, says,

But the heavens and the earth, which are now, by the same word are kept in store, ***reserved unto fire*** *against the day of* ***judgment and perdition of ungodly men****.* (KJV)

God's wrath simmers today. But, the day will come when it will overflow and be poured out on man and on the earth alike. People find this very hard to accept, but it most certainly will come. False and insipid preaching from many pulpits has, no doubt, fueled a good deal of the delusion and false security about this. People have been told that God is all "sweetness and light" and that he would never *punish anyone!* But, the Bible tells a far different story. It is true that God is love (First John 4:4), but he is also righteous and holy ... and he has promised vengeance on all unbelievers and persecutors of his people. You can take it to the bank, there will be retribution on all those who hate God and God's people and who have flatly rejected God's love offered to them in his Son. As you have it in *Second Thessalonians 1:7-9,*

And to you who are troubled rest with us, when the Lord Jesus shall be revealed from heaven with his mighty angels, in flaming fire taking ***vengeance on them that know not God****, and that* ***obey not the gospel*** *of our Lord Jesus Christ who shall be punished with everlasting destruction from the presence of the Lord, and from the glory of his power.*

The implications of that scripture are enormous. It means that men and women have the opportunity, the capacity and the responsibility ... to know God. And, if they do not respond, they will be held accountable for it.

THE FOURTH BOWL ... SCORCHING HEAT

Rev. 16:8-9

*Then the **fourth** angel poured out his bowl on the sun, and **power was given to him to scorch men with fire**. And men were scorched with great heat, and **they blasphemed the name of God** who has power over these plagues; and **they did not repent** and give him glory.*

Isaiah also prophesied this judgment saying,

*Therefore the curse has devoured the earth, and those who dwell in it are desolate. Therefore the inhabitants of the earth are **burned**, and few men are left. Isaiah 24:6*

Malachi spoke of it as well,

*'For behold, the day is coming, **burning like an oven**, and all the proud, yes, **all** who do wickedly will be stubble. And the day which is coming shall **burn** them up,' says the LORD of hosts, 'That will leave them neither root nor branch.' Malachi 4:1*

Notice how men will react when this judgment comes. Will they say, "uncle?" Will they turn? Will they repent? No. Rather, we read they **blasphemed the name of God** and **did not repent**. Hard, aren't they? Note, however, that the opportunity for them to repent still exists, even at this late hour. God's hand of mercy is still clearly being extended. Therefore, we must conclude that these judgments are still remedial. The door will still be open for men and women to be saved ... but multitudes will have none of it. This judgment will parallel the seventh plague on Egypt.

*And Moses stretched out his rod toward heaven; and the LORD sent thunder and hail, and **fire** darted to the ground. And the LORD rained hail on the land of Egypt. Exodus 9:23*

THE FIFTH BOWL ... UTTER DARKNESS

Rev. 16:10-11

*Then the **fifth** angel poured out his bowl on the throne of the beast, and his kingdom became full of **darkness**; and they gnawed* their tongues because of the pain. They blasphemed the God of heaven because of their pains and their **sores**, and did not **repent** of their deeds.

This judgment confirms that the Bowl judgments will come in very quick succession because it informs us that Earth-dwellers will be still suffering from the results of the first Bowl's sores when the fifth Bowl is poured out upon them. Back in 8:12, at the fourth Trumpet, a third of the nights and days were darkened. Now, utter darkness will spread out over all the face of the earth ... twenty-four seven. This judgment will parallel the ninth plague of Egypt.

*Then the LORD said to Moses, 'Stretch out your hand toward heaven, that there may be **darkness** over the land of Egypt, darkness which may even be felt.' So Moses stretched out his hand toward heaven, and there was thick darkness in all the land of Egypt three days. Exodus 10:21-22*

We read here that men ***did not repent of their deeds***. God's tender mercy is still being extended. It will still be available for any who want it.

THE SIXTH BOWL

THREE DEMON GATHERERS GO FORTH

Rev. 16:12-16

*Then the **sixth** angel poured out his bowl **on the great river Euphrates**, and its water was dried up, so **that the way of the kings from the east might be prepared**. And I saw **three unclean spirits** like frogs coming out of the mouth of the dragon, out of the mouth of the beast, and out of the mouth of the false prophet. For they are **spirits of demons**, performing signs, which go out to the kings* [NU omits *"of the earth and"*] *of the whole world, to gather them to the battle of that great day of God Almighty. Behold, I am coming as a thief. Blessed is he who watches, and keeps his garments, lest he walk naked and they see his shame. And they gathered them together to the place called in Hebrew, **Armageddon**.*

16:12

When the sixth angel pours out his Bowl, the hornet's nest of Antichrist's followers will be more than ready to storm back in great anger. However, notice that it is not their anger that will send Earth-dwellers racing to the Holy Land. Rather, it will be because of God's sovereign call. The sixth Bowl will release three demon spirits who will motivate wicked Earth-dwellers to march to war against the Lamb in the land of Palestine. Let's look at it a bit closer. When the sixth Bowl was poured out, John says:

...the great river Euphrates, and its water [were] *dried up.* The vast bulk of the world's population lies to the east of Israel. Countless multitudes in China, India and other Asian nations reside there. At the pouring out of the sixth Bowl, the entire Euphrates river, north to south, will be dried up for hundreds of miles so that these swarming masses of humanity can march unabated into the holy land without so much as getting their feet wet. As I read this, I thought of our own military's battles in Iraq. Many of those battles were centered on critical and strategic bridges over this same river. That war certainly clarified the importance of God's move here to dry it up.

16:13-14

...I saw three unclean spirits like frogs coming out of the mouth of the dragon, out of the mouth of the beast, and out of the mouth of the false prophet. Fascinating. Satan, Antichrist, and the False Prophet will each vomit forth, as it were, an unclean spirit. Then, these demonic spirits will go out to coerce and deceive the nations. Someone has called these spirits the *unholy trinity.* They will go out to the nations of Antichrist's kingdom and bring their armies to Palestine. Once again, God will use the Devil and the Devil's own to do his will.

16:15

At this point, the account of the sixth Bowl judgment is suddenly interrupted by the Lord's voice. I believe he interrupts because, time-wise, we are at the very door of his coming. Suddenly, he booms out, **Behold, I come as a thief. Blessed is he who watches and keeps his garments, lest he walk naked and they see his shame.** This final warning comes from Christ himself. It is also found in the gospels where Jesus taught about the Tribulation and the beginning of his kingdom on Earth. Those passages are often greatly misunderstood and misapplied because Jesus was not speaking about the Rapture ... he was speaking about his Second Coming at the end of the Tribulation. In those scriptures, Jesus taught it was imperative that his covenant people, the Jews, be ready to meet him at his appearing or they would lose out on eternal life and his Kingdom. The Jews who are ready, however, he says will enter into the joy of their Lord. Those who are not ready will be rejected and lost forever.

In Matthew 25, for example, we find two parables, the Parable of the Ten Virgins and the Parable of the Talents. Both are directed squarely at the Jews who will be living at the time of Christ's Second Coming. In the parable of the ten virgins, Jesus said there were ten virgins who took their lamps and went out to meet the bridegroom. Five of them were prepared for the bridegroom's coming, having acquired oil for their lamps. Five others, however, were slothful and were not prepared for his coming. They had made no effort to acquire oil for their lamps. Suddenly, at midnight, they all heard the voice of the bridegroom coming. The five who were ready, met him gladly and went away with him to the wedding, but the five who were unprepared went off to see if they could find oil somewhere. Jesus ended this parable saying,

Afterward, came also the other virgins, saying, Lord, Lord, **open to us**. *But he answered and said, Verily I say unto you,* **I know you not**. **Watch therefore**, *for ye know neither the day nor the hour wherein* **the Son of man cometh**. *Matthew 25:11-13* (KJV)

His teaching is clear. When he appears at his Second Coming, only those Jews who are prepared to meet him will gain entrance to his Kingdom. This is the same theme as the parable of the talents. There, the unprofitable servant who hid his talent and did nothing to prepare for his Master's return, was in a world of trouble! Of this man, Jesus said,

And **cast ye the unprofitable servant into outer darkness**; *there shall be weeping and gnashing of teeth. Matthew 25:30* (KJV)

The Lord has bestowed a tremendous amount of gifts, talents and resources upon his people, the Jews. And, one day, he will surely hold them accountable for them. As you have it in *Romans 9:4-5*,

*Who are **Israelites**; **to whom** pertaineth the **adoption**, and the **glory**, and the **covenants**, and the giving of **the law**, and **the service of God**, and **the promises**; whose are **the fathers**, and **of whom as concerning the flesh Christ came**, who is over all, God blessed forever. Amen.*

If they are caught at their Messiah's Second Coming, having done nothing with these great blessings and advantages and having not even received God's great gift of salvation offered them by faith in his Son, Christ Jesus (Romans 6:23), their fate will be ***outer darkness***. The voice of Christ that interrupted the sequence of the Bowl judgments exclaimed, ***Behold, I am coming as a thief.*** This is the last warning in the Word of God to his covenant people, the Jews. At that point in Earth's history ... the hour will be very very late. Christ will be standing at the very door. And, when he appears, all who are not prepared ... will be lost forever.

16:16

*...**And they gathered them together to the place called in Hebrew, Armageddon**.* This Hebrew word, ***Har*** means ***mountain***. ***Armageddon*** then, means ***Mountain of Megiddo***. The combination of these two words is only found here in the Bible. The ancient town of Megiddo guarded the main entrance to a great valley located in the plain of Esdraeleon. The Old Testament Hebrew name is, *Jezreel*. This great plain cuts the central range of Palestine into two parts and runs all the way from Galilee in the north to Samaria in the south. It has been the site of many battles, both related and unrelated to Jewish history. Several passes enter this valley making it easily accessible. It is here that the great climactic battle of history will occur. Here, godless Satan-instigated men will attempt to take on the Lamb of God. It would be of value to look at some key scriptures that predict this great and fast approaching battle of ***Armageddon***. The prophet Joel spoke of it in amazing detail saying,

*Proclaim this among the nations: '**Prepare for war**! Wake up the mighty men, let all the men of war draw near, **let them come up**.' Beat*

your plowshares into swords and your pruning hooks into spears; let the weak say, 'I am strong.' **Assemble and come**, *all you nations, and gather together all around. Cause your mighty ones to go down there, O LORD.* **Let the nations be wakened, and come up to the Valley of Jehoshaphat; for there I will sit to judge all the surrounding nations**. *Put in the sickle, for the harvest is ripe. Come, go down; for the winepress is full, the vats overflow; for their wickedness is great.* **Multitudes, multitudes in the valley of decision**! *For the day of the LORD is near in the valley of decision. The sun and moon will grow dark, and the stars will diminish their brightness.* **The LORD also will roar from Zion**, *and utter his voice from Jerusalem; the heavens and earth will shake; but the LORD will be a shelter for his people, and the strength of the children of Israel.* **So you shall know that I am the LORD your God, dwelling in Zion my holy mountain. Then Jerusalem shall be holy, and no aliens shall ever pass through her again**. Joel 3:9-17

Jeremiah spoke of this as well saying,

Therefore prophesy against them all these words, and say to them: 'The LORD will roar from on high, and utter his voice from his holy habitation; he will roar mightily against his fold. He will give a shout, as those who tread the grapes, **against all the inhabitants of the earth**. *A noise will come to the ends of the earth; for the LORD has a controversy with the nations;* *he will plead his case with all flesh. He will give those who are wicked to the sword,' says the LORD.* Jeremiah 25:30-31

Isaiah said,

Who is this *who comes from* **Edom**, *with dyed garments from Bozrah, this One who is glorious in his apparel, traveling in the greatness of his strength?;* **'I who speak in righteousness, mighty to save.'** *Why is your apparel red, and your garments like one who treads in the winepress?* **'I have trodden the winepress alone, and from the peoples no one was with me. For I have trodden them in my anger, and trampled them in my fury; their blood is sprinkled upon my garments**, *And I have stained all my robes. For* **the day of vengeance is in my heart**, *and* **the year of my redeemed has come**. *I looked, but there was no one to help, and I wondered that there was no one to uphold; therefore my own arm brought salvation for me; and* my own fury, it sustained me. *I have trodden down the peoples in my anger*, *made them drunk in my fury, and brought down their strength to the earth. Isaiah 63:1-6*

We learn from these scriptures that although the battle of Armageddon will begin in the north at Mount Megiddo, it will run to its final conclusion far to the south at Bozrah, the ancient site of the chief city of Edom. At the conclusion of the conflict, Christ will return from there with his *glorious* garments stained red with blood.

THE SEVENTH BOWL ... A WORLDWIDE EARTHQUAKE ACCOMPANIED BY IMMENSE HAILSTONES

Rev. 16:17-21

*Then the **seventh** angel poured out his bowl into the air, and a loud voice came out of the temple of heaven, from the throne, saying, 'It is done!' And there were noises and thunderings and lightnings;* **and there was a great earthquake, such a mighty and great earthquake as had not occurred since men were on the earth.** *Now the great city was divided into three parts, and the cities of the nations fell. And great **Babylon** was remembered before God, to give her the cup of the wine of the fierceness of his wrath. Then every island fled away, and the mountains were not found. And* **great hail from heaven fell upon men**, *each hailstone about the weight of a talent. Men blasphemed God because of the plague of the hail, since that plague was exceedingly great.*

16:17

Because of the rapid succession of the Bowl Judgments, while the armies of Earth are in the process of gathering to Armageddon, the seventh angel will pour out his final Bowl striking the earth with a worldwide earthquake of mammoth proportions. It will utterly destroy Babylon, Antichrist's capital city, as well as all the rest of his worldwide empire. The utter annihilation of Antichrist's Babylon by the seventh Bowl judgment will be seen in further detail in chapter 18.

When the Lord Jesus returns to Earth, as set before us here in chapter 19, the armies of all the nations will have arrived to do battle with him. Timewise, when the seventh angel pours out his Bowl, immediately thereafter, Christ will descend from Heaven upon the armies gathered at Armageddon. That is why, when this seventh Bowl was poured out, John says *a loud voice came out of the temple of heaven, from the throne, saying, 'It is done'*. This is the same Greek word that Jesus uttered on the cross when he said, *it is finished* (John 19:30). It is the word, Γέγονεν (*tegonen*). The remedial judgments of the first six Bowls will be capped off with one last, great, punitive judgment, when God's angel pours out his seventh Bowl. Let's examine this all-important and final judgment a bit closer. The central part of the seventh Bowl judgment will be a worldwide earthquake as never before experienced by mankind. Our text says ... *such a mighty and great earthquake as had not occurred since men were on the earth*. In the *for what it's worth* department, there are four earthquakes foretold in the book of Revelation. They are as follows:

1. The earthquake that will occur at the breaking of the sixth Seal (Rev. 6:12)
2. The earthquake that will occur at the breaking of the seventh Seal, when the angel took fire from the brazen altar and cast it down upon the earth (Rev. 8:5)
3. The earthquake that will occur at the resurrection of the two witnesses. It will knock down a tenth part of the city of Jerusalem (Rev. 11:13)
4. And, the granddaddy of them all ... the *great earthquake* that will occur at the pouring out of the seventh Bowl (Rev. 16:18)

No Richter Scale will be able to measure this final earthquake. The text says *the cities of the nations fell* and *great Babylon was remembered before God*. The pouring out of the seventh Bowl is the *coup de grace* for Antichrist's Babylon and his dictatorial world system. Babylon, along with all the rest of the cities of Earth, will be smashed to piles of rubble by the earthquake of the seventh Bowl judgment. The devastation at this time will be almost unimaginable. We read here that the *islands* will sink and every *mountain* on the face of the earth will be leveled. On top of that, we read that with fierce rage the Lord will cast one hundred seventeen pound hailstones upon the remaining blasphemous people below. This is not the first time God will have cast such hailstones on his enemies, by the way. When Joshua and the armies of Israel were conquering the Promised Land, a king named Adonizedec, king of Jerusalem, gathered an army of confederate kings against them. We read, in *Joshua 10:11*,

And it happened, as they fled before Israel and were on the descent of Beth Horon, that **the LORD cast down large hailstones from heaven on them** *as far as Azekah, and they died. There were more who died from the* **hailstones** *than the children of Israel killed with the sword.*

Isaiah, quoting the Lord's words, also prophesied about the hailstones of the seventh Bowl...

Also **I will make justice the measuring line**, *and righteousness the plummet; the* **hail** *will sweep away the refuge of lies, and the waters will overflow the hiding place. Isaiah 28:17*

The pouring out of the seventh Bowl will completely abolish Antichrist's kingdom (and glorious capital, Babylon) on Earth.

REVELATION 17

THE GREAT WHORE ON THE SCARLET BEAST

Rev. 17:1-2

Then one of the seven angels who had the seven bowls came and talked with me, saying, [**NU** omits *"to me"*] *'Come,* ***I will show you the judgment of the great harlot*** *who sits on many waters, with whom the kings of the earth committed fornication, and the inhabitants of the earth were made drunk with the wine of her fornication.'*

We come now to the **fourth** and final **interlude** in this section of Revelation that deals with the Tribulation. It takes up all of chapter 17. This chapter, like chapter 12, will give us a history lesson, taking us back in time and then bringing us forward with its subject to the final days of the Great Tribulation. It will explain to us the complex history and nature of The Great Whore. The vision began when one of the angels of the seven Bowl judgments came to John and said, ***Come, I will show you the judgment of the great harlot***. No doubt, this angel was the angel of the Seventh Bowl ... sent to explain the reason for the pouring out of his Bowl (chapter 17), and the effects of it (chapter 18). The angel begins by stating three things about the ***great harlot***. He says:

...She is one who **sits on many waters**. This symbol will be explained in verse fifteen.

...She is one **with whom the kings of the earth committed fornication**.

...She is one with whom ***the inhabitants of the earth were made drunk with the wine of her fornication***.

Rev. 17:3-6

*So he carried me away in the Spirit into the wilderness. And **I saw a woman sitting on a scarlet beast** which was full of names of blasphemy, having seven heads and ten horns. The woman was arrayed in purple and scarlet, and adorned with gold and precious stones and pearls, having in her hand a golden cup full of abominations and the filthiness of her **fornication**. And on her forehead a name was written: **MYSTERY, BABYLON THE GREAT, THE MOTHER OF HARLOTS AND OF THE ABOMINATIONS OF THE EARTH**. I saw the woman, **drunk with the blood of the saints** and **with the blood of the martyrs of Jesus**. And when I saw her, I marveled with great amazement.*

Now here is a drunk indeed, and she is driving! John saw *a **woman sitting on a scarlet colored beast*** and he says the beast upon which she sat, was ***full of names of blasphemy, having seven heads and ten horns***. Do you recognize her trusty steed? We have already encountered it back in chapters 12 and 13. There, we learned that it is a complex symbol representing Satan in chapter 12 and Satan's Antichrist as well as Antichrist's political/economic system in 13.

The vision begins with its focus on the ***woman***. Her appearance was mesmerizing. John says that she caused him to marvel ***with great amazement***. Let's examine her characteristics and see if we can discern what she represents.

First, she has a fourfold ***name*** emblazoned on her forehead. Let's break it down. Her name is:

...***MYSTERY*** ... she is something that has not been revealed before.

...***BABYLON THE GREAT*** ... she is part and parcel of Satan's historic, as well as Antichrist's yet future, system and kingdom. They are two peas in a pod.

...***THE MOTHER OF HARLOTS*** ... her "prostitute" image is one that is frequently used in Scripture to depict man's departure from the true and living God when he goes whoring after false gods and other manmade religions. As ***the mother of harlots***, this ***woman*** is the epitome of man's false religions. Here are a few examples of this analogy in Scripture:

When the LORD began to speak by Hosea, the LORD said to Hosea: 'Go, take yourself a wife of **harlotry** *and children of harlotry, for the land has committed great* **harlotry** *by departing from the LORD.' Hosea 1:2*

They say, 'If a man divorces his wife, and she goes from him and becomes another man's, may he return to her again?' Would not that land be greatly polluted? But **you have played the harlot** *with many lovers; yet return to me," says the LORD. Jeremiah 3:1*

The LORD said also to me in the days of Josiah the king: 'Have you seen what backsliding Israel has done? She has gone up on every high mountain and under every green tree, and there **played the harlot.***'... So it came to pass, through her casual* **harlotry**, *that she defiled the land and* **committed adultery with stones and trees**. *Jeremiah 3:6, 9*

Ezekiel also used the prostitute analogy when he prophesied against Israel, the Northern Kingdom, which was carried away into captivity by the Assyrians in 722 BC. He says,

You also **played the harlot** *with the Assyrians, because you were insatiable; indeed you played the* **harlot** *with them and still were not satisfied. Ezekiel 16:28*

The word of the LORD came again to me, saying: 'Son of man, **there were two women**, *the daughters of one mother. They committed* **harlotry** *in Egypt, they committed* **harlotry** *in their youth; their breasts were there embraced, their virgin bosom was there pressed. Their names: Oholah the elder and Oholibah her sister; they were mine, and they bore sons and daughters. As for their names,* **Samaria is Oholah, and Jerusalem is Oholibah**. *Oholah* **played the harlot** *even though she was mine; and she lusted for her lovers, the neighboring Assyrians, who were clothed in purple, captains and rulers, all of them desirable young men, horsemen riding on horses. Thus she committed her* **harlotry** *with them, all of them choice men of Assyria; and with all for whom she lusted,* **with all their idols, she defiled herself. She has never given up her harlotry brought from Egypt, for in her youth they had lain with her, pressed her virgin bosom, and poured out their immorality upon her**. *Therefore I have delivered her into the hand of her lovers, into the hand of the Assyrians, for whom she lusted. They uncovered her nakedness, took away her sons and daughters, and* *slew her with the sword; she became a byword among women, for they had executed judgment on her. Ezekiel 23:1-10*

So, the harlot image is used in the Bible to picture any person or people who leave the true and living God to go after false gods and false religions. As such, all manmade religions are, in reality, spiritual harlotry. They are all false and antithetical to the worship of the true and living God who has revealed himself in creation, history and Scripture. Men have a long history of spiritual prostitution. As you have it in *Romans 1:21-25,*

... because, although they knew God, they did not glorify him as God, nor were thankful, but became futile in their thoughts, and their foolish hearts were darkened. Professing to be wise, they became fools, and **changed the glory of the incorruptible God into an image made like corruptible man; and birds and four-footed animals and creeping things**. *Therefore God also gave them up to uncleanness, in the lusts of their hearts, to dishonor their bodies among themselves,* **who exchanged the truth of God for the lie, and worshiped and served the creature rather than the Creator**, *who is blessed forever. Amen.*

So, this name, THE MOTHER OF HARLOTS, speaks of the fact that she represents the epitome of man's religious whoring away from the true and living God.

*...**AND OF THE ABOMINATIONS OF THE EARTH** ...* she is also the mother of all the abominations that false religion has perpetrated on mankind. There are several things to note about this part of the harlot's name...

First, she will be the epitome of all the abominable things that have been done in the name of religion throughout history. This future **Mother of Harlots** will perpetrate, and even exceed, all of those abominations.

Second, as with most false religions, she will be filthy rich. She is **arrayed in purple and scarlet, and adorned with gold and precious stones and pearls**. Purple and scarlet are colors often used in ecclesiastical trappings. She is gilded and beautiful to look upon. She is decked out with all the trappings that man uses to adorn his false religious systems. It is amazing how quickly people will fall for counterfeit religions when they present themselves so appealingly to the eye.

Third, the cup she was holding was filled with things that are utterly filthy and disgusting ... a ***golden cup full of the abominations and filthiness of her fornication***. This symbol portrays how eager she will be to partake of such things. False religion is a gateway to immorality, murder and countless other abominations. In the Old Testament, when Israel went whoring after the idols of the heathen around them, they immediately became involved in all kinds of gross immorality (Exodus 32:16). They even began to practice the abomination of sacrificing their own children to dumb idols (Second Chronicles 28:13)! The further they got into idol worship, the more ungodly they became. Such is the downward path that is all too often trod by those who pursue man's trumped up false religions.

Fourth, John says she was ***drunk with the blood of the saints and with the blood of the martyrs of Jesus***. Because of its satanic origin, false religions are ruthless and murder prone. I refer the reader to your morning newspaper and ***Foxes Book of Martyrs*** if you would like to read up on the subject. Two groups of the woman's victims are mentioned here. The ***saints*** refer to God's people prior to the Church Age. The ***martyrs of Jesus*** refer to believers during the Church Age, as well as believers during the Tribulation. This gives us a heads up that the ***woman*** represents something far greater than first meets the eye. This old ***whore*** has been around for a long time. She has a long history of the shedding of the blood of the people of God. Her rap sheet is extensive. She has been responsible for all that false religion has done to God's people all the way back to her beginning. She was responsible for the murder of the prophets. She crucified the Lord of Glory and killed his apostles. She murdered hundreds, if not thousands, of believers in the World Trade Centers, perpetrated by her religious automatons. Pure and simple, she represents FALSE RELIGION. During the days of the Tribulation, she will come forth in her last two manifestations ... first, in the form of a worldwide false religion during the first three and a half years of the Tribulation and then, second, in her final and ultimate form as Antichrist-worship, during the second half of the Tribulation (the Great Tribulation). In chapter 18 we will see her ultimate demise when her center of

Antichrist-worship lies in smoldering ruins from the seventh Bowl judgment.

Rev. 17:7-14

But the angel said to me, 'Why did you marvel? ***I will tell you the mystery of the woman and of the beast that carries her****, which has the seven heads and the ten horns. The* ***beast*** *that you saw* ***was, and is not, and will ascend out of the bottomless pit and go to perdition****. And those who dwell on the earth will marvel, whose names are not written in the Book of Life from the foundation of the world, when they see the beast that was, and is not, and yet is. Here is the mind which has wisdom:* ***The seven heads are seven mountains*** *on which the woman sits. There are* ***also seven kings****. Five have fallen, one is, and the other has not yet come. And when he comes, he must continue a short time. And the beast that was, and is not, is himself also the eighth, and is of the seven, and is going to perdition.* ***The ten horns which you saw are ten kings*** *who have received no kingdom as yet, but they receive authority for one hour as kings with the beast. These are of one mind, and they will give their power and authority to the beast. These will make war with the Lamb, and* ***the Lamb will overcome them****, for he is Lord of lords and King of kings; and those who are with him are called, chosen, and faithful.'*

17:7-8

The angel begins his explanation of this vision, starting with the **beast** upon which the woman rode. At first glance, his words are an interpreter's nightmare, are they not? But, be patient. It will become manageable if we take his words apart, statement by statement. This is a *complex symbol*. That is, some of it represents two different things at the same time. So, let's break it apart.

First, the angel emphasizes that the beast upon which the woman was riding alludes to a person. He says, **The beast that you saw was, and is not, and will ascend out of the bottomless pit and go to perdition**. These words allude to the death and miraculous recovery of

Antichrist that we studied back in chapter 13. To refresh our thinking, it reads as follows:

*And I saw one of his heads as if it had been **mortally wounded**, and his **deadly wound was healed**. And all the World marveled and followed the beast. So they worshiped the dragon who gave authority to the beast; and they worshiped the beast, saying, 'Who is like the beast? Who is able to make war with him?' Revelation 13:3-4*

Antichrist will be a counterfeit Christ and, apparently, he will seek to even imitate Christ in his resurrection. As we learned from Revelation 13, his miraculous recovery from a mortal head wound will be all that is needed to persuade the world to grant him wholehearted allegiance. I believe that the words, **and will ascend out of the bottomless pit**, point to his return from the other side of the grave. The angel says, however, that he will *go to perdition*. This word, **perdition**, refers to *punishment* or *judgment*. Judas, who was Satan's instrument, was a *type* of Antichrist. As you have it in *Luke 22:3-4*,

*Then **Satan entered Judas**, surnamed Iscariot, who was numbered among the twelve. So he went his way and conferred with the chief priests and captains, how he might betray him to them.*

In *John 6:70b*, Jesus, said of Judas,

*Did I not choose you, the twelve, and **one of you is a devil**?*

Jesus also called Judas the **son of perdition**, a term that means *the heir of judgment*. As you have it in *John 17:12*,

*While I was with them in the world, I kept them in thy name: those that thou gave me I have kept, and none of them is lost, but the **son of perdition**; that the scripture might be fulfilled.*

The only other place in the Bible where this term is used is in *Second Thessalonians 2:3-4*. There, Paul uses it as a name of Antichrist.

*Let no one deceive you by any means; for that day will not come unless the falling away comes first, and the man of sin is revealed, the **son of perdition**, who opposes and exalts himself above all that is called God or that is worshipped, so that he sits as God in the temple of God, showing himself that he is God.*

Antichrist will be the epitome of all that Judas Iscariot was, a man possessed by Satan and diametrically opposed to the Son of God. But, the angel says, he is doomed.

Strange Work

He continues, *And those who dwell on the earth will marvel, whose names are not written in the book of life from the foundation of the world*. This is a repetition of the point made back in 13:3, where it was said that the world **wandered after the beast** and **worshipped** him. To sum up, the **scarlet beast**, upon which the woman was riding, represents a person. It is the same **beast** we saw back in chapter 13. It is Antichrist.

Rev. 17:9-11

Here is the mind which has wisdom: The **seven heads** *are* **seven mountains** *on which the woman sits. There are* **also seven kings**. *Five have fallen, one is, and the other has not yet come. And when he comes, he must continue a short time. And the* **beast** *that was, and is not, is himself also the* **eighth**, *and is of the seven, and is going to perdition.*

17:9

The angel continues his explanation of the **scarlet beast**, upon which the woman rode, saying, **Here is the mind that has wisdom: The seven heads are seven mountains on which the woman sits.** In other words, the mind that has wisdom will be able to catch on to the intricacies of the beast's seven heads and its ten horns. As we study this, we will discover that its seven heads actually represent two separate things at the same time. In verse nine, the angel says they are **seven mountains**. Then, in verse ten, he says they are also **seven kings**. This is pretty heavy treading, aye? But, hang in there … we are making headway. Let's look closer now at these two separate meanings of the beast's **seven heads**.

Second, the angel says the seven heads are **seven mountains on which the woman sits**. In ancient times, the city of Rome was referred to as, *the city on seven hills*. Roman coins pictured its seven hills. Victorinus, one of the first commentators on Revelation, says of this verse, *That is the city of Rome*. I believe Victorinus was correct. This leads me to believe that, after the Rapture and early in the Tribulation, a unified world religion (**the woman**), as well as Antichrist (**the beast**) will both make their headquarters in Rome.

17:10-11

Third, the angel says, **There are also seven kings.** So, the second thing that the seven heads of the scarlet beast represent, are **seven kings**. The best reading in the Greek here is simply ... **and seven kings**. Now, we know that Antichrist's empire will arise out of the ancient Roman Empire, as prophesied in Daniel 7. So, the seven kings, spoken of here, are probably seven specific Roman emperors that typified the Antichrist who was yet to come. We may not be able to pinpoint them exactly, but it is clear that the seven heads also represent seven specific Caesars of the ancient Roman Empire. In order to be true *types* of Antichrist, however, these seven ancient Caesars would have to have at least three things in common with him. I believe they are as follows:

...Each would have to have died by assassination. The angel's statement here that *five are fallen* indicates that the first five kings (Caesars) suffered violent deaths.

...Each one would have had to rule the world by absolute dictatorship.

...Each one would have had to make an open and blasphemous claim to deity.

I am no expert on Roman history, and perhaps an exact list of just which individual Caesars the Holy Spirit has in mind here may not be completely knowable. However, I believe he is definitely thinking of seven historical Roman Caesars who were types of the Antichrist to come. In my study, I found seven Roman Caesars that seem to meet the criteria sufficiently to be historic types of Antichrist. They are Julius Caesar, Gauis, Claudius, Nero, Galba, Domitian and Diocletian. All seven of these men were assassinated. All seven enjoyed absolute dictatorships (although Galba's was an extremely short-lived one). And, all seven blasphemously declared that they were a god. These seven Caesars fit the angel's description. He says:

...*five have fallen*. Speaking from the perspective of the time of John's writing (the early AD 90s), the five who were fallen would have been Julius Caesar, Gauis (*Caligula*), Claudius, Nero and Galba. Out of Rome's twelve recorded Caesars, only three died natural deaths and refused to be deified. They were Augustus, Vespasian and Titus.

...*one is*. This would be the one who was reigning at the time when John was writing Revelation. That would be Domitian, AD 81 to 96. This is one we can tag down for sure.

...*the other has not yet come*. Diocletian, I believe, best fits the bill here. He reigned much later, however, from AD 284 to 305.

...*the beast ... is himself also the eighth and is of the seven*. This is clearly referring to Antichrist who will reign much further down in history during the last days of the Great Tribulation. He will be the *eighth* king (or Caesar) and the arch-type of the seven who were before him, epitomizing their Satanic natures and attributes. To sum up, Antichrist's person and reign will be rooted in the tradition and mold of seven blasphemous Roman Caesars who went before him. By their pride and actions, each of them presented as types of Antichrist, **foreshadowing that last great Roman Emperor who was yet to come** and who is the *eighth* and may well be alive on Earth right now today.

Rev. 17:12-14

The **ten horns** which you saw are **ten kings** who have received no kingdom as yet, but they receive authority for one hour as kings with the beast. These are of one mind, and **they will give their power and authority to the beast. These will make war with the Lamb**, and the Lamb will overcome them, for he is Lord of lords and King of kings; and those who are with him are called, chosen, and faithful [this is talking about you and me, dear saint].

17:12

The angel continues his explanation of the complex symbol of the *scarlet beast*. He will now supply us with additional information on its government/political aspects. He says, **The ten horns which you saw are ten kings, which have received no kingdom as yet; but receive power as kings one hour with the beast**. As we have previously discussed, during

Antichrist's reign there will be **ten kings** who will reign under and with him. The angel says they do not exist as yet, but will become kings for **one hour** (meaning a short time) with Antichrist. Some have speculated that the European Union may be the beginnings of this prophetic ten-king alliance. Whether that is true or not, remains to be seen. However, we know from this prophecy that Antichrist will participate, lead and dominate such a confederation when he has his day on Earth. The *"ten kings"* aspect of Antichrist's reign is not new. It was prophesied way back in the days of the prophet Daniel. Here is that key passage.

*After this I saw in the night visions, and behold, a fourth beast, dreadful and terrible, exceedingly strong. It had huge iron teeth; it was devouring, breaking in pieces, and trampling the residue with its feet. It was different from all the beasts that were before it, and **it had ten horns**. I was considering the **horns, and there was another horn, a little one, coming up among them, before whom three of the first horns were plucked out by the roots**. And there, in this horn, were eyes like the eyes of a man, and a **mouth** speaking pompous words. Daniel 7:7-8*

The interpretation is given further down in that passage at verses twenty-four and twenty-five:

*The **ten horns are ten kings** who shall arise from this kingdom. And **another shall rise** after them; he shall be different from the first ones, and **shall subdue three kings**. He shall speak pompous words against the Most High, shall persecute the saints of the Most High, and shall intend to change times and law. Then the saints shall be given into his hand for **a time and times and half a time** [a Hebrew idiom that means three and a half years. See Daniel 4:32].*

17:13-14

The angel continued ... **These have one mind, and they will give their power and authority to the beast**. The **ten kings** will back Antichrist and will delegate all their power and authority to him. According to Daniel 7:24, above... during Antichrist's rise to world domination ...he will subdue three of these kings who, logically, he will then replace. The angel concludes, **these will make war with the Lamb, and the Lamb will overcome them, for he is the Lord of lords and King of kings**. Antichrist's **ten kings** will be archenemies of Christ. The **war** that the angel refers to here is the battle of Armageddon, which will be fought when Christ returns to Earth (Revelation 19). It is important to remember that battle begins with the pouring out of the sixth Bowl judgment (16:12-16), which you will remember, precipitated the gathering of the nations *to the battle of the great day of God Almighty*. Antichrist and his ten kings will pick themselves up from the ravages of the seventh Bowl and hurry their armies on to Palestine where they will ultimately *make war with the Lamb*. Upon arriving at Megiddo, they will be confronted by the descending *Lord of lords and King of kings* and will raise their weapons against him as he descends to take dominion over the earth. But, the angel says, *the Lamb will overcome them*. As we will soon see, boy is that an understatement! That brief conflict will be the most lopsided battle of all time.

Rev. 17:15-18

*Then he said to me, 'The **waters** which you saw, where the harlot sits, are peoples, multitudes, nations, and tongues. And the **ten horns** which you saw* **[Nu omits "on"]** *and the beast, these **will hate the harlot**, make her desolate and naked, eat her flesh and **burn her with fire**. For God has put it into their hearts to fulfill his purpose, to be of one mind, and to give their kingdom to the beast, until the words of God are fulfilled. And **the woman** whom you saw is that great **city** which **reigns over the kings of the earth**.*

17:15

Here, we come to the angel's final explanations of these complex symbols. At the beginning of the vision, John saw the woman seated *upon many waters*. The angel explains that this means she will dominate *peoples, multitudes, nations, and tongues* (languages). This will be the powerful position of the false religion that will exist throughout the Tribulation. Her first manifestation will come immediately after the Rapture of the Church in the form of a confederation of the world's religions. This vision of the *Mother of Harlots* confirms the view that the world's religions will one day unite into one. The World Council of Churches would probably applaud this, even today. This imminent religion of the first three and a half years of the Tribulation, will no doubt be the fulfilled dream of many. The fact that she is riding upon the ***scarlet beast***, which is the symbol of Antichrist and his empire, suggests that she will be supported by him and will dominate him during the first half of the Tribulation. But, that short manifestation of false religion will be short lived, as we will see.

17:16

The angel says the ten kings will ***hate the harlot for God has put it into their hearts to fulfill his purpose***. This is important information concerning the relationship between the political realm, (Antichrist and his confederation of ten kings) of that future day and the ecclesiastical realm (the one-world religion that will dominate during the first half of the Tribulation). This age old clash between church and state will come to a head when Antichrist and his ten kings rise up and destroy the harlot. That is what the angel means when he says they are going to:

...***make her desolate and naked*** ... they will seize her headquarters

...***eat her flesh*** ... they will confiscate her assets

...***burn her with fire*** ... they will burn her houses of worship

At first, Antichrist and his kings will use this post-rapture, great unifying world religion for their own political gain but, they will subsequently get rid of her when God puts it into their hearts to do so. This will bring the first phase of the *harlot* to an end. No doubt, its demise will be coordinated with Antichrist's seizing of the Jew's temple at Jerusalem. Then, the second phase of the harlot ... the worship of Antichrist himself ... will begin. That will be the final and ultimate manifestation of Satan's false religion on Earth.

17:17

In the midst of all of this, verse seventeen brings out a wonderful truth concerning the true and living God. The angel says that the destruction of the ***harlot*** and the desire of the ten kings to ***give their kingdom to the beast*** will all come to pass because ***God has put it into their hearts to fulfill his purpose***. Although all these political and ecclesiastical intrigues will be going on during those last dark days of Earth's history, ultimately it is God who will be directing it all according to his own will and purpose. Make no mistake about it, history unfolds according to his sovereign plan and purpose and no one else's. The one true and living God is sovereign over all. He directs kings, kingdoms and everything else according to his own inscrutable and irresistible will ... including Antichrist and his future Babylon system. As you have it in *Proverbs 21:1,*

The king's heart is in the hand of the LORD, *like the rivers of water; he turns it wherever* **he wishes***.*

And again, as you have it in *Ephesians 1:11,*

In him also we have obtained an inheritance, being predestined according to the purpose of him **who works all things according to the counsel of his will***.*

17:18

In conclusion, the angel says, **And the woman whom you saw is that great city which reigns over the kings of the earth***.* Returning to the **woman**, he says there is yet another meaning to her symbol as well. Although she represents the worldwide religion of the first half of the Tribulation ... as well as Antichrist worship during the second half ... she is also symbolic of an ecclesiastical *city* that, according to the angel, **reigns over the kings of the earth**. This tells us that the ecclesiastical center for the whole world will change locations after the first half of the Tribulation. Whereas it was at Rome during the first half, its new location, during the second half, will be at Jerusalem. Therefore, at that time, the ancient harlot will also be a *city* during the closing days of the Tribulation. She has often sat there in the past, by the way ... in one form or another ... even as she does today. Jerusalem has a history of fostering false religions and rebellion against God. As Jesus put it in *Matthew 23:37-39,*

O Jerusalem, Jerusalem, the one who kills the prophets and stones those who are sent to her! *How often I wanted to gather your children together, as a hen gathers her chicks under her wings, but you were not willing! See! Your house is left to you desolate; for I say to you, you shall see me no more till you say,* **'Blessed is he who comes in the name of the LORD!'**

During the days of the early Church, it was from Jerusalem (primarily through the Jews) that the persecution of God's people came. Ultimately, it will become the seat of Satan and Antichrist worship, as we learned from chapter 13. In that context, Jerusalem, prior to our Lord's intervention, will continue to be the stronghold of man's false religions and Bastian of the enemies of God. We saw that expressed back in *11:8,* when Christ's two witnesses were killed there. We read,

And their dead bodies will lie in the street of ***the great city which spiritually is called Sodom and Egypt****, where also our Lord was crucified.*

So, the grotesque symbol of the *harlot* has yet another meaning as well. She also represents Jerusalem, as it will exist as the center of Satan and Antichrist worship one day during the Great Tribulation.

Here in chapter 17, we have been given a great deal of information about the past and future of that old, hellish *harlot* ... false religion. We have been told about her two manifestations that will prevail on the earth during the Tribulation. We have also been given a good deal of information about the political intrigues that will swirl around her during those days. We have concluded that the initial manifestation of the *harlot* will come in the form of a one world religion that will dominate the whole earth as well as Antichrist and his ten kings during the first half of the Tribulation. At that time, it will be centered at Rome where it will thrive with Antichrist and his ten kings' support and blessing. However, they will *hate* her and will violently eliminate her at the middle of the Tribulation when Antichrist makes his move to set up his own blasphemous worship at Jerusalem. Then, the great harlot's second and final manifestation will emerge. Ultimately, ***MYSTERY, BABYLON THE GREAT, THE MOTHER OF HARLOTS, AND OF THE ABOMINATIONS OF THE EARTH*** ... will arise one last time and flourish at Jerusalem in the form of undisguised Satan and Antichrist worship. That is why she is said to represent a *city* ... because her final manifestation will be at Jerusalem during the dark days of the last three and a half years of Satanic Gentile reign and religion on planet Earth.

REVELATION 18

THE REMAINS OF FALLEN BABYLON

Rev. 18:13

After these things *I saw another angel coming down from heaven, having great authority, and the earth was illuminated with his glory. And he cried mightily with a loud voice, saying,* ***'Babylon the great is fallen, is fallen****, and has become a dwelling place of demons, a prison for every foul spirit, and a cage for every unclean and hated bird! For* ***all the nations have drunk of the wine of the wrath of her fornication****, the* ***kings*** *of the earth have committed fornication with her, and the* ***merchants*** *of the earth have become rich through the abundance of her luxury.'*

18:1

Back in chapter 14, you will remember that God sent forth his proclaiming angel to circumvent the globe and cry out to all Earth-dwellers, **Babylon the great, is fallen, is fallen** (14:8). The angel's prophecy has now come to pass. In prophetic sequence here, we come to the striking description of the destroyed Babylon System, epitomized by the smoking ruins of its capital city, Jerusalem. The chapter begins with the familiar and significant words, ***after these things***, Μετὰ ταῦτα (*Meta touta*). This tells us that this is a distinct new vision following the interlude of chapter 17. Chapter 17, dealt with the historic origin and development of false religion in the world and how it will reach its peak in Antichrist's kingdom. Here, in chapter 18, we come to its end and utter demise. Here we will visually see the end of the ***great harlot***, false religion, along with the complete annihilation of Babylon, as embodied in Antichrist's capital city and center of man-worship, Jerusalem.

John says, ***I saw another angel coming down from heaven, having great authority, and the earth was illuminated with his glory.***,

Notice here that God's angel came forth to illuminate the scene as well as to proclaim a message. By this point in time, Earth's atmosphere will doubtless be filled with megatons of pollutants from the devastating effects of the Seal, Trumpet and Bowl judgments. Due to the aftermath of those twenty-one judgments, it will be surprising if those who survive are able to see much beyond the end of their noses. Not too long ago, I recall a major forest fire in southern Mexico that resulted in a substantial reduction of visibility over the entire eastern half of the United States. That was nothing compared to the atmospheric conditions that will exist by the end of the Great Tribulation. The seventh Bowl alone will cause major fires in every town and city on Earth. This angel of **great authority** and **glory** will be sent by God just so John would be able to see what has happened to Antichrist's Babylon!

18:2-3

Having illumined the earth, the mighty angel proceeded to announce, ***Babylon the great is fallen, is fallen, and has become a dwelling place of demons, a prison for every foul spirit, and a cage of every unclean and hated bird***. This angel's opening declaration parallels the words of the proclaiming angel back in 14:8. Now, however, his words are no longer prophetic, they are reality. Nothing is left of Babylon but debris, birds of prey and a hornet's nest of demons. What a picture is set before us here. The angel continues, ***All nations have drunk of the wrath of her fornication***. The wrath of God, through his seventh Bowl judgment, has completely annihilated Antichrist's capital, Babylon, along with all the other cities of the whole earth! Next, like a prosecuting attorney at a murder trial, the angel begins his indictment. He says, ***the kings of the earth have committed fornication with her ... and the merchants of the earth have become rich through the abundance of her luxury***. They all had greedily shared in Babylon's spiritual whoredom, immorality and materialism. They had all prospered and waxed rich because of her. Everyone, from kings to street venders, had grown fat together through Antichrist's Babylon.

Rev. 18:4-8

And I heard another voice from heaven saying, **'Come out of her, my people**, *lest you share in her sins, and lest you receive of her plagues. For her sins have reached to heaven, and God has remembered her iniquities. Render to her just as she rendered to you, and repay her double according to her works; in the cup, which she has mixed, mix double for her. In the measure that she glorified herself and lived luxuriously, in the same measure give her torment and sorrow; for she says in her heart, 'I sit as queen, and am no widow, and will not see sorrow.' Therefore* **her plagues will come in one day;** *death and mourning and famine. And she will be utterly burned with fire, for strong is the Lord God who* **[NU changes *"judges"* to *"has judged"*]** *her.*

18:4

John says he heard *another voice from heaven saying, 'Come out of her, my people, lest you share in her sins, and lest you receive of her plagues.'* There is much here in the book of Revelation that is addressed to the people who will actually be living during the dark days that it describes. This is a warning to them. Especially, it is a warning to the Jews of that day to not make their home in Babylon (Jerusalem). It is good advice. For a Jew, or any child of God, to reside in Babylon during the days of the Great Tribulation will be a foolish decision indeed. To do so will be to subject one's self to great pressure to share in her sins as well as to put one in harm's way when she is judged by God. I have always wanted to visit Jerusalem, but I must confess, I wouldn't want to live there, even today. It is a place marked for misery, destruction and Gentile domination ... until Shiloh comes. Her present troubles with Islamists, Arabs and Palestinians clearly attest to this.

May we step aside for a moment? There is a very important spiritual application that can be made here. Take care, child of God. Don't allow yourself to be entangled in this world's system. It will seriously injure you, both spiritually and physically. We live in the kingdom of darkness down here. It is a kingdom wherein the essence of Antichrist's Babylon system already thrives. As you have it in *First John 2:15-16*,

Do not love the world or the things in the world. *If anyone loves the world, the love of the Father is not in him. For all that is in the world; the lust of the flesh, the lust of the eyes, and the pride of life; is not of the Father but is of the world.*

Far too often, believers become entangled in the *world* and, like these *merchants* and *kings*, are easily consumed with its money and materialism, immorality and flesh, pride and selfishness, position and advancement and even the deceptions of its cults and counterfeit religions. Walking hand in hand with the *world* is dancing with the beast. Someone has said, *Sin will take you where you don't want to go. Sin will keep you longer than you wanted to stay. Sin will make you pay more than you wanted to pay.* Guard yourself against the lures of this present dark kingdom, dear saint. God hates it and you and I need to hate it as well. It produces nothing but misery, bondage and death to all those who succumb to its enticements.

18:5-8

Now, let's look a bit more closely at this illuminating angel's indictment of Babylon. He says:

*...**her sins have reached to Heaven***. Sin, from the standpoint of Babylon's international identity, will reach such a point of saturation and sophistication that God will no longer tolerate it. It will become so bad that its stench will literally fill the nostrils of God up in the Heaven of Heavens. Keep in mind here, that **there is a great deal of difference between the way God deals with individuals concerning sin and the way he deals with nations concerning sin**. He is not in the judgment business today in relation to individuals and their sins. He does, however, judge nations for theirs. This is a very important distinction. Here are two scriptures to consider in this regard:

And all things are of God, who hath reconciled us to himself by Jesus Christ, and hath given to us the ministry of reconciliation; to wit, that God was in Christ, reconciling the world unto himself, ***not imputing their trespasses unto them****; and hath committed unto us the word of reconciliation. Second Corinthians 5:18-19*

*The wicked shall be turned into hell, and all the **nations** that forget God. Psalm 19:17*

*...**Render to her just as she rendered to you, and repay her double according to her works**.* Babylon will attack God and his laws at every turn and in every way possible. It will do so through Antichrist worship, unjust laws, immorality, abominations and murders. Therefore, God's angel calls for her to be paid back in her own coin and according to her own deeds. As she has so lavishly dished out her evil ... now she must be paid back ... double.

*...**she says in her heart, 'I sit as queen, and am no widow, and will not see sorrow.'*** Babylon's pride will make her ... oh, so cocky. She will proclaim that nothing can touch her but, as *Proverbs 16:18*, declares,

***Pride** goes before **destruction**, and a haughty spirit before a **fall**.*

*...**her plagues will come in one day**.* Babylon's judgment will come all at once and with amazing swiftness. Like the dropping of a great millstone into the sea, she will sink in **one day** because, the angel says, **strong is the Lord who has judged her**.

Rev. 18:9-10

*The **kings** of the earth who committed fornication and lived luxuriously with her will weep and lament for her, when they see the smoke of her burning, standing at a distance for fear of her torment, saying, 'Alas, alas, that great city Babylon, that mighty city! For in one hour your judgment has come.'*

What a vivid picture of Babylon's utter ruin is put before us here. Standing fearfully at a distance, the remaining kings of the earth weep and wail as they look upon their once magnificent, but now decimated, darling ... **Babylon**. The greatest Gentile, political, religious and commercial city that the world has ever seen lay before them as so much smoldering rubble ... destroyed forever by the omnipotent hand of Almighty God! They cried, **Alas, alas, that great city Babylon, that mighty city!** The fact that they refer to Jerusalem here by the name of **Babylon**, by the way, is proof positive that that will be her name in that day.

Rev. 18:11-17a

And the **merchants** *of the earth will weep and mourn over her, for no one buys their merchandise anymore: merchandise of gold and silver, precious stones and pearls, fine linen and purple, silk and scarlet, every kind of citron wood, every kind of object of ivory, every kind of object of most precious wood, bronze, iron, and marble; and cinnamon and incense, fragrant oil and frankincense, wine and oil, fine flour and wheat, cattle and sheep, horses and chariots, and bodies and* **souls of men***. The fruit that your soul longed for has gone from you, and all the things which are rich and splendid have* [**NU changes** *"gone from you"*] **been lost to you** *and you shall find them no more at all. The* **merchants of these things, who became rich by her, will stand at a distance for fear of her torment, weeping and wailing***, and saying, 'Alas, alas, that great* **city** *that was clothed in fine linen, purple, and scarlet, and adorned with gold and precious stones and pearls!* **For in one hour such great riches came to nothing***...*

This word, **merchants**, literally means *one who travels*. All the traveling salesmen of that day will also look on the devastated city and mourn for her as well. The huge and highly organized economy of the Babylon system, with her economic stranglehold on the world, will have been irretrievably shattered after the Lord lowers the boom on her with his final Bowl judgment. Like a head-on car crash, her crass commercialism will have come to a screeching and violent halt. Her merchants will weep. The text says that she will no longer be able to traffic in:

...merchandise of gold and silver, precious stones and pearls ... No more jewelry stores, Dr. McGee points out.

...fine linen and purple, silk and scarlet ... no more of her dry goods stores.

...citron wood, ivory, precious wood, bronze, iron, and marble ... no more luxury furniture stores.

...cinnamon and incense, fragrant oil, and frankincense ... no more cosmetic departments.

...wine ... no more of her liquor stores.

...oil, fine flour and wheat ... no more of her grocery stores.

...*cattle and sheep* ... no more of her slaughter houses and livestock yards.

...*horses and chariots* ... no more of her transportation businesses.

...*bodies and souls of men* ... no more brothels and slave markets. There is a great deal of prostitution and slavery going on in the world today, by the way. These two things are often inseparably linked. The Babylon system will be big on earning money by means of them. We first read about it back in *13:16,*

*He causes all, both small and great, rich and poor, free and **slave**, to receive a mark on their right hand or on their foreheads...*

Antichrist's Babylon was willing to do anything for a buck. This is one of the hallmarks of Satan's dark kingdom and his ministers. Because of their greed, they are always busy as bees working at their money-making schemes. As you have it in *Second Peter 2:3,*

*By **covetousness** they will **exploit** you with deceptive words; for a long time their judgment has not been idle, and their destruction does not slumber.*

Dear saint, please be wary of religious promoters whose every effort is to make money. There are a lot of them around today. God will judge their crass, religious commercialism one day, as well as those who have built their lives upon it. *Proverbs 11:4,* says,

***Riches** do not profit in the day of wrath, But **righteousness** delivers from death.*

The only real riches worth having in this whole wide world are riches in Christ. Dr. McGee asks the question, *Would it break your heart, like its breaking these fellows' hearts, if all of your material things went up in smoke? Or, is your treasure safe and sound in heaven with Christ?* That is a great question. Jesus said,

*Do not lay up for yourselves **treasures** on earth, where moth and rust destroy and where thieves break in and steal; but **lay up for yourselves treasures in heaven**, where neither moth nor rust destroys and where thieves do not break in and steal. For where your treasure is, there your heart will be also. Matthew 6:19-21*

Don't let it be said of your life's work what will be said of Babylon's someday, dear saint, namely ... **For in one hour such great riches came to nothing**.

Rev. 18:17b-19

*Every **shipmaster**, all who travel by ship, sailors, and as many as trade on the sea, stood at a distance and cried out when they saw the smoke of her burning, saying, 'What is like this great **city**?' They threw dust on their heads and cried out, weeping and wailing, and saying, 'Alas, alas, that great **city**, in which all who had ships on the sea became rich by her wealth! For in one hour she is made desolate.*

When Babylon is destroyed, all of its ministers of transportation will mourn. When Christ gets through with Babylon, there won't be anything left to ship. What a sight that will be when all the ship merchants are crying and mourning over Babylon in that day. To those fellows ... it was all about being ***rich***.

Rev. 18:20-23

***Rejoice** over her, O heaven, and you* [NU changes, *"holy apostles and prophets"* to *"saints and apostles,"*] *for God has avenged you on her! Then a mighty angel took up a stone like a great **millstone** and threw it into the sea, saying, '**Thus with violence the great city Babylon shall be thrown down, and shall not be found anymore**. The sound of harpists, musicians, flutists, and trumpeters shall not be heard in you anymore. No craftsman of any craft shall be found in you anymore, and the sound of a millstone shall not be heard in you anymore. The light of a lamp shall not shine in you anymore, and the voice of bridegroom and bride shall not be heard in you anymore. For your merchants were the great men of the earth, for by your sorcery all the nations were deceived.'*

18:20

The angel's words bring us to yet another great contrast between the realities of Heaven and the realities of Earth. While mourning for Babylon occupies the Earth-dwellers below, rejoicing will be the emotion of the day in Heaven. Have you noticed there seems to be a lot of that that goes on up there? When the call went forth to, **Rejoice over her, O heaven, and you saints and apostles**, I suspect that everyone in Heaven just started dancing! They had all suffered greatly at the hands of the Babylon system in their own day. Stephen was stoned to death by Babylon's forerunners (Acts 7); the Apostle James was put to the sword by her (Acts 12); tradition tells us that Peter was crucified upside down by her ... and all the rest of the apostles were put to death by her in one gruesome way or another. All the **saints** will join in this celebration ... saints like Jim Elliot, the twentieth century missionary who was speared to death by her in the jungles of South America. The list is endless. Heaven is really going to "rock" when Babylon finally gets her due!

18:21-23

What a graphic illustration John was provided when he saw the angel pick up a **great millstone** and cast it into the sea crying, **Thus with violence the great city Babylon shall be thrown down, and shall not be found anymore!** In one fell swoop:

...her music will cease.

...her greedy merchandising will come to a grinding halt.

...her lights will literally be punched out.

...her endless weddings will be no more. Apparently, there will be an endless procession of weddings at Babylon during Antichrist's reign. No doubt, they will come from all over the world to seek his blessing, much like those who travel to Rome today to be blessed by the Pope. But, in that day, they will be seeking to be married by the False Prophet so they can go home and brag about how they were married in Babylon by the big Poobah himself! Jesus spoke of these endless weddings as well, saying,

*Just as it was in the days of Noah, so also will it be in the days of the Son of Man. People were eating, drinking, **marrying and being given in marriage** up to the day Noah entered the ark. Then the flood came and destroyed them all. Luke 17:26*

Rev. 18:24

*And **in her was found the blood of prophets and saints**, and of all who were slain on the earth*.

The question arises, *Does she deserve this severe a judgment*? Dr. McGee says, *like searching the pockets of a dead murderer, the evidence of who Babylon really is ... is discovered*. And, it is found that her wicked influence dated all the way back to the Garden of Eden. Every murder of God's **prophets and saints** is attributed to the Babylon system here. An amazing, and yet unfulfilled prophecy in this regard is found in *Jeremiah 51:49-50*. There, we read,

*As **Babylon** has caused the slain of Israel to fall, so at **Babylon** the slain of all the earth shall fall. **You who have escaped the sword, Get away! Do not stand still!** Remember the LORD afar off, and **let Jerusalem** come to your mind.*

Beloved, this matter concerning God's future dealing with Babylon is a *done deal*. Satan and his Antichrist will have their day, but it will be a brief one, and then will come its violent and devastating end. When the Lord Jesus Christ ... the Judge of the whole earth ... steps in ... Antichrist and his scurrilous Babylon, will be *a gonner*!

This brings us to the end of this section. It has taken up the lion's share of the book of Revelation ... all of chapters 4 through 18. It is THE VISION OF JESUS CHRIST IN JUDGMENT.

REVELATION 19

THE SECOND COMING

OF THE LORD JESUS CHRIST

We have arrived now at the amazing section and account of THE VISION OF JESUS CHRIST IN RETURN (Chapters 19-20). The Second Coming of Jesus Christ has been long awaited and much anticipated by the people of God. It is a major theme in both the Old and New Testaments. Here in chapter 19, we have the description of exactly what it will be like when Christ himself descends from Heaven to Earth, destroying his enemies and placing his precious feet once again on the Mount of Olives.

Rev. 19:1-6

After these things I heard **[NU adds *"something like"*]** *a loud voice of a great* **multitude** *in heaven, saying, 'Alleluia! Salvation and glory and honor and power belong to* **[NU omits *"the Lord"*]** *our God! For true and righteous are his judgments, because he has judged the great harlot who corrupted the earth with her fornication; and he has avenged on her the blood of his servants shed by her.' Again they said, '**Alleluia**! Her smoke rises up forever and ever!' And the twenty-four elders and the four living creatures fell down and worshiped God who sat on the throne, saying, 'Amen! **Alleluia**!' Then a voice came from the throne, saying, '**Praise our God**, all you his servants and those who fear him* **[NU omits *"both"*]** *small and great!' And I heard, as it were, the voice of a great multitude, as the sound of many waters and as the sound of mighty thunderings, saying, '**Alleluia**! For* **[NU changes *"the"* to *"our"*]** *Lord God Omnipotent reigns!'*

This chapter has been called the *Hallelujah* chapter of the Bible. The word, *'Alleluia,* is voiced five times here in the first six verses. This ancient Hebrew word means *praise ye Jah.* It is found many times in the Psalms. In fact, fifteen of them begin with it.

Our focus is directed back up to Heaven now ... away from the burning ruins of Babylon down below. Up there, a party is going on. It began in the last chapter at verse 21. All of Heaven is rejoicing because God has arisen and taken devastating action against Satan and Antichrist's dark kingdom. John says that he heard the voice of a **great multitude [ὄχλου (*oxlou*)]**, shouting, *'Alleluia*! Then, he heard them crying, **salvation and glory and honor and power belong to the Lord our God! For true and righteous are his judgments, because he has judged the great harlot who corrupted the earth with her fornication; and he has avenged on her the blood of his servants shed by her**. This great victory chant was followed by another booming *'Alleluia* which apparently came from the angels. In addition, they added, **Her smoke rises up forever and ever**. The angels could see the smoke of Satan's kingdom below as it was ascending continuously upward.

A third *'Alleluia* was boomed out by the **twenty-four elders** and the four **living creatures** fell down to worship before the throne. Out of this great act of worship, a fourth *'Alleluia* came, which was the greatest of all. It had been called for by a **voice** from the throne ... most likely the voice was that of one of the living creatures who surround it. The voice said, **Praise our God, all you his servants, and you that fear him, both small and great.** The response ... well, it was deafening! John says it rolled forth like **the voice of a great multitude, as the sound of many waters and as the sound of mighty thunderings**. Now that's a *'Alleluia,* brother. It will fill Heaven's atmosphere one day, like the roar of a mighty cataract. With peals like thunder, multitudes of God's creatures and servants, angels, and Old Testament saints, Living Creatures, the Church and all the Tribulation Saints lifted their voices and hearts as one exclaiming, **the Lord God Omnipotent reigns**! What celebration and praise that day will bring, aye? And, the amazing thing is ... you and I were actually there that day participating in it. John was actually witnessing it, you see, by way of this vision. So, strange as it may sound, among the voices that John actually heard that day ... was your voice and mine!

Rev. 19:7-10

Let us be glad and rejoice and give him glory, for **the marriage of the Lamb has come***, and his wife has made herself ready. And to her it was granted to be arrayed in* ***fine linen****, clean and bright, for the fine linen is the* **righteous acts of the saints***. Then he said to me, 'Write:* **'Blessed** *are those who are called to* **the marriage supper of the Lamb***!' And he said to me, 'These are the* **true sayings of God.***' And I fell at his feet to worship him. But he said to me, 'See that you do not do that! I am your fellow servant, and of your brethren who have the testimony of Jesus. Worship God! For the testimony of Jesus is the spirit of prophecy.'*

19:7-8

While Babylon continued to smolder below, a marriage was being consummated up above. We learn here that, time-wise, the **marriage of the Lamb** will take place just prior to our Lord's Second Coming to Earth ... just after the destruction of the seventh Bowl judgment.

Jesus came into our world as a Jew, made under the Law (Galatians 4:4-5). Then, by his death on the cross, he instituted a New Covenant between God and the Jewish people, sealed by his own blood. We Gentiles have been grafted into that Covenant like a **wild olive branch** (Romans 11:13-21) is grafted into a natural olive tree. This is why the Church's marriage feast with their Lord will follow Jewish marriage custom. And, believe me, it will be the greatest wedding feast of all time. When Jesus was on Earth, he likened himself to a **bridegroom**. In *Matthew 9:14-15,* we read,

Then the disciples of John came to him, saying, 'Why do we and the Pharisees fast often, but your disciples do not fast?' And Jesus said to them, 'Can the friends of the bridegroom mourn as long as the **bridegroom** *is with them? But the days will come when the* **bridegroom** *will be taken away from them, and then they will fast.'*

The Apostle Paul described the Church as, *"the bride of Christ."* As you have it in *Second Corinthians 11:2,*

... for I am jealous for you with godly jealousy. For ***I have betrothed you to one husband,*** *that I may present you as a chaste virgin to Christ.*

In *Ephesians5:25-32*, he says,

Husbands, love your wives, just as Christ also loved the church and gave himself for her, that he might sanctify and cleanse her with the washing of water by the word, that he might present her to himself a glorious church, not having spot or wrinkle or any such thing, but that she should be holy and without blemish. So husbands ought to love their own wives as their own bodies; he who loves his wife loves himself. For no one ever hated his own flesh, but nourishes and cherishes it, just as the Lord does the church. ***For we are members of his body, of his flesh and of his bones.*** *For this reason a man shall leave his father and mother and be joined to his wife, and the two shall become one flesh. This is a great mystery, but* ***I speak concerning Christ and the church***.

Now, in Jesus' day, a Jewish marriage had three parts. They were as follows:

...First, a marriage contract was signed. It was sometimes entered into by the parents of Jewish children when the prospective bride and bridegroom were still very young. At that point, as far as Jewish law was concerned, they were legally married.

...Next, came the retrieving of the bride. This took place when the couple became of age or after a reasonable waiting period. Then, the groom and his friends would go to the bride's home to fetch her and bring her to live permanently in the bridegroom's home.

...The third and final step was the marriage celebration and feasting. This great celebration took place at the groom's home. It usually lasted for a week. Jesus was attending one of these feasts at the wedding in Cana (John 2), when the host ran out of wine. Jesus performed his first miracle there, helping the host out by changing water into wine. And, as it turned out, it was the best wine they had yet consumed!

We who have trusted in the Lord Jesus Christ as our personal Lord and Savior will also experience all three phases of this Jewish customary wedding ceremony. First, when we receive Christ, we are formally wed to Christ ... having been immediately *baptized* into his Body by his Holy Spirit (First Corinthians 12:13). At that first moment of belief in Christ, we became **members of his body, of his flesh and of his bones** (Ephesians 5:30). This was our marriage contract ... signed, sealed and delivered by our now indwelling Christ. All true believers are spiritually married to the Lamb of God (Ephesians 5; II Corinthians 11). What remains however, is the second and third steps of the process ... namely, his coming to get us and then our sitting down with him at the marriage celebration and feast he has prepared for us in his home above.

One glorious day, our Bridegroom and his friends will come to get us and escort us to he and his Father's house in Heaven (First Thessalonians 4:16-17; John 14:23; 17:24). Then, as we have it here in Revelation 19, we will sit down at the great celebration of the *marriage supper of the Lamb*. There is a place reserved for you and me at that table, dear believer. At that time, we will all sit down together with Him and celebrate the final phase of our marriage to Christ in our new home above. Won't that be wonderful? I suspect there will be more looking, listening, talking, introducing and rejoicing than eating though.

John was actually at that future day, as he described to us here in our text. Notice, he says, ***his wife has made herself ready***. He says she (the Church) was resplendent in the clothing that had been **granted** to her. Significantly, the text calls these garments, **the righteous acts of the Saints**. There is something very important for us to understand here. All of Christ's Church saints will be at the marriage supper of the Lamb and all will be dressed in the beautiful robes that he has provided for them. However, the unique design of each individual's garment will actually reflect the good things that they have done while they were living for Christ on Earth. That is why their robes are said to be, *the righteousnesses* (the word is a plural in the Greek) of the saints. So, at the marriage supper of the Lamb, Christ's saints are going to be actually and visibly wearing their good works. Now, tell me how we live down here doesn't matter! It's going to matter a great deal when we sit down at the **marriage supper of the Lamb**. We need to really take this to heart, dear saint. It is so very important to take great care in how we build our lives on Christ while we are living down here. *Philippians 2:12,* says,

Wherefore, my beloved, as ye have always obeyed, not as in my presence only, but now much more in my absence, **work** *out your own* **salvation** *with* **fear** *and trembling.*

In *First Corinthians 3:11-15,* we read,

For no other foundation can anyone lay than that which is laid, which is Jesus Christ. Now ***if anyone builds on this foundation with gold, silver, precious stones, wood, hay, straw, each one's work will become clear****; for* ***the day will declare it****, because it will be revealed by fire; and the fire will test each one's work, of what sort it is. If anyone's work which he has built on it endures, he will receive a reward. If anyone's work is burned, he will suffer loss; but he himself will be saved, yet so as through fire.*

The crucial question then becomes, *Am I really building my life on Christ? Am I living in the light of who I really am and who I'm going to be for all eternity? Have I been making ready for the marriage supper of the Lamb?* Build your life of good deeds purposefully, beloved. Lay them carefully and thoughtfully, because one day, you and I will be wearing them to the wonderful occasion that is set before us here.

Therefore, my beloved brethren, be **steadfast***, immovable,* ***always abounding in the work of the Lord, knowing that your labor is not in vain*** *in the Lord. First Corinthians 15:58*

19:9

One last thought before we leave this subject, the angel told John, **Write: 'Blessed are they who are called unto the marriage supper of the Lamb.'** Now, we Church saints are the Bride of Christ and this is our wedding supper. We are not *called* to this occasion, it is our wedding. We do the inviting. The Bridegroom and the Bride issue the invitations to their wedding. Those who are *called* to the marriage supper of the Lamb refer to the guests who are going to be invited. Do you know who they might be? Well, Jesus will do the inviting. So, I would expect to see Adam and Eve there, Seth and Enoch and Noah,

Abraham and Sarah and Isaac and Rebecca, Jacob and Rachel, Joseph and Moses and Joshua, King David, Job and Ezra, Nehemiah and Isaiah, Jeremiah and Ezekiel and Rahab and all the rest of God's Old Testament saints ... and all the Tribulation saints as well. There will be many historic, unique and happy guests at *the marriage supper of the Lamb*. Being a guest at this great event will be a *blessing* for all concerned.

Finally, the angel solemnly proclaims ... *These are the true sayings of God*. He is emphasizing that these things are sure and certain. We have the Word of God on it.

19:10

John says, *And I fell at his feet to worship him*. Poor fellow, he was so overcome by all of this that he committed a very human blunder. Don't be too hard on him. I say that for at least three reasons. First, it must have been very difficult for John, still in human flesh and burdened with human frailties, to consistently respond in the right way in the heavenly realm. Second, angels are incredibly awesome beings, brother. The book of Hebrews says, *he makes his angels ministers of fire* (Hebrews 1:7). If you or I found ourselves in the presence of one of these awesome creatures, I suspect we might become a bit *discombobulated* as well! And third, the nature of all the revelations that John had been receiving had to have been so disturbing that, like Daniel of old (Daniel 8:27; 10:8-9), he no doubt became temporarily unhinged by them.

The angel immediately corrected John saying, *I am your fellow servant, and of your brethren who have the testimony of Jesus. Worship God*. By the way, did you know that Jesus never once turned down worship? This is solid evidence that he was indeed who he said he was ... God of very God. Jesus is worthy to receive worship.

There were many occasions in Jesus' life when he readily and openly received worship. One that comes to mind is found in *John 9:38*. There, a blind man confessed, *Lord, I believe!'* Then, we read, *And he worshiped him*. Receiving worship is the sole privilege and realm of God Almighty, beloved. The fact that our Lord always received it, tells us that he was fully aware of just who he was

(John.1:1,14). *Hebrews 1:6,* quotes the Father's decree about this in relation to angels,

But when he again brings the firstborn [Jesus] *into the world, he says: 'Let all the angels of God **worship** him.'*

The angel concluded, ***Worship God: For the testimony of Jesus is the spirit of prophecy****.* In effect, he was telling John, *Don't fall before me. Fall before Jesus. He is the one of whom all the prophets speak*!

Rev. 19:11-13

*Now I saw heaven opened, and behold, a white horse. And he who sat on him was called **Faithful and True**, and in **righteousness** he judges and makes war. **His eyes were like a flame of fire**, and on his head were many crowns. He had a name written that no one knew except himself. He was clothed with a **robe dipped in blood**, and his name is called **The Word of God**.*

O Lord Jesus how long, how long?... go the words of that great old hymn of the faith, *Christ Returneth*. Here in John's vision, the wait is over. Here he is at last! This is what the people of God have looked and prayed for, for millennia. It is that wonderful day when their God and Savior will have risen up from his throne and come at last to intervene upon the earth. This is also that great work of Messiah that the faithful among the Jewish people have so long looked and longed for. All the orthodox Jews of Jesus day were waiting for their conquering Messiah and **Deliverer** to appear. Unfortunately, they didn't catch the truth of their many scriptures that taught that, at Messiah's first appearing, he would come as the meek and lowly One to die for their sins (Isaiah 53, Psalm 22, et. al.). But, as recorded here in Revelation 19, the great conquering Messiah and Deliverer of Israel will have come at last. Let's take a moment and look at a few of the prayers and prophecies in scripture that speak of this Second Coming of the Messiah and Savior. Isaiah said,

The LORD shall go forth like a mighty man; he shall stir up his zeal like a man of war. He shall cry out, yes, shout aloud; he shall prevail against his enemies. ***'I have held my peace a long time, I have***

been still and restrained myself. Now I will cry *like a woman in labor, I will pant and gasp at once. I will lay waste the mountains and hills, and dry up all their vegetation; I will make the rivers coastlands, and I will dry up the pools.' Isaiah 42:13-15*

Isaiah prayed,

Oh, that you would rend the heavens! That you would come down! *That the mountains might shake at your presence; as fire burns brushwood, as fire causes water to boil; to make your name known to your adversaries that the nations may tremble at your presence! Isaiah 64:1-2*

David, the sweet Psalmist of Israel, prayed,

Bow down your heavens, O LORD, and **come down***; touch the mountains, and they shall smoke. Psalm 144:5*

Let God arise*, let his enemies be scattered; let those also who hate him flee before him. Psalm 68:1*

Let the heavens rejoice, and let the earth be glad; let the sea roar, and all its fullness; let the field be joyful, and all that is in it. Then all the trees of the woods will rejoice before the LORD. **For he is coming, for he is coming to judge the earth***. He shall judge the world with righteousness, and the peoples with his truth. Psalm 96:11-13*

These prophecies and prayers encapsulate the hopes and dreams of all of God's people of all ages. They will be answered in spades when Christ Jesus returns to Earth at the end of the Great Tribulation. And, by means of John's vision here, we are given the privilege of seeing it as if we were actually there.

Now, the positioning of the Second Coming of the Lord Jesus Christ here in chapter 19 of the book of Revelation, clearly teaches us that the Lord's Second Coming to Earth will take place at the **end** of the Great Tribulation. Christ will return to Earth, only after Antichrist's Babylon is lying in smoldering ruins. When that occurs in time … just north of Antichrist's ruined city, a great army will have gathered in the valley of Megiddo. You will remember that this was initiated by the pouring out of the Sixth Bowl judgment (16:12-16). The massive army that will assemble will have come from all over the world. Doubtless, they will be seething with anger. Their homes, their cities and their livelihoods, will all be laying in smoking ruins from the knock-out punch of the seventh Bowl. No doubt, the personal cost to each combatant will have filled their hearts with a burning desire for revenge. All the vast armies of the east ... China, India and Asia ... will be on hand, just as predicted back in *16:12*,

*Then the sixth angel poured out his bowl on the great river Euphrates, and its water was dried up, so that the way of the **kings from the east** might be prepared.*

These ungodly armies will have gathered in the valley of Megiddo to do or die! They will have come to the Holy Land on behalf of Antichrist's throne. What an awesome stage will have been set in the valley of Megiddo in that future day. It is described to us in verses eleven through sixteen. This is the climactic event toward which all history will have been moving from time immemorial.

19:11

Then, at last, there He will be. Suddenly, majestically, the great Lord of Glory will appear in the skies above Earth. As we have it in *Psalm 24:7-10*,

***Lift up your heads**, O ye gates; and be ye lift up, ye everlasting doors; and **the King of glory shall come in**. Who is this **King of glory**? **The Lord strong and mighty, the Lord mighty in battle**. Lift up your heads, O ye gates; even lift them up, ye everlasting doors; and **the King of glory shall come in**. Who is this **King of glory**? **The Lord of hosts, he is the King of glory**. Selah* (KJV)

Doubtless, Christ's enemies will instinctively lift their weapons at him. As we had it back in *17:14*,

***These will make war with the Lamb**, and the Lamb will overcome them, for he is Lord of lords and King of kings; and those who are with him are called, chosen, and faithful.*

What an awesome scene! When Jesus came into our world the first time, he entered it as a baby wrapped in swaddling clothes. He lived and walked among us as the ***meek and lowly*** one. He lived out his life as a poor peasant. He rode into Jerusalem on a donkey's colt, the picture of humility and peace. Without the slightest resistance, he allowed himself to be nailed to a Roman cross, to die the ignominious death of a common criminal for the sins of the world. He had come to Earth as the ***Lamb slain from the foundation of the world***. But ... what a contrast we see in him here! He appears in the skies above Antichrist's wicked and blasphemous armies ... astride a great white stallion and surrounded with the roiling *Shekinah* glory clouds of Heaven. As we have it in his own words,

Immediately after the tribulation of those days the sun will be darkened, and the moon will not give its light; the stars will fall from heaven, and the powers of the heavens will be shaken. ***Then the sign of the Son of Man will appear in heaven, and then all the tribes of the earth will mourn, and they will see the Son of Man coming on the clouds of heaven with power and great glory.*** Matthew 24:29-30

First Timothy 6:14-15 says,

*...that you keep this commandment without spot, blameless until our Lord Jesus Christ's **appearing**, which he will **manifest** in his own time, **he who is the blessed and only Potentate, the King of kings and Lord of lords**.*

On that day, there will be no mistake about who Jesus is, nor will there be for a good long while after! This time, he will not appear as the Lamb of God. Rather, he will ride forth as the ***Lion of the Tribe of Judah*** ... ***King of kings and Lord of lords*** ... the God-Man ... Lord of Glory ... Lord of Hosts and Creator of the whole earth.

Christ's great warhorse was the first thing that caught John's eye as came forth stamping and prancing proudly across the skies. Then, as John focused in on its Rider, he recognized him and exclaimed this is the one who is called ***Faithful and True***. Never has anyone had a name so befitting of their person as this Man. Let's think further on that name for a minute...

...His name is ***Faithful***. Jesus always is and always will be, the completely faithful One. He was always faithful to his Father. As we have it in *Hebrews 3:1-2,*

*Therefore, holy brethren, partakers of the heavenly calling, consider the Apostle and High Priest of our confession, Christ Jesus, who was **faithful to him** who appointed him, as Moses also was faithful in all his house.*

He has always been completely faithful to you and me as well. As we have it in *Hebrews 2:17,*

*Therefore, in all things he had to be made like his brethren, that he might be a merciful and **faithful High Priest** in things pertaining to God, to make propitiation for the sins of the people.*

...His name is **True**. Those who have taken the time to carefully examine the person of the Lord Jesus Christ have invariably discovered that he is **Truth** incarnate. As he himself put it in *John 14:6,*

*I am the way, **the truth**, and the life. No one comes to the Father except through me.*

John 1:17, says,

*For the law was given through Moses, but grace and **truth** came through Jesus Christ.*

...***in righteousness he judges and makes war***. I'm certainly glad for that, aren't you? He never errs in his judgments. He never makes mistakes. He is always exactly right. I don't know about you, but I will be glad for my Lord's judgment of me personally, because for better or worse, he will get it right. He will make no mistakes. He will know my every motive and be cognizant of every action and event in my life. In absolute righteousness and complete mercy and understanding ... he will correctly evaluate and reward each of his saints. Though we may be inclined to shrink from such an examination now ... when the day actually comes ... I believe most, if not all, of his saints will find it to be a day of unprecedented blessing. *Isaiah 11:2-4,* says,

*The Spirit of the LORD shall rest upon him, the Spirit of **wisdom and understanding**, the Spirit of counsel and might, the Spirit of **knowledge** and of the fear of the LORD. His delight is in the fear of the LORD, and **he shall not judge by the sight of his eyes, nor decide by the hearing of his ears;** But **with righteousness** he shall judge the poor, and decide with equity for the meek of the earth; he shall strike the earth with the rod of his mouth, and **with the breath of his lips he shall slay the wicked**.*

And, as you have it in *First Corinthians 4:5,*

*Therefore judge nothing before the time, until the Lord comes, who will both bring to light the hidden things of darkness and reveal the counsels of the hearts. Then **each one's praise will come from God**.*

19:12

...***His eyes were like a flame of fire.*** As John continued to watch, again he was struck by the fiery eyes of Heaven's cloud Rider above.

He first described them to us back in chapter 1. You will remember that they speak of the fact that this is the Omniscient (all knowing) and Holy One of God. He is the one who will carry out God's fiery-eyed and righteous wrath against the wicked. He will be able to simultaneously see into the heart of every human being arrayed against him at the battle of Armageddon and know each and every one of them completely!

...*He had a name written, that no one knew except himself*. This mysterious name speaks of Christ's deity. He is God of very God, you see, embodying all the mystery and incomprehensibleness which that implies. This is the Inscrutable One. For many hundreds of years, the Jews, out of respect for their God, would not pronounce the name that he had revealed through Moses at the burning bush in Exodus 3. That Hebrew *tetragrammaton* consisted of four consonants, YHWH. It is translated *I Am* in Exodus 3:14. Much later, the Jews began to pronounce it only when their scholars supplied it with the first three vowels of the Hebrew alphabet. After that, its pronunciation became *YAHOWEH* which, when transliterated into English, becomes *Jehovah*. There is no record of how Moses heard it pronounced, however. To this day, no one knows that exact pronunciation except God himself. I strongly suspect this was the name that John saw **written that no one knew except himself**. Jesus took the Greek form of this name to himself in John 8, when he told the Pharisees, **before Abraham was, I Am**. They knew exactly who he was saying he was ... and they immediately took up stones to kill him for it.

19:13

...*clothed with a robe dipped in blood.* The garment that John saw on Heaven's Cloud Rider was bloodied from top to bottom. I believe that was because he had just come from his judgment of wicked Israel ... having tramped out the vintage of **the great winepress of the wrath of God** outside the City above (14:19-20). He will be wearing the same judgment robe at his Second Coming because of the similar business of physical judgment he is about to take care of at the battle of Armageddon. Isaiah quoted this Judge of all the earth as saying,

I have trodden the winepress alone, and from the peoples no one was with me. For I have trodden them in my anger, and trampled them in my fury; **their blood is sprinkled upon my garments, and I have stained all my robes.** *Isaiah 63:3*

...**His name is called The Word of God.** This certainly tags down the Rider's identity beyond question, does it not? The Lord Jesus Christ alone is called **The Word of God** in Scripture. As you have it in *John 1:1* and *14*,

In the beginning was the **Word***, and the* **Word** *was with God, and the* **Word was God***. ... And the* **Word** *became flesh and dwelt among us, and we beheld his glory, the glory as of the only begotten of the Father, full of grace and truth.*

Rev. 19:14

And the **armies** *in heaven, clothed in* **[NU changes *"fine"*]** *pure white linen, white and clean,* ***followed him on white horses***.

As John's eyes shifted away from Heaven's Cloud Rider, he now observes that there were armies following him. Who might they be? Well, for one, his angels are going to be accompanying him. *Second Thessalonians 1:7-8*, says,

...and to give you who are troubled rest with us when the Lord Jesus is revealed from heaven ***with his mighty angels****, in flaming fire taking vengeance on those who do not know God, and on those who do not obey the gospel of our Lord Jesus Christ.*

Now, I hope you know how to ride because you and I are going to be with him on that day. We are in the other army John saw. Not to worry though, you can be sure that we will have no problem riding on that day and we will not have to lift a finger in battle either. Since we are looking at the actual scene of this future event, if John had taken a photograph of it and had the photo enlarged, you would find your face and the horse you will be riding in this scene! The saints will be following Christ when he descends from Heaven on that day so that they can witness their vindication and, also, witness his awesome justice and power. Here are a few scriptures that speak to this:

Now Enoch, the seventh from Adam, prophesied about these men also, saying, 'Behold, the Lord comes with ten thousands of his saints, to execute judgment on all, to convict all who are ungodly among them of all their ungodly deeds which they have committed in an ungodly way, and of all the harsh things which ungodly sinners have spoken against him.' Jude 14-15

*Then you shall flee through my mountain valley, for the mountain valley shall reach to Azal. Yes, you shall flee as you fled from the earthquake in the days of Uzziah king of Judah. Thus **the LORD my God will come, and all the saints with you**. Zechariah 14:5*

*Wait on the LORD, and keep his way, and he shall exalt you to inherit the land; when the wicked are cut off, **you shall see it**. Psalm 37:34*

*Only with your eyes shall you look, and **see** the reward of the wicked. Psalm 91:8*

Rev 19:15

*Now out of his **mouth** goes a **sharp sword**, that with it he should strike the nations. And **he himself will rule them with a rod of iron**. **He himself treads the winepress of the fierceness and wrath of Almighty God**.*

The *sword* that John saw coming from Christ's mouth is the same symbol that we saw back in 1:16. It needs no explanation. But, as a reminder, here is *Hebrews 4:12*, once again:

*For the **word of God** is living and powerful, and sharper than any **two-edged sword**, piercing even to the division of soul and spirit, and of joints and marrow, and is a discerner of the thoughts and intents of the heart.*

Christ's Word will be his weapon on that future day. He will need no other. And, what an awesome weapon it will be in the day of battle. He will not need to strike or exert himself for ... just as it was when he created all that exists in the first place ... He will simply speak and it will be done. He is the one who spoke the universe into existence and is the one who is presently holding it together by the word of his power (Genesis 1; Colossians 1:16; John 1:3; Hebrews

Strange Work

2:10). When he descends to Earth on that future day, he will take on the armies of Antichrist below with the pure and awesome weapon of the Word of his mouth, fulfilling many prophecies in Scripture in the process. Here are a few of them.

*He shall strike the earth with the rod of his **mouth**, and **with the breath of his lips he shall slay the wicked**. Isaiah 11:4b*

*For behold, the LORD will come with fire and with his chariots, like a whirlwind, to render his anger with fury, and his rebuke with flames of fire. For by fire and by his **sword** The LORD will judge all flesh; and the slain of the LORD shall be many. Isaiah 66:15-16*

You have also given me the necks of my enemies, so that I destroyed those who hated me. They cried out, but there was none to save; *even to the LORD, but he did not answer them. Then* **I beat them as fine as the dust before the wind; I cast them out like dirt in the streets.** *Psalm 18:40-42*

...and he himself will rule them with a rod of iron ... And, he himself treads the winepress of the fierceness and wrath of Almighty God. This is a clear reference to *Psalm 2:8-9*. There, the Father speaking to the Son says,

*Ask of me, and I will give you the nations for your inheritance, and the ends of the earth for your possession. You shall break them with a **rod of iron**; you shall dash them to pieces like a potter's vessel.*

...he treadeth out the winepress of the fierceness and wrath of Almighty God. Make no mistake about it ... Jesus is the Judge of the whole Earth. He pronounces judgment and he carries it out. He is the one who said, **Vengeance is mine, says the Lord, I will repay** (Romans 12:19). And, so he shall.

Rev. 19:16

And he has on his robe and on his thigh a name written: **KING OF KINGS AND LORD OF LORDS**.

What a sight it will be when Christ Jesus rides across the skies of Earth with these awesome inscriptions on his robe and thigh! *Psalm 95:3*, says,

For the LORD is the great God, and the great King above all gods.

Zechariah 14:9, says,
   And the LORD shall be King over all the earth. In that day it shall be; 'The LORD is one, and his name one.'

Rev. 19:17-21

Then I saw an angel standing in the sun; and he cried with a loud voice, saying to all the birds that fly in the midst of heaven, 'Come and gather together for the **supper** *of the great God,* ***that you may eat the flesh of kings, the flesh of captains, the flesh of mighty men, the flesh of horses and of those who sit on them, and the flesh of all people, free and slave, both small and great.'* *And I saw the* **beast***, the* **kings** *of the earth, and* **their armies, gathered together to make war against him who sat on the horse and against his army.** *Then the beast was captured, and with him the false prophet who worked signs in his presence, by which he deceived those who received the mark of the beast and those who worshiped his image.* **These two were cast alive into the lake of fire** *burning with brimstone. And the rest were killed with the* **sword** *which proceeded from the* **mouth** *of him who sat on the horse. And all the birds were filled with their flesh.*

19:17-18

John heard an angel call out to the birds of prey that **supper** was ready! He calls them to eat the flesh of kings and captains and mighty men and **horses and those that sit upon them**. The angel knew the outcome of this battle was a foregone conclusion, you see. What misguided illusions mere humans and their lord, Satan, think they possess! But, up against *El Shaddai*, how shall they possibly stand? What utter fools. In Second Kings 19, when the Assyrian king, Sennacherib, came into Israel with his mighty army to do harm to good king Hezekiah and his people, God sent one solitary angel to deal with them. And, when the sun arose the next morning, all that was left of Sennacherib's army was a hundred eighty five thousand corpses. If that is the power of just one of God's angels, what might be the result of the wrath of the omnipotent Son of God himself? We are about to see the answer to that question.

19:19

John says ... ***And I saw the beast, the kings of the earth, and their armies, gathered together to make war against him who sat on the horse and against his army***. What utter insanity! Never, in all of Earth's long history, will there have been so many fools gathered together in one place as will be congregated in the valley of Megiddo when Christ Jesus returns. Solomon *hit the nail on the head* when he said,

*Even when a fool walks along the way, he lacks wisdom, and **he shows everyone that he is a fool**. Ecclesiastes 10:3*

To a man, they are all foolish adherents of Antichrist's money grubbing empire and Satan's depraved religion and will all perish together at Armageddon. When they said, ***No***, to Christ, they said, ***Yes***, to their own foolishness, delusion, bondage, misery, judgment and death. What a horrendous day of reckoning that day will be for them. The scene before us is incredible. *Psalm 110:5-6,* says,

The Lord is at your right hand; ***he shall execute kings*** *in the day of his wrath. He shall judge among the nations,* ***he shall fill the places with dead bodies, he shall execute the heads of many countries***.

19:20

Notice the brevity of this battle. Verse twenty simply says that the ***beast*** and the ***false prophet*** were ***captured***. Like a big cat snatching up two mice, Christ will grab those two reprobates and, with one shake, he will cast them ***alive into the lake of fire***. Daniel predicted this would be Antichrist's end, by the way.

Through his cunning he shall cause deceit to prosper under his rule; and he shall exalt himself in his heart. He shall destroy many in their prosperity. ***He shall even rise against the Prince of princes****; but* ***he shall be broken without human means***. *Daniel 8:25*

Isaiah also predicted it saying,

...that you will take up this proverb against the ***king of Babylon****, and say: 'How the oppressor has ceased, the golden city ceased! The LORD has broken the staff of the wicked, the scepter of the* ***rulers****; he who struck the people in wrath with a continual stroke,* ***he who ruled the nations in anger****, is persecuted and no one hinders. The whole*

earth is at rest and quiet; they break forth into singing. Indeed the cypress trees rejoice over you, and the cedars of Lebanon, saying, "Since you were cut down, no woodsman has come up against us. **Hell from beneath is excited about you, to meet you at your coming***; it stirs up the dead for you, all the chief ones of the earth; it has raised up from their thrones all the kings of the nations."* **You will not be joined with them in burial***, because you have destroyed your land and slain your people. The brood of evildoers shall never be named.' Isaiah 14:4-9, 20*

Did you notice that Isaiah said that Antichrist would not be buried? The text here in Revelation 19:20, agrees. As for what actually happens to Antichrist's armies, Isaiah addresses that issue as well.

Woe to the multitude of many people who make a noise like the roar of the seas*, and to the rushing of* **nations** *that make a rushing like the rushing of mighty waters! The nations will rush like the rushing of many waters; but* **God will rebuke them and they will flee far away***, and be chased like the chaff of the mountains before the wind, like a rolling thing before the whirlwind. Then behold, at eventide, trouble! And before the morning, he is no more.* **This is the portion of those who plunder us, and the lot of those who rob us***. Isaiah 17:12-14*

He saw that there was no man, and wondered that there was no intercessor; therefore his own arm brought salvation for him; and his own righteousness, it sustained him. For he put on righteousness as a breastplate, and a helmet of salvation on his head; **he put on the garments of vengeance** *for clothing, and was clad with zeal as a cloak. According to their deeds, accordingly* **he will repay, fury to his adversaries***, recompense to his enemies; the coastlands he will fully repay. So shall they fear the name of the LORD from the west, and his glory from the rising of the sun; when the enemy comes in like a flood, the Spirit of the LORD will lift up a standard against him.* **The Redeemer will come to Zion, and to those who turn from transgression in Jacob***, says the LORD. Isaiah 59:16-20*

Our text simply says, **And the rest were killed with the sword that proceeded from the mouth of him who sat upon the horse**. Zechariah, however, tells us a good bit more.

And this shall be the plague with which the LORD will strike all the people who fought against Jerusalem: **their flesh shall dissolve** *while they stand on their feet, their eyes shall dissolve in their sockets, and their tongues shall dissolve in their mouths.* It shall come to pass in that day that a great panic from the LORD will be among them. Everyone will seize the hand of his neighbor, and raise his hand against his neighbor's hand; Judah also will fight at Jerusalem. And the wealth of all the surrounding nations shall be gathered together: gold, silver, and apparel in great abundance. **Such also shall be the plague on the horse and the mule, on the camel and the donkey, and on all the cattle that will be in those camps.** So shall this plague be. And it shall come to pass that everyone who is left of all the nations which came against Jerusalem shall go up from year to year to worship the King, the LORD of hosts, and to keep the Feast of Tabernacles. And it shall be that whichever of the families of the earth do not come up to Jerusalem to worship the King, the LORD of hosts, on them there will be no rain. Zechariah 14:12-17

    John concludes ... **And all the birds were filled with their flesh**.

REVELATION 20

THE THOUSAND YEAR REIGN OF CHRIST

We come now to the aftermath of that great turning point in Earth's history when Christ fought the battle of Armageddon and returned again to Earth. Now, Revelation will take up the subject of Christ's long anticipated and prophesied thousand year reign. The theological term for this reign is the Millennium. This is a word that comes from the Latin word for one thousand. The Greek word is χίλια (*chilia*). It is used six times here in the first nine verses. Some theologians call those who believe in Christ's literal thousand year reign on Earth, **Chiliasts**. There are three major theological positions in the Church today in connection with the millennial reign of Christ. They are as follows:

Post-millennialism is the view that says that Christ will return **after** the Millennium. This position originated with Augustine who felt that the Church would dominate the world for a thousand years and then, afterwards, Christ would return. Many people hold various forms of post-millennialism. For many years, liberal Christianity held a humanistic post-millennialism that taught that man would get better and better until man himself would bring the Kingdom of God on Earth. However, they didn't believe Christ would ever literally return. This position was popular early in the twentieth century but lost most of its adherents because of world wars I and II.

A-millennialism believes that there will be **no** Millennium. A-millennialists do not believe that Christ will literally reign on Earth but they do believe in his return. They simply see Christ as coming one day, judging the wicked and then, everything simply moving straight on into the **new heavens and the new earth**.

Pre-millennialism says that Christ will return **before** the Millennium. It is based on the literal, grammatical, historical interpretation of Scripture that simply interprets Scripture for what it says. It follows the basic hermeneutical principle that says, *If the* *literal sense makes sense seek no other sense.* So, Pre-millennialists believe that Christ's return to Earth will be followed by a literal thousand year reign just as the Bible predicts here in Revelation 20:4-5. The pre-millennial view is the correct view, in my opinion, since it alone strictly adheres to consistent principles of biblical interpretation. In other words, it is based on sound biblical hermeneutics. If you would like to read up on these very important principles of interpretation, you could begin by reading Bernard Ramm's book, *Protestant Biblical Interpretation*.

The Old Testament is replete with prophecies that predict the future millennial reign of Christ on Earth. Before we proceed with our study here, it would be profitable for us to look at a few from an Old Testament prophet that had a great deal to say about Christ's millennial reign ... the prophet Isaiah. He said,

There shall come forth a Rod from the stem of Jesse, and a Branch shall grow out of his roots. The Spirit of the LORD shall rest upon him, the Spirit of wisdom and understanding, the Spirit of counsel and might, the Spirit of knowledge and of the fear of the LORD. His delight is in the fear of the LORD, and he shall not judge by the sight of his eyes, nor decide by the hearing of his ears; but with righteousness he shall judge the poor, and decide with equity for the meek of the earth; he shall strike the earth with the rod of his mouth, and with the breath of his lips he shall slay the wicked. Righteousness shall be the belt of his loins, and faithfulness the belt of his waist. **The wolf also shall dwell with the lamb, The leopard shall lie down with the young goat, the calf and the young lion and the fatling together; and a little child shall lead them. The cow and the bear shall graze; their young ones shall lie down together; and the lion shall eat straw like the ox. The nursing child shall play by the cobra's hole, and the weaned child shall put his hand in the viper's den. They shall not hurt nor destroy in all my holy mountain, for the earth shall be full of the knowledge of the LORD as the waters cover the sea. And in that day there shall be a Root of Jesse, who shall stand as a banner to the people; for the Gentiles shall seek him, and his resting place shall be glorious**. *It shall come to pass in that day* **That the LORD shall set his hand again the second time to recover the remnant of his people who are left**, *From Assyria and Egypt, From Pathros and Cush, From Elam and Shinar, From Hamath and the islands of the sea. He will* *set up a banner for the nations, and* **will assemble the outcasts of Israel, and gather together the dispersed of Judah from the four corners of the earth.** *Also the envy of Ephraim shall depart, and the adversaries of Judah shall be cut off; Ephraim shall not envy Judah, and Judah shall not harass Ephraim. But they shall fly down upon the shoulder of the Philistines toward the west; together they shall plunder the people of the East; they shall lay their hand on Edom and Moab; and the people of Ammon shall obey them. The LORD will utterly destroy the tongue of the Sea of Egypt; with his mighty wind he will shake his fist over the River, and strike it in the seven streams, and make men cross over dry-shod.* **There will be a highway for the remnant of his people** *who will be left from Assyria, as it was for Israel in the day that he came up from the land of Egypt. Isaiah 11*

I will open rivers in desolate heights, and fountains in the midst of the valleys; I will make the wilderness a pool of water, and the dry land springs of water. I will plant in the wilderness the cedar and the acacia tree, the myrtle and the oil tree; I will set in the desert the cypress tree and the pine and the box tree together, that they may see and know, and consider and understand together, that the hand of the LORD has done this, and the Holy One of Israel has created it. *Isaiah 41:18-20*

For the LORD will comfort Zion, he will comfort all her waste places; he will make her wilderness like Eden, and her desert like the garden of the LORD; joy and gladness will be found in it, thanksgiving and the voice of melody. *Isaiah 51:3*

Instead of the thorn shall come up the cypress tree, and instead of the brier shall come up the myrtle tree; *and it shall be to the LORD for a name, for an everlasting sign that shall not be cut off. Isaiah 55:13*

As you can see from these words of Isaiah, the Old Testament scriptures speak in no uncertain terms about the future glorious and literal reign of Messiah on Earth. The Jewish people were, and still are, correctly anticipating it.

Rev. 20:1-3

Then I saw an angel coming down from heaven, having the key to the bottomless pit and a great chain in his hand. **He laid hold of the** *dragon, that serpent of old, who is the Devil and Satan, and bound him for a thousand years; and he cast him into the bottomless pit, and shut him up, and set a seal on him, so that he should deceive the nations no more till the thousand years were finished. But **after these things he must be released for a little while**.*

Following the battle of Armageddon, Christ will literally set foot on the Mount of Olives. And, as he touches down there, he will cause huge topographical changes to the entire area. Then, he will proceed on into Jerusalem through the Eastern Gate and proceed on up to the temple. There, he will remain to govern and reign over all the Earth for one thousand years. As you have it in *Zechariah 14:3-4,*

*Then shall the Lord go forth, and fight against those nations, as when he fought in the day of battle. And **his feet shall stand in that day upon the mount of Olives**, which is before Jerusalem on the east, and the Mount of Olives shall cleave in the midst thereof toward the east and toward the west, and there shall be a very great valley; and the half of the mountain shall remove toward the north, and half of it toward the south.* (KJV)

After that, Christ's next order of business will be to remove Satan from the earth and confine him to the Abyss for **a thousand years**. Back in chapter 12, you will remember that Satan was tossed out of Heaven and restricted to the earth at the beginning of the Great Tribulation. You will also remember from that passage that it was Michael the archangel and the other good angels of God who bodily expelled Satan and his demons from Heaven. I strongly suspect that the angel we find here ... the angel **with a great chain** ... is **Michael** as well. My, how Satan will hate that, aye!? Satan's demons will also be confined to the Abyss during the Millennium. Isaiah supplies us with that information.

*It shall come to pass in that day that **the LORD will punish on high the host of exalted ones**, and on the earth the kings of the earth. **They will be gathered together, as prisoners are gathered in the pit, and will be shut up in the prison**; after many days they will be punished. Then the moon will be disgraced and the sun ashamed; **for the LORD of hosts will reign on Mount Zion and in Jerusalem and before his elders, gloriously**. Isaiah 24:21-23*

In addition, our text tells us that the purpose of Satan's confinement will be so *that he should deceive the nations no more till the thousand years were finished*. The presence of Satan on Earth complicates the nature of man's sin problem today. Without Satan's presence and influence, however, the manifestation of man's sin nature will become much more apparent and predictable. During the Millennium, no one will be able to say, *The Devil made me do it!* On the contrary, the only thing anyone will be able to say about their wickedness will be, *Yes, I did it*. So, for one thousand years, the nature of man will be tested and displayed for what it truly is and man's total depravity will clearly be demonstrated apart from any interference or influence from Satan whatsoever (Romans 3:9-18).

Now, let's consider the identity of the *nations* that our text mentions, who the Devil will no longer be able to deceive. Who might they be? Well, Jesus said there would be a judgment of the nations that would take place at the beginning of his reign on Earth. As we have it in *Matthew 25:31-46*,

When the Son of Man comes in his glory, *and all the holy angels with him, then he will sit on the throne of his glory.* **All the nations will be gathered before him**, *and* **he will separate them one from another**, *as a shepherd divides his sheep from the goats. And he will set the* **sheep** *on his right hand, but the* **goats** *on the left. Then the* **King** *will say to those on his* **right hand**, *'Come, you blessed of my Father, inherit the kingdom prepared for you from the foundation of the world: for I was hungry and you gave me food; I was thirsty and you gave me drink; I was a stranger and you took me in; I was naked and you clothed me; I was sick and you visited me; I was in prison and you came to me.' Then the righteous will answer him, saying,* **'Lord, when did we see you hungry and feed you**, *or thirsty and give you drink? When did we see you a stranger and take you in, or naked and clothe you? Or when did we see you sick, or in prison, and come to you? And the* **King** *will answer and say to them,* **'Assuredly, I say to you, inasmuch as you did it to one of the least of these my brethren, you did it to me**. *Then he will also say to those on the* **left hand**, *'Depart from me, you cursed, into the everlasting fire prepared for the devil and his angels: 'for I was hungry and you gave me no food; I was thirsty and you gave me no drink; I was a stranger and you did* *not take me in, naked and you did not clothe me, sick and in prison and you did not visit me.' Then they also will answer him, saying,* **'Lord, when did we see you hungry** *or thirsty or a stranger or naked or sick or in prison, and did not minister to you? Then he will answer them, saying,* **'Assuredly, I say to you, inasmuch as you did not do it to one of the least of these, you did not do it to me.'** *And these will go away into everlasting punishment, but the righteous into eternal life.*

This famous passage is probably one of the most misunderstood, and often taken out of context, passages in the Bible. Jesus was not speaking about the Rapture of the Church, as is so often taught and preached on that passage. He was not talking to the Church at all. As far as the Church is concerned, there will never be any dividing of saints from non-saints, anywhere, or at any time. Christ specifically says that this judgment of the nations will **follow** his coming in *glory* with **all his holy angels** ... a clear reference to his Second Coming at the end of the Tribulation. As we have it in *Second Thessalonians 1:7-9,*

And to you who are troubled rest with us, when the Lord Jesus shall be revealed from heaven **with his mighty angels***, in flaming fire taking vengeance on them that know not God* [battle of Armageddon]*, and obey not the gospel of our Lord Jesus Christ:* [after the preaching of the 144,000, the two witnesses and God's angel who circumvented the globe] *who shall be punished with everlasting destruction from the presence of the Lord, and from the glory of his power...*

So, Matthew 25, is all about the aftermath of Christ's Second Coming and what will take place at the beginning of his millennial reign. At that time, those who are left alive at the end of the Great Tribulation, will be gathered before Christ Jesus to be divided like **sheep** being separated from **goats**. This is the Judgment of the Nations. The actual Greek word translated **nations** there is εθνη **(*ethnay*)**. It refers to people from every ethnic group. This will be a very unusual and unique judgment. The sole criteria for this judgment will be how each remaining person from every remaining ethnic group on Earth has treated Christ's brethren during the dark days of the Great Tribulation. On that basis alone, individual people will either enter the Millennium or be sent away to the Lake of Fire. In reality, this will be the final separation of the remaining Tribulation saints from the surviving wicked Earth-dwellers at the end of the Tribulation. At this judgment, the **righteous** (those saints who cared for and helped Christ's **brethern** during the Tribulation), will be welcomed into his Millennial reign. Their faith, you see, was demonstrated by their actions. Real faith always demonstrates itself by its good works and, also, its love for the people of God. As you have it in *First Peter 1:22,*

Seeing ye have purified your souls in **obeying the truth** *through the Spirit* **unto unfeigned love of the brethren***, see that ye love one another with a pure heart fervently...* (KJV)

As a result of the Judgment of the *ethnos*, many people from a wide variety of ethnic groups and nations will enter the Millennium and preserve their national identities there. Both Zechariah and Jeremiah speak about these leftover seed nations who will constitute the new populations of the earth during Christ's reign...

And it shall come to pass that **everyone who is left of all the nations** (following the Judgment of the Nations cited above) *which came against Jerusalem shall go up from year to year to worship the King, the LORD of hosts, and to keep the Feast of Tabernacles. Zechariah 14:16*

At that time Jerusalem shall be called The Throne of the LORD, and all the nations shall be gathered to it*, to the name of the LORD, to Jerusalem. No more shall they follow the dictates of their evil hearts. Jeremiah 3:17*

Rev. 20:4-6

And I saw **thrones***, and they sat on them, and judgment was committed to them. Then I saw the* **souls of those who had been beheaded for their witness to Jesus and for the word of God***, who had not worshiped the beast or his image, and had not received his mark on their foreheads or on their hands. And* **they lived and reigned with Christ for a thousand years***. But the rest of the dead did not live again until the thousand years were finished.* **This is the first resurrection***. Blessed and holy is he who has part in the* **first resurrection***. Over such the* **second death** *has no power, but they shall be priests of God and of Christ, and shall reign with him a thousand years.*

20:4

There are two different groups of saints mentioned here who will have important administrative roles during the Millennium. The first group, John saw seated upon **thrones**. He says, **judgment was committed to them**. This group is the Church. The scriptures are clear about the fact that the Church will one day sit on **thrones** and **judge the world**. During the Millennium, this will come to pass. Consider the following scriptures:

*Do you not know that the **saints will judge the world**? And if the world will be judged by you, are you unworthy to judge the smallest matters? First Corinthians 6:2*

*If we endure, **we shall also reign with him**. If we deny him, he also will deny us. Second Timothy 2:12*

*And he who overcomes, and keeps my works until the end, **to him I will give power over the nations**; 'He shall rule them with a rod of iron; they shall be dashed to pieces like the potter's vessels'; as I also have received from my Father... Revelation 2:26-27*

*So Jesus said to them, 'Assuredly I say to you, that in the regeneration, **when the Son of Man sits on the throne of his glory, you who have followed me will also sit on twelve thrones**, judging the twelve tribes of Israel.' Matthew 19:28*

Matthew 19:28, above, speaks of the special position that the Apostles, the founders of the Church, will hold in regard to Israel during the Millennium.

The second group, who will reign with Christ, are the Tribulation Saints. Our text identifies them as, **those who had been beheaded for the witness to Jesus who had not worshiped the beast or his image**. It says that they also **lived and reigned with Christ for a thousand years**.

This vision caused John to exclaim ... **Blessed and holy is he who has a part in the first resurrection. They shall be priests of God and of Christ, and shall reign with him a thousand years**. Notice that these saints are also said to be immune to the **second death**. Verse 14, defines what the **second death** is for us.

Both of the above mentioned groups will have a part in the **first resurrection** and will serve Christ on the earth during the Millennium. It is important to understand that the **first resurrection** is not one single event in time. Rather, it is a concept that incorporates more than one event and more than one time. It is a theological term that refers to **the resurrection of all righteous people** regardless of when, where or how their individual resurrection might occur. The *first resurrection* has been called *the resurrection of the just*, as opposed to the *second resurrection*, which could be called, the *resurrection of the damned*. Dr. McGee likens the *first resurrection* to a parade. At the beginning of the parade is the Grand Marshal, the Lord Jesus Christ. He was the *firstborn from the dead*. There will be many others who will follow him. Paul writes, in *Acts 26:23*,

*...that the Christ would suffer, that he would be the **first to rise from the dead**, and would proclaim light to the Jewish people and to the Gentiles.*

Next in line in the parade of the *first resurrection* ... are the *dead in Christ* who will be resurrected at the Rapture of the Church. As you have it in *First Thessalonians 4:16*,

*For the Lord himself will descend from heaven with a shout, with the voice of an archangel, and with the trumpet of God. **And the dead in Christ will rise first**.*

Following them, still other saints will experience their part in the *first resurrection*. There will be the resurrection of pre-Mosaic Old Testament Saints (Adam to Moses). And, there will be the resurrection of Israel (Moses through the last Israelite who died during the Great Tribulation ... Daniel 12:2). And, finally, there will be the resurrection of the Tribulation Saints. Although we are not given the exact times in Scripture as to these last three resurrections, nevertheless it seems certain they will take place at or near the end of the Great Tribulation. Daniel, speaking of the resurrection of Israel at the end of the Great Tribulation says,

*At that time Michael shall stand up, the great prince who stands watch over the sons of your people; and there shall be a time of trouble, such as never was since there was a nation, even to that time. And **at that time your people shall be delivered**, everyone who is found written in the book. **And many of those who sleep in the dust of the earth shall awake, some to everlasting life, some to shame and everlasting contempt**. Daniel 12:1-2*

Notice that this prophecy, given to Daniel in the context of the events of the Great Tribulation, clearly places the resurrection of Israel at the end of the Great Tribulation. At that time, godly Israelites who were under the Old Covenant will be resurrected to enter Messiah's Kingdom on Earth, just as the Scripture promised them. For example, Ezekiel said that David himself would one day enter the kingdom to rule over Israel once again. We read,

*Therefore I will save my flock, and they shall no more be a prey; and I will judge between cattle and cattle. And **I** will set up **one shepherd over them**, and he shall feed them, **even my servant David**; he shall feed them, and he shall be their shepherd. And I the Lord will be their God, and **my servant David a prince among them**; I the Lord have spoken it. Ezekiel 34:22-24* (KJV)

The resurrection of the pre-law saints will also occur at the Lord's Second Coming, at or near the end of the Great Tribulation. Job fills in this piece of the puzzle when he says,

*For I know that my redeemer liveth, and that **he shall stand at the latter day upon the earth**: and though after my skin worms destroy this body, yet **in my flesh shall I see God**; whom I shall see for myself, and mine eyes shall behold, and not another; though my reins be consumed within me* [i.e. 'frightened out of his wits']. *Job 19:25-27*

20:5

Our passage states, **But the rest of the dead did not live until the thousand years were finished**. All other people who have died, from Adam's day to the last day, who did not have a part in the **first resurrection**, will not be resurrected **until the thousand years are finished**. This vast multitude of peoples will not experience their resurrection until all the ranks of the wicked of all time have been completely filled. Many in this group, I'm sorry to say, will die during the reign of Christ on Earth. This entire group's resurrection is called, by default, **the second resurrection** or *the resurrection of the damned*. It will consist exclusively of wicked human beings from all of human history. We will read the sobering account of it at the end of this chapter.

20:6

Without comment, let's simply read this wonderful verse again. **Blessed and holy is he who has part in the first resurrection. Over** *such the second death has no power, but they shall be priests of God and of Christ, and shall reign with him a thousand years.*

THE MILLENNIUM

Let's pause here for a minute and think a bit more about the thousand year reign of Christ. Revelation does not concern itself with this subject because its main theme is the presentation of how the world will be subdued leading up to the Millennial reign of Christ. Therefore, in our text here, the Millennium is only referred to briefly by the simple statement, *And **they lived and reigned with Christ for a thousand years**.* This future 1000 reign of the Messiah has been the Jews' biblically rooted hope for hundreds and hundreds of years. It was the first thing on Jesus' disciple's minds after his resurrection. They questioned him about it saying,

*"Lord, **will You at this time restore the kingdom to Israel?**" And He said to them, "It is not for you to know times or seasons which the Father has put in His own authority."Acts 1:6-7*

Notice, Jesus did not deny their understanding that his widely prophesied Kingdom would actually come to Earth one day. He simply said that the timing of it was solely in his Father's hands. This future literal reign of Messiah on Earth is a major theme of the Old Testament scriptures. Here are a few of my favorites from Isaiah that refer to it.

There shall come forth a Rod [Jesus] from the stem of Jesse,
    And a Branch shall grow out of his roots.
        The Spirit of the LORD shall rest upon Him,
The Spirit of wisdom and understanding,
The Spirit of counsel and might,
The Spirit of knowledge and of the fear of the LORD.
        His delight is in the fear of the LORD,
And He shall not judge by the sight of His eyes,
Nor decide by the hearing of His ears;

> *But with righteousness He shall judge the poor,*
> *And decide with equity for the meek of the earth;*
> *He shall strike the earth with the rod of His mouth,*
> *And with the breath of His lips He shall slay the wicked.*
> *Righteousness shall be the belt of His loins,*
> *And faithfulness the belt of His waist.*
> *The wolf also shall dwell with the lamb,*
> *The leopard shall lie down with the young goat,*
> *The calf and the young lion and the fatling together;*
> *And a little child shall lead them.*
> *The cow and the bear shall graze;*
> *Their young ones shall lie down together;*
> *And the lion shall eat straw like the ox.*
> *The nursing child shall play by the cobra's hole,*
> *And the weaned child shall put his hand in the viper's den.*
> *They shall not hurt nor destroy in all My holy mountain,*
> *For the earth shall be full of the knowledge of the LORD*
> *As the waters cover the sea.*
> *And in that day there shall be a Root of Jesse,*
> *Who shall stand as a banner to the people;*
> *For the Gentiles shall seek Him,*
> *And His resting place shall be glorious."*
> *It shall come to pass in that day*
> *That the Lord shall set His hand again the second time*
> *To recover the remnant of His people who are left,*
> *From Assyria and Egypt,*
> *From Pathros and Cush,*
> *From Elam and Shinar,*
> *From Hamath and the islands of the sea.*
> *He will set up a banner for the nations,*
> *And will assemble the outcasts of Israel,*
> *And gather together the dispersed of Judah*
> *From the four corners of the earth.*
> *Also the envy of Ephraim shall depart,*
> *And the adversaries of Judah shall be cut off;*
> *Ephraim shall not envy Judah,*
> *And Judah shall not harass Ephraim.*

But they shall fly down upon the shoulder of the Philistines toward the west;
Together they shall plunder the people of the East;
They shall lay their hand on Edom and Moab;
And the people of Ammon shall obey them.
The LORD will utterly destroy the tongue of the Sea of Egypt;
With His mighty wind He will shake His fist over the River,
And strike it in the seven streams,
And make men cross over dryshod.
There will be a highway for the remnant of His people
Who will be left from Assyria,
As it was for Israel
In the day that he came up from the land of Egypt. Isaiah 11

. . . .

I will open rivers in desolate heights,
And fountains in the midst of the valleys;
I will make the wilderness a pool of water,
And the dry land springs of water.
I will plant in the wilderness the cedar and the acacia tree,
The myrtle and the oil tree;
I will set in the desert the cypress tree and the pine
And the box tree together,
That they may see and know,
And consider and understand together,
That the hand of the LORD has done this,
And the Holy One of Israel has created it. Isaiah 41:18-20

. . . .

I will rejoice in Jerusalem,
And joy in My people;
The voice of weeping shall no longer be heard in her,
Nor the voice of crying.
No more shall an infant from there live but a few days,
Nor an old man who has not fulfilled his days;

For the child shall die one hundred years old,
But the sinner being one hundred years old shall be accursed.
They shall build houses and inhabit them;
They shall plant vineyards and eat their fruit.
They shall not build and another inhabit;
They shall not plant and another eat;
For as the days of a tree, so shall be the days of My people,
And My elect shall long enjoy the work of their hands.
They shall not labor in vain,
Nor bring forth children for trouble;
For they shall be the descendants of the blessed of the LORD,
And their offspring with them.
It shall come to pass
That before they call, I will answer;
And while they are still speaking, I will hear.
The wolf and the lamb shall feed together,
The lion shall eat straw like the ox,
And dust shall be the serpent's food.
They shall not hurt nor destroy in all My holy mountain,
Says the LORD. Isaiah 65:19-25

Rev. 20:7-10

Now **when the thousand years have expired, Satan will be released** from his prison and will go out to **deceive** the nations which are in the four corners of the earth, **Gog and Magog**, to gather them together to battle, whose number is as the sand of the sea. They went up on the breadth of the earth and **surrounded the camp of the saints and the beloved city**. And fire came down from God out of heaven and devoured them. The devil, who deceived them, was cast into the lake of fire and brimstone where [**NU inserts** *"also"*] the beast and the false prophet are. And they will be tormented day and night forever and ever.

For a thousand years, the Earth will experience unprecedented peace and righteousness under the benevolent but strict reign of the Lord Jesus Christ. I say "strict" because that is what egocentric sinners will continue to require. This is why our text says that the Lord will rule them with a *rod of iron*. Saved sinners will enter the Millennium but multitudes of unsaved sinners will be born during the thousand year reign of Christ. Those offspring will possess the same sin nature that mankind has always possessed and they will need to be saved and sanctified by faith in the Son of God ... just as people today need to be. Death will also exist in the Millennium but, according to the Scripture, it will be rare. Isaiah tells us the world will be repopulated during the Millennium and also that mankind will have its longevity restored. He prophesies that life spans will once again be as they were in the days of Methuselah, who lived nine hundred and sixty nine years (Genesis 5:25-26).

*No more shall an infant from there live but a few days, nor an old man who has not fulfilled his days; for **the child shall die one hundred years old,** but the **sinner** being one hundred years old shall be accursed.* ***They shall build houses and inhabit them**; they shall plant vineyards and eat their fruit. Isaiah 65:20-21*

Doubtless, by the end of the Millennium, there will once again be billions of people on Earth. However, Isaiah also says ... ***But the sinner being one hundred years old shall be accursed***. This statement makes it clear that for many, a thousand years of righteousness and absolute justice will wear very thin indeed. To those people, there will probably be nothing worse, in their thinking, than having to live one more day under the righteous rule of Christ. Zechariah refers to people of that "ilk" as follows:

And it shall be that whichever of the families of the earth do not come up to Jerusalem to worship the King, the LORD of hosts, on them there will be no rain. *If the family of Egypt will not come up and enter in, they shall have no rain; they shall receive the plague with which the LORD strikes the nations who do not come up to keep the Feast of Tabernacles. Zechariah 14:17-18*

This is one example of the exercise of Christ's *rod of iron*.

20:7-8

We come now to an amazing prophecy to consider. We read here that, after the thousand years has expired, ***Satan will be released from his prison and will go out to deceive the nations***. Why would Christ do that? Someone has said, *Well, if you can tell me why God turned* *him loose the first time, I'll tell you why he turns him loose the second time*! There is ample evidence here, however, as to just why Satan will be released. When he is released from the Abyss, this great archenemy of God and his Christ will go forth and act like a giant magnet to once again draw and assemble together all the world's unsaved malcontents. They will gather themselves together for one last desperate rebellion. Incredible as it sounds, once again multitudes will march against the Holy City and against our blessed Lord, just as the armies of their ancient forefathers had done a thousand years before at the great battle of Armageddon. It is at this precise point in time that *Psalm 2*, will be fulfilled in history. Therefore, I give it here in its entirety...

Why do the nations rage, and the people plot a vain thing? The kings of the earth set themselves, and the rulers take counsel together, against the LORD and against his Anointed, saying, **Let us break their bonds in pieces and cast away their cords from us**. *He who sits in the heavens shall laugh; the LORD shall hold them in derision.* **Then he shall speak to them in his wrath,** *and distress them in his deep displeasure: yet* **I have set my King on my holy hill of Zion**. *I will declare the decree: the LORD has said to me, 'You are my Son, today I have begotten you. Ask of me, and I will give you the nations for your inheritance, and the ends of the earth for your possession. You shall break them with a rod of iron; you shall dash them to pieces like a potter's vessel.' Now* **therefore, be wise, O kings; be instructed, you judges of the earth. Serve the LORD** *with fear, and rejoice with trembling.* **Kiss the Son, lest he be angry, and you perish in the way, when his wrath is kindled but a little**. *Blessed are all those who put their trust in him.*

Our text says, when Satan was released he went throughout **the four corners of the earth, Gog and Magog, to gather them together to battle, whose number is as the sand of the sea**. The Old Testament prophecy of **Gog and Magog** is found in Ezekiel 38 and 39. It greatly amplifies this future, amazing and final rebellion against Christ. There, Christ's final battle with the Evil One and his armies is given in great detail. Here are some of its more pertinent parts.

Now the word of the LORD came to me, saying, Son of man, set your face against **Gog, of the land of Magog**, *the prince of Rosh, Meshech, and Tubal, and prophesy against him, and say, 'Thus says* the Lord GOD: 'Behold, I am against you, O Gog, the prince of Rosh, Meshech, and Tubal. **I will turn you** around, put hooks into your jaws, and lead you out, **with all your army**, horses, and horsemen, all splendidly clothed, a great company with bucklers and shields, all of them handling swords. Persia, Ethiopia, and Libya are with them, all of them with shield and helmet; Gomer and all its troops; the house of Togarmah from the far north and all its troops; **many people are with you**. Prepare yourself and be ready, you and all your companies that are **gathered** about you; and be a guard for them. **After many days you will be visited. In the latter years you will come into the land of those brought back from the sword and gathered from many people on the mountains of Israel, which had long been desolate; they were brought out of the nations, and now all of them dwell safely**. You will ascend, coming like a storm, covering the land like a cloud, you and all your troops and **many peoples with you**. 'Thus says the Lord GOD: "On that day it shall come to pass that **thoughts will arise in your mind**, and you will make an evil plan: you will say, **'I will go up against a land of unwalled villages; I will go to a peaceful people, who dwell safely, all of them dwelling without walls, and having neither bars nor gates'**; to take plunder and to take booty, to stretch out your hand against the waste places that are again inhabited, and **against a people gathered from the nations**, who have acquired livestock and goods, who dwell in the midst of the land. Ezekiel 38:1-11

Then you will come from your place out of the far **north**, you and **many peoples with you**, all of them riding on horses, a great company and a mighty army. **You will come up against my people Israel like a cloud**, to cover the land. It will be in the latter days that **I will bring you against my land, so that the nations may know me, when I am hallowed in you, O Gog, before their eyes**. ... And it will come to pass at the same time, when Gog comes against the land of Israel,' says the Lord GOD, 'that **my fury** will show in my face.'... And I will bring him to judgment with pestilence and bloodshed; **I will rain down on him**, on his troops, and on the many peoples who are with him, flooding rain, great hailstones, **fire**, **and brimstone**. Thus I will magnify myself and sanctify myself, and I *will be known in the eyes of many nations.* **Then they shall know that I am the LORD.***'* *Ezekiel 38:15-16, 18, 22-23*

The next chapter, Ezekiel 39, has to do with the aftermath of the battle of God and Magog ... not the battle of Armageddon ... as is so often taught. It is clear from Ezekiel 39, that the Millennium itself will continue the perfecting of Israel. Strange as it may sound, many Jews who will be born during Christ's thousand year reign, will not respond in faith to Christ and therefore will not understand who Jesus Christ truly is (keep in mind that we are still under the *days of the seventh trumpet* here and the *mystery of God* is still not complete). As for these biblical names, *Gog and Magog*, there has been much speculation. They refer to specific ancient cities in the territory of what is now Russia. Apparently, these cities will be restored during the Millennium and will reassume their ancient biblical names. It seems that they will also be hotbeds of discontent and rebellion that will be played out at the end of the Millennium.

20:9

From Ezekiel's prophecy, we learn that Satan's final rebellion and subsequent invasion of the Promised Land (and its *beloved city*, Jerusalem) will come out of the *north*. At that time, just as Ezekiel predicted, (and also as it is seen here in our text) *fire from heaven* will consume Satan's enormous and last army. Then, we read, *the Devil, who deceived them, was cast into the lake of fire and brimstone where the beast and the false prophet are*. PRAISE GOD FROM WHOM ALL BLESSINGS FLOW. Amen? The great tempter, deceiver, accuser of the brethren, liar, murderer and tormentor of the human race will, on that great day, be permanently dealt with ... once and for all ... never to be heard from again! Our Lord will summarily consign him to the *lake of fire and brimstone*, just as easily as he previously deposited the *beast* and the *false prophet* there at the battle of Armageddon. Satan's downward spiral will then be complete. Having fallen from Heaven to Earth, then from Earth to the Abyss, he will ultimately be cast into the Lake of Fire and Brimstone ... which will be his final and eternal abode.

Rev. 20:11-15

Then I saw a great white throne *and him who sat on it, **from whose face the earth and the heaven fled away. And there was found no place for them.** And I saw the dead, small and great, standing before* **[NU omits "God" adds "the throne"]**, *and books were opened. And another book was opened, which is the **Book of Life**. And **the dead were judged according to their works,** by the things which were written in the books. The sea gave up the dead who were in it, and Death and Hades delivered up the dead who were in them. And they were judged, each one according to his works. Then **Death and Hades were cast into the lake of fire. This is the second death**. And anyone not found written in the Book of Life was cast into the lake of fire.*

20:11-12a

After Satan's final rebellion, at least seven months will go by. This is to allot for the time that Ezekiel said would be required to bury all the bodies of those who came up against the Lord. As you have it in *Ezekiel 39:12*,

*And **seven months** shall the house of Israel be burying of them, that they may cleanse the land.* (KJV)

Following that, the dissolving of this present world and its universe will occur ... followed by the judgment of the ***great white throne***. As described here, ***the earth and the heaven fled away. And there was found no place for them***. Peter put it this way,

But the heavens and the earth which are now preserved by the same word, are reserved for fire *until the day of judgment and perdition of ungodly men. ...* ***But the day of the Lord will come as a thief in the night, in which the heavens will pass away with a great noise***, *and the elements will* ***melt*** *with fervent heat;* ***both the earth and the works that are in it will be burned up***. *Therefore, since all these things will be* ***dissolved***, *what manner of persons ought you to be in holy conduct and godliness, looking for and hastening the coming of the day of God, because of which* ***the heavens will be dissolved, being on fire, and the elements will melt with fervent heat?*** *Second Peter 3:7, 10 -12*

Jesus said,

Heaven and earth will pass away, but my words shall not pass away. Matthew 24:35

On the day of which we are reading, these scriptures will be fulfilled. The universe, as we know it, will pass away **with a great noise**. The *Big Bang* theory is only half right. But, they have it backwards. The *Big Bang* comes at the end of the universe, not the beginning. It did not create the universe but it surely will end it! Then, suddenly, like being caught like a thief in the night, the wicked of all time will find themselves resurrected and standing before a **great white throne**. Theologians call this, *The Great White Throne Judgment*. No unsaved and ungodly person who has ever lived will be absent from this event. Verse 13, says, **death, hell and the sea delivered up the dead that were in them**. That just about covers it, doesn't it? All people from all time, who did not have a part in the first resurrection, will be raised at this *second resurrection* to stand for judgment before Almighty God at his **great white throne**.

I had a non-Christian friend once with whom I discussed this judgment. He found it difficult to believe that God would be able to resurrect bodies from the sea after so many years had elapsed. He argued they would have simply disintegrated. I told him that his god was too small. He then replied, partially in jest, but with a disturbing vein of seriousness ... *Well, I won't be judged there because I'm just not going to show up!* The fact remains, however, that unless my college friend has since come to Christ (and I am still praying that he does), he will absolutely have no choice. On that day, after the entire universe has been dissolved, he will find himself standing in the midst of all the rest of the wicked of all time at this fearful and final judgment.

20:12b -13

John says, **and books were opened**. God keeps track of men's deeds. And, He needs no books to do so. These books are for men's benefit to read, not his. If they wish, I suspect they will be free to read in them to their heart's content. Verse 13, says, **And they were judged, each one according to his works**. One can only imagine the sobering and fearful effect this will have on lost sinners as they are shown all the wicked words, thoughts and deeds they have ever been a party to during their lifetimes. All who have been summoned to the Great White Throne judgment will be examined and meticulously evaluated in light of what is written in the books before them. All will be fair. All will be accurate. Now, believe me, I surely would never want to stand before Holy God solely on the basis of my good works, would you?! Let me give you a few scriptures as to why.

*But we are all like an unclean thing, and **all our righteousnesses are like filthy rags**; we all fade as a leaf, and our iniquities, like the wind, have taken us away. Isaiah 64:6*

*...knowing that **a man is not justified by the works of the law but by faith in Jesus Christ**, even we have believed in Christ Jesus, that we might be **justified by faith in Christ** and not by the works of the law; **for by the works of the law no flesh shall be justified**. Galatians 2:16*

*For by grace you have been saved through faith, and that not of yourselves; it is the gift of God, **not of works**, lest anyone should boast. Ephesians 2:8-9*

***Not by works** of righteousness which we have done, but according to his mercy he saved us, by the washing of regeneration, and renewing of the Holy Ghost; which he shed on us abundantly through Jesus Christ our Savior: that being justified by his grace, we should be made heirs according to the hope of eternal life. Titus 3:5-7* (KJV)

Jesus said,

*But I say to you that for **every idle word men may speak, they will give account of it in the day of judgment**. For by your **words** you will be justified, and by your **words** you will be condemned. Matthew 12:36-37*

The second and third stanzas of that great old hymn *Rock of Ages* puts it well:

- *Not the labors of my hands*
- *Can fulfill Thy law's demands;*
- *Could my zeal no respite know,*
- *Could my tears forever flow,*
- *All for sin could not atone;*

- o   *Thou must save, and Thou alone.*
- o   *Nothing in my hand I bring,*
- o   *simply to Thy cross I cling;*
- o   *Naked, come to Thee for dress,*
- o   *Helpless, look to Thee for grace;*
- o   *Foul, I to the fountain fly,*
- o   *Wash me, Savior, or I die!*

Lost souls, who find themselves at the Great White Throne Judgment, will all too quickly discover just how inadequate the ***filthy rags*** of their own perceived good deeds will be. Before Holy God and his righteous gaze, their multitude of evil deeds and words will be exposed to the light. The filthiness of each individual will be glaring and inescapable. Jesus said that not only will every wicked, thoughtless, blasphemous and unloving word be brought up ... but an explanation will be demanded for them as well. When the books are opened at the Great White Throne Judgment, men's puny cases for their own righteousness will evaporate away like tiny puffs of steam in a hurricane.

May we step aside here for a moment? Did you notice that sin wasn't mentioned here at all? Why is that? Well, it's because the sin question was forever settled at the cross ... not just in relation to you and me, beloved, but in relation to the whole world! The whole world has been reconciled to God through the death of his Son, you see. As you have it in *First John 2:2*,

*And He Himself is the **propitiation** for our sins, and not for ours only but also **for the whole world**.*

God's wrath towards sin has already been propitiated (satisfied) at the cross. Sin is no longer an issue between God and man. As you have it in *Second Corinthians 5:18-21*,

*Now all things are of God, who has reconciled us to Himself through Jesus Christ, and has given us the ministry of reconciliation, that is, that **God was in Christ reconciling the world to Himself**, **not imputing their trespasses to them**, and has committed to us the word of **reconciliation**. Now then, we are ambassadors for Christ, as though God were pleading through us: we implore you on Christ's behalf, be* *reconciled to God. For He made Him who knew no sin to be sin for us, that we might become the righteousness of God in Him.*

I repeat ... sin is no longer an issue between God and man. The issue today is ... **How has a person responded to the Son of God and his work on the cross?** As you have it in *John 3:36,*

*He who **believes** in the Son has everlasting life; and he who does not believe the Son shall not see life, but the wrath of God abides on him.*

This is why sin is not taken up at the White Throne Judgment ... just **works** ... followed by the critical issue of whether or not one's name is found in the Lamb's *Book of Life* (verse 16). Notice that the destiny of those who will stand before the Great White Throne will be based solely on the presence or absence of their name in that one all-important book. It will have nothing at all to do with men's works ... which have just been examined. As far as eternal life is concerned, the only thing that God will hold man accountable for is how they have responded to his Son. As you have it in *I John 5:11-12,*

And this is the testimony: that God has given us eternal life, and this life is in His Son. He who has the Son has life; he who does not have the Son of God does not have life.

At the Great White Throne judgment, I believe the books of works will be opened just to demonstrate the true nature of each life that chose to exclude God's Son and live their lives apart from him. This thorough demonstration of the works of each person's life will be fresh on their minds when the Lamb's *Book of Life* is opened to see if anyone present at this judgment is written therein. But, they will not find a single one. Only those who have placed their faith in the Lord Jesus Christ, having accepted the gracious gift of God's salvation through his Son's shed blood, have their names written in that book. That's why it's called the ***Lamb's Book of Life*** (verse 8). It is not a book of works, as were the others. It is a record of faith. It contains the names of all those who have believed in Christ and have had their sins washed away forever in the blood of the Lamb ... having received his free gifts of righteousness and eternal life. Jesus said to his disciples, in *Luke 10:20,*

*Nevertheless do not rejoice in this, that the spirits are subject to you, but rather rejoice **because your names are written in heaven**.*

The Apostle Paul also speaks of this book.

And I urge you also, true companion, help these women who labored with me in the gospel, with Clement also, and the rest of my fellow workers, **whose names are in the Book of Life**. *Philippians 4:3*

Doubtless, it will be a horror beyond description ... after people have lost any hope in their supposed good works ... and they hear the awful words, *No, Lord, his name ... her name ... is not here*. Dear reader, is your name in the Lamb's Book of Life? Believe me, no one will ever enter Heaven on the basis of their good works. Faith in Christ alone fits one for that holy place. *Second Corinthians 5:21,* says,

For he made him who knew no sin to be sin for us, **that we might become the righteousness of God in him**.

Righteousness is a gift, you see. It fits you for Heaven. It is imputed by God to anyone who places their trust and hope, squarely in his Son, the Lord Jesus Christ. Are you a real believer in the Lord Jesus Christ? If so, you have Christ's own righteousness. It has been imputed to you. And, amazingly, you are now as righteous as he is! I say that reverently, because I have God's word on it. We believers have been given God's own righteousness. It has been counted to us as our own (Romans 4:21-24). Isn't that wonderful? What a trade, aye? He took our sin and, in return, we have been given Christ's own righteousness. That's why *Romans 8:1,* can say,

There is therefore now **no condemnation to those who are in Christ Jesus***, who do not walk according to the flesh, but according to the Spirit.*

Let me say one more word about these books of works here at the **great white throne**. I strongly suspect that they will also be used to determine the extent of punishment that each individual will experience in the Lake of Fire. Not all will be punished alike. Jesus spoke of the fact that some will have *fewer stripes* (Luke 12:48). That will be scant consolation, however, to all who must spend eternity in outer darkness. Nevertheless, there will be degrees of punishment there.

20:14-15

Finally here, John says **death and hell were cast into the lake of fire**. I like that. I like that a lot. When my dad and mother died not too long ago ... I came to hate death more than ever. It bothers me to think about their bodies laying out there in the graveyard. But, praise God, death itself will be dealt with at the Great White Throne Judgment. There will be no more purpose for death or Hell after that, you see. There will be no more dying because there will be no more sinning. Hell, the temporary holding place of all the wicked dead today (Luke 16:19-31), will no longer have a purpose. After the Great White Throne Judgment, all death and Hell and judgment will be past. The wicked will have been fairly judged and disposed of and all of Christ's enemies will have been put under his feet ... including death and Hell itself. As you have it in *First Corinthians 15:25-26,*

For he must reign till he has put all enemies under his feet. The **last enemy** *that will be destroyed is* **death**.

THEN ... *THE MYSTERY OF GOD* will be *COMPLETE* (10:6-7)! Now, we have come to the end of the ***days of the sounding of the seventh trumpet***, you see, and everyone ... everyone in whole wide universe will know who Jesus Christ truly is ... whether they are in Heaven or in the Lake of Fire. PRAISE GOD FOR THAT COMING GREAT NEW DAY!

REVELATION 21 - 22:5

THE ETERNAL HOME OF THE SAINTS

We come now to the final section of the book of Revelation. This is THE VISION OF JESUS CHRIST IN ETERNITY. Chapter 20, ended with the dissolving of the old earth and its universe ... followed immediately by the Great White Throne judgment. The God who spoke the universe into existence (Hebrews 11:3; Genesis 1), will do away with it one day ... just as easily and just as completely. As you have it in *Hebrews 1:10-12* (quoting Psalm 102),

And: 'you, LORD, in the beginning laid the foundation of the earth, and the heavens are the work of your hands. **They will perish,** *but you remain; and they will all grow old like a garment; like a cloak you will fold them up, and* ***they will be changed****. But you are the same, and your years will not fail'*

From this point on in Revelation, our Lord will give us a bit of a tour ... a little glimpse beyond our present world and universe to a ***city*** he has been preparing for us (John 14:13) and the new creation in which it will reside. Here in chapters 21 and 22, we find that city described. It is the same city that Abraham and the people of God have been looking forward to for centuries. As you have it in *Hebrews11:10*, speaking of Abraham's hope,

... for he waited for the ***city*** *which has foundations, whose builder and maker is God.*

He will also show us a bit of the ***new earth*** upon which it will set. So, what we are about to read is very special. Our Lord has given this to us to whet our appetites a bit until we actually arrive there. The city of which we are about to read is a real place. It exists today. However, its final location will be on the new ***Earth*** that has yet to be created.

Rev. 21:1-5

Now *I saw a new heaven and a new earth, for the first heaven and the first earth had passed away*. *Also there was no more sea. Then I* **[NU omits "John"]** *saw the holy city, New Jerusalem, coming down out of heaven from God, prepared as a* **bride** *adorned for her husband. And I heard a loud voice from heaven saying,. 'Behold, the tabernacle of God is with men, and he will dwell with them, and they shall be his people. God himself will be with them and be their God. And God will wipe away every tear from their eyes; there shall be* **no more death, nor sorrow, nor crying**. *There shall be* **no more pain**, *for the former things have passed away.' Then he who sat on the throne said, 'Behold, I make all things new.' And he said,* **[NU omits "to me"]** *'Write, for these words are true and faithful.'*

21:1

In this new vision, John says he saw ***a new heaven and a new earth.*** In many ways, this new creation will be quite different from the present one in which we are now living. In other ways, we will find it quite similar. The first difference that caught John's eye caused him to exclaim ... ***there was no more sea.*** That would certainly be striking, would it not? Now if you are wondering ... *Why is there no sea?* I believe the explanation probably lies in two areas. First, about seventy-five percent of our present Earth is covered by water which renders it unusable. But, that will not be the case with the new Earth. All of its vast landmass will be very much available for our use. Second, the vast oceans of this present Earth are, for the most part, left over from the great judgment of the Flood that occurred in Noah's day. As such, they are very grim and visible reminders of judgment. As Peter puts it,

For this they willfully forget: that by the word of God the heavens were of old, **and the earth standing out of water and in the water, by which the world that then existed perished, being flooded with water**. *But the heavens and the earth which are now preserved by the same word, are reserved for fire until the day of judgment and perdition of ungodly men. Second Peter 3:5-7*

Undoubtedly, Earth's original seas were far less extensive than those that exist today. The oceans, then, stand as vivid reminders that

God once judged our world by water. Every wave that roles upon a sandy shore mutters that there is a righteous and holy God who rules over men and who does not allow evil and wickedness to go on and on ... unchallenged and unchecked. I believe this is why God's new Earth will have no sea. It would not fit with the history of that new world. As he says here, *the former things have passed away*.

In August, 2009, my wife and I went on an Alaskan cruise and were privileged to see the famous Glacier Bay. It was wonderful to take in the grandeur and vastness of that part of the world. And, as Carol and I sat eating our breakfast one morning, while gazing out upon the amazing mountains, glaciers and forests around us, the **new earth** that we are reading about here in Revelation 21, came to mind. And, it occurred to me that one of the hallmarks of that new creation will doubtless be its **vastness**. Judging from some of the descriptions here, it will be a great deal larger than this present earth. In fact, I suspect it will be immensely larger ... perhaps as much as a billion or more times larger than our present world. If that is the case, exploring it will be an eternal fascination for all of God's saints. Our God is a very big God and his works are great and amazing.

Now, if you are a water lover, as I am, you will shortly find here that there will be abundant water on the new earth as well. Doubtless, its rivers, streams and lakes will cause its beauty to far surpass that of this old earth ... rendering it a verdant and wonderfully appealing place. Its unsurpassed beauty will, no doubt, be a source of enjoyment for the people of God for all eternity. Can you picture its vast canyons, dells, glades, forests, prairies, hills, streams, rivers and lakes? If you like the outdoors, as I do, you're going to love the new earth. This will be the final resting place of our eternal home, the **New Jerusalem**. At that time, our Lord's words from *Matthew 5:5*, will be abundantly fulfilled.

Blessed are the meek, for **they shall inherit the earth**.

21:2

Then I saw the holy city, New Jerusalem coming down out of heaven. Lo, suddenly, John saw a *city*. It was descending ... descending ... downward to rest upon the new earth. The greatest thing about the **new heavens and the new earth** will most certainly be this city. Jesus told his disciples he was going away to prepare *a place* for them (John 14:12). This is that place. Its name is the *New Jerusalem*. It will be the centerpiece, main attraction and greatest treasure of the *new heavens and the new earth*. What a sight it will present to the eyes of any sojourner in that day when they come into sight of this immense, luminous and magnificent city. As John watched, it continued its descent down to the earth. He says it was like *a bride adorned for her husband*. That certainly is an apt comparison, don't you think? On her wedding day, a bride is one of the most beautiful things that we humans observe down here. This is the simile that the Spirit uses here to describe the wondrous beauty of the eternal home our Lord has prepared and waiting for us.

21:3

Then, a great *voice* spoke out of Heaven. I believe this was the majestic voice of our Lord Jesus Christ. You will remember that when John heard him back in chapter one, he said his voice sounded like the sound of many waters. The *loud voice* declared *Behold, the tabernacle of God is with men, and he will dwell with them, and they shall be his people. God himself will be with them and be their God*. That certainly went right to the heart of it, didn't it? Wow. You see, the very best thing about our new home, the New Jerusalem, will be the fact that we will live there for all eternity in unbroken, intimate fellowship with our God. Isaiah spoke of it this way,

*And in this mountain **The LORD of hosts will make for all people a feast** of choice pieces, a feast of wines on the lees, of fat things full of marrow, of well-refined wines on the lees. And he will destroy on this mountain the surface of the covering cast over all people, and the veil that is spread over all nations. He will swallow up death forever, **and the Lord GOD will wipe away tears from all faces**; the rebuke of his people he will take away from all the earth; for the LORD has spoken. And it will be said in that day: '**Behold, this is our God; we have waited for him, and he will save us. This is the LORD; we have waited for him**; we will be glad and rejoice in his salvation. Isaiah 25:6-9*

21:4

The Lord's powerful voice continued, reiterating once again his words through Isaiah the prophet ... ***And God will wipe away all tears from their eyes***. One day, God's own hand will lovingly wipe away every tear from every stained face of every single one of his dear people. Amazing statement, is it not? See how he loves you, beloved. Have you been able to believe and accept his great love for you? You certainly will at this time and in this city. The great voice of the Lord further assures us here that there will be no more ***death***, ***sorrow***, ***crying*** or ***pain*** there. The ravages of sin will be no more in that happy place. Our deliverance from the very presence of it will be complete there. It is the yet to be experienced installment of the great salvation that is ours in and through our blessed Lord Jesus Christ.

21:5

Following those extraordinary words, the Throne Sitter spoke adding, ***Behold, I make all things new!*** The significance of these words will be extensive and, no doubt, beyond our present abilities to completely comprehend. I believe they extend far beyond our wildest and fondest imaginations. For example, you will remember at the second Bowl judgment, all of the remaining creatures of the sea were destroyed in the old creation. Today, many species which God originally created have already become extinct through man's thoughtless neglect and destructive practices. Now, think about our Father's words here. What did he say he would make ***new***? ***All things***, did he not? On the basis of that statement, I believe we can fully expect that every single thing our Lord made in the old creation will be totally restored in the new. I don't believe a single thing will be missing ... plant, mineral or animal ... from the minutest sea creatures to the largest dinosaurs ... to your old family pet! What a place that will be, aye? More importantly, you and I are going to share in that newness as well. Dr. McGee says that he believes this will be a time and place where each individual child of God will blossom to their fullest potential. Truly, none of us have been all that we would like to have been as a man or woman, father or mother, husband or wife, friend or child ... and certainly not as a Christian and servant of Christ.

Am I right? But in that day, and in that place, our God is going to make you and me new as well. I'm up for that, how about you?

The Father's voice continued, *Write, for these things are faithful and true.* Again, we not only have his spoken word but we have God's written Word on these things. May we step aside once more? The Father's statement here reminds us of what a wonderful thing it is that he has seen to it that his words were written down and preserved for us. As we have it in *First John 5:13,*

*These things I have **written** to you who believe in the name of the Son of God, that you may **know** that you have eternal life, and that you may continue to believe in the name of the Son of God.*

The written Word of God is the source of all truth, faith, fellowship and sanctification for the people of God. Have you been reading it? Is it a habit? It is the source of all blessing, beloved. Don't forget to read your Bible.

Rev. 21:6-8

*And he said to me, '**It is done!** I am the **Alpha and the Omega**, the **Beginning and the End**. I will give of the fountain of the water of life freely to him who thirsts. He who **overcomes** shall **inherit** all things, and I will be his God and he shall be my son. But the cowardly, unbelieving, abominable, murderers, sexually immoral, sorcerers, idolaters, and all liars shall have their part in the lake which burns with fire and brimstone, which is the second death.'*

21:6

Here, in verse six ... just one sentence away from the Lord's command for John to *write* ... the Father proclaims, *It is done*. This is extremely important because, when he said that, I believe **he was referring to the complete revelation of himself as contained in the written Word of God, the Bible**. With this book of Revelation, God is saying to us that his Word to man is finished and complete. In the Greek, he uses the same word here that Jesus exclaimed on the cross, and the same word that he used when he pronounced that his judgments were *finished* back in 16:19 ... Γέγοναν (*tegonan*). In my opinion, this is solid evidence that the canon of scripture is closed. God has said all that he has to say and all that he needs for us to hear. History bears this out as well. Revelation was the last book of Scripture to be written. It was given and written down around AD 96.

He continues, *I am the Alpha and the Omega*. This is the same title he used when we first began to read back in chapter 1. It reminds us afresh that our great God is everything. He is the A and the Z, the *Beginning and the End* and everything in between. Apart from him, there is nothing. He is our all in all and our every sufficiency. Every breath we take comes from him.

He continues, *I will give of the fountain of the water of life freely to him who thirsts*. Isn't he gracious!? A lawyer once asked Jesus, *Master, what must I do to inherit life everlasting?* We read Jesus' answer as follows,

Then Jesus, looking at him, loved him, and said to him, 'One thing you lack: go your way, sell whatever you have and give to the poor, and you will have treasure in heaven; and come, take up the cross, and follow me.' Mark 10:17

Do you want to know how to have eternal life, dear friend? Come to Christ. He will *freely* give it to you. His invitation is so open, wonderful and warm here. He says, *I will give of the fountain of the water of life freely to him who thirsts*. Are you thirsty? One time, Jesus stood up in the temple and literally cried out,

If anyone thirsts, let him come to me and drink. He who believes in me, as the Scripture has said, out of his heart will flow rivers of living water. John 7:37

What a claim! What an invitation! I am sure the Jews in the temple that day said, *Say, what!?* They could not have escaped who Jesus was claiming to be that day ... for he was crying out Jehovah's words from *Isaiah 55:1-3*,

Ho! Everyone who thirsts, come to the waters; and you who have no money, come, buy and eat. Yes, come, buy wine and milk without money and without price. Why do you spend money for what is not bread, and your wages for what does not satisfy? Listen carefully to me, and eat what is good, and let your soul delight itself in abundance. Incline your ear, and come to me. Hear, and your soul shall live; and I will make an everlasting covenant with you; the sure mercies of David.

I ask you again, *Are you thirsty*? Jesus has living water for you. Won't you go to him and get it? **Come**, he says. It's not complicated. He is the Savior. We are lost, needy, thirsty sinners. He is the source of fountains of living waters. As he said in *John 4:14*,

But whosoever drinketh of the water that I shall give him shall never thirst; but the water that I shall give him shall be in him a well of water springing up into everlasting life. (KJV)

In John's gospel, it is written,

*But as many as **received him**, to them he gave the right to **become** children of God, to those who believe in his name: who were **born**, not of blood, nor of the will of the flesh, nor of the will of man, but of God. John 1:12-13*

In *John 10:27-28*, Jesus said,

*My sheep hear my voice, and I know them, and they follow me. And **I give them eternal life**, and they shall **never perish**; neither shall anyone snatch them out of my hand.*

The Spirit of Christ cries out in Isaiah 45:22,

Look unto me, and be ye saved, *all the ends of the earth: for **I am God**, and there is none else.*

One day, this present age of grace will come to a close and every human being will have made their choice. Tragically, multitudes will not have **come** to Christ. A while back, when I was in the ministry in Oregon, the brother of a lady in my church traveled up from California to visit her. She was deeply concerned about his salvation and shared the good news of Jesus Christ with him while he was there. She asked him if he would like to receive Christ and be saved but he said ... *Not right now*. He put it off. Tragically, on his way back home to California, he was killed in a terrible automobile wreck. I don't know if he ever came to Christ. If he did, he is now with the Savior in his **Father's house** (John 14:13). If not ... the thought is unspeakable. Don't delay. The Bible says **today** is the day of salvation (Hebrews 3:7-8). If you have not yet come to Christ and you can hear the Spirit of God inviting you to **come** to Christ, do it right now. Just talk to him. He will know why you have come. Tell him you believe in him. He is the Savior. He will hear. Jesus said,

...him that cometh to me I will in no wise cast out. John 6:36b (KJV)

21:7-8

The Throne Sitter continued ... **He who overcomes shall inherit all things, and I will be his God and he shall be my son.** Then he added, **But the cowardly, unbelieving, abominable, murderers, sexually immoral, sorcerers, idolaters, and all liars** will be consigned to the Lake of Fire **which is the second death.** This unvarnished description of the unbeliever's lifestyle is right on. Unbelief is always confirmed by an ungodly lifestyle. The opposite is also true. Real faith always produces righteousness in a life. It also is imparted to God's children through the process of sanctification which begins the hour they first believe. The Lord makes it crystal clear here that there are only two eternal possibilities for men and women ... those who will come and partake of the *water of life* (Christ) and be transformed (Second Corinthians 5:17) or ... those who continue in their stubborn unbelief, while clinging to their ungodly lifestyles until they find themselves, one terrible day, in the Lake of Fire.

Rev. 21:9-14

Then one of the seven angels who had the seven bowls filled with the seven last plagues came to me and talked with me, saying, 'Come, I will show you the bride, the Lamb's wife.' And he carried me away in the Spirit to a great and high mountain, and showed me the **[NU omits "great"]** *city, the holy* **[NU adds "city Jerusalem"]**, *descending out of heaven from God, having the glory of God. Her light was like a most precious stone, like a jasper stone, clear as crystal. Also she had a great and high wall with twelve gates, and twelve angels at the gates, and names written on them, which are the names of the twelve tribes of the children of Israel three gates on the east, three gates on the north, three gates on the south, and three gates on the west. Now the wall of the city had twelve foundations, and on them were the* **[NU adds "twelve"] names of the twelve apostles of the Lamb.**

21:9-10

Following the Lord's invitation to life, one of the angels of the Bowl judgments approached John and said, *Come, I will show you the bride, the Lamb's wife*. Then, John says, *he carried me away in the Spirit to a great and high mountain, and showed me the great city, the holy Jerusalem, descending out of heaven from God*. John was taken to a **high mountain** and to a vantage point where he could observe *the Lamb's wife* as she majestically descended down to the earth below. What a panorama it must have afforded. I like mountains, by the way. They are one of my all-time favorite places. I like their smells and the sound of the wind through their trees. I'm glad they will be a part of the new earth. I suspect that we will be able to climb this very mountain that John stood upon and look down upon our home as he did. Won't that be a kick!? It will take a very **high mountain** indeed, however, to enable someone to view such a spacious and magnificent place as that of our New Jerusalem. From his mountain vantage point, John was able to view the extensive nature of the eternal home of the saints. Beautiful and dazzling she was. Keep in mind, at that point in time all of the Church was in her as she descended to her new and eternal resting place on the new earth. That's why the angel could say that he would show John, *the Lamb's wife*. Inside this great city, every member of the Church of Jesus Christ was present and accounted for, except John of course, when he witnessed it descending down to its beautiful and permanent home. I suspect that when this actually occurs, we who are in the New Jerusalem will be lining the walls, as it were, to get the first look of the amazing new earth upon which we will dwell, aye?

21:11

The first thing that impressed John about the New Jerusalem was the fact that it was lighted by the ***glory of God***. You and I haven't experienced this yet, but we shall. We know from the scriptures that mere light and the glory of God are two very different things. The glory of God is a lighting thing, but light is not the glory of God. John likened it here to ***a jasper stone***, which is crystal clear. I guess we are just going to have to wait to see it for ourselves. By the way, did you know that Jesus greatly desires for you and me to see his glory? When he was praying for us in John 17, he said,

And now, O Father, glorify me together with yourself, **with the glory which I had with you before the world was**. ... *Father, I desire that they also whom you gave me may be with me where I am*, **that they may behold my glory** *which you have given me; for you loved me before the foundation of the world. John 17:5, 24*

What a wonderful prayer request. Can you hear how Jesus' great heart longs to have you and me with him to enjoy his fellowship and see his glory? Our home will be illumined by his glory for all of eternity.

Next, notice that there are a lot of familiar things in that future creation and place as well ... things that are already familiar and warm to us human beings down here. Our Lord could have made it otherwise, but he chose to make our eternal home both warm and not too unfamiliar. Therefore, he has incorporated many things in it that we are acquainted with now. Let's look at them.

21:12-13

...It had a great high **wall.** Heaven's wall is gigantic and magnificent. Its wall speaks of the fact that it is an exclusive place. Also, it is a reminder of God's safekeeping of his people and the security that they have in him. All will truly be utterly safe and secure in our Father's house. As you have it in *First Peter 1:5,*

...who are **kept** *by the power of God through faith for salvation ready to be revealed in the last time.*

...It had twelve **gates**. John counted them ... three gates on each side. The fact that Heaven has gates, by the way, speaks of the fact that its occupants are free to roam and that there will be coming and going there. This means that the personal freedom that we enjoy as God's creatures down here, will continue there as well. When God created you and me, he created us as creatures of freewill and choice. That will not change in his **new heavens and new Earth** and in the **New Jerusalem**.

...There was an **angel** posted at each gate. Fascinating. I believe they will be stationed there to wish us good journey as well as to greet and welcome us home as we come and go upon the **new earth**.

...There was a **name** inscribed on each gate ... one of the names of one of the **twelve tribes of Israel**. Amongst other things, this will ever remind us that our salvation came through the Jews (John 4:22). It also indicates that Israel has access to the city and, no doubt, it is their home as well. And, since these gates are individually named, I suspect they will be useful for orientation purposes ... departures and meeting places and so forth. By the way, these names of the twelve tribes of Israel will also be inscribed on the gates of Jerusalem during Christ's millennial reign on Earth. Did you know that? Ezekiel 48:31-34, lays them out for us. The order given there will very likely carry over to the New Jerusalem as well. Ezekiel tells us they will be labeled as follows:

> North gates ... Reuben, Judah, and Levi
> East gates ... Joseph, Benjamin and Dan
> South gates ... Simeon, Issachar and Zebulon
> West gates ... Gad, Asher and Naphtali

One time or another, you may have heard a brother or sister say, *I'll meet you at the Eastern Gate!* (..referring to meeting them in Heaven one day). Next time someone says that to you, you might answer, *Which one, Joseph, Benjamin or Dan?*

21:14

...Finally, John says it had **twelve foundations and on them were the twelve names of the twelve Apostles of the Lamb**. In *Ephesians 2:19-20*, we read,

Now, therefore, you are no longer strangers and foreigners, but fellow citizens with the saints and members of the household of God, having been **built on the foundation of the apostles and prophets**, *Jesus Christ himself being the chief corner stone...*

All who come to this great city will marvel at the foundations of its wall and will see the names of the twelve Apostles of the Lamb inscribed upon them. Their names will forever be there. I believe they are there to remind us that our faith is built upon the sacrifices and teachings of these twelve great and dear men of God and the huge role they played in the laying of the foundations of the Church. We owe a great deal to them. They gave their lives for Christ, his gospel and for you and me, his Church. So, when we enter or leave our city, we will ever be reminded of these men who were so instrumental in bringing you and me the Word of God and in building us up in our most holy faith.

By the way, there is something here I believe solves an old argument from Acts 1, where, at Peter's suggestion, the Apostles elected a replacement for Judas. You will remember they elected a man named Matthias and it says, **he was numbered with the eleven apostles** (Acts 1:15-26). Many think that, although this was logical and they thought they were acting on scriptural grounds, it was not a Spirit led decision. Therefore, they conclude that Mathias was not a real Apostle. I agree. The wall of the New Jerusalem only has twelve foundations ... each one inscribed with a name of **one** Apostle. There are only twelve. And, since the New Testament is full of evidence confirming Paul as an Apostle, I take this to be evidence that Mathias, though doubtless a wonderful and great brother in the Lord ... was not technically an Apostle.

Rev. 21:15-21

*And he who talked with me had a gold reed to **measure** the city, its gates, and its wall. **The city is laid out as a square**; its length is as great as its breadth. And he measured the city with the reed: **twelve thousand furlongs. Its length, breadth, and height are equal**. Then he measured its **wall**: one hundred and forty-four cubits, according to the measure of a man, that is, of an angel. The construction of its wall was of **jasper**; and the city was pure gold, like clear glass. The **foundations** of the wall of the city were **adorned with all kinds of precious stones**: the first foundation was jasper, the second sapphire, the third chalcedony, the fourth emerald, the fifth sardonyx, the sixth sardius, the seventh chrysolite, the eighth beryl, the ninth topaz, the tenth chrysoprase, the eleventh jacinth, and the twelfth amethyst. The twelve gates were twelve **pearls**: each individual gate was of **one pearl**. And the **street** of the city was pure gold, like transparent glass.*

21:15-16

Psalm 18:19, comes to mind here.

*He also brought me out into a **broad place**; he delivered me because he delighted in me.*

The New Jerusalem is big ... really big! That is what the Lord wants to convey to us here by getting John to measure it. John found it to be 12,000 furlongs on a side and 12,000 furlongs high. In shape then, it is a cube. The word translated *furlongs* in the Greek here is the word σταδίων *(stadion)*. It is the word from which we get our word *stadium*. A stadia was approximately 606 feet long. So, the outside dimensions of the New Jerusalem are approximately 1377.27 miles on a side and 1377.27 miles high. That means that its inside dimensions are over two billion, six hundred twelve million, five hundred twenty one thousand, three hundred eighteen cubic miles (2,612,521,318). That's a lot of room to roam, brother and sister. Our future home contains over two and a half billion cubic miles! And, since its exact height is given, I believe we are to picture it in layers. C. S. Lewis envisioned it that way in his Narnia Tales when his fictional inhabitants called delightfully to one another, *higher up and farther in.*

I once took a course in college titled, *Population Problems.* It was designed to demonstrate how overpopulated the world was and what might be done about it. However, to the professor's credit, he pointed out that if you dug a hole, one mile square and one mile deep, you would be able to put every human being on the face of the Earth at that time into it with room to spare! I bring this up to reinforce how large our New Jerusalem truly is. I repeat, the city contains 2,612,521,318 cubic miles!

21:17

The city's wall measures around 216 feet high. The NIV says *thick* but its footnotes say that it could also mean high. I don't think the Lord would describe a wall to us by merely telling us how thick it was.

21:18-20

Now, the city and its wall are breathtakingly beautiful. John says it was constructed of ***jasper*** and the city itself ***of pure gold, clear like***

glass. Apparently, in the new creation, jasper will have more of a diamond like quality with a golden clarity. Further, he says that the foundations of the wall were encrusted with **all kinds of precious stones**. Were you or I to decide, one day, to walk completely around Heaven's perimeter, we would walk for over 5,500 miles before we returned to the point where we started. And, all along the wall ... mile after mile ... the jewels in its foundations would be refracting the light of the glory of God outward and all around us! Can you imagine what kind of beauty that might be? The twelve stones in its foundations are given to us as follows:

> *jasper* ... green
> *chrysolyte* ... blue-green
> *sapphire* ... blue
> *beryl* ... yellow-green
> *chalcedony* ... green
> *topaz* ... apple-green
> *emerald* ... green
> *chrysoprasus* ... blue
> *sardonyx* ... red and white
> *jacinth* ... violet
> *sardius* ... golden yellow
> *amethyst* ... purple

21:21

John says that the city's gates **were twelve pearls**. Each of Heaven's gates are constructed of a single pearl. *That's a mighty big pearl*, you say. I know. But, it is what it is. *There are no pearls that big*, you say? Oh? And, God couldn't make a pearl that big? Come on.

Then, he says, **the street of the city was pure gold**. First, notice there is only one street in the New Jerusalem. The Greek word here is singular. One broad and magnificent "golden walkway" has been prepared for your feet and mine in the New Jerusalem. I can see it in my mind's eye as it winds its way upward, mile after mile, level after level, through the city. I picture it ... ever inviting the inhabitants of the city onward and upward to the high throne of the Father and the Lamb. John says it is made of ***pure gold***, like ***transparent glass***. So, to walk upon that street, I suspect will be to experience sites and shadows of things below as well as things above, adding greatly to the delightful sights within the city.

Rev. 21:22-27

*But I saw **no temple** in it, for the Lord God Almighty and the Lamb are its **temple**. The city had no need of the sun or the moon to shine in it, for the glory of God illuminated it. **The Lamb is its light**. And the nations of those who are **saved** shall walk in its light, and **the kings of the earth bring their glory and honor into it**. **Its gates shall not be shut at all by day** (there shall be no night there). And they shall bring the glory and the honor of the nations into it. **But there shall by no means enter it anything that defiles, or causes an abomination or a lie, but only those who are written in the Lamb's Book of Life**.*

21:22

The best thing about the New Jerusalem is that it is a place of unbridled fellowship with God and his Son. It has no temple. There is no designated place of worship because there is no need for it. The Greek word used here for ***temple*** is ναὸς (***naos***). This is the word that designated the Holy of Holies (that most sacred inner room of the temple) where God dwelt and which contained the Ark of the Covenant with its Mercy Seat. The New Jerusalem has no such place. From gate to gate, wall to wall, top to bottom and side to side ... the whole city is the ***naos*** ... because God and his Lamb are there, you see. ***The Lord God Almighty and the Lamb are its temple***, our text says.

21:23

The City had no need for the sun or of the moon to shine in it. Also, there is no need for external sources of light in the New Jerusalem. The ***glory of God*** illumines it and ***the Lamb is its light***. That does not necessarily mean that luminaries will not exist in God's new creation, however. They will just not be needed within our great glory-lit city. You will remember, back in the chapter one, when John first saw the glorified Christ, he said, *his countenance was like the sun shining in its strength*.

21:24

The nations of those who are saved shall walk in its light. The New Jerusalem is a place for saved people. Are you saved, my friend? This word *saved* is out of favor today. It's considered old fashioned. It's archaic. It's *Christianese*. It's not *PC*. Some are ashamed of it. However, it has not gone out of favor in the Scripture. In *Acts 4:12*, the Apostle Peter said to a crowd of Jews,

*Nor is there salvation in any other, for there is no other name under heaven given among men by which we must be **saved**.*

Romans 10:13, says,

*For whoever **calls** on the name of the LORD shall be **saved**.*

"*Saved*," is a good Biblical term and it accurately defines what a person is ... or needs to become. It sums it up nicely. It tells it like it is. There is a great deal of truth and spiritual significance packed into that little word. I'll leave it to your judgment as to the appropriate time and place to use it.

The *kings of the earth bring their glory and honor into it*. Verse twenty-six also states, *they shall bring the glory and honor of the nations into it*. Who do you think these kings and their nations will be? And, who do you think *they* are in verse twenty-six? These statements, coupled with 22:5, where it says that the saints shall *reign* forever and ever, make it clear that the new earth will be a populated place. We are not told who *they* will be, however. Will they be a brand new race of beings? Perhaps. It hasn't been revealed yet. But *they* will be there. That's exciting, don't you think? Living for eternity in *the new heavens and the new earth* and reigning with Christ there is certainly not going to be dull, brother.

21:25

The gates of Heaven will never be shut and that there will be no night there. No one will ever have to wait for the New Jerusalem to open. It's open for business at all hours. The significance of not having any night there indicates that, in our glorified bodies, we will not need rest and recuperation like we do now. That will certainly be different, aye? Down here, a third or more of our lives is spent sleeping. But, that will not be the case there.

21-26-27

It also says, **there shall by no means enter it anything that defiles**. **Only those who are written in the Lamb's Book of Life** can enter the New Jerusalem. These scriptures, and also 22:15, are not speaking about sin or evil existing in the new heavens and the new earth. They are referring to the fact that the New Jerusalem exists right now today. No one who has not been washed in the blood of the Lamb will ever have access there. As you have it back in verse ten, it is the **holy Jerusalem**, a holy place for holy people. *Ephesians 5:25-27,* says,

Husbands, love your wives, just as Christ also loved the church and gave himself for her, that he might sanctify and cleanse her with the washing of water by the word, **that he might present her to himself a glorious church, not having spot or wrinkle or any such thing, but that she should be holy and without blemish**.

Every child of God has been washed by the Word of God and the blood of the Lamb and is fit for the New Jerusalem. They heard the Word. They obeyed it, trusting in Christ. They were then made holy. This is each and every believer's **standing** before God. These are facts. Facts are to be believed. Our citizenship is in Heaven, where our Lord is seated at the right hand of the Majesty on High. When we arrive there, this present foreign land in which we live will vanish away from our memories like a wisp of steam in the wind. *Isaiah 65:17-19a,* says,

For, behold, I create new heavens and a new earth: and ***the former shall not be remembered, not come into mind****. But be ye glad and rejoice forever in that which I create: for, behold, I create Jerusalem a rejoicing, and her people a joy. And I will rejoice in Jerusalem, and joy in my people...*

Is your focus there ... more than down here, beloved? We believers need to be a *heavenly minded* people. The description here of our eternal home is given to encourage and help us to be so.

If then you were raised with Christ, **seek those things which are above**, *where Christ is, sitting at the right hand of God.* **Set your mind**

on things above, *not on things on the earth. For you died, and your life is hidden with Christ in God. Colossians 3:1-3*

Rev. 22:1-5

And he showed me a **[NU omits *"pure"*]** *river of water of life, clear as crystal, proceeding from the throne of God and of the Lamb. In the middle of its street, and on either side of the river, was the* **tree of life**, *which bore twelve fruits, each tree yielding its fruit every month. The* **leaves** *of the tree were for the* **healing of the nations**. *And there shall be* **no more curse**, *but the throne of God and of the Lamb shall be in it, and* **his servants shall serve him**. **They shall see his face**, *and his name shall be on their foreheads. There shall be no night there: They need no lamp nor light of the sun, for the Lord God gives them light. And they shall* **reign** *forever and ever.*

22:1

Chapter 22, continues with the description of the New Jerusalem. However, it now gives us something of the warmth and softness of our great jeweled city. We read:

And he showed me a river of water of life... The New Jerusalem has water and trees and fruit. John says that he saw a magnificent ***river of water of life*** there. Can you see it? Smell it? Flowing from its source at the high throne of God ... this amazingly beautiful river cascades down through thousands and thousands of miles of the city. Along the way, it doubtless takes on all of the interesting and lovely forms that such rivers manifest here and now on Earth. I can picture its rapids, waterfalls, deep emerald pools, and meandering streams ... can you? *Psalm 46:4,* speaks specifically of it saying,

There is a ***river*** *whose* ***streams*** *shall make glad the city of God, the holy place of the tabernacle of the Most High.*

I like that word, ***streams***, don't you? I am hoping that one will run right through my back yard! A similar river will flow from the throne of Christ on Earth during his thousand year reign. It is described to us in Ezekiel 47. The reality of it was brought home to Ezekiel when he was told to wade in it. Beginning at its source at the Lord's temple,

Ezekiel began wading and the further he went, the deeper it got. We read there,

And when the man went out to the east with the line in his hand, he measured one thousand cubits, and he brought me through the waters; **the water came up to my ankles**. *Again he measured one thousand and brought me through the waters:* **the water came up to my knees**. *Again he measured one thousand and brought me through;* **the water came up to my waist**. *Again he measured one thousand,* **and it was a river that I could not cross; for the water was too deep, water in which one must swim, a river that could not be crossed**. *He said to me, 'Son of man, have you seen this?' Then he brought me and returned me to the bank of the river. When I returned, there, along the bank of the river, were very many trees on one side and the other. Then he said to me: "This water flows toward the eastern region, goes down into the valley, and enters the sea. When it reaches the sea, its waters are healed.* **And it shall be that every living thing that moves, wherever the rivers go, will live**. *There will be a very great multitude of* **fish**, *because these waters go there; for they will be healed, and everything will live wherever the river goes. It shall be that* **fishermen** *will stand by it from En Gedi to En Eglaim; they will be places for spreading their nets.* **Their fish will be of the same kinds as the fish of the Great Sea, exceedingly many**. *Ezekiel 47:3-10*

That certainly will be an amazing and wonderful river that flows from our Lord's throne during the Millennium. It will be so enticing, so life giving! Wherever its waters go ... it will produce abundant life. What then, do you suppose its final and permanent version in the New Jerusalem will be like? I guess you can tell that I'm a sucker for rivers. As a boy, I waded, fished and floated just about every inch of the Rio Grande river from Elephant Butte Lake to Caballo Lake. Every river and stream I have ever been around fascinated me. From the little stream up at Wall Lake in the Gila wilderness of New Mexico to the mighty Columbia River where I used to live in Oregon, I loved them all. Where rivers and streams are, there is life. The New Jerusalem's river will be a source of life like we won't believe. Its source is *from the Throne of God and of the Lamb*. Can we even begin to imagine what that water might be like ... or produce ... wherever it goes?

22:2

...*And on either side of the river, was the tree of life.* Lining the banks of *the river of life*, the *tree of life* grows. Apparently, it expands along the banks of the river and in the midst of the street like a giant Banyon tree out of Africa. It is just one *tree*, not trees. If I understand the Banyon tree correctly, it just keeps putting down roots from its branches above and those roots eventually becomes a trunk and thus the tree continuously expands and spreads itself. Wikipedia says one *famous banyan tree was planted in 1873 in Lahaina's Courthouse Square in Hawai'i and has now grown to cover two-thirds of an acre.* All along the banks of the river, and in the midst of the street of the New Jerusalem, the *tree of life* grows. And, month by month, it produces twelve kinds of fruit. These fruits were promised to, and reserved exclusively for, Christ's overcomers back in *2:7,*

He who has an ear, let him hear what the Spirit says to the churches. **To him who overcomes I will give to eat from the tree of life**, *which is in the midst of the Paradise of God.*

This tree was also in the Garden of Eden (Genesis 2:9). So, it is found in the first book of Bible and we don't run into it again until we get here in the last book of the Bible. Adam and Eve were barred from it after they had sinned so that they could not eat from it and live forever (Genesis 3:22). You will remember that God stationed a Cherubim and a *flaming sword* to guard the way to it after the fall (Gen. 3:24). The Tree of Life, in the account of Adam and Eve in the Garden of Eden, is no myth. It was a real tree and I, for one, am looking forward to eating its fruit one day, how about you?

Also, notice it says that its *leaves* are for *the healing of the nations*. This refers to the people who will live on the new Earth in that future day. The word *healing* is a poor rendering. There will be no sickness in God's new creation. The Greek word here is θεραπείαν *(therepian)*, from which we get our word *therapeutic*. The idea here is that the leaves of the Tree of Life will be gathered for their invigorating qualities by the Earth-dwellers of that yet future creation. Perhaps they will eat them, rub them on the skin or possibly use them in beverages. In any case, they will be delightfully invigorating and people travel great distances to come to the city to pick them.

22:3

...There will be **no more curse**. You will remember that the curse referred to here, was imposed upon our parents (Adam and Eve) because of the fall. It turned the earth into a non-productive, difficult and dangerous place to live. We read in *Genesis 3:17-19*,

Then to Adam he [God] *said, "Because you have heeded the voice of your wife, and have eaten from the tree of which I commanded you, saying, 'You shall not eat of it':* **Cursed is the ground for your sake**; *in toil you shall eat of it all the days of your life. Both* **thorns and thistles it shall bring forth for you**, *and you shall eat the herb of the field. In the sweat of your face you shall eat bread till you return to the ground, for out of it you were taken; for dust you are, and to dust you shall return.*

It is because of the *curse* that dogs bite, bees sting and weeds grow. God cursed the earth so that man's environment would be a constant reminder to him that things were not right ... that he was out of sync with God and all that God had made. It is because we are sinners that we are continuously out of harmony with the creation, you see. That will no longer be the case in **the new heavens and the new earth**. There, all will be right; all will be in harmony. There will be **no more curse**. What will that be like? I believe that Mark's account of the temptation of Jesus gives us a bit of a hint,

And he was there in the wilderness forty days, tempted of Satan; and **was with the wild beasts**; *and the angels ministered unto him. Mark 1:13*

Notice that the wild animals were in perfect harmony with Jesus. He was not a sinner, you see. He was a perfect man. As such, as far as the animals were concerned, the curse did not apply to him. Can you picture the wild animals crowding about him? Can you see him scratching the lion behind its ear? You and I will enjoy such a relationship with the God's creation one day.

...He continues, **and his servants shall serve him**. I like that. The New Jerusalem is a place of wonderful service and activity. Have you ever wondered where the idea came from that pictures Heaven as a place where people listlessly float about on little clouds while they clutch their little harps ... which, by the way, only have four strings? That sounds more like Hell than Heaven, does it not? One of the most unbiblical and misinformed concepts of Heaven is that it is a place of idleness. NOT! Glory to God, **his servants shall serve him** there. Reminds me of that old song, *There is joy in serving Jesus.* Heaven is a place of real, significant and fulfilling service for the Savior.

22:4

...**and they shall see his face.** Now, that is a mountaintop experience worth waiting for! Amen? We will *see his face.* I don't think we will ever tire of looking upon him, do you? When this becomes a reality, over and over again Jesus' words from *Matthew 5:8,* will be fulfilled in us...

Blessed are the pure in heart, for they shall **see God***.*

...**and his name shall be on their foreheads.** This identifying mark will proclaim to all intelligences for all time ... just who we belong to. May I ask you a question? How do you think of yourself? Do you say, *I'm a child of God, I belong to Christ!*? If so, good for you. Those who see themselves that way are right where they ought to be.

Or do you not know that your body is the temple of the Holy Spirit who is in you, whom you have from God, and **you are not your own***? For you were bought at a price; therefore glorify God in your body and in your spirit, which are* **God's***. First Corinthians 6:19-20*

22:5

...John concludes by restating that there is **no night there**, no need for a **candle** or **sun**, **for the Lord God gives them light. And they shall reign forever and ever.** Again, we are reminded that the New Jerusalem and the new heavens and the new earth will be a place of dominion with Christ. There are many scriptures that back this up. Here is one of them,

This is a faithful saying: for if we died with him, we shall also live with him. If we endure, **we shall also reign with him***. If we deny him, he also will deny us. Second Timothy 2:11-12*

Just before Jesus left our world, he said he was going away to prepare a place for us (John 14:1-3). Here in Revelation 21 and 22, he has given us the thrill of a bit of a tour of it. It has been a wonderful glimpse, has it not? We found it to be a very large, warm, and familiar place, as well as a place of incredible beauty. But the best part of all is, it is a place where we saints will experience wonderful intimacy with our Lord Jesus Christ and his Father. Blessed indeed are they who have the right to enter the gates of this city.

REVELATION 22:6-21

EPILOGUE

We come now to the last recorded words of Christ to the Church. These are his *goodbye until we meet again* words. We should listen carefully, like we would listen to the last words of a dear friend or loved one. In the book of Revelation, Christ has faithfully passed on his Father's words to you and me. It has been eye-opening, has it not? Line upon line, precept upon precept, we have sat at Jesus feet listening to him tell us about himself ... ourselves ... and the things that are to come. His words have been honest, straightforward and encouraging. He has opened our eyes and hearts to many things ... including peoples, politics, players, spirits, personalities and judgments that are to come during the closing days of Earth's history. Then, to top it off, he has led us right on out into eternity so we could get a peek at our eternal home, the New Jerusalem, and the new earth upon which it will rest. Thank you, Lord Jesus. Amen?

Rev. 22:6-11

*Then he said to me, '**These words are faithful and true**.' And the Lord God of the* **[NU omits *"holy"*]** *spirits of the prophets sent his angel to show his servants the **things which must shortly take place**. 'Behold, **I am coming quickly**! Blessed is he who keeps the words of the prophecy of this book.' Now I, John,* **[NU changes *"saw and heard"*]** *am the one who heard and saw these things. And when I heard and saw, I fell down to worship before the feet of the angel who showed me these things. Then he said to me, 'See that you do not do that.* **[NU omits *"For"*]** *I am your fellow servant, and of your brethren the prophets, and of those who keep the words of this book. **Worship God**.' And he said to me, 'Do not seal the words of the prophecy of this book, for the time is at hand. He who is unjust, let him be unjust* *still; he who is filthy, let him be filthy still; he who is righteous, let him* **[NU changes *"be righteous"* to *"do right"*]** *still; he who is holy, let him be holy still.'*

22:6

As the Lord is taking his leave of us here, he first reassures us that the things he has shared with us are absolutely true and dependable. His angel says, **These words are faithful and true.** He is referring to everything he has said in the book of Revelation. Every word of it is *faithful and true*. It has been given to us from the very One whose nature and name itself is **Faithful and True**. He always speaks the truth. Therefore, the angel can confidently proclaim, these things will **shortly take place** and conclude, **blessed is he who keeps the words of the prophecy of this book**. Blessed indeed, aye!?

Child of God ... the only solid, dependable, unchanging, reliable, trustworthy thing in this whole vacillating, ambiguous, truth-starved and deceived world of ours is found between the covers of our Bibles. It contains God's written words to you and me and is absolutely *faithful and true*. It tells us everything we need to know ... from the origin of this universe to its end. It tells us who we are, why we're here, where we're going, where sin came from and how God has and will deal with it. It tells us who God is and how we can come into a real relationship with him. How important God's Word is. Here are a couple of scriptures to remind us of these truths:

Let the word of Christ dwell in you richly *in all wisdom, teaching and admonishing one another in psalms and hymns and spiritual songs, singing with grace in your hearts to the Lord. Colossians 3:16*

All Scripture is given by inspiration of God, and is profitable for doctrine, for reproof, for correction, for instruction in righteousness, *that the man of God may be* **complete**, *thoroughly equipped for every good work. Second Timothy 3:16-17*

22:7

The second thought that our Lord leaves us with here is, **Behold, I am coming quickly**. Jesus wants his followers to be filled with the expectancy and anticipation of His imminent appearing. Three times, he repeats these words ... in verses 7, 12, and 20. Do you think that maybe he feels this is important? Let's take a moment to look at them in greater detail. He says:

...*I am coming.* Jesus Christ is coming again. He says it here in triplicate and his Word trumpets this great truth in many places. Since these words are addressed to his Church here, he is talking about the Rapture (First Thessalonians 4:16-17; John 14:13). To put the doctrine of the Imminent Return of the Lord Jesus Christ into perspective, it simply says that Christ could appear at any moment. From one moment after he left our world ... right on up to this very moment ... Christ could have returned ... at any time. He wants the hope of his return to be a major focal point of each and every one of us believers. It is to be our sure hope, our prophetic certainty and our daily expectation. *James 5:7,* says,

Therefore be patient, brethren, **until the coming of the Lord***. See how the farmer waits for the precious fruit of the earth, waiting patiently for it until it receives the early and latter rain. You also* **be patient***.* **Establish your hearts, for the coming of the Lord is at hand***.*

And again, as we have it in *First John 3:2-3,*

Beloved, now we are children of God; and it has not yet been revealed what we shall be, but we know that **when he is revealed***, we shall be like him, for we shall see him as he is. And* **everyone who has this hope** *in him purifies himself, just as he is pure.*

Do Christ's words *I am coming,* grip your heart and life, dear saint? Will they affect your walk today?

...*quickly.* Granted, this is speaking from our Lord's point of view. Nevertheless, the countdown to the Rapture relentlessly continues today as surely as that of a space shuttle's countdown to launch. Don't you wish we could get a peek at the clock? It has been nearly two thousand years since John first wrote down Jesus' words, *I am coming quickly.* So, here we are ... way down here at the beginning of the twenty-first century. Should we not be anticipating his coming more than all the saints that have gone before us? Peter says,

But, beloved, do not forget this one thing, that with the Lord one day is as **a thousand years***, and a thousand years as one day.* **The Lord is not slack concerning his promise***, as some count slackness,* *but is long-suffering toward us, not willing that any should perish but that all should come to repentance. Second Peter 3:8-9*

Hebrews 9:28, says,

*...so Christ was offered once to bear the sins of many. To those who **eagerly wait for him he will appear** a second time, apart from sin, for salvation.*

Again, as Paul tells the Thessalonians,

*And **to wait for his Son from heaven**, whom he raised from the dead, even Jesus, which delivered us from the wrath to come. First Thessalonians 1:10* (KJV)

And again, as you have it in *Titus 2:13*,

*...**looking** for the **blessed hope and glorious appearing of our great God and Savior Jesus Christ**...*

22:8-9

John continues, ***Now, I John am the one who heard and saw these things.*** This is his personal testimony to the things we have read. He wants us to know that what he has shared with us is his eyewitness account. Then, he says,

*...**I fell down to worship before the feet of the angel who showed me these things.*** My, how powerfully all these things moved the Apostle John. He was overcome by them. And frankly, he is telling on himself here. He shares with us that he repeated the same mistake he made back in 19:10 ... once again falling down to worship at the feet of an angel! Just as before, however, the angel wanted nothing to do with this. He immediately said to John, ***I am your fellow servant, and of your brethren the prophets, and of those who keep the words of this book. Worship God.***

Let's stop and think about this for a moment. Do we ***worship God***? I mean do we really worship him? When there is an opportune moment ... maybe while driving our car or some other occasion presents itself, do we lift up our hearts to him and tell him how much we love him and how wonderful he is? Do we ever get on our knees or lift up our hands or sing to him? When we awake in the night, do we think about him and find that we are glad because he is there and, in those quiet moments, we can bask in the wonder of his presence and worship him without distraction or interruption? David knew the joy of such moments. He said,

My soul shall be satisfied as with marrow and fatness, and my mouth shall praise you with joyful lips. When I remember you on my bed, **I meditate on you in the night watches**. *Psalm 63:5-6*

In the Greek, the angel's words, **Worship God**, are in the imperative tense. This means it is a command. *First John 2:5,* says,

But whoso keepeth his Word, in him truly **the love of God is perfected***: hereby know we that we are in him.*

So, like the Nike commercial says, *Just do it!*, dear saint. Obey this command and your love for God will increase and be perfected. **Worship God.**

22:10-11

The angel continued ... **Do not seal the words of the prophecy of this book, for the time is at hand.** Time is short, beloved. The book of Revelation is intended to be an open book. It is for anyone and everyone to read. No one should be discouraged from reading it. It is very special. Like the rest of the Bible, is not just for the people of God. It is also for those who God is drawing to himself.

He continued ... **He who is unjust, let him be unjust still: and he who is filthy, let him be filthy still; he who is righteous, let him do right still; he who is holy, let him be holy still**. These are sobering and challenging words that Christ instructed his angel to say. I view them as a divine decree. For those who have been made righteous (are **right** and **holy**) in Christ, the decree here is, *Let them continue forever to be*! On the other hand, for those who have been enlightened here by this book of Revelation but are still determined to reject Christ's love and salvation ... the decree is, *Let them continue forever to be*! (**unjust**, still ... **filthy**, still). How sobering. When a heart grows hard towards the Word of God and the Spirit of God who spoke it and applies it ... there is no longer any hope. The time for tenderness and change of attitude towards God must take place before that point is reached ... before the human heart has set itself like concrete against the things of God. *Hebrews 3:7-8*, says,

Therefore, as the Holy Spirit says: 'Today, **if you will hear his voice, Do not harden your hearts** *as in the rebellion, in the day of trial in the wilderness...*

Rev. 22:12-16

'And behold, I am coming quickly, and my reward is with me, to give to every one according to his work. **I am the Alpha and the Omega, [NU reverses** *"the Beginning and the End, the First and the Last"***] *the First and the Last, the Beginning and the End*. *Blessed are those who* **[NU omits** *"do His commandments"***]** *wash their robes that they may have the* **right** *to the tree of life, and may enter through the gates into the city.* **[NU omits** *"But"***]** *Outside are dogs and sorcerers and sexually immoral and murderers and idolaters, and whoever loves and practices a lie.* **'I, Jesus, have sent my angel to testify to you these things in the churches. I am the Root and the Offspring of David, the Bright and Morning Star.'**

22:12

Our Lord's final words continue here in verse twelve. They are words that have to do with our personal relationship with him. They have seven parts:

1. He says **my reward is with me**. While we are waiting for him to appear, He wants us to keep our **Priorities** straight. This is vitally important because, when he appears, it will be his good pleasure to reward each one of us personally. As you have it in *Second Corinthians 5:10*,

For **we must all appear before the judgment seat of Christ**, *that each one may* **receive** *the things done in the body, according to what he has done, whether good or bad.*

22:13

2. He says **I am the Alpha and the Omega, the First and the Last, the Beginning and the End**. While we are waiting for him to appear, he wants each one of us to keep our **Theology** straight. His clear declaration of who he is here is unmistakable. He is our God. The name, **Alpha and Omega**, is the same name used by God the Father back in 1:8 and again in 21:6. Christ takes it to himself here and, also,

the name, ***the First and the Last***. These are titles held by Jehovah God of the Old Testament. We read in *Isaiah 41:4*,

Who has performed and done it, calling the generations from the beginning? 'I, the LORD, am the first; and with the last, I am he.'

22:14

3. He says ***blessed are they that wash their robes that they might have the right to the tree of life and may enter in through the gates of the city***. While we are waiting for him to appear, he wants each one of us to keep our **Soteriology** (doctrine of salvation) straight. In *Second Corinthians 13:5a*, Paul says,

Examine yourselves, whether you are in the faith; prove your own selves.

The only ones to enter Heaven will be those whose robes have been washed in the blood of the Lamb. Have your robes been washed in the blood of the Lamb? Are you sure? If this terminology is foreign to you, it simply means you have put your faith in Christ and asked him save you. He does the washing. Now, there is a problem in the translation at this point in the KJV Bible. This phrase, ***wash their robes***, is correct. But the words, ***keep his commandments are*** an emendation (addition by a copyist). They are not a part of the Word of God. Apparently, some copyist didn't believe that people could be saved solely on the basis of the fact that they were washed in the blood of the Lamb ... so he added the words ***and keep his commandments***. I am grateful for the scholarship that is available to us today so that we can easily tell where the Scripture has been tampered with.

22:15

4. He warns, ***Outside are dogs and sorcerers and sexually immoral and murderers and idolaters, and whoever loves and practices a lie.*** While we are waiting for his appearing, he wants us to keep our **Separation** from the world straight. The things of the world have no place in the life of a Christian. They belong to the lifestyles of those who will forever be ***outside*** the city of God. By the way, these words emphasize the city's existence in John's day as well as our own. Both the NKJV and the NIV use the word ***sorcerers*** to translate the

Greek word **φάρμακοι (farmakoi)** here. In my opinion, it should be translated *druggies*. In any case, the point is that everyone who is **outside** the city of God are lost and unwashed people and are still in their sins, as enumerated here.

22:16

5. He says, ***I, Jesus, have sent my angel to testify to you these things in the churches***. While we are waiting for him to appear, he wants us to keep our **Inspiration** straight. Make no mistake about it, this book is the authoritative Word of God. It is the Word of Christ.

6. He declares, ***I am the Root and Offspring of David***. While we are waiting for him to appear, he wants us to keep our **Covenants** straight. He declares here, in no unequivocal terms, that he is the Messiah of the Davidic Covenant with the Jewish people. Are you a Jew? If so, I pray God has opened your eyes to who Christ Jesus truly is. He is **the Root and Offspring of David**. If you are a Gentile (non-Jew), as I am, keep in mind that we are his adopted and grafted in children. We have been grafted into God's people, the Jews, and thereby have access to their New Covenant. As you have it in *Romans 11:18*, speaking of the Gentiles and using the analogy of a natural **olive tree** for Israel,

...*do not boast against the branches. But if you do boast, remember that you do not support the root, but* ***the root supports you***. *Romans 11:18*

We Gentiles got in by God's grace, combined with the fact that Israel stumbled over Christ (Romans 11). This should generate a great appreciation on our part for our Lord's great mercy toward us. As you have it in *Romans 9:25-26*,

As he says also in Hosea: 'I will call them my people, ***who were not my people****, and her beloved, who was not beloved.* ***And it shall come to pass in the place where it was said to them, 'You are not my people,' There they shall be called sons of the living God.'***

All I've got to say about that is **GLORY!** ... how about you? Everyone needs to keep their Covenants straight. Jesus' words here are aimed at his Jewish people and especially his Messianic Jewish believers. He is the King of Israel, David's direct descendant through

Mary's line (Luke 3:23-31) and legal heir to the throne through Joseph's line (Matt. 1:1).

7. He says, **I am the Bright and Morning star**. While we are waiting for his appearing, he wants us to keep our **Eschatology** (events of the end times) straight. Continuing the theme that he is **the Root and Offspring of David**, he reminds us, by using this Old Testament title, that he, the Messiah, will appear one bright day to rule the world ... just as the Word of God has said that he would. The title, or name, **Star**, is rooted in *Numbers 24:17,* and emphasizes Christ's Second Coming. There we read,

I see him, but not now; I behold him, but not near; **a Star shall come out of Jacob**; *a* **Scepter shall rise out of Israel**, *and batter the brow of Moab, and destroy all the sons of tumult.*

Peter, in his letter to the Jews, also alluded to this prophecy in *Second Peter 1:19,*

And so we have the prophetic word confirmed, which you do well to heed as a light that shines in a dark place, until the day dawns and the **morning star** *rises in your hearts...*

The prophet, Samuel, said,

The God of Israel said, The Rock of Israel spoke to me: 'He who rules over men must be just, ruling in the fear of God. And **he shall be like the light of the morning when the sun rises**, *a* **morning** *without clouds, like the tender grass springing out of the earth, by clear shining after rain.' Second Samuel 23:3-4*

What a blessed event it will be when the **Morning Star** appears for all his covenant people to behold ... and to ever shine before them forevermore!

But to you who fear my name **the Sun of Righteousness shall arise** *with healing in his wings; and you shall go out and grow fat like stall-fed calves. Malachi 4:2*

Rev. 22:17-20

And the Spirit and the bride say, **'Come!'** *And let him who hears say,* **'Come!'** *And let him who thirsts* **come**. *Whoever desires, let him take the water of life freely. For I testify to everyone who hears the*

words of the prophecy of this book: If anyone adds to these things, God will add to him the plagues that are written in this book; and if anyone takes away from the words of the book of this prophecy, God shall take away his part from the Book of Life, from the holy city, and from the things which are written in this book. He who testifies to these things says, 'Surely I am coming quickly.' **Amen. Even so, come, Lord Jesus!** *The grace of our Lord Jesus Christ be with you all. Amen.*

22:17

Here, at verse 17, we come to the closing words of the book of Revelation. The Lord chooses to end his Revelation with an invitation to be saved. He extends it here, three times. What a heart for people Jesus has.

Come, he says. Come to Christ. Come and get the water of life freely. The invitation rises up off this page from three different sources. First, it comes from the **Spirit** (Christ's Holy Spirit). Second, it comes from the **Bride** (Christ's Church). Third, it comes from all who **hear** ... who are able to hear, in other words (all the saints who are other than the Church). All three invite the lost to, **Come**. I have often heard the opinion that Revelation is a book that is far too difficult for unbelievers or new believers to tackle. But do you know what I've discovered? People in general are very interested in this book. When my youngest son was in High School, he said that the young people there were more interested in this book of the Bible than any other. Its words held a peculiar fascination to them. Christ anticipated that God-given curiosity and he takes advantage of it here to lovingly invite all of his unsaved readers to **Come** to him.

...for the Son of Man has **come** *to seek and to* **save** *that which was lost. Luke 19:10*

If you are unsaved, dear reader, it is no accident that you have been reading the book of Revelation. Christ's Holy Spirit has been speaking to you. He is saying, *Won't you come to Christ?* If he is speaking to you right now ... and you are willing ... just bow your head and pray, *Lord Jesus, please save me. Thank you for dying for my sins on the cross. Please wash me in your blood and forgive my sins and make me your child. From this day forward, I wish to give my life* to you and begin looking forward to your appearing. Thank you for saving me, Lord, Amen. Romans 10:13, promises,

For whosoever shall **call** upon the name of the Lord shall be saved. (KJV)

22:18-19

The final words of the book are a warning against tampering with this book of the Word of God. To those who would add to it, he says, **God will add to him the plagues that are written in this book**. To those who would take away from it, he warns, **God shall take away his part from the Book of Life, from the holy city, and from the things that are written in this book**. The penalty for tampering with this book is huge. Not only will it bring punishment, but also, the loss of one's part in the Book of Life. I believe this means that such a one will lose his or her chance to be saved. It is not referring to the salvation of those who already have it. Only an unsaved man or woman would be so dull and presumptuous as to deliberately mess with the Word of the living God. Perhaps one of the saddest illustrations of this is found in the life of Thomas Jefferson, author of the Declaration of Independence. Jefferson's 1820, Bible is preserved at the Smithsonian in Washington, D.C. The amazing thing about it is that Jefferson used a razor to meticulously remove all the passages that had anything to do with miracles or even a hint of the deity of Jesus Christ. When he was done, he pasted what was left into a bound plain page book. Jefferson's new "bible" had no loaves and fishes, no walking on water, no water into wine, no resurrection and no deity of Christ. He eliminated them all. He dismissed such passages as mere *superstition*. He left only those parts in his "bible" that he considered more believable and important, as reflected in his work, *The Life and Morals of Jesus of Nazareth*. Amazing presumption, was it not? An article about him and his bible can be found in the January/February 2009, issue of *AARP* magazine.

22:20

The last words of Revelation come like a sweet refrain and a persistent echo ... **Surely I am coming quickly**. John enthusiastically responded, **even so come Lord Jesus!** John himself says goodbye to us, as well, adding, ***The grace of our Lord Jesus Christ be with you all. Amen.*** Thank you, John. Thanks for everything. Well, there you have it, God's ***strange work*** ... as given by the Father to the Son to his angel to John to show to you and me, his servants, things to come. And strange but wonderful things they will be ... when the words in this book come to pass. Grace and peace, beloved.

Comments, questions, suggestions, and insights welcome at: munsonh@gmail.com. ***Strange Work*** is also available online at: biblebookofrevelation.com.

APPENDIX A

TIME-LINE CHART OF THE 7 YEAR TRIBULATION

THE SEVEN YEAR TRIBULATION PERIOD

The Seal Judgments	The Trumpet Judgments	*.Last Hours
Rev. 6; 8:1	Rev. 8:6-9:2; 11:15	Rev. 14-18

[_____|_____|*_____]

First 3 1/2 years of the Tribulation   Last 3 1/2 years: The Great Tribulation.....

* LAST HOURS above ... expanded *

Removal of the wicked Jews	6 Rapid Bowl Judgments	7th Bowl Judgment/Fall of Babylon
Rev.14:14-20	Rev.16	Rev. 18

*[_____|_____|_____]

APPENDIX B

DANIEL'S 70th WEEK

The question addressed here is, *Where does one find the seven year Tribulation in the Bible?* It comes from Daniel's prophecy of the **seventy weeks** in *Daniel 9:24-27*. There, speaking about both the first and second comings of the Messiah, an angel told Daniel,

Seventy weeks [70] *are determined for your people and for your holy city, to finish the transgression, to make an end of sins, to make reconciliation for iniquity, to bring in everlasting righteousness, to seal up vision and prophesy, and to anoint the Most Holy. Know therefore and understand, that **from the going forth of the command** to restore and build Jerusalem* [fulfilled by Artaxerxes in 445 BC. See Nehemiah 2:5-8) **until Messiah the Prince, there shall be seven weeks and sixty-two weeks** [69]; *the street shall be built again, and the wall* [accomplished under Nehemiah], *even in troublesome times. And **after the sixty-two weeks, Messiah shall be cut off**,* [speaking of the cross] *but not for himself* [speaking of his death for you and me]; *and **the people*** [the Romans] *of **the prince** who is to come* [Antichrist] *shall destroy the city and the sanctuary* [destroyed by the Roman general, Titus, in AD 70]. *The end of it shall be with a flood, and till the end of the war desolations are determined. Then **he*** [Antichrist] *shall confirm **a covenant*** [make a treaty] *with many for **one week**;* [a seven year treaty with the Jews initiated at the beginning of the Tribulation] *but in the **middle*** [3 1/2 years after the treaty, at the beginning of the Great Tribulation] *of the week he shall **bring an end to sacrifice and offering**. And on the wing of **abominations** shall be **one who makes desolate**,* [Antichrist's cutting off of the temple's operations and setting up his own worship there] *even until **the consummation, which is determined**, is poured out on the desolate* [Christ's judgment of Antichrist at the Second Coming, casting him into the Lake of Fire].

As far as exact dates and times are concerned, this is the most amazingly precise prophecy in the entire Bible. Three key portions of it have already been fulfilled, namely:

...the issuing of the decree to **restore and build Jerusalem**.

...the precise fulfillment of the exact date of the coming of Messiah.

...the cutting off of Messiah at the cross.

When Sir Robert Anderson calculated the time between Artaxerxes decree (445 BC) to the first coming of Christ the Messiah, he found that it was exactly 483 years, just as Daniel had predicted when he wrote, *from the going forth of the command to restore and build Jerusalem until Messiah the Prince, there shall be seven weeks and sixty-two weeks* (69 *weeks*). Using simple mathematics, Sir Robert Anderson found that Daniel's **seventy weeks** referred to time periods of seven years each or "prophetic weeks." So, 69 prophetic weeks equaled 7 X 69 = 483 years. He then calculated that from Artaxerxes' decree, in the days of Nehemiah, to the day when Jesus rode into Jerusalem on a donkey's colt and presented himself to Israel as their Messiah, was exactly 483 years. In fact, this turned out to be so precise a prediction that liberal theologians immediately began to say that the book of Daniel was not written by Daniel at all, but must have been written by someone else at a much later time! Careful study of Daniel, however, proves otherwise. The historicity and date of Daniel's writings are beyond question. This is dealt with extensively by Sir Robert Anderson in his classic book, *The Coming Prince*. The following is a quote from that book, citing Sir Robert Anderson's calculations (Anderson, Pickering and Inglis, Ltd., London, 13th Edition, n.d. pp. 127 - 128):

In accordance with the Jewish custom, the Lord went up to Jerusalem upon the 8th of Nisan, 'six days before the passover.' But as the 14th, on which the Paschal Supper was eaten, fell that year on a Thursday, the 8th was the preceding Friday. He must have spent the Sabbath, therefore, at Bethany; and on the evening of the 9th, after the Sabbath had ended, the Supper took place in Martha's house. Upon the following day, the 10th of Nisan, He entered Jerusalem as recorded in the Gospels. The Triumphal entry, the end of the 69 sevens cf. Zech. 9:9. The Julian date of that 10th of Nisan was Sunday the 6th of April, a.d. 32. What then was the length of the period intervening between the issuing of the decree to rebuild Jerusalem and the public advent of 'Messiah the Prince,' -- between the 14th March b.c. 445, and the 6th April, a.d. 32? THE INTERVAL CONTAINED EXACTLY AND TO THE VERY DAY 173,880 DAYS, OR SEVEN TIMES SIXTY-NINE PROPHETIC YEARS OF 360 DAYS, the first sixty-nine weeks of Gabriel's prophecy.

The 1st Nisan in the 20th year of Artaxerxes (the edict to rebuild Jerusalem) was 14th March, b.c. 445.

The 10th Nisan in Passion Week (Christ's entry into Jerusalem) was 6th April, a.d. 32.

The intervening period was 476 years and 24 days (the days being reckoned inclusively, as required by the language of the prophecy, and in accordance with the Jewish practice.)

But 476 x 365 =	173,740 days
Add (14th March to 6th April, both inclusive)	24 "
Add for leap years	116 "
	173,880 days

Add 69 weeks of prophetic years of 360 days (or 69 x 7 x 360) = 173,880 days.

Coming back to Daniel's prophecy, this means that there remains only one **week** (7 years) that is yet to be fulfilled.

When Messiah was *cut off* at the cross, Daniel's prophetic 70 week prophetic clock stopped, leaving its final **week** yet unfulfilled. It will be fulfilled by the Tribulation. In the Old Testament, the mystery of the Church and its time period (from the cross of Christ until now), is not found. The Church was not revealed in the Old Testament, you see. So, the mystery of the Church Age lies between Daniel's 69th and 70th week. When the Rapture of the Church occurs, it will end the Church Age and kick off the beginning of Daniel's 70th week. Daniel's **seventy weeks** will then resume and begin to tick down once again allowing its last week to be fulfilled by the final seven years of Earth's secular history. When those days have run their course, all of Daniel's prophecy will have been fulfilled.

Other references to the 7 year Tribulation come from the scriptures that mention its two 3 ½ year segments. The last 3 ½ years is called *The Great Tribulation*. Here are those scriptures. You can draw your own conclusions about them:

1. Revelation 11:3, says that God's **two witnesses** will prophesy at Jerusalem for **one thousand two hundred and sixty days** (1260 divided by 360 = 3 1/2 years).
2. Revelation 12:6, says that the **woman**, Israel, will be hidden in the wilderness for **one thousand two hundred and sixty days** (1260 divided by 360 = 3 1/2 years).
3. Revelation 13:5, says that the **beast** with the big **mouth** (Antichrist) was granted to **continue** for **forty-two months** (42 divided by 12 = 3 1/2 years).
4. Daniel 7:25, says that the saints will be given into the hands of the **little horn** (Antichrist) for **a time and times and half a time** (a Jewish idiomatic expression where the term **time** means one year) (1 + 2 + 1/2 = 3 1/2 years).
5. Daniel 12:11, says that from the time that the sacrifice is caused to **cease** and the **abomination of desolation** is **set up** (until the end) will be **one thousand two hundred and ninety days** (1290 divided by 360 = 3 1/2 years + an extra 30 days). We don't know what that extra 30 days is all about. It is still a mystery.
6. Daniel 12:12, says that there will be **one thousand three hundred and thirty five days** until the **day** when all who arrive in Israel will be called **blessed** (1335 divided by 360 = 3 1/2 years + an extra 75 days). Apparently, this refers to a particular "red-letter" day that will take place at the beginning of the Millennial Kingdom of Christ … calculated from the day that the sacrifice was stopped by Antichrist at the middle of the Tribulation.

So, Daniel 9:24-27, is the prophecy that lays the foundation for the 7 year Tribulation Period. Several of its predictions and time periods have already been fulfilled with such preciseness and precision that the predictions of the entire prophecy is, in my opinion, beyond question. There is only one piece that is yet to be fulfilled, namely its last 7 year period or final *week*.

In addition, there are the other scriptures quoted above that predict the 3 ½ year segments of the Tribulation that are yet to be fulfilled in history. These fit perfectly with Daniel's 70th week. Together, these scriptures clearly predict that the length of the Tribulation will be seven years.

SCRIPTURES QUOTED IN *STRANGE WORK*

Scripture taken from the New King James Version. Copyright © 1982 by Thomas Nelson, Inc. Used by permission. All rights reserved.

Genesis 1:20-23 (p.260
Genesis 1:26 (p. 196
Genesis 3:4-5 (p. 56
Genesis 3:15 (p. 202
Genesis 3:17-19 (p. 366
Genesis 12:3 (p. 258
Genesis 15:1b (p. 58
Genesis 37:9-10 (p. 200
Genesis 49:9-10 (p. 102

Exodus 3:14 (p. 311
Exodus 7:17-20 (p. 261
Exodus 7:20-21 (p. 150
Exodus 9:8-10 (p. 259
Exodus 9:23 (p. 149, 263
Exodus 10:21-22 (p. 152, 264
Exodus 10:12-15 (p. 164
Exodus 12:13 (p. 134
Exodus 12:29-30 (p. 164
Exodus 20:11 (p. 79

Numbers 24:17a (p. 58
Numbers 24:17 (p. 377

Deuteronomy 11:26-28 (p. 249
Deuteronomy 29:18 (p. 151
Deuteronomy 32:25 (p. 92

Joshua 10:11(p. 271

II Samuel 23:3-4 (p. 377

II Kings 1:9-10 (p. 185

Ruth 2:12 (p. 95

Job 19:25-27 (p. 328
Job 23:14 (p. 239

Psalm 1:1-3 (p. 71
Psalm 1:4-5 (p. 256
Psalm 2 (p. 334
Psalm 2:7-9 (p. 205, 314
Psalm 7:6 (p. 193
Psalm 9:12 (p. 120
Psalm 9:19 (p 193
Psalm 11:6 (p. 148
Psalm 16:10 (p. 68
Psalm 18:19 (p. 358
Psalm 18:40-42 (p. 314
Psalm 19:17 (p. 293
Psalm 24:7-10 (p. 308
Psalm 29:3-4 (p. 21
Psalm 37:10-11 (p. 161
Psalm 37:34 (p. 313
Psalm 46 (p. 141

Psalm 46:4 (p. 363
Psalm 59:12-13 (p. 145
Psalm 63:5-6 (p. 373
Psalm 68:1 (p. 307
Psalm 75:8 (p. 243
Psalm 80:8, 14-15 (p. 251
Psalm 90:2 (p. 5
Psalm 91:4 (p. 95
Psalm 91:8 (p. 313
Psalm 94:23 (p. 161
Psalm 95:3 (p. 314
Psalm 96:11-13 (p. 307
Psalm 110:4 (p. 18
Psalm 110:5-6 (p. 316
Psalm 116:15 (p. 245
Psalm 119:103 (p. 176
Psalm 119:105 (p. 83
Psalm 119:130 (p. 83
Psalm 124 (p. 214
Psalm 132:8-9 (p. 197
Psalm 136:1b, 2b (p. 241
Psalm 138:8 (p. 239
Psalm 139:23-24 (p. 30
Psalm 140:10 (p. 148
Psalm 141:2 (p. 144
Psalm 144:5 (p. 307

Proverbs 1:1-2 (p. 71
Proverbs 8:12, 17 (p. 19
Proverbs 8:34-36 (p. 244
Proverbs 11:4 (p. 295
Proverbs 13:7 (p. 38
Proverbs 15:3 (p. 92
Proverbs 16:4 (p. 164
Proverbs 16:18 (p. 293
Proverbs 21:1 (p. 286
Proverbs 25:2a (p. 172

Proverbs 29:1 (p. 154
Proverbs 30:8-9 (p. 81

Ecclesiastes 9:4 (p. 119
Ecclesiastes10:3 (p. 316

Isaiah 1:10 (p. 188
Isaiah 2:10-21 (p. 125
Isaiah 2:21b (p. 143
Isaiah 6:9-10 (p. 29
Isaiah 9:6 (p. 24
Isaiah 11 (p. 320, 329
Isaiah 11:1-10 (p. 103
Isaiah 11:2-4 (p. 310
Isaiah 11:4b (p. 314
Isaiah 13:10 (p. 153
Isaiah 14:4-9, 20 (p. 316
Isaiah 14:12-15 (p. 210
Isaiah 17:12-14 (p. 317
Isaiah 22:22-23 (p. 68
Isaiah 24 (p. 74
Isaiah 24:6 (p. 263
Isaiah 24:21-23 (p. 322
Isaiah 25:6-7 (p. 174, 191
Isaiah 25:6-9 (p. 348
Isaiah 26:6-7
Isaiah 28:17 (p. 271
Isaiah 28:21-22 (p. xi
Isaiah 40:3 (p. 186
Isaiah 40:11 (p. 140
Isaiah 40:31 (p. 213
Isaiah 41:4 (p. 375
Isaiah 41:18-20 (p. 321, 331
Isaiah 42:1 (p. 94
Isaiah 42:13-15 (p. 306
Isaiah 43:1-3a (p. 214
Isaiah 44:6 (p. 23

Isaiah 45:22 (p. 352
Isaiah 49:14-16 (p. 131
Isaiah 51:3 (p. 321
Isaiah 53:7 (p. 104
Isaiah 55:1-3 (p. 351
Isaiah 55:13 (p. 321
Isaiah 57:15 (p. 5
Isaiah 59:16-20 (p. 317
Isaiah 63:1-6 (p. 268
Isaiah 63:3 (p. 312
Isaiah 63:17 (p. 135
Isaiah 64:1-2 (p. 307
Isaiah 64:6 (p. 339
Isaiah 65:17-19a (p. 362
Isaiah 65:19-25 (p. 331
Isaiah 65:20-21 (p. 333
Isaiah 66:15-16 (p. 314

Jeremiah 2:21 (p. 251
Jeremiah 3:1 (p. 275
Jeremiah 2:21 (p. 251
Jeremiah 3:1 (p. 275
Jeremiah 3:6, 9 (p. 275
Jeremiah 3:17 (p. 325
Jeremiah 13:23 (p. 139
Jeremiah 15:16 (p. 176
Jeremiah 23:24a (p. 20
Jeremiah 25:30-31 (p. 268
Jeremiah 30:5-11 (p. 130
Jeremiah 32:7 (p. 124
Jeremiah 51:49-50 (p. 298

Lamentations 3:33-34 (p. 143

Ezekiel 1:4 (p. 12
Ezekiel 2:9-10 (p. 99, 176
Ezekiel 3:1-4 (p. 176

Ezekiel 3:14 (p. 176
Ezekiel 14:21 (p. 118
Ezekiel 16:28 (p. 275
Ezekiel 20: 35-38 (p. 208
Ezekiel 23:1-10 (p. 275
Ezekiel 33:11 (p. 165
Ezekiel 34:22-24 (p. 328
Ezekiel 38:1-11 (p. 334
Ez. 38:15-16, 18, 22-23 (p. 335
Ezekiel 39:12 (p. 337
Ezekiel 47:3-10 (p. 364

Daniel 7:7-8 (p. 283
Daniel 7:8 (p. 224
Dan. 7:13-14 (p. 12, 17, 19, 101
Daniel 7:21 (p. 120
Daniel 7:24-25 (p. 219, 283
Daniel 7:25 (p. 120, 224
Daniel 7:25-26 (p. 187
Daniel 8:23-27 (p. 114
Daniel 8:23-28 (p. 221
Daniel 8:25 (p. 316
Daniel 9:24-27 (p.383
Daniel 9:26 (p. 213
Daniel 9:27 (p. xv, 179
Daniel 11:31-39 (p. 187
Daniel 11:36-39 (p. xiv, 114
Daniel 11:37-38 (p. xiv, 223
Daniel 12:1-2 (p. 171, 327
Daniel 12:2 (p. 195
Daniel 12:2-3 (p. 250

Hosea 1:2 (p. 275

Joel 1:18-20a (p. 148
Joel 2:1-11 (p. 157

Joel 2:30-31 (p. 126
Joel 3:9-17 (p. 267
Joel 3:13-14 (p. 248
Jonah 1:17 (p. 147

Micah 5:2 (p. 19
Micah 7:15-17 (p. 147

Zephaniah 3:17 (p. 108

Zechariah 2:8-13 (p. 257
Zechariah 12:10; 13:6 (p. 13
Zechariah 13:8-9 (p. 251
Zechariah 13:9 (p. 130
Zechariah 14:3-4 (p. 322
Zechariah 14:4 (p. 11
Zechariah 14:5 (p. 313
Zechariah 14:9 (p. 315
Zech.14:12-17 (p. 318
Zechariah 14:16 (p. 325
Zechariah 14:17-18 (p. 333

Malachi 3:1a (p. 181
Malachi 3:1-3 (p. 178
Malachi 4:1 (p. 263
Malachi 4:2 (p. 377
Malachi 4:5-6 (p. 160, 183

Matthew 2:16 (p. 202
Matthew 3:11-12 (p. 247
Matthew 5:5 (p. 347
Matthew 5:8 (p. 367
Matthew 5:11-12 (p. 39
Matthew 5:15-16 (p. 26
Matthew 5:29-30 (p. 253
Matthew 6:19-21 (p. 295
Matthew 6:24 (p. 80

Matthew 8:20 (p. 38
Matthew 9:14-15 (p. 301
Matthew 10:28 (p. 256
Matthew 10:32-33 (p. 66
Matthew12:34-35 (p. 229
Matthew 12:36-37 (p. 339
Matthew 13:16 (p. 29
Matthew 13:24-30 (p. 248
Matthew 13:36-42 (p. 248
Matthew 13:41-42 (p. 196
Matthew 19:28 (p. 91, 326
Matthew 19:28 (p. 324
Matthew 23:37-39 (p. 286
Matthew 24:6-7 (p. 116
Matthew 24:9 (p. 120
Matthew 24:14 (p. 241
Matt.24:15-16 (p. xiv, 177, 179, 180, 206
Matthew 24:29-30 (p. 13
Matthew 24:22-24 (p. 228
Matthew 24:29-30 (p. 309
Matthew 24:35 (p. 338
Matthew 24:36 (p. 2
Matthew 24:37-42 (p. 249
Matthew 25:11-13 (p. 266
Matthew 25:29-30 (p. 152
Matthew 25:30 (p. 266
Matthew 25:31-46 (p. 323
Matthew 26:52 (p. 227
Matthew 26:63b-64 (p. 13
Matthew 26:64-65 (p. 252

Mark 1:13 (p. 366
Mark 5:35-43 (p. 7
Mark 9:43-44 (p. 244
Mark 10:17 (p. 351
Mark 10:45 (p. 94

Luke 1:19 (p. 144
Luke 1:32-33 (p. 103
Luke 1:35b (p. 67
Luke 6:8a (p. 96
Luke 6:21-23 (p. 245
Luke 7:11-15 (p. 7
Luke 7:27 (p. 183
Luke 8:31 (p. 156
Luke 10:18b (p. 155
Luke 10:20 (p. 225, 341
Luke 15:7 (p. 138
Luke 17:26 (p. 298
Luke 17:36-37 (p. 252
Luke 19:10 (p. 17, 378
Luke 19:46 (p. 182
Luke 21:11 (p. 122
Luke 21:16-19 (p. 225
Luke 21:25-26 (p. 151
Luke 22:3-4 (p. 279
Luke 23:38b (p.19

John 1:1 (p. 95, 312
John 1:3 (p. 173
John 1:12-13 (p. 346, 352
John 1:14 (p. 68, 95, 312
John 1:17 (p. 310
John 1:18 (p. 2, 89, 310
John 1:29 (p. 103
John 1:47b (p. 238
Jn. 3:36 (p. 122, 262, 341, 347
John 4:14 (p. 352
John 5:22-23 (p. 20
John 5:26-29 (p. 24, 195
John 6:36b (p. 353
John 6:70b (p. 279
John 7:16-18 (p. 7

John 7:37 (p. 351
John 8:28-29 (p. 78
John 8:31-32 (p. 71
John 8:43-44a (p. 38
John 8:44a (p. 202
John 8:44b (p. 201
John 9:38 (p. 305
John 10:27-30 (p. 239, 346, 352
John 11:25-26 (p. 41, 256
John 11:43-44 (p. 7
John 14:6 (p. 68, 310
John 14:9 (p. 89
John 14:10b (p. 78
John 15:3 (p. 71
John 15:7-8 (p. 71, 177
John 15:8 (p. 43
John 17:5 (p. 22
John 17:5, 24 (p. 355
John 17:6-8 (p. 2
John 17:12 (p. 279
John 7:16-18
John 17:17 (p. 72
John 17:24a (p. 12
John 20:21b (p. 78

Acts 1:6-7 (p. 329
Acts 1:8 (p. 78
Acts 1:9 (p. 206
Acts 1:11-12 (p. 11
Acts 3:19-21 (p. 102
Acts 4:12 (p. 361
Acts 10:42 (p. 257
Acts 17:10-11 (p. 230
Acts 20:32 (p. 83
Acts 26:18 (p. 203
Acts 26:23 (p. 327

Romans 1:21-25 (p. 115, 276
Romans 1:22-24 (p. 115, 166
Romans 2:28-29 (p. 72
Romans 3:25-26 (p. 96
Romans 4:17b (p. 242
Romans 5:8 (p. 8
Romans 6:14 (p. 9
Romans 6:23a (p. 9, 97
Romans 8:1 (p. 342
Romans 8:11(p. 7
Romans 8:18 (p. 39
Romans 8:19-22 (p. 109
Romans 8:31b (p. 213
Romans 8:33 (p. 204
Romans 8:33-34 (p. 211
Romans 8:38-39 (p. 8
Romans 9:3-5 (p. 200, 267
Romans 9:25-26 (p. 376
Romans 10:9-10 (p. 211
Romans 10:13 (p. 361, 379
Romans 10:13-14 (p. 165
Romans 11:18 (p. 376
Romans 11:25-29 (p. 133
Rom.11:25-29 (p. 128, 197,
Romans 11:26 (p. 238
Romans 12:19b (p. 93, 314

I Corinthians 1:27-29 (p. 70
I Corinthians 1:31 (p. 19
I Corinthians 3:1-2 (p. 30
I Cor. 3:11-15 (p. 50, 304
I Corinthians 4:5 (p. 310
I Corinthians 6:2 (p. 58, 326
I Corinthians 6:19-20 (p. 367
I Corinthians 7:27-29 (p. 237
I Corinthians 11:30-32 (p. 54

I Corinthians 13:34-35 (p. 52
I Corinthians 15:8 (p. 132
I Corinthians 15:20 (p. 7
I Corinthians 15:25-26 (p. 343
I Corinthians 15:51-52 (p. 75
I Corinthians 15:55-57 (p. 24
I Corinthians 15:58 (p. 31, 304

II Corinthians 3:15a (p. 369
II Cor. 5:10 (p. 38, 48, 374
II Corinthians 5:18-19 (p. 292
II Corinthians 5:18-21 (p. 340
II Corinthians 5:19 (p. 121
II Corinthians 5:21 (p. 67, 342
II Corinthians 6:14-15 (p. 46
II Corinthians 11:2 (p. 302
II Corinthians 11:13-15 (p. 222
II Corinthians 12:2 (p. 15
II Corinthians 12:9-10 (p. 70
II Corinthians 13:5a (p. 375

Galatians 2:16 (p. 339
Galatians 4:4 (p. 204
Galatians 5:16 (p. 64

Ephesians 1:7 (p. 139
Ephesians 1:11 (p. 286
Ephesians 1:13 (p. 239
Ephesians 2:6-7 (p. 137
Ephesians 2:8-9 (p. 339
Ephesians 2:19-20 (p. 356
Ephesians 3:3-5 (p. 174
Ephesians 4:11 (p. 26
Ephesians 5:13-16 (p. 62
Ephesians 5:18-19 (p. 71
Ephesians 5:25-27 (p. 362
Ephesians 5:25-32 (p. 302

Ephesians 5:26-27 (p. 211, 356
Ephesians 6:12 (p. 44
Ephesians 6:17 (p. 21

Philippians 1:6 (p. 239
Philippians 1:20-21 (p. 133
Philippians 1:29 (p. 37
Philippians 2:9-10 (p. 8
Philippians 2:9b-11 (p. 175
Philippians 2:12 (p. 304
Philippians 2:15-16a (p. 26
Philippians 3:20-21 (p. 8
Philippians 4:3 (p. 226, 342

Colossians 1:11 (p. 70
Colossians 1:15-16 (p. 79
Colossians 1:16 (p. 21, 173
Colossians 1:18 (p. 6
Colossians 2:8 (p. 75
Colossians 3:1-3 (p. 362
Col. 3:16 (p. 71, 177, 370
Colossians 4:3 (p. 69

I Thes.1:10 (p. 73, 372
I Thessalonians 4:16-17 (p. 10, 12, 88, 327

II Thessalonians 1:7b-8 (p. 1
II Thessalonians 1:7-9 (p. 122, 262, 312, 324
II Thessalonians 2:3 (p. 228
II Thess.2:3-4 (p. xiv, 180, 187, 279
II Thessalonians 2:3-8 (p. 222
II Thessalonians 2:8 (p. 114
II Thessalonians 2:8-10 (p. 187

I Timothy 2:4b (p. 243
I Timothy 2:5 (p. 44
I Timothy 2:11-14 (p. 52
I Timothy 3:16 (p. 44
I Timothy 6:8-10 (p. 80
I Timothy 6:14-15 (p. 309
I Timothy 6:15-16 (p. 22

II Timothy 1:12 (p. 174, 239
II Timothy 2:11-12 (p. 367
II Timothy 2:12a (p. 58
II Timothy 2:12 (p. 326
II Timothy 2:15b (p. xvi
II Timothy 2:26 (p. 203
II Timothy 3:1b (p. xii
II Timothy 3:1-5 (p. 228
II Tim. 3:16-17 (p. 172, 370

Titus 2:13 (p. 372
Titus 2:13-14 (p. 42, 107
Titus 3:5-7 (p. 339
Titus 3:8, 14 (p. 43
Titus 3:10-11 (p. 45

Hebrews 1:1-3 (p. 173
Hebrews 1:2-3 (p. 79
Heb.1:3 (p.22, 70, 88, 89, 104, 206
Hebrews 1:6 (p. 306
Hebrews 1:7 (p. 92
Hebrews 1:10-12 (p. 345
Hebrews 1:13 (p. 2
Hebrews 2:3 (p. 253
Hebrews 2:14-15 (p. 204
Hebrews 2:14, 16-17 (p. 17
Hebrews 2:17 (p. 309
Hebrews 3:1-2 (p. 309

Hebrews 3:7-8 (p. 373
Hebrews 4:12 (p. 21, 313
Hebrews 4:13 (p. 20
Hebrews 4:14-16 (p. 18
Hebrews 5:6 (p. 18
Hebrews 7:25-26 (p. 68, 209
Hebrews 9:12 (p. 9
Hebrews 9:27 (p. 40
Hebrews 9:28 (p. 372
Hebrews 10:26-27 (p. 162
Hebrews 10:28-29 (p. 246
Hebrews 10:31 (p. 254
Hebrews 11:3 (p. 21, 79
Hebrews 11:10 (p. 345
Hebrews 11:36-39 (p. 81
Hebrews 12:5-6 (p, 56
Hebrews 12:6-9 (p. 83
Hebrews 12:22-23 (p. 236
Hebrews 13:17 (p. 60

James 5:7 (p. 57, 371
James 5:19-20 (p. 56

I Peter 1:5 (p. 239, 355
I Peter 1:18-19 (p. 103
I Peter 1:22 (p. 325
I Peter 1:23 (p. 63, 71, 165
I Peter 2:1, 14, 18-19
I Peter 2:2 (p. 71, 177
I Peter 2:4-5 (p. 76
I Peter 2:9 (p. 9, 18
I Peter 4:12-13 (p. 39

II Peter 1:19 (p. 377
II Peter 1:21 (p. 4
II Peter 2:1-2 (p. 47, 53
II Peter 2:3 (p. 295

II Peter 2:4 (p. 156
II Peter 3:5-7 (p. 346
II Peter 3:7 (p. 262
II Peter 3:7, 10-12 (p. 337
II Peter 3:8 (p. 3
II Peter 3:8-9 (p. 371
II Peter 3:9 (p. 143

I John 2:1 (p. 209
I John 2:2 (p 101, 340
I John 2:5 (p. 373
I John 2:15-16 (p. 292
I John 2:18 (p. 114, 188, 221
I John 3:2-3 (p. 371
I John 3:7-8 (p. 55
I John 3:18-19 (p. 63
I John 4:1-3 (p. 229
I John 5:5 (p. 36
I John 5:11-12 (p. 341
I John 5:13 (p. 350
I John 5:14-15 (p. 69

Jude 6 (p. 156
Jude 9 (p. 171
Jude 14-15 (p. 313
Jude 23 (p. 119
Jude 24-25 (p. 240

Revelation 1:5 (p. 139
Revelation 1:6 (p. 18
Revelation 1:18 (p. 173
Revelation 2:7 (p. 365
Revelation 2:26-27 (p. 84, 326
Revelation 3:21 (p. 89
Revelation 6:2 (p. xv
Revelation 6:12-17 (p. xvi
Revelation 7:9-17 (p. xvii

Revelation 11:8 (p. 287
Revelation12:17-13:1a (p. 217
Revelation 13:3-4 (p. 279
Revelation 13:4 (p. 114
Revelation 13:16 (p. 295
Revelation 13:17-18 (p. xvi
Revelation 14:1 (p. 134
Revelation 14:14-20 (p. xvi
Revelation 16:12 (p. 308
Revelation 17:10-11 (p. 219
Revelation 17:12 (p. 219
Revelation 17:14 (p. 308
Revelation19:7-8 (p. 82
Revelation 19:15b (p. 20
Revelation 20:4 (p. 3
Revelation 20:14 (p. 40
Revelation 22:16 (p. 58

Made in the USA
Lexington, KY
26 January 2015